Basic SA Tasks

Starting and Stopping the Server

```
startserver -f runserver_file [-m] [-p]
```

- *runserver_file* contains SQL Server command with appropriate options for locations of master device, interfaces file, SQL Server name, etc.
- d specifies master device name.
- f specifies alternative runserver file.
- m specifies single-user mode.
- p generates password for sso account.

```
shutdown [with nowait]
```

Granting Access to the Server

```
sp_addlogin login_name, password [ ,default_db
          [ ,language]]
```

- *password* required, 6 characters minimum.
- Only user with sso_role can add logins.

```
sp_password caller_password, new_password,
          [ , login_name]
```

- Only user with sso_role should specify *login_name*.

```
sp_droplogin login_name
sp_defaultdb login_name, default_db
```

- Pre-System 10—Assigns or changes *default_db* for specified user.

```
sp_locklogin login_name, {"lock ¦ "unlock"}
```

- Locks the specified *login_name*.

```
sp_configure "password expiration interval",
          #_of_days
```

- Sets number of days passwords will expire after they are changed.
- A value of 0 means no password expiration.
- Only user with sso_role can set password expiration interval.

```
sp_modifylogin login_name, options, value
```

- *options* are defdb, deflanguage, fullname

Defining Physical Resources

```
disk init name = 'logical_name',
          physname = "phys_name",
          vdevno = dev_num,
          size = dev_size
```

- *logical_name* must be unique throughout server.
- *phys_name* disk location of device.
- *dev_num* unique integer < sp_configure devices.
- *dev_siz* in pages (2KB except Stratus (4KB)).

```
disk reinit name = 'logical_name',
          physname = "phys_name",
          vdevno = dev_num,
          size = dev_size
```

- Used to rebuild sysdevices to reestablish a database device after restoring a damaged master database if the device was added since the last database dump of the master database.

```
disk refit
```

- Used after disk reinit to rebuild sysusages and sysdatabases to reestablish databases created or altered since the last database backup of master.

```
disk mirror name = 'logical_name', mirror =
          'phys_name'
```

- K ...me.

```
disk un...
```

- D...

```
disk r...
sp_add...
```

- A...
- *logical_name* is a uniq... ...r for dump device.
- *physical_name* is the physical location of the device of disk file.
- *tape_size* is the capacity of the tape dump device in megabytes.

```
sp_help device [logical_name]
```

- Reports information about the specified or all database and dump devices.

```
sp_diskdefault logical_name, defaulton ¦ defaultoff
sp_dropdevice logical_name
```

- Removes device definition if device is not in use.

Database Management

Basic Commands

```
create database db_name [on device_name = size
          [ , ...] ]
          [log on device_name = size [, ...] ]
          [with override]
          [for load]
```

- with override allows the specification of the same device name for the on and log on clauses. Allows dumping of transaction log even though it is not a separate device.
- for load invokes a streamlined version of create database. Use when recovering from media failure, and database will be loaded from backup immediately following creation.
- *size* is in megabytes.
- *device_name* is any database device in sysdevices.
- Separate log device highly recommended.

```
drop database db_name
alter database db_name [on device_name = size
          [ , ...]]
          [log on device_name = size [ , ...]]
          [with override]
          [for load]
sp_changedbowner login_name
sp_dboption database, options, true ¦ false
```

- *options* are select into/bulkcopy, read only, single user, dbo use only, no chkpt on recovery, trunc log on chkpt, abort tran on log full, allow nulls by default, ddl in tran, no free space acctg.

```
checkpoint
```

- Checkpoint a database (must be in database to be checkpointed).

```
sp_helpdb [database_name]
```

Granting *create database* Permission

```
use master
sp_adduser login_name
grant create database to login_name
```

MEMORY AND RESOURCE ALLOCATION

sp_configure [*option*, *new_value*]

- sp_configure without arguments lists valid options and ranges.
- *option* is any value in description column of sysconfigures.
- *new_value* is any value in valid range for parameter.
- Reconfigure after sp_configure verifies available resources.

reconfigure [with override]

- Instructs server to apply changes.

MONITORING CPU AND I/O USAGE

BASIC COMMANDS

sp_monitor

- Shows CPU usage, I/O usage, and so on, since server came up and since last sp_monitor call.

set statistics io on ¦ off

- Quantity of logical and physical I/O.

set statistics time on ¦ off

- Elapsed system and CPU time for parse, compile, and execute.

set forceplan on ¦ off

MANAGING REMOTE ACCESS

sp_addserver *server_name*, {local ¦ null}, *network_name*
sp_dropserver *server_name* [, droplogins]
sp_addremotelogin *server_name* [, *local_name* [,*remote_name*]]
sp_remoteoption [*server_name*, *login_name*, *remote_name*, 'trusted', true ¦ false]
sp_serveroption [*servername*, *options*, {true ¦ false}]

- *options* are net password encryption, time-outs

sp_helpremotelogin [*servername* [, *remotename*]

MANAGING SYSTEM-DEFINED ROLES

sp_role {"grant" ¦ "revoke"}, {sa_role ¦ sso_role ¦ oper_role ¦ oper_role}, *login_name*

- *login_name* must be a valid SQL Server login.
- User must have sa_role to grant sa_role.
- User must have sso_role to grant sso_role, oper_role.
- sa_role performs SQL Server management tasks:
  - Server configuration.
  - Manage database devices.
  - Create/drop databases.
  - Shut down SQL Server.
  - Kill processes.
- sso_role performs security-related tasks.
  - Add/drop/lock logins.
  - Change passwords.
  - Set password expiration interval.
  - Manage auditing system.
- oper_role can back up and restore any database within SQL Server.

set role {"sa_role" ¦ "sso_role" ¦ "oper_role"} {on ¦ off}

- Disable/enable role for current session.

BASIC *DBO* TASKS

USER AND GROUP MAINTENANCE

sp_adduser *login_name* [, *name_within_db* [, *group_name*]]

- *login_name* is from syslogins.
- *name_within_db* is optional different name within database.
- *group_name* is name of group to place user in.
- Specifying a group name requires specifying a non-null *name_within_db*.
- guest is a special case of user; it gives database access to any non-user.
- Adds a row to sysusers.

sp_addalias *login_name*, *current_user*

- *login_name* is user to add to database.
- *current_user* is existing user who *login_name* will alias to.
- Adds a row to sysusers.

sp_addgroup *group_name*

- Adds group *group_name* to sysusers.

sp_changegroup *group_name*, *user_name*

- Places user *user_name* in group *group_name*.

sp_dropuser *user_name*

- Removes user *user_name* from sysusers and any aliased users from sysalternates.

sp_dropalias *login_name*

- Removes *login_name* from sysalternates.

sp_dropgroup *group_name*

- Removes group *group_name* from sysusers.

sp_helpuser [*user_name*]

- Displays list of database users or detailed user information.

GRANTING AND REVOKING PERMISSION

grant {all ¦ *permission_list*} on *object* [(*column_list*)]
to {public ¦ *name_list* ¦ *role_name*}
[with grant option]
grant {all ¦ *command_list*} to {public ¦ *name_list* ¦ *role_name*}

- *permission_list* may be any combination of select, insert, update, and delete.
- *name_list* may be any combination of users and groups.
- *command_list* may include any of the create commands (create rule, table, view, procedure, default).
- with grant option allows user to grant specified permissions to other users.

revoke [grant option for]
    {all ¦ *permission_list* ¦ execute}
    on *object* [(*column_list*)]
    from {public ¦ *name_list* ¦ *role_name*}
[cascade]
revoke {all ¦ *command_list*} from {public ¦ *name_list* ¦ *role_name*}

- grant option for revokes user's permission to grant specified permissions.
- cascade is required with grant option for if user has granted permissions to other users.
- Revokes those permissions.

SYBASE®
SQL SERVER™ 11 DBA
SURVIVAL GUIDE

Jeffrey R. Garbus
David S. Solomon
Brian Tretter
Ray Rankins

SAMS
PUBLISHING

201 West 103rd Street
Indianapolis, Indiana 46290

TOM BARTON
UNISYS.

I dedicate this book to my wife, Penny, without whose help and support I would never have finished my part, and to my children, Brandon, Devon, Max, and Gillian, for the space I got to write. —JG

For Carola. —DS

For Diane. Her love, understanding, and support mean more to me than she will ever know. —BT

To the two shining beacons in my sea of life, Elizabeth and Jason, without whose love, understanding, and most of all, patience, I would be lost. —RR

COPYRIGHT © 1996 BY SAMS PUBLISHING

SECOND EDITION

International Standard Book Number: 0-672-30888-6

Library of Congress Catalog Card Number: 95-72924

99 98 97 96   4   3   2   1

Interpretation of the printing code: the rightmost double-digit number is the year of the book's printing; the rightmost single-digit, the number of the book's printing. For example, a printing code of 96-1 shows that the first printing of the book occurred in 1996.

Composed in New Century Schoolbook and MCPdigital by Macmillan Computer Publishing

Printed in the United States of America

PUBLISHER AND PRESIDENT	*Richard K. Swadley*
ACQUISITIONS MANAGER	*Greg Wiegand*
DEVELOPMENT MANAGER	*Dean Miller*
MANAGING EDITOR	*Cindy Morrow*
MARKETING MANAGER	*John Pierce*
ASSISTANT MARKETING MANAGER	*Kristina Perry*

ACQUISITIONS EDITOR
Rosemarie Graham

SOFTWARE DEVELOPMENT SPECIALIST
Steve Flatt

PRODUCTION EDITOR
Kristi Hart

TECHNICAL REVIEWERS
Ed Walsh
Martin Ward

EDITORIAL COORDINATOR
Bill Whitmer

TECHNICAL EDIT COORDINATOR
Lynette Quinn

FORMATTER
Frank Sinclair

EDITORIAL ASSISTANTS
Carol Ackerman
Andi Richter
Rhonda Tinch-Mize

COVER DESIGNER
Alyssa Yesh

BOOK DESIGNER
Alyssa Yesh

COPY WRITER
Peter Fuller

PRODUCTION TEAM SUPERVISOR
Brad Chinn

PRODUCTION
Mary Ann Abramson, Stephen Adams, Mona Brown, Michael Brumitt, Jason Hand, Sonja Hart, Clint Lahnen, Paula Lowell, Laura Robbins, Bobbi Satterfield, Laura A. Smith, SA Springer, Mark Walchle, Todd Wente

INDEXER
Brad Herriman

Overview

Contents

Acknowledgments

When there are multiple authors, it seems like we need first to acknowledge each other. Jeff thought up this project and made it happen, and he cracked the whip when things started to sag. Brian added a thoroughness and thoughtfulness to the writing. His experience administering SQL Server in many organizations helped make this book far more real. David gave the book coherence and flow, and he knitted the sections together into a whole.

We want to thank Ray Rankins, who helped put together the sample test questions in Appendix B. Rosemarie Graham at Sams Publishing helped make this a reality and helped us through when the deadlines were looming. Thanks also to Kristi Hart, who had to work much too hard to make this book more coherent.

We would all like to thank those who gave us the push to examine Sybase. Brian would like to thank Bob Kiep, who was his first guide on the road to Sybase expertise. David and Jeff owe a debt to Mike Luckevich, who saw the future and helped us understand how we could play a part in it.

All of us want to thank our wives, Penny, Diane, Carola, and Elizabeth, for their support. And we probably ought to thank our kids (Brandon, Devon, Max, and Gillian Garbus; Zachary and Nicholas Tretter; Adam and Luke Solomon; and Jason Rankins). They were sometimes patient, seldom quiet enough, but they would never go to bed.

Troy, NY
February 1996

About the Authors

Jeffrey R. Garbus is President of Northern Lights Software, Ltd. Since 1989, Jeff has taught thousands of programmers, systems administrators, and database designers about Sybase administration and tuning, based on his experience as a consultant to some of the most complex Sybase installations in the world. His current interests are in design, tuning, and maintenance of Very Large Databases (VLDBs) in Sybase.

David Solomon, President of metis technologies, llc., of Troy, NY, writes, speaks, teaches, and consults on SQL Server design, application, and implementation. With more than five years of experience in SQL Server, he is an expert on query analysis and troubleshooting, logical database design, and application design and implementation. He specializes in advanced SQL techniques and physical database design.

Brian Tretter has put dozens of systems into production in roles ranging from project management to architecture, and database administration to quality assurance. His experience spans multiple industries, including healthcare, hospital, manufacturing, automotive, airport, distribution, financial, publishing, and telecommunications. His expertise in performance tuning and resolution of locking/deadlocking problems has been called on worldwide. When not training, he consults on VLDBs and large user systems, and he also assists organizations in the development of standards and procedures in the use of Sybase.

Ray Rankins is currently a Managing Consultant for Northern Lights Consulting and a Certified Sybase Professional Database Administrator. Prior to joining Northern Lights, he worked for Sybase Professional Services as a consultant and instructor and was involved in the development of the Sybase Performance and Tuning class. Ray has been working with Sybase and Microsoft SQL Server since 1987 as a DBA, application developer, database designer, project manager, consultant, and instructor and has worked in a variety of industries including financial, manufacturing, healthcare, retail, insurance, communications, and state and federal government. His expertise is in SQL Server performance and tuning, SQL Server application design and development, client/server architecture, and Very Large Database design and implementation.

Introduction

Why does the world need a survival guide for Sybase database administrators? If you are like most Sybase DBAs, this is not the first system you have administered. You probably have spent the last five to 20 years becoming an expert in some other system—a mainframe, a minicomputer, or a Local Area Network (LAN). Perhaps your expertise was in database design and administration in another database environment, such as IDMS, DB2, Oracle, or even FoxPro.

If you are like most Sybase DBAs, you also haven't had much exposure to Sybase. You may have gone to a class or two, but you don't really feel any closer to understanding your new job. You are probably skeptical about whether Sybase can really meet the needs of your organization—especially if you are used to operating on a mainframe.

No matter what your experience, your organization has expectations about the performance and reliability of systems. You need to know what tools and resources are out there to help you meet those expectations. You need to understand what is meant by client/server and what Sybase is supposed to bring to the table.

WHO SHOULD READ THIS BOOK

This book is for you, the Sybase database administrator. You've had the classes, you've read the manuals, but you need answers to some basic questions:

- What are the features new to System 11?
- How do all the pieces fit together?
- What is the right way to set up security?
- What is an effective backup strategy?
- Am I getting the most out of SQL Server?
- What do you need to do every day? every week? now and then?
- What approach do you take when something goes wrong?
- Why doesn't bcp ever work the way you expect it to?
- Are there good tools out there?
- (UNIX users only) Why is vi so cryptic?

ABOUT THIS BOOK

Let's consider the answers to these questions. It probably will help you make the best use of this book.

We review client/server in general and Sybase in particular in Chapter 1, "A Brief Introduction to Client/Server and Sybase." You'll learn where this technology comes from and understand some of the broad opportunities Sybase offers in data distribution, data management, and application development. If you are experienced in client/server, you may want to skip Chapter 1 and move on to Chapter 2.

In Chapter 2, "Overview of Systems Administration," you look at the roles and responsibilities of a Sybase systems administrator and how they differ from or overlap with those of a database or operating system administrator. You also learn critical terminology and explore key concepts.

How do all the pieces fit together? Sybase clients and servers communicate over a local area network (LAN). Both the client and the server provide several layers to isolate application programmers from details of the network, making the system modular and portable. The problem for the administrator is finding all of the necessary pieces to make the lights come on. We will show you how in Chapter 3, "SQL Server Installation and Connectivity."

Chapter 3, along with Chapter 4, "Defining Physical and Mirror Devices," and Chapter 5, "Defining, Altering, and Maintaining Databases and Logs," show you how to install the server, database devices, and databases. Most administrators make three or four critical mistakes in the first 10 minutes after installation. We will show you the right steps you need to take from day one.

What is the right way to set up security? There are lots of ways to set up security—many of them are ineffective or hard to manage. Chapter 6, "Security and User Administration," describes Sybase security and provides some recommendations for security implementation.

What is an effective backup strategy? Chapter 7, "Database Logging and Recovery," and Chapter 8, "Backing Up and Restoring the Database and Transaction Logs," help you understand database logs and define some tried-and-true backup approaches for your organization.

Are you getting the most out of SQL Server? Chapter 9, "Configuring and Tuning the SQL Server," helps you understand memory usage and helps you understand how to set the configuration settings to get the best performance.

Chapter 10, "Optimizing SQL Server Configuration Options," presents the configuration options within SQL Server that affect SQL Server performance, including memory configuration, CPU configuration, network configuration, and lock configuration.

Chapter 11, "Database Design Issues," explores physical database design techniques for improving SQL Server performance.

Chapter 12, "Remove Server Management," presents the definition and management of remote servers, privileges, and security.

We don't tackle *query performance* in depth in this book (that's another whole book!), but you will find essential information about query optimization in Chapter 13, "Basic Application Performance and Tuning."

What do you need to do every day? Every week? Now and then? To keep the server running, you need to develop a preventive maintenance program (see Chapter 14, "Periodic Maintenance for Your SQL Server").

What approach do you take when something goes wrong? There are some obvious things to try before panicking. See Chapter 15, "What Do You Do When Things Go Wrong?"

Why doesn't bcp ever work the way you expect it to? Good question! Learn to control bulk copies and use the other Sybase utilities in Chapter 16, "Tools for Sybase Administrators."

Chapter 17, "Managing the Audit System," explains how to use the Audit System to keep tabs on most SQL Server activities.

Chapter 18, "Defining Systems Administration and Naming Standards," focuses on the core standards you need in place as you develop procedures at your environment.

Are there good tools out there? You bet there are! Check out the Aurora Desktop demo on the disk at the back of the book.

You also will want to explore the appendixes. Appendix A, "The Database Consistency Checker (dbcc)," helps you learn to use dbcc like a pro (not an easy task!). Appendix B, "Sample CSP DBA Test," helps you get ready for Sybase's DBA certification process. You can test your knowledge and probably learn a few things, too. Appendix C provides you with the answers to the Sample CSP DBA Test. Appendix D presents several quick-reference tables for many of the DBA tasks and commands presented in this book.

Note

Why is vi so cryptic? If your SQL Server is running under UNIX, you have the vi editor, the basic editing tool provided with most UNIX systems. For the uninitiated, vi is a character editor doing a bad imitation of a full-screen editor. If you're a UNIX jock, it's great—powerful, fast, almost no keystrokes. If you're new to UNIX, vi is a complete mystery. When vi was invented, it was probably the best thing since sliced bread, but for most new users it feels like trying to chop garlic with a jackhammer. We won't teach you anything about vi here, but if you're just learning it, you certainly have our sympathy.

This book answers most of your questions by providing realistic approaches to everyday problems, as well as recommending a maintenance program for keeping your server running year-round.

It's a constant surprise to those who teach systems administration courses to discover how few people responsible for maintaining Sybase systems had a say in the original decision to purchase it. Having been left out of the decision and with no background in client/server or Sybase, administrators don't understand the role of SQL Server in the MIS environment—or what (reasonable or unreasonable) expectations management might have.

CONVENTIONS USED IN THIS BOOK

We've tried to be consistent in our use of conventions here. In the text itself, we have not capitalized the names of objects, databases, or logins/users where that would be incorrect. That has left lots of sentences starting like this, "sysdatabases includes …" with an initial lowercase character.

Names of commands and stored procedures are presented in a special computer typeface.

Code and output examples are presented separately from regular paragraphs and also are in a computer typeface. Here is an example:

```
select id, name, audflags
from sysobjects
where type != "S"

id          name                            audflags
----------  ------------------------------  ----------
144003544   marketing_table                 130
```

When we provide *syntax* for a command, we indicate optional items in square brackets [ ] and items you provide in angle brackets < >, as in the following example:

```
sp_addlogin <login_name>, <password> [, <database_name>]
```

In this case, the *login_name* and *password* parameters are required, but the *database_name* is optional. Note also that items shown in plain computer type, such as sp_addlogin, should be entered literally as shown. Placeholders are presented in italics, such as *database_name*; a placeholder is a generic term for which you must supply a specific name.

Our editors were enormously helpful in finding inconsistencies in how we used these conventions. We apologize for those that remain: they are entirely the fault of the authors.

EPIGRAM

παθη μαθος ...

(Learn by suffering)

Aeschylus

- Roots of Client/Server Computing

- Client/Server to the Rescue!

- The Critical Factor: Cost

CHAPTER 1

A Brief Introduction to Client/Server and Sybase

ROOTS OF CLIENT/SERVER COMPUTING

Strictly speaking, client/server is a style of computing in which a client process requests services from a server process. Client/server processing is a broad area within cooperative processing, a field that looks at interactive computing between systems. What most distinguishes client/server computing is how processing is distributed between independent applications.

That's all well and good, but in the real world of business computing, the term client/server has come to describe the interaction between Fourth Generation Language (4GL) front-end applications and relational database management systems (RDBMS). That is certainly how we will use the term in this book.

Client/server computing represents the marriage of two older processing models: mainframe, or host-based, computing and PC/LAN-based computing. Let's look more closely at these two models to understand the purpose of client/server.

For this discussion, let's break down a typical business data-processing application into four components:

◆ User interface
◆ Application program
◆ Logical data processing
◆ Physical data processing

User interface elements control keyboard and screen features, including the implementation of function keys, the field-to-field behavior of the cursor, and the display of data.

Application program elements manage screen-to-screen behavior of the system and menuing, as well as mapping field information to a logical data model.

Logical data processing is the application of business rules to application data. This includes data validation and referential integrity. Data validation involves ensuring that a provided value is in a valid format or within a valid range of values (Is the "price" greater than $0.00? Is "social_security_number" in the format ###-##-####?). Referential integrity involves verifying that the data "referenced" in one table exists in a "related" table (Does the "pub_id" value in the titles table exist in the publishers table? Is "item_number" found in the "items" table?). It also includes rules particular to a specific organization or application (for example, promised ship dates are always seven days from the date of order; only managers may fill in an "override" column; and so forth).

Physical data processing maps logical data to a physical storage structure. It handles locking, data caching, and indexing, as well as the actual reads and writes from media.

Host-Based Computing

In the host-based environment, almost all processing occurs on the central host. What little local processing does occur (for instance, with an advanced terminal) is restricted to cursor handling from field to field and handling individual keystrokes. Once a screen of data is transmitted, the host resumes control.

In this environment, applications and data are centralized and exist solely on the host computer. Communications are virtually eliminated a bottleneck, even when the host and the terminal are separated by hundreds of miles and only share a relatively slow, asynchronous connection. Application development and maintenance are also centralized, providing an important measure of control and security. Administration of the system (backup, data maintenance) is handled centrally as well.

Host-based computing has been the platform for most business database applications for the past 20 years: mainframes and traditional minicomputers have provided solid, reliable performance, but at a tremendous cost. Purchase prices are stratospheric compared to PCs, but the intolerable burden of mainframes has been the cost of maintenance. The combined effect of high purchase prices and exorbitant maintenance fees was that processing cycles centralized on the host became far more expensive than the processing cycles on a PC.

PC/LAN-Based Computing

When those central mainframe costs were billed to a department manager's budget, the manager turned to a PC to solve departmental problems. The low cost and high availability of PC computing was extremely attractive to people who were forced to wait in line to pay high prices for mainframe processing.

Of course, the real nightmare of host processing has always been the tremendous backlog of applications waiting to be developed and maintained. PC users found they could build their own applications (they were admittedly amateur, but often more usable than the enterprise applications) faster than they could fill out the forms requesting applications from the central MIS group.

Note

> Years ago, a colleague of mine switched to a PC to do all his data analysis and number crunching, even though his data sets were typically large and fairly complex. He explained, "It takes my PC seven minutes to do what the mainframe can do in one-half second, but I have to wait a week to run my job on the mainframe."

The small, private, PC-based databases started to grow into multi-user, LAN-based databases because it made sense—users found ways to share data and be more efficient. Although fileserver-based LANs are well-qualified to handle most office-automation (OA) tasks (word processing document storage, shared printing devices, and central OA application maintenance), performance is problematic when managing databases with large amounts of data and/or increasing numbers of concurrent users.

The performance problem relates to the breakdown of application processing on the LAN. User interface processing is performed entirely on the local PC, as is application processing. Logical data processing also occurs on the PC, which can create a data integrity problem (discussed later in this chapter). Physical data processing is split between the local PC and the central file server.

A file server is a lot like a hard drive attached to your computer by a very long cable (the network), and that cable is usually shared by many users. When your application needs to find a particular record in a database, it retrieves a set of physical blocks from the file server file. It is up to the application to find the required record in the data stream that is transmitted.

The efficiency of each request (defined as the ratio of data required to data returned) depends significantly on the capabilities of the application programmer. Using clever indexing strategies, a skilled programmer can write applications in the file server environment that support hundreds of thousands and even millions of records.

On the other hand, ad hoc query performance can be disastrous. Users without a sophisticated understanding of how to manipulate indexes to improve performance can initiate queries that—although accurate—require that the system return all records for review by the local PC. Not only is this time-consuming, but it also can lock up system resources for the hours it takes to retrieve the results.

The problem is that the file server doesn't know anything about the data itself. All it understands is the physical storage of information on the hard drive. The result is that a simple query could take hours, filling the network with useless traffic and slowing down every other operation at the same time.

Note

Here is a useful analogy to help you understand LAN-DBMS computing.

If you call information to get a telephone number for John Murphy on Cedar Street, the conversation might go like this:

OPERATOR:	"Information. What city, please?"
YOU:	"Murphysville, please. I would like a number for John Murphy on Cedar Street."
OPERATOR:	"Please hold for the number."
[Pause]	
RECORDING:	"Abbott, James, 555-1234."
	"Abbott, Martin, 555-1299."
	"Abby, Philip, 555-9999."
	...

[Two hours later—are you still waiting?]

...

"Murphy, James, 555-8888."

"Murphy, John, 555-6666."

Of course, by this time, John Murphy has probably moved to another city.

You didn't call to have someone play a recorded telephone book—you called to get a specific number. With LAN-based databases, the server sends your application the telephone book and it's up to the application program to find the number you need.

The other problem with the PC/LAN-based approach to database applications is as much cultural as technical. There are plenty of outstanding PC programmers and sophisticated power users, but every shop seems to have its share of dBASE programmers whose background in computer systems left them with no understanding of the craft of software development.

This latter group tends to be very productive in the early stages of development, but software maintenance is another issue. Because data integrity checks are housed in the application software, and application software is distributed, version control and related data integrity control often can fall victim to deadlines and software enhancements.

The fact of life is that application development, report development, and data analysis are gravitating toward individuals with less experience and less training in the information disciplines. This means that the "system" (to be better defined later) needs to become more intelligent, more protective of data integrity, and more efficient.

The host-versus-LAN dichotomy is summarized as follows:

Host	LAN
High speed	Low cost
Central administration	Local processing
Geographical distribution	High-speed communication
Maturity	Opportunity

The issue of maturity versus opportunity is where a lot of people are stuck right now. Mainframes represent a stable, predictable environment, with dependable utilities, well-developed infrastructures, and large budgets. PCs represent a dynamic, uncontrolled world, short on administrative utilities, long on risk, and with very low cost expectations from management.

CLIENT/SERVER TO THE RESCUE!

Client/server computing seeks to merge the best of both worlds: the sheer power and central control of mainframes with the lower cost and better processing balance of PCs. Let's look at how this is achieved.

First, what is client/server computing? For many, client/server is another way of saying cooperative processing. By that definition, any time two separate computers are communicating, you are in a client/server world. Broadly speaking, client/server is a subset of cooperative processing, which is a peer-to-peer architecture.

In the real world (that is, when you see the words in the classified ads), client/server refers to the interaction between user workstations and central database servers. The workstations run application programs that query and update data stored centrally on the database server.

The following are the key points about this client/server model:

◆ The client process and server process may be (but are not required to be) connected by a LAN or a Wide Area Network (WAN). They both could be running on the same computer.

◆ The basic language used to communicate between the client and a database server is through Structured Query Language (SQL).

Note

It's worth understanding a key point about SQL. SQL is a highly abstract language, in which the programmer or user describes his requirements (add a row of data to a particular table, display rows having the following characteristics, and so forth) without needing to understand or define the physical approach to answering the question. The database server is fully responsible for interpreting an abstract request, finding the fastest method to retrieve the data and managing the locking and data integrity.

Because SQL is so abstract, the implementation of client and server software tools and client/server applications does not require the close coordination ordinarily required for cooperative processing. In client/server, both sides write to a common API with some confidence that the final result will provide sufficient functionality and good performance.

Client/server provides a new approach to the central/local distribution of work and responsibility. Like a host-based system, client/server is capable of exerting stringent central control over data integrity, administration, and security. Because data is stored centrally, client/server enables you (the administrator) to back up work centrally and to perform periodic maintenance against data stored in a central and secure location.

Because application programs run entirely on the client systems and only database requests are handled centrally, intricate and processor-intensive user interfaces (for example, Windows applications and highly graphical data presentations) are performed using local processors and local memory.

Note

The other resource that can become a bottleneck is the network, especially in a multiuser environment with graphical applications. Anyone who has tried to execute intricate X-Window applications with multiple X-terminals on a busy network will tell you that executing graphical application processing on a host can cause serious performance degradation on a LAN. (With lots of users, CPU and memory resources on the server quickly can run dry.)

Local application and interface processing (using local CPUs and local memory) make the client/server model work.

Client/server is particularly efficient (when properly implemented) at responding to ad hoc queries. A LAN-DBMS often responds to simple requests by delivering huge amounts of useless data, but client/server systems return an answer. This answer, called a result set, is only the rows and columns of data that you requested from the server in a SQL statement.

As mentioned before, SQL should not dictate a specific method of answering a query; it only defines the data required. How does the server know how to answer the question?

Sybase's RDBMS includes a query optimizer, whose responsibility is to analyze the SQL query, consider the data it is to act on, and decide on an optimization plan. The Sybase optimizer is very powerful and a major factor in the success of SQL Server. (The optimizer is also a fascinating part of the system, and understanding how it works can have a major impact on system performance. For more on the optimizer, see Chapter 13, "Basic Application Performance and Tuning." However, a detailed discussion of query performance and tuning issues falls outside the scope of this book.)

The other implication of client/server computing (particularly under the Sybase model) is that application programming can be distributed without creating complete havoc in the database. Sybase (and now other competitive products) provides several data integrity structures to perform server-side validation and processing within the database. Detailed instructions on building these structures fall outside the scope of this book, but review the following object descriptions so that you understand their purpose.

Sybase provides these database objects for enforcing data integrity within the database server:

- ◆ Rules enforce the domain of values permitted for a column within a database. For example, a rule can require that only the values "red," "green," and "blue" will be permitted for a color column. This rule would be enforced during every insert or update to a table for the column, once the rule is bound to the column.

- ◆ Check constraints, which also enforce the domain of values, are new (System 10 and later only). Declarative check constraints are very similar to rules but with two main differences. First, the constraint is defined as part of the `create table` or `alter table` statement. Second, a check constraint can refer to more than one column in a table (verify that "ship_date" is later than the "order_date").

- ◆ Defaults provide a value for a column when no value is provided during an insert. For example, a default of "blue" can be created and bound to a color column. This default would be inserted whenever an insert is made to the table and no value is specified for the column. In System 10 and later, defaults also can be defined as part of the `create table` or `alter table` statement.

♦ Unique indexes require that a column or set of columns within a table be unique for that table. Indexes also are used to improve query performance. (For more on indexes, see Chapter 13.)

♦ Primary key constraints, in System 10 and later, allow you to identify which column or columns comprise the primary key of a table. These constraints are defined as part of the `create table` or `alter table` command. The columns cannot be nullable, and a unique index will be created automatically when the command is executed.

♦ Unique constraints, in System 10 and later, allow you to identify which column or combination of columns will be unique for each row in the table. These constraints are defined as part of the `create table` or `alter table` command. The columns can be nullable, and a unique index will be created automatically when the command is executed.

♦ Referential integrity (RI) constraints enforce RI between related tables (System 10 and later). For example, a constraint can require that a customer ID exist within a customer's table before allowing an order from that customer in the orders table.

♦ Triggers enable the database administrator to specify a set of SQL instructions to execute after any modification of a table (insert, update, or delete). Triggers are used to maintain referential integrity, to maintain derived or dependent data, and to perform complex data validations. For example, a trigger on the orders table can maintain a running accounts-receivable balance in the customer's table.

♦ Stored procedures enable authorized users to define executable SQL routines to operate on the server. Stored procedures can be specified by name and accept parameters, and they can dramatically improve server performance. Stored procedures often are used to enforce standards in table modification routines. For example, a procedure to handle all inserts to the orders table can check stock, ensure that the customer is in good standing, determine a proper shipping date, and maintain other dependent data.

Because the server is able to manage data integrity, this burden can be lifted (in part or in whole) from the application development at the client. Consider each item in this list. Where was this processing taking place before? Data integrity was managed within the application, not the database. Application programmers were fully responsible for data integrity. An error in implementing data integrity in an application would likely result in having "bad" data in the database. The detection, identification, and clean-up of this data could require hundreds (or thousands!) of hours. DBAs could do no more than provide guidelines, review code, and hope for the best.

The DBA is able to become more active now. The database has extensive capabilities, and the DBA can use the data integrity objects to enforce guidelines on the server side. In many cases, this enables thousands of lines of redundant code to be eliminated from applications. Applications become simpler, they are faster to develop, and it is less likely to be a disaster when they contain an error.

THE CRITICAL FACTOR: COST

Of course, the driving force behind the move to client/server is the cost difference. Mainframe hardware and software is expensive to buy and expensive to keep. Annual maintenance costs alone make MIS managers see red (instead of black), and the rightsizing trend is intended to bring systems cost to an acceptable level. For some organizations, this can mean the elimination of a mainframe or not having to perform an expensive mainframe upgrade to handle new application requirements.

Note

There is some discussion of using mainframes as giant database servers, and some organizations are already doing this. Because UNIX systems are able to provide more storage options in hundreds of gigabytes, they will be more attractive as superservers. As of this writing, mainframe DASD storage costs approximately thirty times what UNIX drives cost for the same capacity (and that gap is actually widening).

Mainframes as database servers represent an enormous integration problem as well: There is a very limited choice of RDBMS software, and sophisticated connectivity on the mainframe is substantially more difficult than on the UNIX and other more open platforms (including Windows NT). The proprietary architecture of mainframes imposes a substantial burden on an integrator because of the problems in transferring knowledge and tools from one environment to the other.

Cost issues extend beyond the purchase and maintenance costs of computing equipment. LANs are not cheap, and they can become enormously complex. On the other hand, most organizations are building LANs and WANs for other uses, including office automation, telephony, and video-conferencing. Client/server creates substantially less traffic on the network than some of these other systems.

Many businesses have bought into client/server to gain access to advanced development tools, such as PowerBuilder, Visual Basic, Visual C++, and many useful query and analysis products as well. The opportunity to develop products in less time does more than reduce development costs; it also enables an organization to move more rapidly into new markets, to improve customer service, and to be more competitive.

Warning

> It is crucial that you understand the business case for client/server in your organization in order to gauge management's expectations of your new systems. Many MIS shops have succeeded in implementing newer technologies, but have failed in the eyes of management because of a marked difference between what was implemented and what management expected.

In the coming chapters, you look at SQL Server from an administrative standpoint so that you can understand the strengths and weaknesses of the product and the background you need to develop an aggressive approach to maintenance and tuning of the server.

SUMMARY

You and your organization have traded in the maturity and stability you were used to with mainframe systems for the dynamism and opportunity of the client/server environment. Maybe you decided to step up from a LAN DBMS to a database capable of supporting hundreds or thousands of users and hundreds of gigabytes of information.

This book provides you with the information you need to bolster the system and to provide the reliable service your organization expects from its data resources.

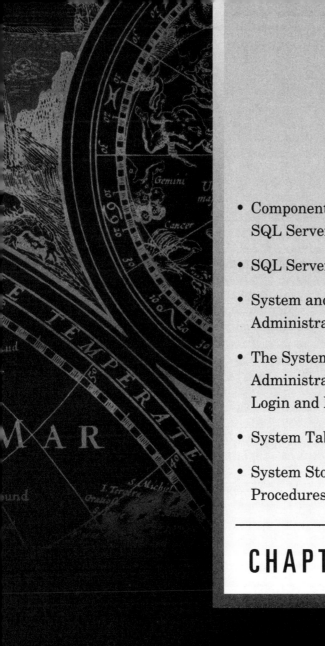

- Components of
  SQL Server

- SQL Server Versions

- System and Database
  Administration

- The Systems
  Administrator (sa)
  Login and Roles

- System Tables

- System Stored
  Procedures

CHAPTER 2

Overview of Systems
Administration

In this chapter, you look at the roles and responsibilities of a Sybase systems administrator and how they differ from or overlap with those of a database or operating system administrator. You learn critical terminology and explore the following key concepts:

◆ Roles (system defined)
◆ System tables
◆ System stored procedures

COMPONENTS OF SQL SERVER

Recall from Chapter 1 that the SQL Server environment consists of clients, servers, and a network that enables them to communicate. Let's review each of these components to understand the broad spectrum of administration required to keep SQL Server operational.

Client components include the following:

◆ Workstation hardware
◆ Network interface card (NIC)
◆ Operating system
◆ Network software
◆ Network library software
◆ Database library software (ct-library/db-library)
◆ Application software

Network components include:

◆ Server and client NIC
◆ Network software
◆ Hubs, routers, and concentrators
◆ Cable

Server components include:

◆ Server hardware
◆ NIC
◆ Operating system
◆ Network software
◆ Network library software
◆ Server library software

- SQL Server software
- Audit System
- Backup Server

As the SQL Server system administrator, you are probably only *officially* responsible for the SQL Server software and the various client libraries, but consider a different question. When the server becomes unavailable, which of these components could be the culprit? The answer: any of them. Client/server requires a mastery of several disciplines to maintain solid, reliable performance day in and day out.

As system administrator, you need to muster a team of experts—in client software, server software, and all the networking layers in between. As you work through this chapter, map the examples to your environment; this will enhance your capability for troubleshooting problems as they arise.

Note

People who are worried about job security in the client/server world should think about all the areas of expertise that are required to make a complex system such as SQL Server really work. Here's a very brief list of specializations:

- Project manager
- Analyst
- Relational database designer
- SQL server administrator
- Server OS (for example, UNIX) administrator
- Network administrator
- Help-desk staff
- Database administrator
- Client OS (for example, Windows) specialist
- Applications programmer

SQL SERVER VERSIONS

SQL Server has been around for a number of years, and many releases and versions are in production in companies around the world. If you bought Sybase SQL Server in 1996, you bought System 11, the version of the software that this book focuses on. If you bought SQL Server from Microsoft, you probably bought (or should get) version 6.0.

Sybase's System 10 release offered a variety of important features for system administrators; most visible are enhanced, faster backup capabilities, roles, and auditing. (This book points out features specific to System 10 and later; older versions of SQL Server and Microsoft releases will not include these advanced features.)

SQL Server runs on several operating platforms, including UNIX, NetWare, Windows NT, OS/2, and Open VMS. UNIX is by far the dominant platform for Sybase SQL Server, but Microsoft is selling thousands of servers on Windows NT. As of this writing, the major UNIX flavors of SQL Server are Sun, HP, IBM, DEC, and AT&T. Sybase's stated policy has been to provide concurrent major releases on each of these platforms, with releases for other platforms following closely behind.

SQL Server clients can run on any of the server platforms. In addition, development libraries are available on MS-DOS, Windows, and Macintosh. It is even possible to develop client software that operates in the MVS environment to enable mainframe terminals to execute applications to modify SQL Server data. (For organizations with well-developed WANs running over mainframe connectivity components, this approach enables a much smoother transition from a centralized model to a client/ server model. Over time and as appropriate, specific sites can convert to intelligent workstations. Until then, users can still operate from existing terminals and over existing lines.)

SYSTEM AND DATABASE ADMINISTRATION

In some organizations, no distinction is drawn between administration of SQL Server and its resident databases. A single individual or group is responsible for all these issues. Certainly, overall system responsiveness and integrity require good coordination between the system and its databases, but there are distinctions between SQL Server and database administration. The systems administrator keeps the server available and focuses on the relationship between the server and its operating system. The database administrator focuses on database query performance, transaction throughput, and concurrency. Chapter 14, "Periodic Maintenance for Your SQL Server," takes a brief look at the database administration issues, but for the most part, this book concentrates on server administration issues.

THE SYSTEMS ADMINISTRATOR (SA) LOGIN AND ROLES

Prior to the System 10 release, all administrative responsibilities needed to be executed by an individual logged in—literally—as sa, for system administrator. System 10 introduced the concept of roles. Now specific user logins can be assigned components of the administrative responsibility, enabling you to track and audit administrative activities.

The three roles are the sa_role (systems administrator) for administrative tasks, sso_role (site security officer) for security tasks, and oper_role (operator) for backup and recovery tasks. See Chapter 6, "Security and User Administration," for more on roles.

RESPONSIBILITIES OF THE SYSTEM ADMINISTRATOR

The Sybase system administrator is responsible for the overall performance and reliability of SQL Server. In System 10 and later, a systems administrator is considered any login that has been granted the sa_role. (Note that the sa login is automatically granted the sa_role upon server installation.) For the purposes of this section, the use of sa really refers to any login granted that role. Here's a list of some of the responsibilities of the system administrator. (This probably is a pretty good place to start defining the job description of an sa for your organization or workgroup.)

SERVER INSTALLATION AND UPGRADE

The system administrator installs the software on the server. (When performing an installation, assistance from a person skilled in the server operating system is always helpful.) A sybase user must be added to the operating system to perform the SQL Server installation. This user is also responsible for applying patches and bug fixes to SQL Server, and for performing major version upgrades. Once installation is complete, the system will contain a login for the sa.

PHYSICAL DEVICE CONFIGURATION

Sybase uses underlying system resources, including disk, memory, and network resources. The system administrator needs to identify physical storage areas, then define logical mappings to those areas.

DATABASE CREATION

After identifying logical devices, the sa creates databases on those devices, then often assigns ownership (and administrative responsibility) to another login.

SYSTEM CONFIGURATION SETTINGS

The system administrator manages system configuration settings, including the amount of server memory and how it is allocated, the number of concurrent user connections and open databases, and the number of locks and system devices. These settings affect system availability and performance.

SERVER MONITORING AND PREVENTIVE MAINTENANCE

SQL Server administration requires a well-defined regimen of preventive maintenance. Activities to include among regular administrative activities are outlined in
Chapter 14.

BACKUP AND MAINTENANCE OF THE SYSTEM DATABASES

The master database is a crucial resource in which systemwide information is
recorded. Model is the template database for all subsequent database creations. All
stored procedures are maintained in the sybsystemprocs database. As system
administrator, you guarantee the availability and integrity of these databases.

SERVER STARTUP AND SHUTDOWN

Only the system administrator is permitted to start and stop the server process. You
may require periodic shutdowns to change system parameters or to repair broken
equipment.

In addition, the system administrator is the backup database administrator (dbo)
for all databases.

RESPONSIBILITIES OF THE SITE SECURITY OFFICER

The Site Security Officer (sso) is responsible for adding logins and administering
the sa_role and sso_role, as well as the audit system (if installed). The sso is
considered to be any login that has been granted the sso_role. (Note that the sa login
is also automatically granted the sso_role upon server installation.) Following is a
list of tasks handled by the sso.

SYSTEM SECURITY

SQL Server provides several levels of security: server login security, database
security, and object security. A user with the sso_role is responsible for server-level
security.

MANAGEMENT OF SITE SECURITY AND OPERATOR ROLES

Only a user with the sso_role may grant others that permission or grant or revoke
the operator role.

MANAGEMENT OF THE AUDIT SYSTEM

The sso is responsible for server auditing. The sso may grant others permission to use and query the audit tables, but only the sso can control what databases, objects, and users are audited.

RESPONSIBILITIES OF THE OPERATOR

An operator is able to back up and load all databases. An operator is considered to be any login that has been granted the oper_role. Note that an operator can even back up and load databases that he cannot access in any other way. For example, a login with the oper_role may not be able to use a database or access any of the underlying objects, but still has the ability to perform a database backup or load.

SYSTEM TABLES

SQL Server stores almost all configuration, security, and object information in its own *system tables*. There are system tables within each individual database, as well as in the master database.

Note

The system tables are sometimes referred to as the system catalog or data dictionary. It's crucial to remember that system tables are stored within each individual database (including master). *Additional tables* appear in the master database to store systemwide information.

DATABASE-LEVEL SYSTEM TABLES

These databases are stored in every database, *including master:*

sysalternates	User "aliases" for logins whose database access is granted through another login
syscolumns	Names and characteristics of every column in every table and view in the database
syscomments	Contains the creation text of every view, rule, default, trigger, and procedure. This text is accessed through sp_helptext.
sysconstraints	Names and characteristics of table constraints
sysdepends	Relationships between dependent objects (views to tables, stored procedures to tables, and so forth)

sysindexes	Index and space allocation information for every table
syskeys	Documented keys for each table
syslogs	Transaction log, a non-readable record of each logged modification performed within the database (this is the only system table stored in the log segment—see Chapter 5, "Defining, Altering, and Maintaining Databases and Logs," for more on segments)
sysobjects	Object definitions (tables, views, procedures, triggers, rules, defaults, constraints)
sysprocedures	Preparsed optimization trees for code-based objects (views, procedures, triggers, rules, defaults, constraints)
sysprotects	Permissions for users on objects (tables, views, procedures)
sysreferences	Names and characteristics of each referential integrity constraint declared on a table or column
sysroles	Maps the server-wide roles to local database groups
syssegments	Database partitions for storing different types or categories of objects and managing object growth below the level of the entire database
systypes	System- and user-defined datatypes available for columns when creating tables
systhresholds	Contains information on each threshold defined for the database
sysusermessages	User-defined messages, added with sp_addmessage, for use with the raiserror statement (this is the only system table that is stored in a user data area)
sysusers	Authorized logins who may access the database

Note

Don't confuse the keys in syskeys with index columns or with primary and foreign keys in constraints. Index columns determine the contents of an index, as well as the physical sort order of data (if clustered) and a unique identifier (if unique). Primary and foreign keys constraints define an enforced referential integrity relationship between tables.

Keys recorded in syskeys (established with `sp_primarykey`, `sp_foreignkey`, `sp_commonkey`) define the structure of tables *as system documentation only*. Their only real use comes when an application examines these values to suggest a join or to learn about the structure of the tables, but the keys defined in syskeys are never enforced by SQL Server itself.

SYSTEM-LEVEL SYSTEM TABLES

These databases are stored in master:

syslogins	Name, password, and configuration information about each server login
sysloginroles	Administrative roles for each login
syssrvroles	Available administrative roles
sysconfigures	System configuration values to be used at next system startup
syscurconfigs	Current system configuration values
sysdatabases	Database name, owner, status, and other information
sysdevices	Physical storage resources available to SQL Server (both active database devices and backup devices)
sysusages	Data allocations and mappings of physical storage areas to individual databases
sysengines	Information about available CPUs (primarily for the SMP version of SQL Server)
sysprocesses	Process IDs, login information, and current status of each logged-in user
syslocks	Current locks (this is a memory table only—if the server goes down for any reason, all locks are released)
syslanguages	Installed language sets (in the U.S., this is usually only `us_english`)
syscharsets	Installed character sets
sysmessages	Server-wide error messages
sysservers	All servers involved in remote procedure calls
sysremotelogins	Mappings and login identifiers for users logging in from remote SQL Servers

AUDIT SYSTEM TABLES

These databases are stored in sybsecurity:

sysauditoptions	Global auditing option settings
sysaudits	Detailed audit information

SYSTEM STORED PROCEDURES

SQL Server enables the database developer to store SQL routines within the database; these are *stored procedures*. Stored procedures provide faster performance, reduced network traffic, better control for sensitive updates, and modular programming.

Although stored procedures often support user table processing, Sybase provides several stored procedures called *system stored procedures,* which support system table processing. For example, the sp_helpdb stored procedure returns a complete listing of all system databases. Other system stored procedures (for example, sp_addlogin and sp_bindrule) modify system tables.

Note

When I first encountered SQL Server, I called a technical contact to find out how to retrieve the columns from a table. I'm not quite sure what she thought I was asking (she must have thought I knew more than I did), but this is what she told me to type:

```
select c.name, c.colid
From syscolumns c, sysobjects o
where c.id = o.id
and o.name = "employers"
```

The query worked, but I couldn't help thinking that it was an awfully inconvenient way to get table information. I didn't learn about the sp_help stored procedure until several days (and lots of typing!) later.

SPECIAL CHARACTERISTICS

Names of system stored procedures start with the characters sp_ and are stored in the sybsystemprocs database. By naming a stored procedure with sp_ and storing it in sybsystemprocs, you can create your own system stored procedures, or procs.

When you execute a stored procedure whose name starts with sp_, the server first looks in your current database to find the proc. If the proc is not found in your current database, the server looks for it in sybsystemprocs.

Note

> Users of SQL Server prior to System 10 should note that earlier versions stored system stored procedures in the master database.
>
> By moving system stored procs out of master, Sybase enables master database backups to run more quickly and leaves more room in the master database for system configuration information.

Ordinary stored procedures are interpreted in terms of the current database when the procedure is created. For example, if you create a stored procedure in a user database, the stored procedure is immediately bound to the tables within the database. Note that in the following examples, any characters embedded inside a /* and */ are interpreted as comments and are ignored by SQL Server:

```
/* create proc in user1db */
use user1db
go
create proc show_objects
as
select name, user_name(uid)
from sysobjects
go
```

You can execute this procedure from any database, but you will always see a listing of objects in user1db, the database in which the procedure was created. To invoke a procedure in one database from a different database, you must qualify the procedure name. The format is *database.owner.procedure*. If the database name is not provided, the object is assumed to be in the current database. If the owner is not provided, it first looks for an object owned by you; if you don't own an object of that name, it then looks for an object owned by the user dbo, the database owner. Assuming the previous procedure was created by dbo, you would execute the procedure like this:

```
/* sample execution of procedure from database user9db */
use user9db
go
user1db..show_objects
go
```

System procedures always are interpreted in terms of the current database *when the procedure is executed.* Create a similar system procedure in sybsystemprocs:

```
/* create this proc in sybsystemprocs */
use sybsystemprocs
go
create proc sp_show_objects
as
select name, user_name(uid)
from sysobjects
go
```

When the procedure runs, the system returns the contents of sysobjects in the current database at execution time. Remember, you don't need to fully qualify the procedure name with its database and owner if you have prefixed it with sp_:

```
/* sample execution from user9db */
use user9db
go
sp_show_objects
go
```

Note

With some practice, you will be creating these stored procedures yourself, without giving it much thought. Do not forget, however, that a stored procedure must be prefaced by execute (or exec) if it is not the first command in a batch. Here is an example:

```
/* From user9db, execute the */
/* show_objects proc in user1db */
/* AND the sp_show_objects proc */
use user9db
go
user1db..show_objects
exec sp_show_objects
go
```

USEFUL SYSTEM PROCEDURES

The following are system procedures you will find useful:

sp_who	Current logins and operations (from sysprocesses in master database)
sp_lock	Current locks and table identifiers (from syslocks in master database)
sp_help	Objects in the database or detailed object information (from sysobjects, syscolumns, sysindexes, syskeys)
sp_helpdb	Databases on the server (from sysdatabases in master database)
sp_configure	Current system configuration settings (from syscurconfigs, sysconfigures in master database)
sp_helpdevice	Physical storage and backup devices on the server (from sysdevices in master database)

Note

> If you plan to write your own system stored procedures, you probably want to identify your procs to avoid future versions of SQL Server from overwriting important, working procs with new standard system procedures. For example, if your company name is "ABC Corp.," you may want to prefix all your developed stored procs with sp_abc_.

SUMMARY

As an administrator of a Sybase SQL Server, you have several areas of responsibility. These responsibilities can be assigned to other logins using roles. System tables record configuration and object information, and system stored procedures enable you to query and modify those system tables. (Although it is possible to update the system tables by hand, Sybase strongly recommends against bypassing the system stored procedures to make changes directly to system tables unless instructed to do so by Sybase Technical Support.)

In the coming chapters, you examine the many responsibilities of the system administrator, explore the system tables involved in maintenance, and learn the proper usage of most of the system stored procedures.

- Server Selection and Configuration

- Server Installation

- Server Startup, Login, and Shutdown

- Client Installation

- Networking and Connectivity

- Troubleshooting

- Changing Defaults: The Top Ten Items To Address Upon Installation

- Environment Checklist

CHAPTER 3

SQL Server Installation and Connectivity

In this chapter, you take a look at installation and connectivity with SQL Server. You explore some broad guidelines and learn about the traps at this stage. This chapter does not give detailed instructions, because so many of the choices you need to make relate to your specific environment: your version of SQL Server, your platform, and your choice of client operating system. There are, however, several areas that may be of immediate interest:

◆ If you are trying to decide on a database server environment for your organization, see the section titled "Server Selection and Configuration."

◆ If you've already decided on your environment and are ready to install, you can find out some things to look out for in "Server Installation."

◆ If the server is already installed, but you want more information on how to bring the server up or down, see "Server Startup, Login, and Shutdown."

◆ Of course, you can't ignore the client side of client/server. Preparing clients to communicate with the server is often an area of much confusion for many people. See "Client Installation" for more information.

◆ If you have the client and the server but want to know how they communicate, see "Networking and Connectivity" for an overview on the various protocols used in the industry.

◆ Looks like all the bases are covered, right? The system is going to work the first time and every time. It's always nice to be optimistic, but, just in case, we've included a "Troubleshooting" section to help you identify the problem and get the system running again.

◆ Even if your system is up and you haven't changed a thing, do not leave this chapter without reviewing "Changing Defaults—The Top Ten Items To Address Upon Installation." You'll be glad you did.

◆ Finally, at the end of the chapter is a "Checklist" of the items that are part of a normal installation.

SERVER SELECTION AND CONFIGURATION

Before setting up SQL Server, you must understand the version and platform on which you are running—the characteristics of SQL Servers, the various operating systems they run under, and the versions of SQL Server that have been released in the last several years.

This is not meant to be a buyer's guide to Sybase versions. Your choices will de-pend most on the following crucial organizational issues:

◆ What operating systems are installed? If you already are running 500 NetWare servers in your organization, you should take a long, hard look at

SQL Server NLM. If you are an all-UNIX shop, you should consider a UNIX implementation of SQL Server. New operating systems create new problems for MIS staffs, but a particular version of SQL Server may integrate connectivity features that help in other aspects of your project.

♦ What network protocols are installed? If you already have networked heavily with TCP/IP, using the UNIX version of SQL Server won't add complexity or create new RAM problems on client workstations. If you are using Named Pipes to communicate with Windows NT servers, you may consider a Windows NT implementation.

♦ What are the required performance characteristics? At the time of this writing, there are limitations in the capabilities of Intel-based hardware for providing effective symmetric multiprocessing (SMP), and the bus architecture continues, for the most part, to be inappropriate for applications that move big blocks of data.

♦ How large are the databases you will implement? For a very large database (VLDB), you should consider the availability, cost, and reliability of very large storage devices for your platform.

♦ What other Sybase products do you plan to implement? Some newer products, such as Replication Server and Navigation Server, were available only for UNIX at the time this book went to press. If your architecture might benefit from these capabilities, you may find it easier or more manageable to bring up all Sybase applications under a single operating system.

♦ What is your budget? If your budget is very tight, you may want to look at one of the Intel-based versions (NetWare, SCO UNIX, or Windows NT).

SERVER HARDWARE CHARACTERISTICS

SQL Server itself needs to be fast enough to handle the work of several users concurrently, and to manage all the overhead involved in running a complex product. The speed of the bus is critical so that data can move quickly between memory, CPU, disk, and network.

The memory capacity also is critical. Once Sybase has set aside the minimal memory it needs for users, devices, and databases, the remaining server memory is used for cache. There is a simple rule about Sybase and memory: more is better. The larger your tables, the more indexes you plan to create, and the more users you expect, the greater the memory you should plan to install.

Here are some quick RAM guidelines:

♦ Development systems can run with only 16MB of actual RAM in the system, although occasionally that is not enough memory even to start the server.

- ◆ Production systems can have as much as 1GB.
- ◆ On Intel-based systems, the lowest reasonable RAM is probably 32MB.

SQL SERVER PLATFORMS

Sybase runs as a process under several operating systems. The encouraging part is that, aside from installation, disk configuration, and setup of the backup devices, SQL Server is the same across all releases.

This chapter describes installation generally and some of the common environments. First, however, here is a review of the major platforms on which SQL Server is available.

The one critical difference between the platforms is that UNIX enables Sybase devices to be mapped directly to unformatted, "raw" physical drives or drive sectors. If you can't write to a raw device, your devices are mapped to the operating system's file system. For example, Sybase on a NetWare server maps physical devices to specific pathnames in the NetWare file system (NFS). Most environments enable you to optimize the system to avoid additional overhead and to turn off cached writes (additional caching between SQL Server and the drive, which can cause data integrity problems if the server goes down). If you use file system devices, it is critical to explore these issues to guarantee both performance and data integrity.

UNIX (WHERE IT ALL BEGAN)

Sybase SQL Server was first released under UNIX and that continues to be the first operating system (or set of operating systems) where new releases are developed. Sybase focuses on five primary UNIX flavors when developing new versions, with other flavors of UNIX appearing in a second wave along with other major platform releases. These are the five mainstream UNIX flavors:

- ◆ Sun OS and Solaris (Sun)
- ◆ HP/UX (Hewlett-Packard)
- ◆ AIX (IBM)
- ◆ Ultrix (Digital)
- ◆ UNIX System V (AT&T/NCR)

Nearly all hardware vendors in the UNIX arena can tell you about major Sybase applications running on their products. When choosing your hardware platform for a UNIX implementation, your criteria must include performance benchmarks, customer referrals, and internal experience with the UNIX product.

Warning

> Customer referrals are very important. The critical issue in client/ server (as in all open, multivendor architectures) is the compatibility and supportability of all the components. Ask vendors for names of others running Sybase on their platforms. Call those users and get detailed configurations: What specific products are you using? How are you using them? Do they work well together? Is each vendor's technical support group aware of the other products you use?
>
> The fact is, there is no way to avoid being a pioneer in at least some part of your work with client/server. You will use at least one new untested product, or a new version, or a unique combination of products and features. Every implementation is a little different.
>
> The critical point is to know in advance which elements are new or experimental and to make time for testing, experimentation, and even some backtracking if critical elements fall short.

WINDOWS NT

Windows NT is a portable operating system that runs on a variety of hardware platforms, from small, single-processor PC clones to very large, multiprocessor RISC systems. SQL Server ports along with Windows NT to all those platforms, although it is probably even more important to be certain that another organization has tried to make your planned configuration work.

SQL Server can be used for Windows NT exclusively for in-house development. It is inexpensive to implement on an Intel box, and the server also can run other work at the same time. This is the only Intel environment where SQL Server runs well even when users are doing other work at the same time.

Microsoft also sells a version of SQL Server for Windows NT. (For more about that version, see the sections, "SQL Server Versions" and "Microsoft SQL Server," later in this chapter.)

OS/2

The original version of SQL Server for OS/2 presented an interesting problem. It provided all the features of other versions, but, *if you tried to do anything else in OS/2 while SQL Server was running,* multitasking resulted in either extremely poor performance or complete server lockup. It was discouraging.

Preliminary work with the System 10 implementation shows that Sybase has really addressed the OS/2 market with a solid product. You should still be aware of serious performance degradation when running another process on the server while the server is handling queries.

Most organizations who have implemented SQL Server on OS/2 chose it because of the following:

◆ They are 100 percent IBM shops.
◆ They need the promised integration between OS/2 and their existing mainframes.
◆ They like the low cost (compared to UNIX).
◆ They have a fear and loathing of UNIX.

NetWare

Organizations with thousands of NetWare servers like the fact that the Sybase implementation of SQL Server uses IPX/SPX, meaning that client systems do not need to add another protocol. The proprietary NLM architecture does mean that client/server applications that do more than query a static SQL Server are harder to write, but the server is fairly reliable, provides acceptable performance, and supports a moderate-size work group.

Warning

Do not use the server for file services, print services, or anything else if it's a production SQL Server. Performance will be atrocious.

Open VMS

For organizations with large networks of VAXes and strong organizational experience with DEC, Sybase on Open VMS might make sense. VMS is a capable multitasking environment, and many of the systems provide good throughput. This environment has proven itself to be very reliable and easy to manage and network. On the other hand, it's rare to find any organization interested in buying into a new VAX to run SQL Server.

SQL Server Versions

The Sybase SQL server is intended to be a fully operational online transaction processing (OLTP) database. Organizations that implement OLTP systems in SQL Server are understandably nervous about upgrades to the server. Sybase is no different from any other software vendor when it comes to new releases; along with all the fabulous new features come all the fabulous new bugs.

Here are a few of the important Sybase releases you may encounter, along with the important features introduced with the release:

- Version 4.2 (released around 1989) introduced unions.
- Version 4.8 (1990) introduced multiprocessor architecture.
- Version 4.9x (1992) introduced stable symmetric multiprocessing, and some maintenance features were introduced in anticipation of System 10.
- System 10 (1993) introduced server cursors, auditing, improved security, better maintenance features, and backup server.
- System 11 (1996) provides better memory management for performance.

Note

What's with these version numbers—4.1, 4.2, 4.8, 4.9, System…11? The rumor is that Sybase was preparing for the big release of System 5 after version 4.9. (According to a Sybase engineer, it even says it's version 5 in the code!) Oracle released their version 7, however, and the rest is history. (DBMS Customer: "Hmm, 5 is less than 7, so Oracle must be better. I'll buy Oracle!" Now there's respect for your customer!) System 11 came out as a new, fuller product.

MICROSOFT SQL SERVER

Microsoft and Sybase cooperated for years on the SQL Server product line. Microsoft was responsible for Intel versions of the software (OS/2 and later Windows NT); Sybase handled everything else. The products were based on the same core code, and their architectures were identical. Microsoft releases typically trailed Sybase releases by about six months. From the standpoint of developers and users, it was ideal: there was a straightforward path from less expensive, less capable servers from Microsoft to more expensive, fire-breathing systems from Sybase.

Things got confusing when Sybase started selling an NLM version, because this armed Novell to compete with Microsoft in certain circumstances. It all fell apart in early 1994 when Sybase and Microsoft agreed to disagree. Microsoft has announced that it will remain compatible with the 4.2/4.8 release of SQL Server but that it will feel free to provide enhancements to that product, now 6.0, soon to be 6.5.

Sybase has already introduced a slew of enhancements, including new keywords and subtle variations from the 4.2/4.8 platform. The differences between the Microsoft and Sybase products will continue to grow.

Which version is right for you? That call is getting harder with the release of Windows NT on high-end RISC boxes. Microsoft has rewritten some of the multitasking/multiprocessing code in SQL Server to take better advantage of the multithreading architecture of Windows NT. On the Intel platform, there have been dramatic performance improvements with NT over Sybase on the same platform; with limited memory and CPU resources, Microsoft can provide startlingly good performance. As of this writing, however, Sybase continues to offer a more mature product with better features and solid performance across a range of platforms.

Which company will ultimately win? Never bet against Microsoft in this industry. It remains in both companies' best interests to continue to maintain compatibility. Both companies probably will continue to benefit so long as the uneasy cease fire between them can hold.

SERVER INSTALLATION

All the activities in this section vary dramatically from platform to platform. The installation routines and utilities vary, and the methods of identifying the server and defining its environment are completely different among the various implementations of SQL Server. Starting and stopping the server is sometimes performed by typing a command, sometimes by clicking on an icon.

On UNIX platforms, you typically have to type a series of commands at the console. In Windows NT, you execute a setup program and follow the on-screen instructions.

Nevertheless, the fundamental installation procedures and the information you must provide are fairly similar.

When you install a SQL Server, you follow the explicit instructions provided in the installation guide for your server.

Warning

The instructions should indicate the version of SQL Server provided, as well as the expected version of the operating system you are using. If your version of SQL Server or the operating system is different from the version specified by the installation manual, it is likely that some of the information in the manual is incorrect.

It's possible that you might install the 4.2.2 version of SQL Server on NetWare version 3.12 but have documentation for a 3.11 version of NetWare. Certain detailed instructions will be incorrect and others unnecessary and misleading.

Sometimes you will find installation supplements or some other document that helps you determine in what way your environment differs from the expected environment.

Just keep in mind that SQL Server places extreme demands on operating systems. There often are patches, utility updates, or other materials that enable the operating system to function properly. The best way to ensure smooth installation and operation is to call Sybase to get information about patches, releases, and other fixes to make your system work. It's also helpful to find another user with *exactly* your set of product releases and find out what that user went through to accomplish an installation. A good place to find these users is in the Sybase Forum (GO SYBASE) on CompuServe. It is an excellent arena to pose questions, access information, and communicate with other Sybase users. This forum is monitored by Sybase employees and can be an alternative source of technical or general information.

Server installation consists of three general steps: gathering information, copying files, and installing the software.

OPERATING SYSTEM USER PRIVILEGES

Sybase needs access to specific user privileges in each operating system environment. Your documentation will tell you the user requirements for your server. On UNIX, you may be able to install SQL Server as the root, but you inevitably will have problems and ultimately will need to rerun the entire installation as sybase. Create the sybase user and log in as sybase to run the installation.

On most other platforms (NT and NetWare, for example), SQL Server runs as a process owned by the administrative login (SUPERVISOR in NetWare, administrator in NT). The installation directories are owned by the administrative login.

STEP 0: FILLING OUT THE FORMS

When you run the installation program, the server asks whether you have completed all the forms before beginning installation. If you answer "No," the server exits the installation program. (The typical next step is to answer "Yes" without filling in the forms.)

The server is going to ask you for some very detailed information about your server. If you are the system administrator for the operating system on which you are installing SQL Server, go ahead and install without filling in the forms. Chances are good that you will know the answers as they arise.

Note

> When I first installed SQL Server on HP/UX, I knew absolutely nothing about HP UNIX, or about the specific system I was running on. My first step was to find someone who really knew UNIX well (and had "root" authorization) and could help me get the answers I needed. It is normal and efficient to seek help in defining the values you will need to complete the installation.

SQL SERVER INSTALLATION PATH

Installation copies a number of files to the operating system file system, including the installation program, the server software itself, installation scripts, and utility files. You need to tell the server where this installation path is located in your directory structure.

In UNIX, you have to grant the full set of rights to the directory to the sybase user. On other platforms, the administrator should have sufficient privileges to run the installation. (Later, you may choose to grant users access to the utility programs, the errorlog, or other parts of the server environment that they might find helpful.)

MASTER DEVICE LOCATION AND SIZE

The next value required by the server is a location and size for the master device. Under UNIX, the master device can be mapped to a file or raw device (in Open VMS, this is a foreign device). Generally, mapping to a raw device provides better integrity and performance. On all other platforms, the master device is a file in the file system.

Mirror the master device (for more information, see Chapter 4, "Defining Physical and Mirror Devices"). You may need to make a provision for a small raw partition to mirror the master device under UNIX. If you are using a file system, the master device probably should be set apart from the other devices, in its own directory. Secure the directory well to prevent other users from stumbling on the master device. Name the file master.dev or something similar that makes its purpose unmistakable.

Tip

> How large should the master device be? It's *very hard* to expand the master device, so it needs to be large enough for everything that will ever be installed on the device.
>
> Typically, the only databases residing on the master device are master, model, and the first 2MB of tempdb. Model, unless you expand it,

is also 2MB. How large will the master database grow? The answer depends on your version of SQL Server.

The growth of the master database was a serious problem prior to the release of System 10. In earlier versions, the system stored procedures were stored in the master database. With each release, there were more and larger stored procedures, and master was stretched to its absolute capacity. There was no way to keep the size of the master database under control.

With System 10, Sybase has moved all the system stored procedures into a separate database, sybsystemprocs, which you should almost always install separately on its own device. This will avoid the hassle of having to move sybsystemprocs once you begin to run out of space in the master device. The contention for space in the master database has been resolved.

The official minimum size of the master device is 17MB. The master device should be no smaller than 30MB, and it certainly doesn't need to be larger than 40MB unless you are planning to write a lot of large, complex system stored procedures in a pre-System 10 server (or if the sybsystemprocs database is created on the master device).

SERVER NAME

The default server name is Sybase. This name is appropriate for only the first server you install on your hardware. Many sites have several servers installed, but they are usually on their own dedicated hardware. Decide on a distinct server name now (see Chapter 18, "Defining Systems Administration and Naming Standards," for recommendations). The name can be no longer than 30 characters, although a shorter name is probably easier to type and remember. The name will be installed in the interfaces file for your server.

PORT NUMBER OR NAMED PIPE

Depending on your network protocol (TCP/IP, IPX/SPX, or Named Pipes), you need to decide on a listening port within the server. Processes that communicate with SQL Server send a message to the host operating system network address. The message is keyed with the internal address of the SQL Server process. The address you establish will be used by every client and every server that needs to communicate with this SQL Server.

3

INSTALLATION AND CONNECTIVITY

In Named Pipes, the internal address of the process is a pipe name—usually, the following; where SERVERNAME is the published name of the host computer:

`\\SERVERNAME\PIPE\SQL\QUERY`

In IPX/SPX, the server is assigned a standard port address within NetWare. There is a default value (normally 0x08bd) included with the server installation. If that value is already assigned, Sybase provides several other values you can try. (It is unlikely that you will encounter any other process with that identifier. Novell has assigned that number to Sybase for SQL Server processes, and you will never find two SQL Servers running on a single NetWare Server.)

In TCP/IP you identify a single integer port address within the server. For UNIX installations, contact an administrator for a value to use.

Tip

If you are installing many SQL Servers at your organization, it is helpful to install Sybase with the same port address everywhere, for the sake of consistency. If you choose not to standardize port addresses, publish port addresses to help those who do workstation setup and administration.

You can use 5000, for example, unless that number is used. If you are installing several SQL Servers on the same hardware, increment this number by 100 for each new server (check with the administrator to ensure that each value is available).

SYBSYSTEMPROCS SIZE AND PATH

The sybsystemprocs database (System 10 and later only) contains the system stored procedures. The database needs to be at least 10MB, although the rate of growth of Sybase stored procedures from version to version indicates that 20MB may be more appropriate. You need to provide a name and location for the *device* where sybsystemsprocs should be stored.

BACKUP SERVER NAME

You need to provide a name and port address for the backup server as well. You must install a local backup server on the system where SQL Server will run. Even if the actual tape device where the data will be recorded is attached to a remote server, you still must install a local backup server to perform any database or transaction dump. In UNIX, the default name is SYB_BACKUP, which should be satisfactory.

STEP 1: FILE TRANSFER

On UNIX servers, the first step of the installation is to load the installation program from the tape. On other systems, the installation program is directly executable from the SQL Server distribution disk or CD-ROM.

When installing on UNIX, log in as the sybase user so that all the files transferred from the tape will have the correct ownership. Follow your installation instructions closely to unload the installation files from the tape.

STEP 2: INSTALLATION

The installation program has several names, depending on the platform. On UNIX platforms, it is normally called sybinit, although sybconfig or sybinstall are sometimes used, especially in earlier versions of the server. On NetWare, the program is called setup.nlm.

The Windows NT install program is named setup.exe.

The installation program prompts you for the information you recorded in Step 0. After this information is provided, it executes the following:

- ◆ Initializes the master device
- ◆ Creates four databases (three, prior to System 10)
- ◆ Runs installmaster to set up the master database (or sybsystemprocs database in System 10 and later)
- ◆ Runs installmodel (to set up the model database)
- ◆ Starts the server
- ◆ Starts the backup server, if installed
- ◆ Sets up the system tables in each of the installed databases (master, model, and sybsystemprocs)

Note

The tempdb database is created, but system tables actually are copied from the model database every time you restart the server.

When the installation step is complete, the server is up and running.

SERVER DIRECTORIES

The installation program copies several files into directories beneath the Sybase directory. The following sections explore some of the important files.

SYBASE ROOT DIRECTORY

The Sybase root directory is the reference point for the other directories that follow. One important file in this root directory is the interfaces file. It lists the names and access paths for the server and backup server. You can run `sybinit` to add additional servers to the interfaces file or you can add them manually.

Tip

Maintain a single interfaces file with a listing of all the servers in your organization. Copy the file to all your servers to simplify maintenance. (If you do not want the users on a particular server to be capable of accessing certain servers, remove those entries from the file.)

INSTALL

The install directory contains files commonly used to start the server as well as a file to house messages from SQL Server. The contents of the install directory are as follows:

`startserver` (or `sqlsrvr`)	The normal program for starting the server.
`runserver`	A file with detailed information about how to start a server. There probably are two runserver files in the install directory—one for the server, one for the backup server. The SQL Server runserver file invokes the `dataserver` executable; the backup server runserver file invokes the `backupserver` executable.
`errorlog`	The file in which the server records important changes to the server's configuration and lists critical error messages. The errorlog can be installed in a different directory and/or be given a different name, if desired. The `-e` parameter to the `dataserver` executable dictates the name and location. (Note: although `dataserver` can be called from the command line, it normally is called from the runserver file. This is where you should verify the correct directory and name of the errorlog file.)

BIN

The following are tools installed in the bin directory (for more information about these tools, see Chapter 14, "Tools for Sybase Administrators"):

isql	An interactive utility used to submit queries to the server and read results.
bcp	The high-speed data load utility.
buildmaster	Provides access to less-used configuration options and is critical if you need to restore the master database.
defncopy	Enables you to export the definition of Sybase objects from the server.
dataserver	The executable used to invoke a SQL Server.
backupserver	The executable used to invoke a backup server.

SCRIPTS

The scripts directory provides SQL scripts that can be executed with the isql utility. The following are three of the install scripts:

installmaster	Installs the master database during installation.
installmodel	Installs the model database during installation.
installpubs2	This optional script installs the pubs2 database during installation or later.

BACKUP SERVER INSTALLATION (SYSTEMS 10 AND 11)

The installation of the backup server is optional during normal installation, but it's a good idea to go ahead and install backup server when you install SQL Server. Otherwise, you will need to rerun the installation program later to enable backup.

Note

Remember, all backups under Systems 10 and 11 require a local backup server, whether you are backing up locally (to a locally connected tape drive or disk file) or remotely (to a tape drive or disk file on another system on your network).

To install the backup server, you need to specify a name for the backup server and a listening port (see the earlier section, "Port Number or Named Pipe"). By default, the name of the backup server is SYB_BACKUP in UNIX, Novell, and Open VMS. In Windows NT, the name used is the same as the SQL Server name, with an extension of _BS. For example, if the server name is ACCOUNTING, the backup server name is ACCOUNTING_BS.

Server Environmental Values

Although the implementation varies from platform to platform, SQL Server always must be able to find mappings to other servers, including the backup server. Environmental values help SQL Server find a list of servers and addresses (usually stored in an interfaces file on UNIX systems), and enable it to identify itself within that list. Those same values are used to enable client programs to map to servers as well. (See the section titled "Client Installation" later in this chapter for more on this topic.)

Server Startup, Login, and Shutdown

Once the server is installed, there are a few activities you'll perform frequently in the normal use of SQL Server. You'll need to be able to start the server, log in to the server once it is up and running, and shut down the server.

Starting the Server

Your installation manual gives the name of the server startup program. Here are the startup methods for four major platforms:

Platform	Startup Method(s)
UNIX (logged in as Sybase user)	startserver -f <run_servername>
NetWare	load sqlsrvr
Windows NT	sybase.bat
Open VMS	startserver/server = <servername>

In the UNIX and Windows NT cases, you call an operating system batch or script file from the operating system prompt. You also can execute the literal statements that are in the named script file. For example, in the case of Windows NT, the sybase.bat batch file provides the parameters required to start a server on any platform:

```
d:\SQL10\bin\sqlsrvr.exe -dd:\SQL10\data\master.dat -sSYBASE
                  -ed:\SQL10\install\errorlog -id:\SQL10\ini -Md:\SQL10
```

Note

Although the command does not fit on one line, it must be typed on a single line.

The components of the `startup` command are as follows:

◆ SQL Server executable (`sqlsrvr.exe`)
◆ Name and location for the master device (`-dd:\SQL10\data\master.dat`)
◆ Name of the server (`-sSYBASE`)
◆ Name and location of the errorlog (`-ed:\SQL10\install\errorlog`)
◆ Location of the interfaces file (`-id:\SQL10\ini`)
◆ Location of the Sybase directory (`-Md:\SQL10`)

AUTOMATIC STARTUP

In most environments, you can execute the startup program automatically as part of the operating system startup procedure (for example, you can insert the `load sqlsrvr` statement into the AUTOEXEC.NCF in NetWare, or insert each of the explicit statements in the runserver file in the automatic startup file in UNIX). (In Windows NT, use the Control Panel Services Manager to set the Sybase SQL Server to automatic startup.)

There are three potential problems with automatic startup:

◆ On UNIX servers, the SQL Server process must be started by the `sybase` user, not the root user. Because the root user is running the startup procedure, you need to `su` to Sybase during startup in order to make the process start properly.

◆ On some servers, the network may not be completely started before SQL Server attempts to access it. If that happens, the SQL Server process fails to start.

◆ If the Sybase process tries to start up before drives are really available (for example, an external drive array may take a minute or two to power up), the automatic startup may try to access the drives too early. If that happens, any databases on those drives will be marked as SUSPECT, and you need to remove that flag by directly modifying the sysdatabases table (see Chapter 9, "Configuring and Tuning the SQL Server," on enabling updates) and restarting SQL Server.

Obviously, you don't get much benefit from an automatic start if more than half the time you need to shut down and restart the server manually. If you experience this problem, you have a couple of options.

First, you can always start the server manually. Although it is no problem to execute the `startserver` statement manually in the middle of a weekday afternoon, answering a page in the middle of a weekend night after a power interruption can be irritating.

Second, you can establish a protocol for starting the drives first and enabling them to warm up for 30 seconds before starting the server. This is useful, but also may not work in an automated environment.

Third, and probably the best, start SQL Server last of all services, guaranteeing the most possible time to enable other devices and services to fully install. If necessary, insert a brief delay in the startup (30 seconds ought to do it in most cases).

VERIFYING WITH *SHOWSERVER*

On character-driven systems such as UNIX, Open VMS, and NetWare, there is a command-line utility to determine whether SQL Server is running (for example, the UNIX showserver utility returns a list of SQL Server processes). On graphical systems, there is an icon-driven program to display the status of SQL Server, Backup Server, and SQL Monitor.

TIME TO LOG IN!

You have installed SQL Server. The server is running. It's time to log in, look around, and see what's left to do. You'll use the isql (interactive SQL) command on the server to log in (for additional information on isql, see Chapter 16, "Tools for Sybase Administrators"). Your installation guide should tell you how to start isql if your platform is not listed here:

Platform	Starting isql
UNIX (logged in as sybase user)	isql -Usa -P
NetWare	load isql -Usa -P
Windows NT	Double-click the isql icon in the SQL Server group. Press Enter when prompted for a password.
Open VMS	isql /username = "sa"

> *Note*
>
> The only initial usable login on the server is sa, which has no password upon installation. (See the section titled "Changing Defaults" later in this chapter.)

You must get the capitalization right in the isql statement. Notice that the U means user, and it must be uppercase, but sa is a user name, and it must be lowercase. If the isql command works, within a few seconds you'll see the standard isql prompt:

1>

Run `sp_who` to see a list of connections. Enter these commands (not the numbers—they are prompts that the system provides):

```
1> sp_who
2> go
```

You should see your own login listed, as well as three or four system connections.

Now log out of SQL Server:

```
1> quit
2> go
```

Congratulations, you have installed SQL Server!

IF THE LOGIN DIDN'T WORK

When `isql` running on the server fails to work, there are a few simple problems to check, based on the error message you receive.

Because SQL Server is case-sensitive, the most common problem in invoking `isql` is an error in capitalization. Try retyping the `isql` command, carefully checking how you spell and capitalize each word.

The easiest messages to resolve are `Login Incorrect` or `Login Failed`. Both of these messages mean that you found the server, but your combination of name and password were entered incorrectly. If you just installed the server, you probably typed something wrong. If you installed the server a while ago, the sa password may have changed, or the sa login may have been disabled. If you really can't get in, make sure the SQL Server process is running. In the worst case, you may have to reinitialize the master database (run `buildmaster -m` in UNIX—see Chapter 16. This is an extreme measure and likely will require a reload of master!).

Another common message is `Unable to Connect: SQL Server is not available or does not exist`. SQL Server is probably not running. Run the `showserver` command to see the status of SQL Server. If necessary, restart the server and try again.

Note

> This really is a more difficult message to interpret. Troubleshooting the `Unable to connect` message is discussed in detail later in the chapter, but most of the issues there relate to proper addressing and network connectivity. When you execute `isql` from the physical SQL Server and cannot find the server process, the usual problem is that the server process is not started yet.

3

INSTALLATION AND CONNECTIVITY

If you are still stumped, see "Troubleshooting" later in this chapter. There may be a useful hint on how to resolve the problem.

SHUTTING DOWN WITH *SHUTDOWN*

To shut down the server, you execute the SQL statement shutdown after connecting to the server.

> *Note*
>
> There is no operating system command to shut down the Sybase process gracefully (except for the stop server command in Open VMS). You can kill the Sybase process with the UNIX kill command (or the equivalent on other platforms), but this is not an orderly shutdown (it's really no different from pulling the plug out of the wall as far as SQL Server is concerned) and could result in data integrity problems, especially if you are using file devices. There are times when SQL Server hangs and must be killed from the operating system. Sometimes, the UNIX kill command does nothing or the hardware itself hangs, requiring you to reboot the hardware.
>
> This situation is not normal and, if occurrences are frequent, may indicate a serious problem with your system. Do not consider occasional hangups to be normal, expected, or acceptable. Contact technical support and report the problem. They may direct you to new patches or versions or help you identify a configuration problem.

The shutdown command instructs the server to disable all logins except sa, waits for currently executing transactions and procedures to complete, checkpoints all databases, and exits the server executable process. This is an orderly shutdown, which manages data integrity before downing the server.

The shutdown with nowait command shuts everything down immediately, without regard to process status. Transactions are not allowed to continue to completion and are rolled back upon restart. Databases are not checkpointed and need to do additional work to recover. This is not considered an orderly shutdown; data integrity is not damaged by a shutdown with nowait.

If you execute the shutdown statement and remain logged in while it proceeds, you lose your connection when the server shuts down and are notified of the dropped connection by your application program. Other users are not notified until the next time they try to use their connection. To avoid user panic and annoying calls, inform users before executing a shutdown.

Although SQL Server is considered a round-the-clock, 24×7 server, there are some common administrative tasks requiring a server shutdown:

◆ *Changing configuration options.* There are a handful of *dynamic* configuration options that can change while the server is up. Most configuration options require modifications in the allocation of memory or resources that can be made only when the server is restarted.

◆ *Removing aborted transactions from the log.* If a client disconnects leaving a noncommitted, non-rolled-back transaction in the log, that transaction may prevent a truncation of the database log. During the database recovery, aborted transactions are marked for rollback and the server is free to clean up the log.

◆ *Setting server trace flags.* Server trace flags enable you to access dbcc and monitoring features. They must be set during server startup. (Sybase Technical Support will instruct you on setting trace flags.)

◆ *Configuring mirroring of the master device.* The mirror parameter must be supplied to the dataserver executable before startup.

◆ *Killing certain user connections.* The SQL Server kill statement can kill certain user processes, but other connections (for example, sleeping processes in earlier versions of SQL Server) simply cannot be killed without restarting the server.

CLIENT INSTALLATION

Getting workstations ready for client/server is a big job, and the more workstations there are, the more logistic problems overshadow technical ones. If you have existing workstations that require work before they are ready for SQL Server, you have a more complicated problem in making changes to workstation configurations without impacting current capabilities.

In this section, you examine the Open Client and Open Server implementations to understand how SQL Server provides openness, portability, and modularity to application programmers. You learn the differences between programming in db-library and CT-library and discuss when to implement either one. Finally, you review some of the installation and application issues with some of the major client platforms.

It's important to realize that you need to install completely the appropriate Open Client product on your server as well as your client workstations. For example, if you are running a UNIX server with Windows clients, you must install the UNIX Open Client on the server for two reasons:

◆ You are likely to need to run utilities from the server (isql, bcp). Without Open Client, these tools cannot access the server.

◆ The server also is capable of accessing other servers. To do that, it maintains hooks to Open Client itself.

OPEN CLIENT AND OPEN SERVER

Sybase provides network transparency, code portability, and modularity with the Open Client and Open Server components of SQL Server. Figure 3.1 shows a single set of application code using Open Client function calls: that code can port easily between Windows and UNIX.

Figure 3.1.
CT-library provides
code portability to the
application developer.

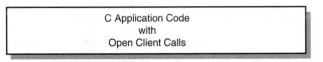

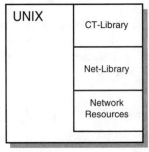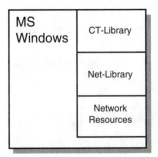

Note

Just how portable is SQL Server application code from UNIX to Windows to Macintosh to DOS? The SQL Server code is completely portable. The function calls and their parameters are the same. There are fine differences in datatypes between the environments that probably can be handled with varying header files.

The real portability problem comes in the application itself. Anyone who has made the transition from UNIX or DOS to Windows or Macintosh knows that the environments are completely different. So you can speak all you want about code portability; the fact is you still have some work to do to make your application look even vaguely familiar to an experienced user of the system.

Open Server provides the same measure of code portability and openness as Open Client. Application programmers can write Open Server programs to handle the special needs of client programs.

Note

The most interesting Open Server programs can interact directly with real-time devices such as scientific test equipment, stock tickers, and pagers. Other Open Server applications are able to interact with non-Sybase database sources, including mainframe flat-file databases and other similar systems.

DB-LIBRARY AND CT-LIBRARY

Every SQL Server application uses Open Client calls to interact with the server. A typical Open Client application will perform the following tasks:

1. Get a pointer to a login structure (a memory-resident record stored as a variable).
2. Set up the login structure.
3. Submit the login structure to a named server to get a pointer to a connection structure.
4. Set up a query in a buffer of the connection structure.
5. Submit the query to the server.
6. Process results sets (processing results rows).
7. Close the connection.

Each numbered item corresponds to a specific C function call (or set of calls).

If you are already running a SQL Server application, or have started to program one using a product such as PowerBuilder, Visual Basic, or Access, you did not see the Open Client function calls. All these products provide a transparent mapping between their own database functions (for example, login to server) and the SQL Server function (steps 1, 2, and 3). Whether it is your product or theirs, however, somewhere along the way, a client application is issuing an explicit function call to Open Client.

The original Open Client interface was called db-library, and it is still in use in almost all SQL Server installations. With the release of System 10, Sybase introduced CT-library to take advantage of System 10's newer features and to provide a better application architecture. Sybase also released a version of db-library in System 10 that is able to access some of System 10's advanced features. These all work with System 11 as well.

DB-LIBRARY COMPONENTS

The following two components comprise db-library:

- ◆ db-lib
- ◆ net-lib

db-lib is the set of functions directly accessible to the application, including calls to set up information in the login record (DBSETLUSER), log in (dbopen), store a query in the buffer (dbcmd), execute the command (dbsqlexec or dbsend), and process result rows (dbresults, dbnextrow).

db-lib is implemented differently on different platforms. UNIX and DOS applications call a LIB file in a mapped directory; Windows applications use resources in a dynamic link library (W3DBLIB.DLL for Windows version 3.*x*).

net-lib provides network transparency (see Figure 3.2). There are typically several net-libs available for each supported client operating platform. The net-lib receives the name of a Sybase server from db-library and transforms that into a full address and port identifier (or named pipe) for network communication. Applications written for db-library name only the server; the rest of the network implementation is managed entirely through net-lib.

Figure 3.2.
net-lib provides
network transparency
to the application
developer.

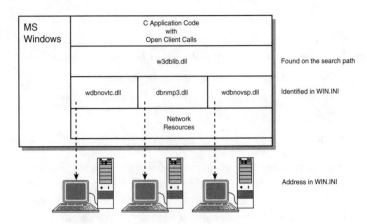

Each net-lib applies to a specific protocol and, if appropriate, a version of that protocol. For example, there is a specific net-lib for Windows for several different versions of TCP/IP (Novell, FTP, Microsoft, and so forth), as well as net-libs for Named Pipes and IPX.

CT-Library Components

Sybase released CT-library with System 10. CT-library will ultimately replace db-library as the standard method of writing applications to communicate with Sybase SQL Server, although there is no indication yet whether Microsoft plans for SQL Servers to support the advanced features of CT-library.

CT-library offers many improvements over db-library, mostly in application structure. Sybase also adds substantial improvements in asynchronous architecture and support for server-side cursors within Client-library:

- ◆ Client-library is a collection of routines for writing client applications and provides the same code portability as db-library.
- ◆ CS-library (Client/Server library) is a collection of routines for writing both client and server applications. All client-library applications call at least one CS-library function to access a structure stored within CS-library.
- ◆ Net-library is a collection of network routines for handling the accessing of a specific network type. Net-library corresponds to net-lib and provides the same benefit of network transparency to the application programmer.

db-Library or CT-Library?

For programmers, the choice of library depends on applications experience and system requirements, so the answer is fairly straightforward. Most programmers are using CT-library whenever possible. On the other hand, the answer is not completely cut and dried for administrators.

The problem is that applications meant to run with db-library do not work with CT-library and vice versa. You need to install the library used by the programmers or referred to by the application. Expect to need to install both db-library and net-library until early 1997 (at least).

Remember, the installation depends on your client configuration. Open Client is shipped with an installation manual, which is your best resource. If you have questions about your configuration, contact Sybase or seek help from another user.

Once the installation is complete, you need to make certain that all the configuration settings are in place to enable a client to communicate with the server.

UNIX

UNIX clients use a combination of text files and environmental variables to find a server address. The SYBASE environmental variable points to the location of the Sybase home directory (this variable should be set up in your .profile or .cshrc file):

```
SYBASE=/home/sybase
```

Stored in the Sybase home directory is the `interfaces` file, a map to all the Sybase servers on the network. Here is a fragment from an interfaces file:

```
A sample interfaces file
#
SYBASE_1
        query tcp sun-ether rose 5000
        master tcp sun-ether rose 5000
DEVEL
        query tcp sun-ether tulip 5000
        master tcp sun-ether tulip 5000
```

Warning

Be careful when you modify the interfaces file, if you do. The query and master entries must each be prefaced with a tab character, or db-library will interpret the line as a new server name.

The DSQUERY environmental variable identifies a default server entry within the interfaces file. If the user fails to specify a server name when logging in, the application will log in to the server named in DSQUERY.

For example, a user has a SYBASE variable of /home/sybase and a DSQUERY value of Devel. Now the user logs into isql, but does not specify a server name:

```
isql -Ujoey
```

Using this example, the Client-library identifies the Devel section of the interfaces file and uses the server address provided in the query line for Devel to find port 5000 in a server named TULIP using TCP/IP over Sun's version of Ethernet. To work with the server running on the ROSE server, the user types this:

```
isql -Ujoey -SSYBASE_1
```

By naming the server at startup, the user overrides the default server name and finds the correct SQL Server.

Note

Remember! Even if you are using UNIX only as SQL Server and using some other OS for client workstations, you still need to install and maintain an Open Client for UNIX clients.

WINDOWS

Under Windows, you record the names of servers in a text file in the format of a Windows initialization file. With db-library, you store server names and addressing schemes in the WIN.INI file (in the Windows directory) under the heading [SQLSERVER] (see Figure 3.3).

Figure 3.3.
db-library uses the
WIN.INI section,
[SQLSERVER], as a
central resource to
locate servers.

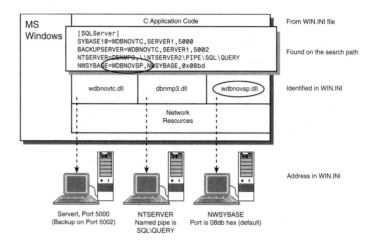

If you have a DSQUERY value listed in the .INI file, it is used by default if no server is named. Here is the SQLSERVER section from a sample WIN.INI file:

```
[SQLServer]
DSQUERY=DBNMP3,\\SYB2\PIPE\SQL10\QUERY
BACKUPSERVER=DBNMP3,\\SYBASE_10\PIPE\SQL10\BACKUP
MSSQLV4_2=DBNMP3,\\SYBASE_10\PIPE\SQL\QUERY
```

With CT-library, server names and addresses reside in the file SQL.INI (in the INI subdirectory within the SYBASE directory). The following is a sample SQL.INI file:

```
[SQLSERVER]
WIN3_QUERY=WNLWNSCK,SYBASE_10,5000
[SQL10NMP]
WIN3_QUERY=WNLNMP,\SYBASE_10\PIPE\SQL10\QUERY
[SQL10IPX]
WIN3_QUERY=WNLNOVSP,SYBASE_10
```

MACINTOSH

Recall that Macintosh uses an interfaces file identical in form and content to the UNIX interfaces file to map login attempts to servers. The interfaces file is stored in the System folder and can be accessed through the control panel. There is no DSQUERY value so all logins need to specify a server. Macintosh has no isql utility.

NETWORKING AND CONNECTIVITY

Let's start with an agreement. If you are not a "networking person," you are going to have to make friends with one pretty soon. Client/server is as dependent on

3

INSTALLATION AND CONNECTIVITY

the network as on any other component, and networks are a huge mystery to most Sybase administrators. In this section, you get up to speed on some of the impor-tant terms and concepts, but you are going to know enough only to be entertaining at cocktail parties or a little dangerous.

Like most client/server products, SQL Server is open, modular, and flexible about its networking options.

NETWORK TYPES

You probably won't need to choose the network type; that decision will have been made by your LAN Administrator. Just keep in mind that when you pick a network type (Ethernet, Token Ring, or something else) you are talking about *hardware*: network interface cards in PC clients and servers, network cabling, central hubs, concentrators, routers, and other specialized equipment to improve performance.

The world is made up of three kinds of people: Ethernet people, Token Ring people, and everyone else.

ETHERNET

Ethernet people think you ought to keep Big Brother out of networking. If you want to send a message, see whether anyone's on the line and send your message. If two systems try to send a message at the same time, they cause a collision, and both back off for a brief (but random) period. While they are backed off, they jam the network to keep other users not involved in the collision from jumping ahead in line.

Ethernet is a freewheeling approach to networking, wherein moderate numbers of users sending large amounts of data from time to time get outstanding performance. However, performance tends to fall off rapidly if too many users need to send data too frequently and generate huge numbers of collisions.

Don't get the wrong idea. Ethernet can support networks of hundreds and thou-sands of users without problems, but performance under a very high load can sometimes be problematic. It really depends on your configuration. With the correct combination of routers to localize traffic, Ethernet is a highly effective and simple network type.

Tip

If you want to impress the network administrator, ask what frame type you are using with Ethernet. (Not that you will know what to do with that information!)

Ethernet is the standard network type for most UNIX systems (the exception is IBM RS/6000, which also supports Token Ring).

Token Ring

Token-passing environments are more structured. A token is passed from user to user, with each connection having the chance to send a message. There are no collisions because you never transmit if you don't hold the token. Token Ring is only one implementation of a token-passing environment, but it is by far the most common.

Token Ring provides adequate performance with few users and low volume, but it really shines when there are many users, all transmitting frequently. The lack of collisions provides much steadier and more predictable throughput than Ethernet under load. Token Ring can feel slow when compared to Ethernet.

If your organization uses Token Ring, you may find the implementation easiest if you use OS/2, Windows NT, NetWare, or AIX (IBM's flavor of UNIX running on the RS/6000). If you want to use another UNIX system with Token Ring, talk to your hardware salesman first, then the Sybase representative or another Sybase customer already using it.

Network Protocols

Network protocols provide an addressing and data packaging method for sending information between systems. There are lots of network protocols out there, but only a few major players. The choice of a protocol also is probably not yours, but note that your choice of a server may be closely linked to internal policies about network protocols. The following sections present the primary protocols used to talk to SQL Server and the implementation issues with each.

Protocols are implemented through software. Often software to support a standard protocol is provided by the manufacturer of the hardware. Specialized software to support nonstandard protocols may be purchased separately.

TCP/IP

Terminal Control Protocol/Internet Protocol (TCP/IP) is getting a lot of press nowadays. Just a few years ago, it looked as if TCP/IP's days were numbered, but then lots of people started hooking into the Internet and there was a resurgence of support for this stately old method of interacting with the world.

TCP/IP requires that you manually assign addresses to each network connection. A classic problem in TCP/IP arises from duplicate addresses. Manage addresses carefully to avoid this error.

3

Installation and Connectivity

TCP/IP grew up on UNIX, so the networking software is part of the standard system. Novell started supporting and routing TCP/IP in the 3.1x versions (check to see whether it is included or provided at an additional charge). Windows NT includes TCP/IP at no additional charge.

On DOS and Windows clients, however, you need to find third-party TCP/IP software to enable you to communicate with a TCP/IP network. Some of the TCP/IP software comes from Novell (LAN WorkPlace for DOS), NetManage (Chameleon and Newt), and FTP (PC/TCP).

If you plan to have Macintosh workstations or UNIX servers, TCP/IP is your best bet.

IPX/SPX

Novell invented the Internetwork Packet Exchange/Simple Packet Exchange (IPX/SPX) protocol to provide a simple method of transporting packets quickly across interconnected networks. Today, there are millions of workstations using IPX in existing Novell networks.

Certainly, the capability of communicating using IPX was a major factor in the selection of NetWare-based SQL Servers for many organizations. (Changing the network configuration of hundreds and thousands of workstations is not something a LAN administrator does lightly.)

IPX is fast and efficient, but support for IPX among UNIX systems is still fairly weak. Windows NT, DOS, and Windows for Workgroups all provide support for IPX right out of the box.

NAMED PIPES

Named Pipes enables interprocess communication over networks. It was originally implemented as part of LAN Manager and OS/2, and it is the easiest protocol to implement on small Windows NT networks.

Named Pipes is supported on Novell servers, although you are usually better sticking with IPX.

OTHERS (DECNET, SNA, APPLETALK)

There are other protocols available, but their use in SQL Server systems is rare. If you plan to do something out of the ordinary, remember to find others who have already been successful with your planned combination of pieces.

TROUBLESHOOTING

Client/server works great—once you get it working. Then it works until someone changes something.

Troubleshooting client/server is no different from troubleshooting any other kind of system, except that the vendors are unbelievably non-useful. Why? Because there are simply too many products (and too many combinations of products) for them to be smart about all of them.

You need to be single-minded about isolating the problem:

◆ Is the problem on the server, the client, or the network?

◆ Is the problem in the workstation application or the operating system?

◆ Is the problem in the connectivity software or the equipment?

And so forth. We're not going to troubleshoot performance, locking, or other such problems here. (See Chapter 15, "What Do You Do When Things Go Wrong?", for more advice on these topics.) This section presents some of the steps you can take to isolate problems, such as: you can't log in at all; you can log in but can't send a query; and you can log in, but periodically your connection hangs.

STEP 1: DOES SQL SERVER WORK?

Let's start simple. Run `showserver`. If the server isn't started, you can't log in. If the server was started but isn't showing up, it may not be able to start. Look at the errorlog.

STEP 2: CAN YOU ACCESS SQL SERVER FROM *ISQL*?

The server is working, so now let's see whether anyone can log in. Remove the network and all the client issues and try to log in from the server. Log in to the hardware where SQL Server resides and invoke `isql` (see how to log into the server using the server-based `isql` program earlier in this chapter). If you can't log in, you may be out of maximum connections (the message for this is quite specific).

You also may have a problem in your addressing on the server itself. Remember the port you assigned to the server when you ran the installation? That's also how your client will address the server. Look in the interfaces file (or the equivalent) on the server to make sure that the port address listed there is correct. You also may have to set server environmental variables to make this work.

Tip

> In UNIX, the environmental variables SYBASE and DSQUERY should be
> set in your .profile or .cshrc file for your login. If you change these
> files, you may need to log out and log back in to change your session
> settings.

At any rate, don't bother trying to get a client process to talk to the server over the
network until an isql session can communicate with the server locally.

STEP 3: CAN YOU TALK TO THE PHYSICAL SERVER AT ALL OVER THE NETWORK?

If a client is having a problem initiating a SQL Server session, first try to initiate
a non-SQL Server connection. If you are using NetWare or Windows NT, try to
access the file or print services of the server. Run slist in NetWare to see whether
the Sybase server is listed. If you are running Windows and Named Pipes, see
whether an NT server shows up in your workgroup under File Manager's Disk
Connect Network Drive option.

In UNIX, use the TCP/IP ping utility (this is shipped with every TCP/IP toolset—
"ping" comes from the sonar method of detecting ships underwater). The utility
sends a packet to a specific address. If a network node is using that address, it
returns an acknowledgment packet.

If you can't find or ping the server at the operating system level, then you have a
network problem. The problem could be a loose or bad cable connection, a bad
Ethernet card, out-of-date or incompatible network software, incorrect Ethernet
frame types, bad packet sizes... well, you get the idea. This is the part where you call
your networking friend and say, "Fix it. It's broken."

Again, don't bother attempting to log in to SQL Server until this problem is solved.

STEP 4: CAN YOU PING SQL SERVER?

The next step is to make certain that you can ping SQL Server. Every Open Client
product comes with a dbping (or sybping, wsybping, or wdbping) utility to perform at
SQL Server level what was described at the server level before.

If you can connect to the physical box and SQL Server is running, you should be able
to connect to SQL Server. Period. If it doesn't work, the problem is in db-library or
CT-library and net-library.

The easy solution may be in your interfaces file (or equivalent) on the workstation. Look for addressing problems or even missing references. The addresses should match what you see in the server interfaces file. If not, you almost certainly won't connect.

The worst problems can be with old or incompatible versions of db-library and net-library in Windows. The db-library program, W3DBLIB.DLL, has gone through dozens of interim releases. It's likely that you have a couple of different versions of db-library on each of your workstations, with varying sizes and release dates.

The question is, which db-library is being used? Ideally, you should have the same release on each workstation and it should be the latest release.

Note

> There has been a case where a single workstation needed access to two different versions of db-library to work well with two applications, but that is the exception. Generally, use only one version of db-library throughout the organization.

First, inventory all versions of SQL Server. Then test them in order, starting with the most recent version first.

Note

> Sybase has just begun to talk freely about version control with db-library. DBAs have known for a long time about the importance of these versions. There are SQL Server DBAs with a disk having six or seven versions of db-library just in case something new arises.

STEP 5: IT WORKED YESTERDAY...WHAT CHANGED?

This is one of the most perplexing problems you will face. It is especially problematic in Windows.

A Windows workstation worked yesterday, does not work today, but the user swears nothing changed—except that he "did install Excel."

Microsoft (and a lot of other vendors) ships db-library with many of its products. (Some vendors ship really old, horrible versions.) If the installation program also changes the workstation search PATH (which unfortunately is common), the new db-library jumps to the front of the path and sabotages any attempt to find SQL Server.

3

INSTALLATION AND CONNECTIVITY

Step 6: Can you log in to SQL Server?

If you can't log in, first check the capitalization and spelling of your name and password. Your sso (in charge of SQL Server security) should be able to give you a new password if that appears to be the problem. If you are the sso, you have bigger problems.

Step 7: Does it happen only when the number of users increases?

One of the simplest solutions to occasional server lockups or problems with logins is duplicate client TCP/IP addresses. These conflicts cause the server to go completely berserk, so manage those addresses carefully.

Changing Defaults—The Top Ten Items To Address Upon Installation

There are some things you should do as soon as you can log in. SQL Server is a great product, but sometimes you have to wonder. Some default settings are just senseless and you need to change them just as soon as you log in as sa.

Securing sa Access

The sa has no password and complete control over the server. You need to fix that—*pronto*. (For more on security, see Chapter 6, "Security and User Administration.")

Prior to System 10, sa privileges were nontransferrable, so you merely set a password. Log in as the sa and execute the following command:

```
sp_password null, my_secret
```

With Systems 10 and 11, you put a password on the sa account as previously. Then read about the sa_role and sso_role (see Chapter 6) and grant those roles to actual logins for named administrators. When those roles are set up, disable the sa account.

Turning Off the Master Device Default Status

If you don't change this value, you can mistakenly install user databases on the master device. Ultimately, this could mean a painful database recovery if you have to reinitialize the master device, and you may have to free up the space later to make additional room for the master database.

To turn this value off, use the following command:

```
sp_diskdefault master, defaultoff
```

For more on default disks, see Chapter 4, "Defining Physical and Mirror Devices."

REMOVING THE *DISKDUMP* BACKUP DEVICE

In versions prior to System 10, Sybase provided a backup device called `diskdump` that maps to the local null device—a "bit bucket." (Imagine a long wire, attached to nothing, with electrons pouring out all over the floor.)

When you back up to `diskdump`, the backup is amazingly fast and equally fruitless. Nothing is backed up because there is no physical device attached. To avoid tragic mistakes, remove the `diskdump` device:

```
sp_dropdevice diskdump
```

INCREASING THE SIZE OF TEMPDB

You probably don't know how large tempdb will need to be yet, but 2MB certainly won't be enough. Use `disk init` to set up a logical device for tempdb (see Chapter 4) and alter the database to extend tempdb onto the new device (see Chapter 5, "Defining, Altering, and Maintaining Databases and Logs"). For now, 20MB might be a good place to start.

NAMING THE SERVER

Although installation records the name of the server in the interfaces file, it may not set that name up in the sysservers table. To name the server, follow this example:

```
sp_addserver GEORGE, local
```

Other settings to enable remote server management are reviewed in Chapter 12, "Remote Server Management." *You must set up remote servers to enable backups.*

SETTING OBVIOUS CONFIGURATION SETTINGS

In Chapter 9, "Configuring and Tuning the SQL Server," you review the configuration and tuning settings in detail, but here are three values that are always wrong:

◆ Open databases
◆ Memory
◆ User connections

Databases don't consume much server memory, so set this value near the maximum number of databases you expect to create on the server, with additional room for master, model, tempdb, and sybsystemprocs:

```
sp_configure "open databases", 20
go
reconfigure
go
```

The memory setting probably needs to be changed. The correct value depends on your server. Don't forget that memory is specified in 2KB pages (10240 = 20MB).

Connections should be set as low as reasonable because connections do consume memory (about 50KB each in Systems 10 and 11):

```
sp_configure "user connections", 25
```

SETTING UP THE MODEL DATABASE OBJECTS, USERS, AND DATATYPES

You may want to set up the model database with all the objects (rules, defaults), users (guest, others) and user-defined datatypes you will want in every database on this server. This is optional.

If this is your first server in your organization, it is really unlikely that you have made any of these decisions yet. If you have other servers, you may already have a set of standards. Make certain you create everything in model before you create your first user database. Otherwise, you need to copy everything manually into both model and the user database(s) later on.

INSTALLING THE pubs2 DATABASE

The pubs2 database is provided with every server, and you should install it on most servers. pubs2 contains sample tables, views, and data that you can query to observe how the SQL works or how to implement special objects or concepts. This also is optional. All of the examples in the Sybase documentation—and in most articles you read—use pubs2 objects.

Note

In versions of SQL Server such as NetWare and Windows NT in which you're limited to eight-character filenames, the name of the pubs2 script is instpbs2.

INSTALLING THE SYBSYNTAX DATABASE

SQL Server can provide help on Transact-SQL syntax with the sp_syntax stored procedure. Detailed help and syntax information is stored in the optional system database, sybsyntax, which you install with a script in the scripts directory (the script name depends on your operating system). This also is optional. To install the sybsyntax database in Windows NT, use the following:

```
isql -Usa -iinssyndb -oinssyndb.out
```

Tip

You may want to modify the pubs2 and sybsyntax scripts slightly to change the device where the database is installed. Otherwise, the database will be installed on your default device (which should not be the master device). (For more on devices, see Chapter 4.)

SUMMARY

If you already have decided on SQL Server, you still need to find all the pieces to make it work. Think of client/server as a scavenger hunt. One medium-size client eventually bought more than 100 products from more than 40 vendors to build a client/server system.

Your client/server installation will depend on your ability to find high-quality components and knit them together into a seamless system. It's not a one-day job; it's a continuous process of building a reliable, functional, simple system.

Use the Checklist at the end of this chapter to make sure you have addressed all of the major points covered in this chapter.

3

INSTALLATION AND CONNECTIVITY

CHECKLIST

DECIDING ON YOUR SQL SERVER ENVIRONMENT

- ☐ Server operating system (UNIX, NetWare, Windows NT, OS/2, Open VMS)

- ☐ Server vendor and configuration (IBM, Sun, HP, Compaq, DEC, and so on)

- ☐ Network type (Ethernet, Token Ring)

- ☐ Network protocol (TCP/IP, IPX, Named Pipes)

- ☐ Network operating system (NetWare, UNIX, Windows NT, VINES)

- ☐ Client workstation operating system (UNIX, OS/2, DOS, Windows, Macintosh)

- ☐ Client workstation configuration (CPU, Speed, RAM, and so on)

- ☐ Client development and reporting products (PowerBuilder, Visual Basic, C++, Forest & Trees, ReportSmith, Clear Access, and so on)

- ☐ Server administration tools (Aurora Utilities)

- ☐ Network administration tools

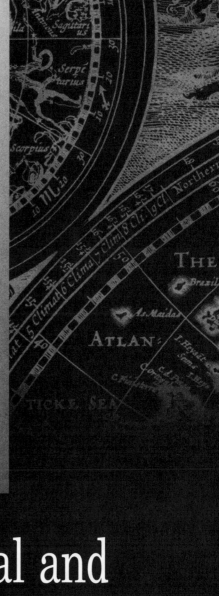

- Disk Initialization
  with disk init

- Default Disks

- Disk Mirroring

- Software Mirroring,
  Hardware Mirroring,
  and RAID

- Device SQL

CHAPTER 4

Defining Physical and Mirror Devices

The server is installed. Now what? In order for the server to be useful you need to be able to create and load user databases. On a Sybase SQL Server, you must first define the physical area that is to be used for the databases; this is done with the `disk init` statement, as shown in Figure 4.1.

Figure 4.1.
You must set up devices
before setting up
databases.

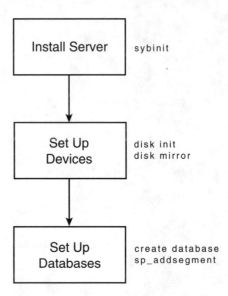

In this chapter, you explore device mirroring at the software level. When you mirror devices, Sybase keeps an exact copy of each used page from one device on another that you specify. You set up mirroring with the `disk mirror` statement. You also compare advantages and disadvantages of hardware-level mirroring, software-level mirroring, and RAID (Redundant Array of Inexpensive(!) Devices) devices.

DISK INITIALIZATION WITH *DISK INIT*

Chapter 5, "Defining, Altering, and Maintaining Databases and Logs," discusses database creation and configuration. Before you can set up databases, Sybase needs to map logical device names to physical disk resources. The logical names you assign here ("devices") are used again at database creation (and segment placement) time.

Note

Upon server installation, you will have a device initialized to house the master, model, tempdb, and, optionally, sybsystemprocs databases. The logical name of this device varies from platform to platform, but some common names are `master` and `the_master_device`.

Note

Although you can create user databases on this device, it is strongly recommended that you use this device only for the databases previously mentioned, especially for production servers.

Several databases can reside on a single physical device, and storage for a single database may span many devices. (Also, a single physical disk can contain several devices.) Figure 4.2 illustrates the many-to-many relationship between devices and databases (discussed at length later in this chapter).

Figure 4.2.
A physical device is defined to Sybase as a logical device, on which may reside 0, 1, or many databases. A database can span several physical devices.

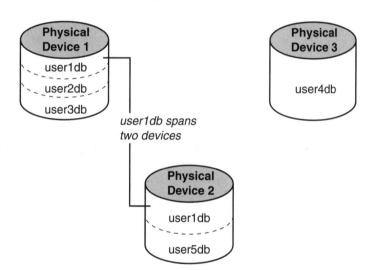

The disk init statement provides the server with a method of mapping databases to physical drives. You will use databases to contain (provide a context for) data objects such as tables, indexes, and stored procedures.

Note

Because disk init is used only when defining physical resources to the server, it is easy to forget the syntax. If you are unsure, look it up rather than guessing at it.

When working with the parameters, remember that the tricky parts are getting the physical name right, making sure the vdevno is unique on the server, and stating the size parameter in pages (not megabytes).

4

SYNTAX

```
disk init
name = 'logical_name_of_device',
physname= 'os_location_of_device',
vdevno= virtual_device_number,
size=size_of_device_in_pages
[, vstart = virtual_address, cntrltype= controller_number]
[, contiguous]
```

PARAMETERS

The first parameter for disk init is the logical name:

```
name = 'logical_name_of_device',
```

The logical name of the device is the name you use to refer to the device when creating or altering a database on it, mirroring it (succeeding topic), or using the sp_diskdefault command (discussed later) to make it a default disk for database creation.

Device names must be unique within a Sybase SQL Server. Limitations on device names are the same as with any other Sybase SQL Server object: the name must be unique among devices and thirty characters in length with no spaces or punctuation (data_device, log_device, index_device). Don't forget that the server treats device names (like other meaningful identifiers) as case-sensitive.

The second parameter is the physical name:

```
physname = 'os_location_of_device',
```

The physical name of the device is its actual location within the operating system. The address here may be a raw partition (UNIX) or foreign disk (Open VMS), a file system name, or an address of some other type of device. Raw partition and file system devices are discussed later in this chapter.

Note

> Until recently, Sybase SQL Server used only disk devices. Third-party vendors created other media addressable by Sybase, including optical disk jukeboxes (for archival purposes) and solid state disk (memory) devices.

The third parameter of disk init is the virtual device number:

```
vdevno= virtual_device_number,
```

The virtual device number is a unique identifier used by SQL Server to identify unique page numbers (it is the high-order byte of an address, hence the 255-device limitation on the servers). These addresses are used to help map the many-to-many relationship between the system tables, sysdevices, sysusages, and sysdatabases.

The virtual device number must be less than the `devices` parameter in the sysconfigures system table. If, for example, you configure devices to 10 as follows, the device number must be 9 or less:

```
sp_configure "devices", 10
reconfigure
```

(Device numbering begins with 0, and device 0 is set at installation time to be the master device.)

Tip

Memory is assigned for devices at server startup. This means that if you configure for 255 devices, memory is allocated for 255 devices, even if you use only 2. Devices normally require around 0.5KB of memory (which is not terribly significant). However, on certain Sybase platforms, you can externalize your I/O devices. This requires a process (thread), which normally requires 50KB of memory (100 times as much!). If this is the case, over-configuring the number of devices can be a significant waste of memory (20 devices would require 1MB of memory), which could be better used for cache (see Chapter 9, "Configuring and Tuning the SQL Server").

If you need to add more devices, change the `devices` parameter with `sp_configure`, then restart the server. Note that the server does not free up dropped virtual device numbers until the server is restarted. This applies even to many failed `disk init` statements. You may have to restart the server to free up a virtual device number after `disk init` fails.

DETERMINING THE AVAILABLE *VDEVNO*

Because it can be extremely frustrating trying to find an available `vdevno`, especially under pressure, we recommend that you build the following Store Procedure so you can easily determine the available `vdevno`:

```
/* sp_vdev : reports all SQL devices and how much free space there is for
** further allocation to databases.

** Orginally Written by: Ramakrishna Raju, Tech Support, Emeryville.
** Oct 12th,1993.
** WARNING: The magic number 16777216 is valid only for 32-bit machines.
**          It may or may not be valid for 64-bit machines, depending on
```

```
**              whether we decide to use short or long for low,high and
                vstart.
*/
use sybsystemprocs
create proc sp_vdevus
as
begin
 set nocount on
  declare @magic int, @mbfactor float
     select @magic=16777216 /* may need to recalc for 64 bit machines */
   select @mbfactor=low/4 from master..spt_values
          where type='E' and number=1
     create table #tmp ( nam char(32) null, dev int, ize float null  ,
                         full )
     if @@error != 0
begin
        print "Error encountered in creating temp table. Cannot
               proceed."
             return 1
      end

   insert #tmp
   select null, vstart/@magic, null, sum( size )/@mbfactor
          from master..s
group by vstart/@magic

 update #tmp set nam = name, ize = (high-low+1)/@mbfactor
      from master..sysdevices
where #tmp.dev = low/@magic and ( status&2>0 or status&4>0 )

   insert #tmp
    select name, low/@magic, (high-low+1)/@mbfactor, 0  from
      master..sysdevices a
    where a.low/@magic not in ( select vstart/@magic from
          master..sysusages )
    and ( a.status&2>0 or a.status&4>0 )

   print "DEVICE-ALLOCATION SUMMARY."
     print "***************************"
     select "VDev #"= convert(char(3),dev),"Device" = nam,
           "Size (MB)" = s,
           "Allocated (MB)"= str(full,8,2),
           "Free (MB)" = str(ize - full,8,2)
     from #tmp
     order by dev
   set nocount off
return 0
end
```

Here is some sample output:

```
DEVICE-ALLOCATION SUMMARY.
***************************
VDev # Device                          Size (MB) Allocated (MB) Free (MB)
------ ------------------------------- --------- -------------- ---------
0      master                            30.02        14.00        16.02
1      sysprocsdev                       50.20        50.00         0.20
```

```
2       sybsecurity                30.02     20.00        10.02
3       devc1t0d1s1               400.00    386.00        14.00
4       devc1t1d1s0               300.00    300.00         0.00
5       devc1t2d1s1               300.00    240.00        60.00
6       devc1t1d2s0               150.00    150.00         0.00
7       logc1t3d2s0               100.00    100.00         0.00
8       devmd5                    150.00    150.00         0.00
9       devmd2                    500.00    500.00         0.00
10      devmd3                   1000.00   1000.00         0.00
11      logc1t4d1s0               300.00    270.00        30.00
12      devmd4                    150.00    150.00         0.00
13      devmd10                  1000.00    970.00        30.00
14      logmd6                    100.00    100.00         0.00
15      devmd9                    150.00    150.00         0.00
16      devmd8                    100.00    100.00         0.00
17      logmd11                   250.00    150.00       100.00
```

The fourth parameter is the size, which is the size of the device in pages:

```
size=size_of_device_in_pages
```

(A page is 2KB on all platforms except Stratus, where it is 4KB.) It also has been rumored that the page size will be variable in the future.

Tip

Sybase generally is excellent at performance, throughput, and a host of other things, but leaves much to be desired in consistency with administration commands. Sometimes turning flags on means setting them to 1, sometimes it means setting them to true, sometimes setting them to default on, and so forth.

In this case, note that size is in pages. At installation time, depending on version and platform, you may have been prompted for the size of your master device in megabytes, pages, or sectors. When you create a database, the sizes will be in megabytes.

Moral: If you are unsure about the units, consult your Sybase documentation. There is a reference card in the front of this book to help you figure out what SQL Server is looking for in many situations.

The sixth line of `disk init` specifies these parameters:

```
[, vstart = virtual_address, cntrltype= controller_number]
```

It is unusual to have to specify this set of parameters. They default to zero; leave them alone unless directed by Sybase Technical Support.

4

The final option is the following:

```
[, contiguous]
```

This option (in Open VMS only) is used to enable software mirroring of a disk file.

The following example of `disk init` creates a raw partition device in the UNIX environment:

```
disk init
name = 'data_device_1',
physname = '/dev/rsd03',
vdevno=3,
size = 512000
```

In this example `disk init` statement creates a device whose logical name is `'data_device_1'`. The device is mapped to a physical location `'/dev/rsd03'` (which is likely to be a raw partition, but this is something that would need to be verified at the operating system level). The virtual device number is 3, and its size is 1GB (= 512000 × 2KB).

How long does `disk init` take? That varies with your version of SQL Server. At one point in its evolution, `disk init` would zero out every page and could take hours. With more recent releases of the server, a `disk init` of 2GB takes only a couple of minutes.

Note

In the case of many SQL Server commands (`disk init` is one of these), no news turns out to be good news. If there is an error with a `disk init` statement, you will hear about it. If the command appears to take a few seconds and there is no error, it probably worked. Just run `sp_helpdevice` to make sure (see an example later in this chapter).

After a while, you will get used to it, but for now just make a note: If you don't get an error message, it probably worked.

RAW-PARTITION AND FILE-SYSTEM DEVICES

What is the difference between a raw partition and an operating system file (besides the fact that raw partitions are more difficult to create)?

With a file system, when you write a page, SQL Server instructs the operating system to write a page. Figure 4.3 illustrates the relationship between SQL Server and a file system device.

Figure 4.3.
When SQL Server
requests data from a
file system device, the
request must pass
through the operating
system's I/O process.

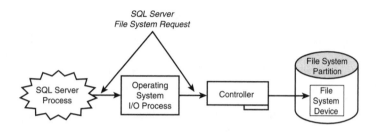

With a raw partition, SQL Server instructs the controller to write a page. Figure 4.4 illustrates the relationship between SQL Server and a raw partition.

Figure 4.4.
SQL Server requests
from a device on a raw
partition go directly to
the controller.

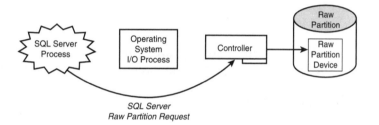

In addition to the overhead and performance penalty of writing through the OS, the use of a file system device introduces a level of risk in the SQL Server commit process. The problem is that operating systems cache I/O (both reads and writes in some cases) for efficiency. This would be fine if your only concern was speed, and you didn't care about losing data. But for writes, you have the following scenario:

Sybase: Here, write this page.

[Operating System writes the page to cache.]

Operating System: OK. It's written.

[Is it really written? Not necessarily.]

Sybase: Thank you.

Before the operating system has the chance to write from its internal cache to a disk device, any number of catastrophic events could occur. The OS could crash, there could be a power surge or blackout, or SQL Server itself could come down, and the OS file will not be written. When SQL Server comes back up, the page will not have been written by the operating system.

For a single page, this problem may be surmountable. But what happens when thousands of pages are written to the operating system, and the OS manages to write only some of these before a crash? There is no guarantee that they were written to disk in the order that Sybase requested, or that that would help anyway.

Referential integrity is probably lost and, if the wrong pages were lost, data could be orphaned or destroyed.

Note

Oddly, the most common problem in using file systems is index corruption.

Use your operating system's equivalent of a raw partition, if it is available. It's safer in the long run, and you will probably get better performance.

Warning

Be sure to use an appropriate partition on UNIX. If you use the c partition (meaning the whole disk), most versions of the server over-write the UNIX disk label (partition a), reinitializing the disk. When the server goes down and then comes back up, the disk will be unaddressable.

If you are still determined to use a disk file as your device, you must meet two criteria:

◆ The file must not already exist (it will be created by the disk init process).

◆ The file must be writeable by the process that is running SQL Server. This means that if you started the server when logged in as sybase, as you normally would, the sybase user would have to have write permission in the directory and file permission on the file after creation. It is irrelevant (and probably a bad security idea) to enable access to the file at the operating system level to any user other than sybase or any process other than the SQL Server dataserver process (including the sa who issued the disk init command!).

In the next example, a file system disk of 40MB (20,480 pages) is created on a UNIX file system. A file of 40MB is created during initialization and an entry is made in the sysdevices system table:

```
disk init
name = 'data_device_2',
physname = '/home/user/sybase/diskfile/data_dev1.dat',
vdevno=4,
size = 20480
```

Note

Errors from file system `disk init` statements are normally not very descriptive, for example:

```
Error 5123: DISK INIT encountered an error while attempting to
open/create the physical file. Please consult the SQL Server errorlog
(in the SQL Server boot directory) for more details.
```

When you do consult the errorlog, you usually find one of three errors:

◆ The directory or filename is invalid.

◆ The file already exists.

◆ There is not enough space to create the file.

Here are some sample errorlog entries after a `disk init` error:

```
94/10/29 13:26:30.25 kernel   udcreate: Operating system error 112
(There is not enough space on the disk.) encountered
94/10/29 13:26:38.61 kernel   udcreate: Operating system error 80
(The file exists.) encountered
```

Normally, you can delete a physical file that was created during a filed `disk init`. If you can't delete it, SQL Server failed to release the locks on the file. To delete the file and reclaim the space, you may need to cycle the server and try again. Before doing that, make absolutely certain that the `disk init` didn't actually work. You may be trying to delete a valid device!

EFFECTS OF *DISK INIT*

The `disk init` command can be performed only by the `sa` or by a login with the `sa_role`. After the disk initialization is complete, the space described by the physical address is available to SQL Server for storage, and a row is added to the sysdevices table in the master database.

Figure 4.5 shows the contents of a small sysdevices table (use `select * from` sysdevices).

4

DEFINING DEVICES

Figure 4.5.
The contents of the
sysdevices table in an
Aurora Utilities
window.

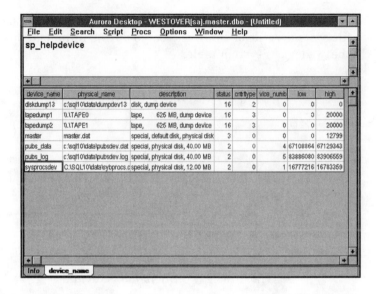

The sysdevices table contains one row for each device that the server can access. (Devices include disks for storage of data and tape and file devices for backups.) Relevant columns in sysdevices include the name of the device (and its mirror, if it has one—you learn about that later), device status, and page range. Can you find the virtual device number? It is actually the high-order byte of the "low" column.

The status is a bitmap describing what the device is used for and what options have been set (if any). The layout of the status byte is provided in Table 4.1.

TABLE 4.1. BITMAP VALUES FOR THE STATUS COLUMN OF SYSDEVICES.

Decimal	Hex	Description
1	0x01	Default disk
2	0x02	Physical disk
4	0x04	Logical disk
8	0x08	Skip header
16	0x10	Dump device
32	0x20	Serial writes
64	0x40	Device mirrored
128	0x80	Reads mirrored
256	0x100	Secondary mirror side only
512	0x200	Mirror enabled

For instance, the status of the master device is 3 (= binary 00000011), which corresponds to "database device" and "Default disk" (1 + 2 = 3).

By far the easiest way of decoding the status bit and virtual device number is to use the system stored procedure sp_helpdevice.

Here is the syntax of sp_helpdevice:

```
sp_helpdevice [<logical_device_name>]
```

sp_helpdevice can be used without parameters to get a list of defined devices. Figure 4.6 shows two devices for data storage (master and data_device_2):

Figure 4.6.
The master and
data_device_2 devices
in an Aurora Utilities
window.

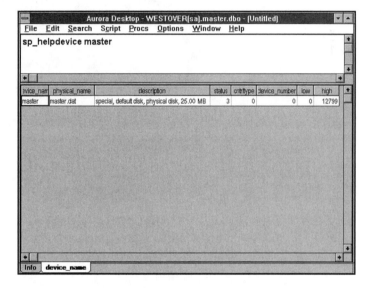

Pass sp_helpdevice the name of the disk device to get information on a specific disk. The information retrieved is shown in Figure 4.7.

The master device status is 3 (disk device + default device), its controller type is 0 (a device for storage, not backup), its virtual device number (device) is 0, and its low and high values represent the logical page numbers that define the space to be used on the device (12,800 pages = 25MB).

4

Figure 4.7.
Specific disk informa-
tion in an Aurora
Utilities window.

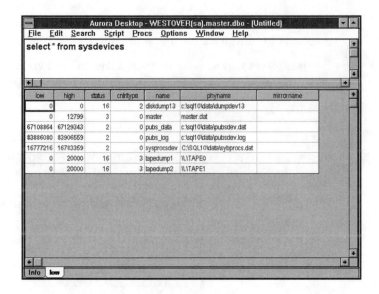

REMOVING DEVICES WITH *SP_DROPDEVICE*

Once a device has been defined, it remains permanently in the data dictionary in the master database until you decide that it has served its purpose and should be removed. A typical reason for this might be that you are replacing a small or slower, older device with a newer one.

Devices cannot be removed if databases have been defined on the device; any databases must be dropped first. (The server will check sysusages for any allocated fragments for the device.)

A device may be dropped with the sp_dropdevice command.

SYNTAX

```
sp_dropdevice <logical_device_name>
```

EXAMPLE

```
sp_dropdevice data_device_1
```

If your device was created as an operating system file, you must execute the necessary commands to remove the file (dropping the device will not automatically delete the file). Also, to be able to use that space, you must shutdown and restart the server to release its pointer to the device.

DEFAULT DISKS

The point of defining disks with `disk init` is to store data on them. The data will be stored in databases, which actually allocate space on disks for tables of data, their indexes and related objects, database transaction logs, and so forth. At database creation time, a database must have a disk to reside on; if there are no devices available (no space left on any defined device), a database cannot be created.

When creating databases, you can (and usually do!) specify the devices where the database will reside. In some cases, you may want the server to determine the devices where the database will reside; in those cases, the server may use only disks you have indicated to be default disks. In other words, if a database is created and no device is specified, each default disk may be used as a database device. In a moment, you examine more closely how the server decides which default disk(s) to use.

SYNTAX

```
sp_diskdefault "device_name", {defaulton ¦ defaultoff}
```

EXAMPLES

```
exec sp_diskdefault data_device_1, defaulton
exec sp_diskdefault master, defaultoff
```

Note

You use `execute` or `exec` before any stored procedure that is not the first statement on the batch. This is a rule for the Sybase parser.

In the previous example in which you issue two procedure requests in a single batch, the first use of `exec` is optional; the second is required.

In the first example, you instruct the server that `data_device_1` may be used as a default device.

In the second example, you tell the server that you do not want database space on the master device unintentionally. This does not mean the master cannot be used; it does mean that the space cannot be used unless it is specifically allocated.

4

DEFINING DEVICES

Note

The only device whose default status is on automatically is the master device. (Master is the "default default device.") This means that if you issue a simple `create database` command and do not specify a device, the database may end up on the master device.

You do not want the master device cluttered up unintentionally. (It's a real problem if the master device becomes full—especially if you need to increase the size of the master database.) So turn off the default bit of your master database right now!

Because the `sp_diskdefault` command affects server-wide resources, it is limited to systems administrators only (those with the `sa_role`, which is discussed later in the security section).

The net effect of the `sp_diskdefault` command is that the 2^0 bit in the status bit of the sysdevices table for that device is set to 1 (if `defaulton`) or 0 (if `defaultoff`).

In most systems, a default is the single option chosen when no selection is made by the user. Because you can set the default bit on or off independently for each database, you can end up with several default disks (or none).

It probably seems a little strange to have several default disks. How does the server decide which default disk to use? Space on default disks is assigned to databases alphabetically, exhausting all space on each default disk, then proceeding to the next, until all requested space is allocated.

For example, consider the following `create database` command, which requests that 100MB be assigned to database `newdb` on a default disk (or disks):

```
create database newdb on default = 100
```

Assume that you have the default disks and available space on each as outlined in Table 4.2. (Okay, it doesn't follow the Greek alphabet correctly, but then neither does SQL Server.)

TABLE 4.2. DEFAULT DISKS.

Disk Name	Available Space
alpha_disk	10MB
beta_disk	10MB
delta_disk	10MB
gamma_disk	1000MB

Where will the server place newdb? The obvious answer is, "There is room on the gamma_disk, so it will go there." But this is not the way default disks are allocated. Remember: Space on default disks is assigned to databases alphabetically.

Here's what happens:

◆ 10MB is allocated on alpha disk.

◆ 10MB is allocated on beta disk.

◆ 10MB is allocated on delta disk.

◆ The remaining 70MB is allocated on gamma disk.

The net effect is the same as if you had issued the create database command:

```
create database newdb
   on alpha_disk = 10,
      beta_disk = 10,
      delta_disk = 10,
      gamma_disk = 70
```

and the effect on the disks is the following:

Disk name	Available space
alpha_disk	0MB
beta_disk	0MB
delta_disk	0MB
gamma_disk	930MB

Note that this is not necessarily a performance problem. In fact, it is an advantage to spread active tables across disk controllers.

Tip

If you want to find out whether a specific device is a default device, you can check the device status bit in sysdevices (if the status is odd, the 2^0 bit is set and it is a default device). Alternatively, use the sp_helpdevice command. It specifies whether the device is a default device.

It's normally not a good idea to use default disks. Whatever work it saves you in remembering physical device names is nullified by the enormous pain you will endure to fix one bad command. Turn off all your default statuses and specify device names in your create database statements.

In fact, it is unusual to have default disks defined. Systems administrators tend to want to keep a very tight control on physical server resources.

4

DEFINING DEVICES

DISK MIRRORING

Occasionally, devices fail.

You can ensure against problems caused by device failures by instructing the server to mirror two devices, keeping them in complete sync at all times. You can mirror devices at the hardware, operating system, or SQL Server level. In the last case, SQL Server handles all the disk mirroring work.

Warning

Disk mirroring at the hardware level may work, and may reduce the load on the CPU, but it is necessary to stress-test the hardware mirroring before counting on it to work with SQL Server in a production environment.

You should mirror, at a minimum, the master device and all your log devices. A failed master device without backup is agony; a failed master device with backup is merely a pain in the backside. (You learn more about this in Chapter 8, "Backing Up and Restoring the Database and Transaction Logs.") Failed log devices cook the database; if the log devices do not fail, data device failures can be mitigated at least through log recovery (again, more in Chapter 8).

If you mirror devices across controllers (see Figure 4.8) as well as across physical disks, you reduce potential single points of failure.

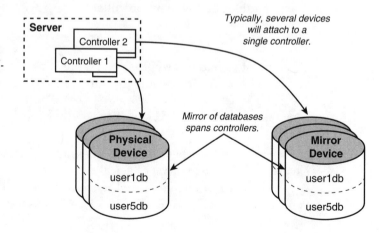

Figure 4.8.
Mirroring across devices still leaves you vulnerable to a controller failure. Mirroring across controllers protects against controller failures as well.

Note

Pages are written to both devices, synchronously or asynchronously, at your choice (the default is synchronously). Prior to System 10, reads could be across both devices, an option called mirrored read (splitting reads across both disks of a mirrored pair). This option was removed for System 10, because Sybase technical support and development determined that mirrored reads were not a substantial improvement in performance.

Sybase currently has a limitation of 255 physical devices. Mirroring does not take up any of these device connections. (Note the syntax.)

Finally, please note that a mirror device must be at least as large as the device it is mirroring.

SYNTAX

```
disk mirror
name = 'logical_device_name',
mirror = 'physical_device_name'
[ , writes = {serial | noserial } ]
[ , contiguous ]
```

In the disk mirror syntax, *logical_device_name* is the name of the device you initialized (on which you used the disk init command). The *physical_device_name* is the device that holds the contents of the mirror. Serial writes, the default, ensures that in case of a power failure, the write will go to at least one of the physical devices if the mirrors are on separate physical devices (they should be). The contiguous option is available on Open VMS only.

EXAMPLE

```
disk mirror
name = 'data_device_1',
mirror = '/dev/rsd05'
```

In the example, you mirror a device that you initialized and to which you assigned the logical device name data_device_1. A copy of all writes to the disk are also written to the physical device at address /dev/rsd05.

4

DEFINING DEVICES

SEQUENCE OF EVENTS

There are three steps in the disk mirror sequence of events:

1. The secondary device (mirror device) is initialized.
2. All used pages on the primary device are copied to the secondary device. Note that, as expected, this is not a fast process.
3. Bits are set in sysdevices, bit 2^6 (device mirrored) and 2^9 (mirror enabled).

Note

Sybase mirrors at the device level, not the database level. If a database is spread across many devices, and any one device used by the database is not mirrored, the database is at risk from a physical failure. For a database to be fully protected, every device associated with that database must be mirrored.

DISK MIRRORING INFORMATION

The easiest way to check on disk mirroring for a device is with the sp_helpdevice command.

Warning

With some versions of the server (prior to System 10), sp_helpdevice does not report disk mirroring information 100 percent accurately. If you suspect the values in sp_helpdevice, you have to select the row from sysdevices and decode the data bits.

Alternatively, rewrite sp_helpdevice and fix it.

Alternatively, you can identify all the disk devices (devices with cntrltype of 0—others are backup devices) using the SQL statement:

```
select * from sysdevices where cntrltype = 0
```

DEACTIVATING DISK MIRRORING

Devices become unmirrored in two ways:

◆ You, as the sa or using the sa_role, issue the disk unmirror command.
◆ Sybase, in an attempt to write to a primary or secondary device of a mirror pair, is unable to write to one of the devices.

The server maintains the bit flags within the device status in sysdevices to report on the status of the mirror. When mirrors fail or are disabled for any reason, the server updates the bit flags to indicate which mirror failed. Table 4.3 summarizes the bit flags as they relate to mirror devices. Note that other status flags (default or reads mirrored) could be set in addition to the flags described in the table.

TABLE 4.3. STATUS FLAGS RELATING TO MIRROR DEVICES.

State of Mirror	Status Value	Decoded Status
Not mirrored	2 (2)	Physical disk
Mirrored	578 (2 + 64 + 512)	Mirrored, mirror-enabled
Secondary failed	66 (2 + 64)	Mirrored
Primary failed	322 (2 + 64 + 256)	Mirrored, half-mirrored

Unmirroring a device has the effect of modifying status bits and instructing the server to write to only one specific device of a mirrored pair.

If the mirroring is automatic, the server checkpoints the master database so that changes in the sysdevices table are permanently reflected on the disk. Additionally, any processes that are awaiting a mirrorexit event are enabled.

Note

The waitfor command is a Transact-SQL enhancement that is effectively an event handler. Here is an example:

```
waitfor mirrorexit
print "A mirror primary or secondary device has failed! Take action."
```

In this example, the process executing the SQL sleeps until the event specified (the waitfor command) occurs. For more information, see the waitfor command in volume one of the SQL Server Reference Manual, because it is beyond the scope of a systems-administration book.

SYNTAX

```
disk unmirror
name = 'logical_name'
[ , side = { "primary" ¦ secondary } ]
[ , mode = { retain ¦ remove } ]
```

The parameter logical name is the device that you initialized with the disk init command; the "primary" side is the device that you initialized; the secondary is the mirror that you specified. You may unmirror either the primary or the secondary device. Defaults are secondary and retain.

4

DEFINING DEVICES

If you specify `retain`, the names of the unmirrored devices are kept in the sysdevices table indefinitely, and you may remirror (you will see remirror shortly). Automatic unmirroring uses the `retain` option.

EXAMPLE

```
disk unmirror
name = 'data_device_1',
side = 'primary',
mode = remove
```

In the example, you are telling the server that you want to permanently remove the definition of the primary device from the `data_device_1` device. The effect is that the mirror side becomes the primary (only) device.

```
disk unmirror name = 'data_device_1'
```

In this example, the server unmirrors the secondary device, and keeps the definition of the device in sysdevices. In this case, you can use the `disk remirror` command.

DISK REMIRRORING

After a device becomes unmirrored automatically, or manually with `mode = retain`, you, the `sa`, can instruct the server to restart the software mirroring. The `disk remirror` statement will fail unless the device was previously mirrored and the definition still remains in sysdevices.

SYNTAX

```
disk remirror name = 'logical_name'
```

Note that it is not necessary to specify anything else. The *logical name* in sysdevices already has the necessary information in the row or the command will fail (and you should have used the `disk mirror` command instead).

EXAMPLE

```
disk remirror name = 'data_device_1'
```

Note

Regardless of the elapsed time of the `disk unmirror` (one second unmirrored, with no updates occurring!), an unmirrored disk is considered to be out of synchronization with the primary, and the mirroring process begins anew. This means that the entire device is recopied onto the mirror (or primary, if that was the side unmirrored). Remember that this is not a fast process.

What happens when you have an older device that is being replaced because it is too old, small, or slow? What if you have several databases on the device (or parts of several databases on a device)? One technique is to execute the following steps:

1. Dump all the databases.
2. Drop all the databases. (You cannot drop a device if a database is on it.)
3. Drop the "old" device.
4. Cycle the server. (Remember, the device numbers are not reusable.)
5. Recreate the device.
6. Recreate the databases.
7. Reload the databases.

This is a lot of work. It also needs to be done when your users are not on the system (and you'd rather be home in bed). It is possible to use the disk mirroring commands to migrate data from one device to another. This may be extremely useful.

Here is the easy way (see Figure 4.9):

1. Mirror the current disk onto the new disk (or an appropriate slice of the new disk).
2. Unmirror the device, side = primary, mode = remove.

Figure 4.9.
It usually is more
efficient to migrate data
with mirroring than
with a backup and
restore.

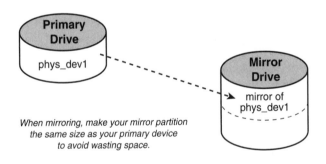

When mirroring, make your mirror partition
the same size as your primary device
to avoid wasting space.

You should mirror at least the master device and all log devices. With the low cost of disk space, there is little excuse not to mirror everything. Think about the cost of having the system down compared to the cost of a 2GB SCSI drive. When it comes time to mirror the master device, there are two steps to follow:

1. Mirror the device like any other.
2. At startup, the dataserver command must be made aware that it has another place to look if the primary master device is unavailable. You can do this with the -r option on the dataserver command in the runserver file. Following is an example of a UNIX runserver file:

```
/sybase/bin/dataserver -d /dev/rsd06 -r /dev/rsd08
```

4

There are a few things to note about this command. First, even if your master device has failed, you need to specify it before the mirror device to enable the server to recognize the mirrored master device properly.

Second, every platform or version offers subtle variations on maintaining a mirror on master; check your installation manual and troubleshooting guides for more information.

Third, mirroring the master device is important. If you lose master after a substantive change to your system configuration (but before a backup), you have to piece it back together. If you can't piece it back together, you may lose all contact with your user database(s).

Software Mirroring, Hardware Mirroring, and RAID

Sybase mirrors data at the software level to ensure that mirroring is possible, regardless of hardware platform or configuration. There are alternatives, however. Many hardware vendors enable mirroring at the controller level. Alternatively, RAID provides an alternative to mirroring every device, along with a concurrent performance throughput benefit. Here are the advantages and disadvantages of each.

Software Mirroring

Software mirroring guarantees database stability against hardware failure. It is guaranteed by Sybase, so if there is a problem, it is handled by Sybase Technical Support. In addition, software mirroring enables you to mirror across controllers, minimizing single points of failure.

However, software mirroring requires additional writes, which require more CPU cycles. Sybase does not admit to a substantial performance degradation, but other vendors talk about a 10 percent performance hit from software mirroring.

Hardware Mirroring

Hardware mirroring reduces CPU work. (Hardware mirroring is handled by the controller.)

However, hardware mirroring is guaranteed by the hardware vendor. This means that if the mirroring does not work out, the hardware vendor will blame the software vendor, and the software vendor will blame the hardware vendor. This is not a pretty picture when all you want is your data back. (You learn about restore techniques later.)

Tip

> If you are going to mirror at the hardware level, be sure to test the mirroring. When the server is under load, pull out one of the drives and see what happens. After mirroring is re-enabled, pull the other drive out and see what happens. (If you smell smoke or ozone, consider software mirroring.)
>
> Network administrators have been pulling the plug on uninterruptible power supplies (UPS) for years, to make sure the server can run even when the UPS has suffered a lapse in power from the power company. However, when you pull the power cord on the UPS, you can sometimes damage the UPS and it stops working immediately.

RAID

With RAID, there are typically five devices: four contain data, and the fifth has redundant hash information. If any device fails, the RAID device notifies the operator, and acts as if nothing happened as far as data transmission goes. The operator will replace the bad drive with a "hot" backup. The RAID device will automatically bring the new device up to speed.

The RAID architecture handles all mirroring automatically, and at the hardware level. It is a nifty technology.

However, RAID is expensive. You might spend some time looking into advantages at the different RAID levels that you can set. You may decide that performance advantages are outweighed by an inconvenience factor.

Typically, you have to set RAID to level 5 to get the protection you want, and on many platforms you may find that SCSI was faster after all.

Device SQL

It can be important to determine what devices are available, how much space is initialized on the devices, and how much space is actually utilized. This SQL returns that specific information in a neat report:

```
select 'Database device name' = name,
'In use by databases' = sum (size / 512),
'Space initialized' = (high-low+1)/512
from sysdevices, sysusages
where vstart between low and high
and cntrltype = 0
group by name
```

4

DEFINING DEVICES

Warning

Some Sybase documentation incorrectly states that sysdevices and sysusages are joined with 1start; vstart is correct.

SUMMARY

You've learned how to implement storage devices using SQL Server and looked at the use of internal and external mechanisms to provide fault tolerance and ensure data reliability and availability. In the next chapter, you create databases using the space created on these devices.

CHAPTER 5

Defining, Altering, and Maintaining Databases and Logs

This chapter addresses how to create and maintain databases and database logs. You will learn several approaches to managing disk space on various versions of SQL Server. You also will learn about Sybase segments. If you are familiar with the term segment from a different database management system, you need to disregard your preconceived definition when reviewing this chapter. It is likely that what is defined as a segment for some other database management system is different than how Sybase defines segments.

WHAT IS A DATABASE?

The database concept is central to almost all implementation and administration tasks in SQL Server. During the database design phase of a project, you define the tables of interest to your organization. From a logical perspective, these related tables are collectively considered a single database. From a physical perspective, however, you can implement these tables in one or many Sybase databases. The Sybase database is important because it determines how data is stored physically—how data is mapped to physical devices. Physical space is assigned to a database during database creation, and additional space can be assigned to the database when the need arises.

Several key areas are based at the database level. All Sybase objects must exist within the database—often refered to as "in the context of a database." Therefore, the limits on how large an object can grow is dependent on the amount of space allocated to the database. (At a detailed level, limits on object growth are truly dependent on the amount of space available to a segment in the database, which is described in the section titled "Segments and Object Placement" later in this chapter.) The database is also an important element in your security strategy because you must be a user of a database to be able to access objects within. Some analysis tools, such as dbcc (the Database Consistency Checker), act at the database level. Also, backups are conducted only at the database level, which means a database is the only unit of recovery available in Sybase (table-level backups are not currently supported).

DATABASES AND SPACE MANAGEMENT

Logical devices (see Chapter 4, "Defining Physical and Mirror Devices") make space usable to the SQL Server, and databases organize that space, making it available to Sybase tables and their indexes, as well as other objects. Databases cannot span physical SQL Servers, nor can tables and their indexes span databases. Therefore, the size of a database will limit the size of any tables and indexes it contains. However, if a table or index grows too large, you can increase the size of the database on the fly.

Note

Later in the chapter, you will look at database segments and how they are used to manage table and index sizes within the database. Although people usually refer to the size of the database as determining the maximum size of a table or index, this is not fully accurate. Each object is created on a segment in a Sybase database, and objects cannot span segments. Therefore, it is the amount of space available to the segment that determines the maximum size of an object.

DATABASES AND SECURITY

The owner of a database maps a system login to a database user. This is accomplished in one of four ways and is described in detail in Chapter 6, "Security and User Administration." Permission to access objects is granted to a database user (either explicitly—to the user, or implicitly—to a user group. See Chapter 6 for more information). Therefore, if you do not allow a SQL Server login to be associated with a database user, you have eliminated the ability for that user to access the objects within that database.

DATABASES AND BACKUP

You will see later that Sybase utilities allow you to back up a database only. This can either be a full backup (copy of the entire database) or an incremental backup (copy of the transactions that have occurred since the last backup). Because transactions are logged in a table within a database, you need to be careful when creating related tables in different databases. For example, consider a table called "customer" in the customerdb database and a table called "purchase" in the purchase_db database. As part of a transaction, you add a new customer to the customer table and that customer's purchases to the purchase table. Each database will log the addition of rows in their own transaction log. If a disaster occurs and you lose the customer_db database, you may be forced to reload this database from backup (assume the purchase_db database was fine). It is possible that you would not be able to restore the customer_db database to the point at which the disaster occurred. Therefore, the purchase table would contain purchases for customers that are not in the customer table. When you decide how to distribute related tables in different databases, remember that you are possibly putting your data integrity at risk.

SYSTEM DATABASES

A system database is a database created to support the operation of the server or a Sybase facility. When the SQL Server is installed, it creates at least three system databases—master, model, and tempdb. In a System 10 or 11 installation, there is a fourth database created called sybsystemprocs. However, you also can install other system databases to support additional capabilities. There is a new syntax database, sybsyntax, which allows the user to execute the sp_syntax command (System 10). Also, if you install auditing, the sybsecurity database is added.

- The *master database* records all of the server-specific configuration information, including authorized users, devices, databases, system configuration settings, and remote servers.

- The *model database* is a template database. The contents of model are copied into each new database created after the system is installed.

- *tempdb* is the temporary database. This database is used as an interim storage area. It is used by the server (automatically) to resolve large or multistep queries or to sort data before returning results to the user (if a query contains an order by clause). Programmers also can use it (programmatically) to provide a worktable to support application processing.

- *sybsystemprocs* contains all system-stored procedures, such as sp_who, sp_helpdevice, sp_help, and sp_dropdevice.

Note

Before the release of System 10, system-stored procedures were stored in the master database.

DATABASE CREATION

A primary task of the system administrator is to create databases. In this section, you'll learn the syntax of the create database statement as well as some of the implementation issues involved with database creation.

Tip

As you implement databases, remember that database creation can take a long time. Creation time depends mostly on your physical disk speed—the server initializes every page in a database—and can take between 20 and 60 minutes per gigabyte, depending on your platform. If you are implementing a very large database, this could impact your project schedule.

SYNTAX

```
create database <db_name>
[on <device_name> [= <size>] [, ...]]
[log on <device_name> [= <size>] [, ...]]
[for load]
```

When creating a database, you must provide a database name. Database names must be 30 characters or less, cannot include any punctuation or other special characters, and must be unique within the server.

Note

The naming conventions for database names vary widely between organizations. Some shops limit themselves to four or eight characters so that the database can easily map to DOS or MVS filenames. Others use long descriptive names. Some shops standardize on encoded names, such as ACTV94TST01 (for "1994 activity test 1").

Database names are case-sensitive (for example, you could create two databases, "customer_db" and "CUSTOMER_DB"). Many organizations standardize on uppercase—for database names and object names—to allow easier portability to other environments. (I prefer to use lowercase because writing in all uppercase usually looks like someone is shouting at me.)

I recommend that you keep database names short. After all, people will need to type them. And keep them meaningful and memorable. Names like "AU149305" don't mean much to most mortals. Use names like "accounting" or "acctg," which are easy to remember and easy to type, so your users and programmers won't be cursing you six times a day. For more on naming standards, see Chapter 18, "Defining Systems Administration and Naming Standards."

A database is created on one or more physical devices. Specifying the device is optional—but is highly recommended. When indicating the device, you use the logical name you specified as part of disk init. (See Chapter 4, "Defining Physical and Mirror Devices," for more on setting up database devices.)

Note

If you do not specify the device on which to create the database, a default device will be used (see the section titled "Default Disks" in Chapter 4). Most DBAs like to know up front where a database is going to be placed. Therefore, always supply the device where you want the database to be created.

You also can specify the size of the database, in megabytes. If a size is not indicated, the server will use the larger of the default size (a configurable value set to 2MB upon installation) or the size of the model database (because the contents of model is copied into each new database created). It is a good standard practice to always provide size to create database.

Note

You specify disk size in pages, but you specify database size in megabytes.

If you request more megabytes than are available on a device, the server will allocate all remaining space on the device, as long as there is enough room to make a complete copy of the model database.

EXAMPLES

Note

We have written the examples to improve readability: each individual device is listed on its own line. This does not affect how the command works, but it certainly makes it easier to read later on. And don't forget that you are saving all create statements in a script in case you need to execute them later.

This first example sets up a 12MB (8 + 4) database called "marketing." In this database, 8MB is allocated for tables, indexes, system tables, and other objects (all of which are broadly classified as *data*), and 4MB is allocated for the transaction log.

```
create database marketing
on data_device_1 = 8
log on log_device_4 = 4
```

Note

The transaction log is used by Sybase to log certain activity within a database. Examples of logged activity includes creating objects, adding or deleting database users, or adding, deleting, or modifying data in tables.

Note

In general, you should set up your log segment on a separate drive and controller, if possible. Performance will be better, you will be able to perform incremental backups, and you will be better able to recover after a disaster. Please see Chapter 7, "Database Logging and Recovery," for more on transaction logs.

The following example sets up a 30MB (12 + 8 + 10) database called "accounting." It provides 20MB for data and 10MB for the transaction log.

```
create database accounting
on data_device_1 = 12,
data_device_2 = 8
log on log_device_1 = 10
```

This `create database` statement includes several devices and sizes. If you include several devices, SQL Server acquires on each device a fragment of the size you specify. If there is not enough space on any single device listed, SQL Server will allocate as much space as it can on the device.

The next example includes the keywords, `for load`. Create a database `for load` if you are creating the structure for the sole purpose of restoring a database from a backup where the structure does not exist.

```
create database newdb
on data_device_3 = 12,
data_device_4 = 8
log on log_device_2 = 10
for load
```

For example, consider the situation where you have encountered a database corruption and are forced to load from a backup copy. Normally, a corrupt database must be dropped—completely removed from the physical device(s). However, you must load the backup copy into an existing database. Because the `load` process is going to replace the existing structure with the data in the backup, there is no need to go through the time-consuming activity of initializing all the database pages. See

Chapter 8, "Backing Up and Restoring the Database and Transaction Logs," for more information on restoring databases.

After a `create database ... for load`, the only permitted operation on the database is `load database`, the SQL Server method of restoring a database from backup.

WHAT HAPPENS WHEN YOU CREATE A DATABASE?

The server performs the following actions when you create a database:

1. Immediately allocates database space.
2. Inserts one row in sysdatabases (a system table in the master database) for the database. You will have a row in sysdatabases for every database in a server.
3. Inserts one row in sysusages (master database) for each device fragment.
4. Physically marks each extent. An extent is comprised of eight data pages (pages are normally 2KB, except on Stratus hardware where the page size is 4KB). This activity is what takes the bulk of the elapsed time for a database creation.
5. Copies the model database into the new database.

If the database is created `for load`, the server allocates the space from the specified devices, but does not mark the extents or copy the contents of the model database into the structure. The actual marking of extents is an automatic part of the restore process (`load database`). If you do not create the database `for load`, you are performing the most time-consuming part of the create process needlessly.

Note

A hospital system using Sybase experienced a database corruption. Minimizing downtime was critical. By using `for load`, I was able to create the database structure in a few minutes—instead of performing a "normal" database create which had originally taken over seven hours. This allowed the system to be up and running almost a full business day sooner than if I had not used `for load`.

Here are the steps to take when you specify `for load`:

1. Immediately allocate database space.
2. Insert one row in sysdatabases for the database.
3. Insert one row per device fragment in sysusages.
4. Set the database status bit 5 (value = 32), indicating that the database was created `for load`.

SIZING DATABASES

By definition, the size of the database is the size of all data fragments plus the size of all log fragments. The data area needs to be large enough to hold all of the system tables and your user tables, as well as any indexes. The log needs to be large enough for the transaction log.

MINIMUM SIZE

The minimum database size is the greater of the setting in `sp_configure` (2MB is the default value) or the size of the model database (also 2MB by default). If the model database will not fit into the allocated space, the database creation will fail.

DEFAULT DEVICES AND SIZES

You don't need to specify a device name or a size. If you don't specify the size, the default size is the greater of the size of the model database and the value of "database size" in sysconfigures. For example, if "database size" is 2MB but the model database is 8MB, the default database size is 8MB.

Note

> To change the minimum database size, you can either increase the size of the model database (with `alter database`, see the section titled "Making Databases Larger" later in this chapter) or change the configured value (this is the recommended approach).
>
> To change the configuration setting to 8MB, use the `sp_configure` stored procedure:
>
> ```
> sp_configure "database size", 8
> reconfigure
> ```
>
> You will need to restart your server before the new setting takes effect.

HOW BIG SHOULD THE DATABASE BE?

When you create a database, remember that the data area needs to be large enough to contain the system tables, user tables, and all indexes. You probably want to leave about 25 percent free space in your database as well. To estimate the eventual size requirements of tables, use the stored procedure `sp_estspace`.

Note

Use sp_estspace whenever you need to estimate how large a table and its indexes will grow. The stored procedure is shipped with System 10 and is available on the Sybase CompuServe forum, OpenLink. You will also find the script on the disk in this book; look for the file named estspace.sql.

It is important to remember that databases can get larger (you'll see how in a moment), but they cannot get smaller. If you oversize a database, the only way to recover the additional space is to drop the database and re-create it, re-create all the database objects, then reload each table individually. The general approach is to start the database small and let it grow as necessary.

HOW BIG SHOULD THE LOG BE?

The transaction log records all database modifications. If the log is full, no further modifications are permitted in the database. Under ordinary production circumstances, the only time SQL Server clears the transaction log is after an incremental backup.

The factors influencing log size are database activity level, the frequency of incremental backup, and the volume of simultaneous updates. Because these factors vary dramatically from one system to another, it is impossible to establish firm guidelines on sizing a database log. As a starting point, you may want to consider creating logs that are between 10 and 25 percent of the database size.

Long-running transactions also influence log size. If your system will be updating large amounts of data in a single transaction, the log will need to be large enough to hold the entire transaction. In that case, you may need the log to be 200 percent or more of the size of the data. If you want your logs to be smaller, you will need to break up large updates into smaller transactions (which is usually a good idea anyway), then dump the transaction log in between the transactions to free up space in the log.

SETTING UP A SEPARATE AREA FOR THE TRANSACTION LOG

Most of the examples of database creation in this chapter include a separate allocation for the transaction log. This is accomplished by providing log on information to create database. Transaction logging and log management are discussed in great detail in Chapter 7 but it's important to understand now some of the characteristics of transaction logs.

A Sybase transaction log is a record of all modifications made to a database. Every object creation, every security implementation, every row modification (insert, update, delete) is logged in a transaction log. (There are a handful of non-logged activities, which are discussed later, but in a true production environment, all activities are fully logged.)

The transaction log is a *write-ahead log,* which means logged activity is written to the transaction log before the modifications are made to the tables and indexes themselves. In most cases, the only information that is written to disk at the time of update is the logging information; the data will only be brought up to date at checkpoint time.

There are several crucial benefits to separating your log from your data in your `create database` statement.

First, Sybase incremental backups are actually just copies of the transaction log. If the data and log areas are not separated, the server cannot perform incremental backups; all backups for database with integrated log and data areas will be full backups.

Second, you can get some performance benefits by separating log and data activity, especially if the devices are attached to separate physical disk drives in the server.

Third, without separate logs, recovery is more difficult. One implication of writing the log first is that the log is the unit of data integrity in Sybase. If you lose your data but have your log, up-to-the-transaction recovery is possible (even likely). If you lose your log but still have your data, up-to-the-minute recovery is not possible, and you can only recover up to the point of your last backup.

The best method of ensuring fault tolerance is to mirror all the devices, but sometimes that is not feasible. If you can mirror at least your log devices (which are always smaller than all database devices), you can ensure recoverability. If any log device fails, you still have an alternative device from which you can work. (See Chapter 4 for more information on mirroring.)

How Big Should You Make tempdb?

The tempdb database is a temporary work area used by the SQL Server to resolve large queries or queries requiring the creation of a worktable. (Queries that may need a worktable include those with order by or distinct clauses. The group by clause always uses a worktable.) Users can also direct SQL Server to create temporary tables with create table or select ... into statements.

Temporary tables are identified by the number sign (#) in the first character. For example, the following statement creates a temporary table, #authors_and_titles, in tempdb:

```
select au_lname, au_fname, title
into #authors_and_titles
from authors a, titleauthor ta, titles t
where a.au_id = ta.au_id
and ta.title_id = t.title_id
```

The size of the temporary table depends on the size of the tables referenced in the query (authors, titleauthor, and titles).

You cannot restrict users from creating temporary tables. The temporary tables will persist until the user explicitly drops the table (drop table #titles_and_authors) or until the user creating the temporary table logs out. Temporary tables created by stored procedures are dropped when the procedure ends.

Sizing tempdb depends on a number of factors: how often users create ad hoc temporary tables, whether application programs or stored procedures create temporary tables, how many concurrent users will need to create these tables at one time, and so forth.

Tip

The typical motivation for a programmer to use a temporary table is to avoid a second pass through a large table. By copying a small subset of the data to another location, the user can save many disk operations and improve performance. In general, you want to encourage programmers to think this way because it will improve overall system performance.

If you properly select indexes on the primary tables, it may not be necessary to create a worktable to resolve a query. For example, a programmer may want to retrieve data from a table in a particular order. If there was a clustered index created on the columns the programmer wants to order the data by, the data could be retrieved directly from the primary tables. (The creation of a clustered index on a column or columns of a table will physically store the data in the table in the sort order specified.)

Note

If tempdb runs out of space, the transaction aborts and an error is reported in the errorlog.

At first, make tempdb about 25 percent of the size of your largest database, unless you have reason to expect you will need substantially more.

DATABASE CREATION AUTHORITY AND DATABASE OWNERSHIP

Normally, databases are created by the system administrator—who historically has logged into the server as sa. In System 10 and later, however, the capabilities of the system administrator can be granted to individual logins through the use of Sybase roles. The sa_role is granted to an individual login, enabling the the server to treat that login as a system administrator. Any login that has been granted the sa_role is permitted to perform database creations.

Whoever creates a database owns it. However, ownership of a database can be transferred.

ALLOWING OTHERS TO CREATE DATABASES

Someone other than the system administrator can create a database if the system administrator grants that person the ability to execute the create database command. (See the section titled "Command Permissions" in Chapter 6 for more information.)

Ordinarily, you will not assign the database creation ability to others, and you should not. Because database creation allocates system resources, you want to manage this task carefully and thoughtfully. Database creation should be a "system administrators only" task.

If you really need to allow others to create databases, do the following:

1. Use the master database:

   ```
   use master
   go
   ```

2. Add a database user in the master database for the particular login:

   ```
   sp_adduser john
   go
   ```

3. Grant the create database privilege to the user:

   ```
   grant create database to john
   go
   ```

TRANSFERRING DATABASE OWNERSHIP

Whoever creates a database is designated as its owner. It is very common to transfer ownership of a database to another user, once the database is created. Database ownership is often transferred to distribute responsiblity—a person other than the sa is responsible for the normal operations of the database (adding users, granting permissions, and so on).

Note

The database is the only object that can change ownership. If you try to change the ownership of a table or other object, the system usually marks the entire database "suspect" and you will need to drop the database and restore from tape. I know; I tried it.

MAKING DATABASES LARGER

Use the alter database command to make databases larger. You can enlarge a database while the system is online and the database is in use.

Note

Don't forget that databases can get larger, but not smaller.

SYNTAX FOR *ALTER DATABASE*

The alter database command is similar to create database.

```
alter database <db_name>
[on device_name [= size], [...]]
[log on device_name [= size]]
```

Specify the additional amount of space to be allocated, not the ultimate size of the database. The default increment is 2MB. You cannot allocate less than 1MB at a time.

Consider the following examples of create and alter database commands.

```
create database market_db
on device1 = 50,
device_2 = 100
log on logdev1 = 35

alter database market_db
on device1 = 50
```

In this example, a 185MB database is created on three devices. The alter database command adds an additional 50MB, for a total of 235MB.

ADDING LOG SPACE

Adding log space to a database requires the `log on` keywords (found in System 10 only) in the `alter database` statement.

```
alter database market_db
log on logdev2 = 35
```

This statement adds 35MB of space to the log of the market_db database.

ASSIGNING SPACE TO THE LOG

Typically, you assign log space with the `log on` clause in the `create database` or `alter database` statement. It is also possible to assign database space on a specific device to the log retroactively (that is, after a `create` or `alter` statement) with the `sp_logdevice` stored procedure, as in the following:

```
sp_logdevice <databasename>, <devicename>
```

Consider the following examples:

```
create database test_db
on device1 = 50,
device2 = 100
log on logdev1 = 35

alter database test_db
on newdevice = 50
```

After the `alter` statement, the database is 235MB, with 200MB of space for data and system tables (50MB on `device1`, 100MB on `device2`, and 50MB on `newdevice`) and 35MB of space for the transaction log (on `logdev1`).

The space allocation on additional database devices is assumed to be used for data in SQL Server versions 4.8 and later. In the preceding example, the allocation on newdevice is for data because there was no previous allocation of space for the database on the device. If you want to make newdevice a log device, use the `sp_logdevice` statement.

```
sp_logdevice test_db, newdevice
```

Note

In the previous example, the `create database` statement sets aside 35MB on `logdev1` for the transaction log. All subsequent allocations of space on that device will also be used for the log. The `sp_logdevice` procedure sets aside any space allocations on newdevice for the log as well.

> This is really the crucial point about space utilization: space is assigned for data or log by device. This is a special case of the general use of database segments, which will be examined in detail a little later in this chapter.

EXPLORING DATABASES

It's useful to get down under the covers when it comes to databases, particularly if you ever need to do creative work with the system tables to enable a recovery. In the next sections, you're going to explore databases using standard stored procedures, then examine the system tables in more detail.

SP_HELPDB

The system stored procedure, sp_helpdb, provides information about databases on the server. If you don't provide a parameter, the system provides a list of all databases on the server.

```
sp_helpdb
```

name	db_size	owner	dbid	created	status
fred	4.0 MB	sa	9	Jan 18, 1995	no options set
master	3.0 MB	sa	1	Jan 01, 1900	no options set
model	2.0 MB	sa	3	Jan 01, 1900	no options set
perftune	15.5 MB	sa	6	Jan 06, 1995	select into/bulkcopy
pubs2	2.0 MB	sa	8	Nov 23, 1994	no options set
sybsecurity	8.0 MB	sa	7	Nov 10, 1994	trunc log on chkpt
sybsystemprocs	20.0 MB	sa	4	Nov 05, 1994	trunc log on chkpt
tempdb	2.0 MB	sa	2	Jan 05, 1995	select into/bulkcopy
testdb	4.0 MB	sa	5	Nov 07, 1994	no options set

If you provide a parameter, you get detailed information about a single database, as in the following example:

```
sp_helpdb pubs2
```

name	db_size	owner	dbid	created	status
pubs2	2.0 MB	sa	8	Nov 23, 1994	no options set

device_fragments	size	usage	free kbytes
master	2.0 MB	data and log	480

The detailed information from sp_helpdb includes a list of database fragments, which are specific allocations of space on each device.

DATABASE SYSTEM TABLES

When you create and modify databases, three system tables in the master database are involved: sysdatabases, sysusages, and sysdevices (see Figure 5.1).

Figure 5.1.
The sysusages table resolves the many-to-many relationship between sysdatabases and sysdevices.

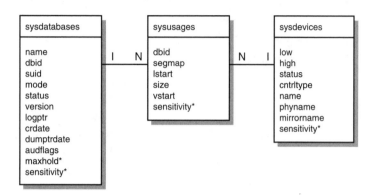

SYSDATABASES

The server adds a row to sysdatabases for each new database. The user specifies the name, but the server automatically selects the next available integer ID for dbid. There are several important columns in sysdatabases:

name	The name of the database, assigned by the database creator.
dbid	The system-assigned identifier for the database.
suid	The ID of the database owner; at database creation time, this is set to the ID of the login who issued the create database statement. To change the database owner, use the sp_changedbowner stored procedure.
status	An integer consisting of several control bits with information about the database. See the section, "The Database Status Flags," later in this chapter.
dumptrdate	The date of the last dump transaction. The server marks this date on the next transaction dump to ensure that all dumps are loaded in order during a restore from backup.

Note

The sysdatabases table also has additional columns used to record audit settings for the database itself, as well as default audit settings for tables, views, and procedures. (See Chapter 18 for more information.)

SYSDEVICES

The create database statements do not affect the sysdevices table, but each named device must exist in sysdevices. Information in sysdevices is used to build detailed rows in sysusages, so it is useful to look at sysdevices now. The important columns for this discussion are cntrltype, low, high, and name.

The maximum size of a device on SQL Server is 16 million pages (32GB). A unique range of 16 million pages is allocated to each device upon allocation; these are *virtual page numbers*.

> ## Note
>
> The virtual page range is determined by multiplying the virtual device number assigned in the disk init statement by 2^{24}, or approximately 16 million.

Following is a description of some of the important columns in sysdevices:

cntrltype	This differentiates between dump devices and database devices. A value of zero is assigned to all database devices.
low	The first virtual page number available on the device.
high	The last virtual page number available on the database device. Although the system reserves the entire range of 16 million pages to the device, the high value will reflect the device's actual capacity. To determine the number of pages on a device, use high - low + 1. To determine the number of megabytes, use (high - low + 1) / 512.
name	The logical name of the device.

The following is a sample listing from the sysdevices table for all physical database devices (cntrltype = 0). Values in the low column are even multiples of 16777216.

```
select cntrltype, low, high, name
from sysdevices
where cntrltype = 0
order by low

cntrltype low        high       name
--------- ---------- ---------- -----------------------------
0         0          12799      master
0         16777216   16787455   sysprocsdev
0         33554432   33558527   sybsecurity
0         67108864   67112959   testdevice
0         100663296  100665343  test_dev
0         1342177728 134230015  introdev
0         150994944  151000063  instruct2_data
```

Tip

To determine the virtual device number, divide the low value by 16777216; the virtual device number for testdevice is 4.

The size of the testdevice is (67112959 − 67108864 + 1) = 4096 pages = 8MB.

SYSUSAGES

The `create database` statement automatically adds one row in sysusages for each allocation of space on a device. For example, the following `create database` command:

```
create database market_db
on DATA_1 = 100, DATA_2 = 100
log on LOG_1 = 50
```

allocates space on three devices, DATA_1, DATA_2, and LOG_1. Each of these allocations is recorded in a separate row in sysusages.

Take a closer look at the useful columns in sysusages:

dbid   The database identifier. It is used to relate information in sysusages with sysdatabases (dbid exists in sysdatabases as well).

segmap   This is used to map database fragments to segments (see the section "Segments and Object Placement," later in this chapter).

lstart   The first database (logical) page number, is the logical page start within the database.

size   The number of contiguous pages.

vstart   The starting virtual page number enables you to map the database fragment to a specific virtual device. The fragment is located on the device if the vstart value falls between the low and high page numbers for the device in sysdevices.

USING SQL TO QUERY THE SYSTEM TABLES

The trick to joining sysdevices, sysdatabases, and sysusages is to understand how virtual device numbers in sysdevices are mapped to the vstart column in the sysusages table.

The following output displays the rows in sysusages for a single database. There are three fragments in the database, all on the same virtual device. sysusages includes one row per device fragment per database.

```
select *
from sysusages
where dbid = 9
order by lstart

dbid   segmap    lstart    size    vstart       pad    unreservedpgs
9      7         0         1024    67110912            664
9      7         1024      512     67111936            512
9      7         1536      512     67112448            512
```

The vstart value for each fragment falls between the low and high page numbers (67108864 and 67112959) for the testdevice, so each of these fragments is stored on the testdevice.

The actual SQL used to join sysusages to sysdevices uses a between test, as in the following fragment:

```
where sysusages.vstart between sysdevices.low and sysdevices.high
  and cntrltype = 0
```

Note

> Some older Sybase documentation tells you to join sysusages to sysdevices with the lstart column. This is wrong. Use vstart to make the join to sysdevices.

The following is the SQL used to list allocations of space on devices for each database:

```
select 'Database' = d.name, 'Device' = v.name, u.size
from sysdatabases d, sysusages u, sysdevices v
where d.dbid = u.dbid
  and u.vstart between v.low and v.high
  and cntrltype = 0
order by d.name
compute sum(u.size) by d.name
```

DATABASE SPACE USAGE

Use sp_spaceused to determine the amount of space used (and space available) in your database. If the database runs out of space for objects, you will not be able to add data to tables or indexes. You may not be able to add new views or procedures as well, depending on where the space shortfall occurred.

The database only runs out of space when it tries to allocate a new extent to an object. For example, the server determines that a page split is required in an index, but the current extent is full. At that time, the server attempts to allocate a new extent

(8 pages, which is usually 16KB) to the index. If all extents for the segment are reserved, the update fails and rolls back and the server reports an error ("out of space on segment...").

You usually want about 25 percent free space in your database at any time. This will help you avoid major work stoppages when you are hurrying to add additional space to the database.

The sp_spaceused procedure can report on the space allocated to a table, if you pass the tablename as a parameter (sp_spaceused *tablename*). However, you should be more concerned with database space usage and availability at this time. No parameters are required to get database space usage for the current database, as in the following example:

```
sp_spaceused

database_name                database_size
-------------------------    --------------------
master                       8 MB
(0 rows affected)

reserved       data           index_size       unused
-------------  -------------  --------------   -------------
5230 KB        4232 KB        208 KB           790KB
(0 rows affected)
```

Warning

sp_spaceused can be off by as much as two extents per table.

The output from the procedure can be somewhat misleading, so review it closely. Database size is the total database size, including data and log allocations, but the reserved value is only based on data usage (not logs). If you have allocated data and log separately, you can subtract from the total database size the space allocated to the log to get the total data allocation.

To determine how much space is reserved for objects within the data allocation, take the reserved value in the previous example (5230) and subtract the pages reserved for the log (run sp_spaceused syslogs). That is the space reserved for objects.

To arrive at the space available for allocation to objects, subtract from the total allocation for data the amount reserved for objects.

In the case of the master database, where you cannot separate the data and log segments, you may have to add the space reserved by syslogs to the reserved value to get a total for the space being utilized. Then, subtract the total space utilized from the total size of the database to get the amount of space available for allocation.

Database Options

Use sp_dboption to enable or disable a database option for a database. Internally, this command sets a status flag for the database. The following list contains several options you can use to define standard processing or to support special requirements:

abort tran on log full	Enables the database administrator to determine whether transactions should be placed on hold or rejected when the free space threshold is crossed in the transaction log. For more on the free space threshold, see Chapter 8, "Backing Up and Restoring the Database and Transaction Logs."
allow null	Permits the database owner to decide whether columns that do not specify nullability will permit nulls. For example, the following create table statement does not specify whether col_1 permits nulls or not:

```
create table table_1 (col_1 int)
```

Normally, col_1 would not permit nulls. If you set allow null to true before executing the create table statement, the column will permit nulls.

dbo use only	After setting a database to dbo use only, only the database owner (dbo) may issue the use statement for this database.
ddl in tran	Permits the use of create, drop, grant, and revoke statements within begin tran ... commit tran structures.
disable free space acctg	Suppresses free-space accounting and execution of threshold actions for non-log segments. This option does not affect log segments.
no chkpt on recovery	Prevents a checkpoint record from being written to the log after the recovery process is complete.
read only	Enables database users to select from the tables, but prevents all modifications. This option may provide a performance enhancement to decision-support systems.

`select into/bulkcopy`	Enables fast, non-logged actions in a database, including `select ... into`, non-logged `writetext`, and fast `bcp`.
`single user`	Limits database access to one user at a time.
`trunc log on chkpt`	Automatically truncates the transaction log after every system-generated checkpoint.

Warning

We have experienced a curious problem with `trunc log on chkpt` on certain systems. A checkpoint clears a portion of the cache to free space or update the data segments of the database. There are three kinds of checkpoints:

◆ Checkpoints explicitly requested by the database owner

◆ Checkpoints generated by the server to free space in the cache

◆ Checkpoints issued by the server checkpoint process based on the server recovery interval

On some SQL Server platforms, the `trunc log on chkpt` option only truncates the log after the third kind of checkpoint—a manual checkpoint did not truncate the log.

For more about checkpoints, see Chapter 7. For now, try to understand the potential problem with truncation.

Consider a long-running transaction, like an update of all rows in a large table.

```
update titles
set price = price * 1.02
```

In this transaction, the titles table contains several million rows. The transaction is likely to be larger than the total capacity of the transaction log. You have two choices: you can increase the size of the log (ignore that choice), or you can try to run the transaction in smaller pieces, presumably clearing the log after each statement, as in the following:

```
update titles
set price = price * 1.02
where title < "P"
checkpoint
update titles
set price = price * 1.02
where title >= "P"
```

> If the checkpoint results in a truncation, all is well. On some servers, the dbo-initiated checkpoint does not truncate the log and the log will fill up. What's worse, the explicit checkpoint reduced recovery time, further delaying the server-generated checkpoint that would otherwise have truncated the log.

Default Database Options

Upon server installation, the following items are true concerning database options:

♦ All database options are set to false in model and in all user databases.

♦ No options can be set for the master database (and master has no options set).

♦ select into/bulkcopy is always true in tempdb.

♦ Any option enabled in the model database at the time a new database is created will also be enabled for this new database.

Setting Database Options

To set database options, use sp_dboption.

Syntax

```
sp_dboption <databasename>, <option>, {true ¦ false}
```

Example

```
sp_dboption market_db, "select", true
```

Notes

♦ You must be using the master database when you execute the sp_dboption stored procedure.

♦ You may abbreviate the name of the database option, as long as the server can distinguish the option from all others. Note that all keywords (such as "select") must be placed in quotation marks when they are passed as a parameter to a stored procedure.

♦ Options may be set true or false.

♦ If you attempt to enable a database option for the master database, the command will have no effect (no options can be set for master).

♦ You must explicitly checkpoint the database after setting an option.

♦ `sp_dboption` without parameters will list all possible parameters.

♦ Only the `dbo`, `sa`, or `sa_role` may set database options; `dbo` aliases may not set options.

Typically, changing an option involves the four steps shown in the following code:

```
use master  /* only set options in the master database */
go
sp_dboption market_db, "select into/bulkcopy", true
go
use market_db /* issue the checkpoint from within the target database */
go
checkpoint
go
```

EXAMINING DATABASE STATUS

Use `sp_helpdb` to determine the value of status flags on a database. The status values are decoded to the far right in the output, and you may need to scroll to the end of the report to see the information.

THE DATABASE STATUS FLAGS

The status column in sysdatabases (and status2 in System 10) records information about a database in a bit field. Table 5.1 displays the bit representations of the status column and Table 5.2 displays the bit representations of the status2 column.

TABLE 5.1. STATUS COLUMN BIT REPRESENTATION.

Value	Status
4	Select into/bulkcopy
8	trunc log on chkpt
16	No chkpt on recovery
32	Crashed during load
256	Database suspect
512	ddl in tran
1024	Read-only
2048	dbo use only
4096	Single user
8192	Allow nulls by default
16384	dbname has changed

TABLE 5.2. STATUS2 COLUMN BIT REPRESENTATION.

Value	Status
1	Abort tran on log full
2	No free space acctg
4	Auto identity

HOW TO TURN OFF THE *SUSPECT* FLAG ON A DATABASE

If you start the SQL Server before giving external storage devices a chance to warm up, or perhaps if a drive came unplugged, the server will detect a failure of the device and mark all databases mapped to that device as SUSPECT (status column, bit value $2^8 = 256$). That value in the status column will prevent the server from ever trying to recover that database. In order to regain access to the database, you will need to turn off the bit and restart the server.

In a minute, you will learn how to manually update the sysdatabases table and remove the SUSPECT bit. Before you do anything unreasonable, though, you should check to make sure that you correctly understand the problem. If the server is up, run sp_helpdb on your database. Is the SUSPECT flag set? If not, but you still cannot access your database, you have a different problem.

If the database is marked SUSPECT, take a look at the errorlog. You want to see, fairly early in the server startup process, that it failed to start the device where the database is loaded. If you find this message, you are ready to roll. If not, keep reading and try to understand why the database was not recovered.

You will need to log in as sa, or with a login granted the sa_role, in order to be allowed to manually update the sysdatabases table. The following example shows the necessary commands to enable you to directly update the status bit in the sysdatabases table:

```
use master
go
sp_configure "allow updates", 1
reconfigure with override
go
update sysdatabases
set status = status - 256
where dbname = "your database name here"
and status & 256 = 256
go
sp_configure "allow updates", 0
reconfigure
go
```

Now shut down and restart the server. If the drives are working, the system should come right up and the databases should be available.

THE MODEL DATABASE

Whenever a database is created, the contents of the model database are copied to the new database. It is typical to place in the model database any objects that you intend to be located in all databases. Typically, model contains rules, defaults, user-defined datatypes, and any logins (for example, guest) that will be created in all databases.

Tip

User-defined datatypes are stored in systypes in each individual database. As new types are created in each database, each type is assigned a new integer identifier.

For example, if ssn_type was the first user-defined type created in one database and age_type was first in another, each would be assigned the same identifier, 100. This would create a problem when you move information between databases, especially when you use the select ... into command, where the datatype identifier (the numeric value) is copied to the new table structure.

The same problem is more severe in tempdb, where the lack of any matching type identifier typically causes sp_help to fail.

We recommend that you define user-defined types first in the model database before creating any user databases. Then, when the user database is created, the user-defined types will be copied to this new database. We further recommend that as individual databases need to add further data types, you should create these data types in the model database first, then re-create them in each user database.

Bear in mind that tempdb is created every time the server restarts. When tempdb is created, it also gets a copy of the model database, which means that it gets a complete library of user-defined datatypes.

You should consider creating a system-stored procedure to handle centralized functions, rather than creating a procedure in model to be propagated to all databases. You should also consider placing lookup tables in a single, central database, rather than propagating lookup tables into every database.

DROPPING DATABASES

To drop a database, simply issue the drop database command. Dropping a database will remove all of the appropriate entries from the various system tables and the structure will be removed—making that space available to other databases. Only the dbo (or sa, or sa_role) can drop a database, and nobody can be using it at the time it is dropped.

The syntax for the `drop database` command is as follows:

```
drop database <database_name>
```

When you drop a database, you remove all objects, all data, and all logs associated with the database. The server removes all references to the database in sysdatabases and sysusages.

Sometimes you won't be able to drop a database; for example, SUSPECT databases cannot be dropped. To remove a corrupt or damaged database, use `dbcc dbrepair`, as in the following:

```
dbcc dbrepair (<db_name>, dropdb)
```

The following is an example of how to remove a corrupt database called corrupt_db:

```
dbcc dbrepair (corrupt_db, dropdb)
```

SEGMENTS AND OBJECT PLACEMENT

If you have a database with space allocated for data on two different physical devices, it is important to understand where the server will place tables, indexes, and other objects as they are created and expand. For example, a database was created on devices `DATA_1` and `DATA_2` as follows:

```
create database market_db
on DATA_1 = 100, DATA_2 = 100
log on LOG_1 = 50
```

When you create a table in the database, as in the following example, where does the server place the table, on `DATA_1` or `DATA_2`?

```
create table Customer
(name char(30) not null,
 address char(30) not null)
```

The simple answer is: If you haven't set up any segments in your database, it doesn't matter. The server allocates space freely within the data area of the database until all of the allocations for data are full.

Note

By specifying in the `create database` statement that the 50MB on `LOG_1` was for log use only, you have already set up a *log segment*, a predefined segment that is for the exclusive use of the syslogs table. In this section you will learn to create your own user-defined segments for storing tables you want to isolate.

A *segment* is a label that identifies a set of storage allocations within a database. By using segments, you can control where the server places database objects, enabling those objects to expand only within specifically defined areas within the database. Segments can provide two broad benefits: improved performance and greater control over object placement and growth within the database.

> ## Note
>
> Segments are not widely used in the SQL Server community. An estimate is that less than five percent of all SQL Server sites use any segments beyond those provided as part of SQL Server (see the section "Predefined Segments," later in this chapter).
>
> Consider the following discussion and look at the examples before deciding to implement segments. They provide some benefit, but require a little more administrative attention and can sometimes complicate database restores.

SEGMENTS FOR PERFORMANCE

Typically, when segments are used to improve performance, the segments point to Sybase devices that are mapped to different physical disk drives. The performance improvements typically seek to distribute database activity across disks (and controllers). Some examples of how activity can be distributed are

- ◆ Non-clustered indexes can be stored on one segment, while the table itself is stored on another. This can improve both read and write performance because index I/O can run parallel to table I/O.

  Note that clustered indexes always reside on the same segment as the table indexed. This requirement arises because the leaf level of the clustered index is the table itself.

- ◆ A large table can be divided among segments (and disks) to allow different parts of the table to be read at one time.

- ◆ Text and image data (Binary Large OBjects, or BLOBs) can be placed on a segment, apart from the standard data pages. This may improve read performance when the table is heavily used.

SEGMENTS FOR CONTROL

Segments also enable you to manage the size of objects within the database. Without segments, each object can grow to the full size of the data allocations in the database, contending for space with all other objects. In the previous example, the customer table and its indexes could grow to 200MB, unless other objects also were consuming space in the database.

When you use segments, objects can only grow to the size of the segment. In addition, by implementing segments, you will be able to place thresholds on each segment and define the necessary action when the objects in a segment come near to filling the segment.

SEGMENT DEFINITION

Use the sp_addsegment stored procedure to add a new segment to a database. Use sp_extendsegment to add other device allocations for the database to an existing segment.

SYNTAX

```
sp_addsegment <segmentname>, <databasename>, <devicename>
sp_extendsegment <segmentname>, <databasename>, <devicename>
```

EXAMPLES

```
sp_addsegment Seg1, market_db, DATA_1
sp_extendsegment Seg1, market_db, DATA_2
```

Take careful note of the parameters of the sp_addsegment and sp_extendsegment stored procedures: segment name, database name, device name. Two characteristics you must understand about segments are

◆ Segments are database-specific. When you create a segment, you establish a mapping to the usage of space on a specific device or set of devices for a database. Fragments of other databases on that device are not part of that segment.

◆ Segments refer to all fragments on a device or set of devices for a database.

Take a look at two examples. In the first example, the accounting database is 240MB, with 200MB for data, 40MB for log. The first segment, Seg1, includes 50MB on DATA_1 and 100MB on DATA_3. The second segment, Seg2 includes 50MB on DATA_1 and 100MB on DATA_3.

```
use master
go
create database acctg_db
on DATA_1 = 50, DATA_2 = 50, DATA_3 = 100
log on LOG_1 = 40
go

use acctg_db
go
exec sp_addsegment Seg1, acctg_db, DATA_1
exec sp_addsegment Seg2, acctg_db, DATA_2
exec sp_extendsegment Seg2, acctg_db, DATA_3
exec sp_extendsegment Seg1, acctg_db, DATA_3
go
```

In the second example, add an additional 50MB to acctg_db on DATA_3. Now Seg1 includes 50MB on DATA_3 and 150MB on DATA_3.

```
alter database acctg_db
on DATA_3 = 50
```

NOTES

◆ Segment definitions are database specific, so Seg1 for acctg_db does not conflict with Seg1 for market_db (see "Examples" above).

◆ Segment definitions are database specific, so the fact that Seg1 in acctg_db extends to the DATA_3 device does not affect the mapping of the similarly named segment in market_db (see Figure 5.2).

Figure 5.2.
A segment is database-specific. Two segments, each with the same name, are created for different databases. They uniquely identify usages on devices for that database.

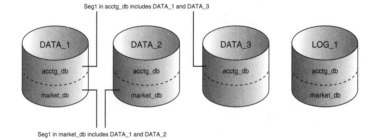

Segments refer to all fragments on a device or set of devices for a database. When you add 50 additional megabytes to the database on DATA_3, the additional space is automatically incorporated into every segment that refers to that device for the database (see Figure 5.3).

Figure 5.3.
Segments refer to all fragments on a device or set of devices for a database. Additional space allocated on a device already mapped to a segment becomes part of that segment.

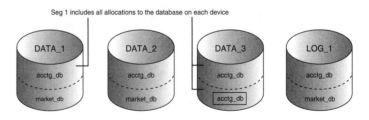

Note

> There is a many-to-many relationship between segments and devices. A single segment can include mappings to many devices. A single device can be part of many segments, even within a single database. The section "Segment System Tables," later in this chapter, talks about how this mapping is recorded in the sysusages table.

PREDEFINED SEGMENTS

Whenever you create a new database, the server automatically creates three segments in the database:

- ◆ default, for tables and indexes
- ◆ system, for system tables (including all object definitions)
- ◆ logsegment, for storing syslogs

The default and system segments are mapped to all data allocations. The logsegment is mapped to any allocations for log. In the following three lines, the allocations on DATA_1 and DATA_2 were mapped to the default and system segments:

```
create database market_db
on DATA_1 = 100, DATA_2 = 100
log on LOG_1 = 50
```

Allocations for LOG_1 were mapped to the logsegment (see Figure 5.4).

Figure 5.4.
When a database is created, default, system, and logsegment segments are defined automatically.

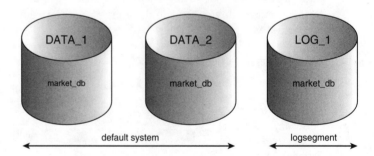

PLACING OBJECTS ON SEGMENTS

Every object is placed on a segment when the object is created. System tables (except syslogs) are placed on the system segment and the transaction log (syslogs) is placed on logsegment segment. Everything else (specifically, tables and indexes) is placed on the default segment automatically.

To create an object on a specific segment, add the following to your `create` statement:

```
on <segmentname>
```

This example places the Customer table (market_db database) on Seg1. As the table grows, it will use space on DATA_1 and DATA_2, the devices mapped to Seg1.

```
create table Customer
(name char(30) not null,
 address char(30) not null)
on Seg1
```

The next example creates a non-clustered index on Customer on a different segment, Seg2. A table and its non-clustered indexes may be on separate segments.

```
create index Customer_nci1
on Customer(name)
on Seg2
```

This final example explicitly places a table on the default segment:

```
create table lookup
(code int not null,
 value varchar(20) not null)
on "default"
```

Note

The word *default* must be enclosed in quotes: `"default"` is a keyword referring to a type of system object.

CHANGING AN OBJECT'S SEGMENT

Use `sp_placeobject` to place all of an object's future growth on a specific segment.

Note

SQL Server allocates space to objects in eight-page (usually 16KB) extents. `sp_placeobject` instructs the server that all future extent allocations should come from devices mapped to the new segment. It does not prevent newly inserted rows from being added to pages that have already been mapped to the earlier segment.

SYNTAX

```
sp_placeobject <segmentname>, <objectname>
```

EXAMPLE

```
sp_placeobject Seg3, Customer
sp_placeobject Seg3, "Customer.Index03"
```

After these statements are issued, all additional space allocations to the Customer table and to the Customer table Index03 index will come from Seg3.

> **Note**
>
> Placing the clustered index on a different segment, as in the following:
>
> ```
> sp_placeobject Seg3, "Customer.ClusteredIndex"
> ```
>
> has the same effect as placing the table on the new segment: all future space allocations to the table or clustered index will come from devices mapped to Seg3.

One way to use segments is to spread a large table across several devices. To distribute the table evenly, you need to create the table on one segment, load a segment of the data, then run sp_placeobject to point to the next segment, as in the following example:

```
create table spread_table ( ... ) on Seg1
```

Now load 50 percent of the data:

```
sp_placeobject Seg2, spread_table
```

Now load the rest of the data. At this point, the data is evenly distributed between the two segments.

```
sp_placeobject Seg3, spread_table
```

All future allocations will come from Seg3.

> **Note**
>
> The interesting question is, when should the clustered index be created? If you create the clustered index after the last sp_placeobject, the entire table will reside on the Seg3 segment. So you need to create the clustered index early and enable it to grow across all three segments. To optimize the load, you will probably choose to create the clustered index after you load the first half of the data, but before you place the table on Seg2.

MOVING AN OBJECT TO A NEW SEGMENT

The method you use to move an object to a new segment, including all existing allocations, depends on the object. To move a table without a clustered index to a new segment, create a clustered index on the new segment, then drop the index.

```
create clustered index temp_index on Table1(key) on New_Seg
drop index Table1.temp_index
```

The first statement moves the table to New_Seg and builds a clustered index along the way. The second statement drops the index (if the sole use of creating the index was to enable you to move the table).

Note

Whether this is an efficient way to move a table to a new segment depends in part on the size of the table and the resources you have available to you. It may be faster to create a new table on the desired segment, insert rows from one table to the other, then drop the old table and rename the new one. It may also be faster to use bcp to copy the data out, then in.

Keep in mind that you cannot use the clustered index method to move a table that contains fully duplicate rows: clustered index creation will fail if duplicate rows are discovered in the table.

To move a table that has a clustered index, drop the clustered index first, then re-create it on the new segment:

```
drop index Table1.clustered_index
create clustered index clustered_index on Table1(key) on New_Seg
```

To move a non-clustered index to a new segment, drop the index and re-create it on the new segment:

```
drop index Table1.nc_index
create index nc_index on Table1(nckey) on New_Seg
```

Tip

Try to remember that sp_placeobject only affects the future growth of an object; it does not affect existing allocated space.

REMOVING A DEVICE FROM A SEGMENT

Use sp_dropsegment to remove a device from a segment definition or to remove a segment from a database. Remember, every object is created on a segment. If you remove a device from a segment defintion, you control which objects can exist on a physical device.

There are some limitations to using sp_dropsegment:

◆ You cannot drop the last segment from a device.

◆ You cannot use sp_dropsegment on a segment if you have previously created or placed objects there.

◆ You cannot completely drop the predefined segments, default, segment, and logsegment.

When you create a database, all data allocations are mapped to the default and system segments. When you create a new segment for a specific device, you probably want to remove the default and system segment mappings to that device to ensure that only objects explicitly placed there use the segment device(s).

For example, to create a segment to use with indexes in this database, you would create the index segment, then drop the default and system segments from the device, as in this example:

```
create database market_db
on DATA_1 = 50, DATA_2 = 50
log on DATA_3 = 25

exec sp_addsegment index_segment, market_db, DATA_2
exec sp_dropsegment "default", market_db, DATA_2
exec sp_dropsegment "system", market_db, DATA_2
```

Figure 5.5 illustrates the segment mappings at the end of this process.

Figure 5.5.
You may drop the
default *and* system
segments from a data
device once you have
created a new segment
on that device.

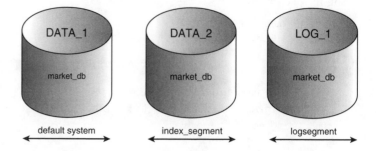

DATA_1	DATA_2	LOG_1
market_db	market_db	market_db
default system	index_segment	logsegment

INFORMATION ON SEGMENTS

Use sp_helpsegment to get information about segments in your current database. If you do not pass the segment name parameter, sp_helpsegment lists all segments in the database. If you pass the name of a segment as a parameter, you get detailed information about the segment, including a detailed list of fragments on devices and the fragment size, as well as a list of all objects stored on the segment.

Tip

Don't forget that "default" is a keyword. To find out about the default segment, pass the name in quotes:

```
sp_helpsegment "default"
```

SEGMENT SYSTEM TABLES

Segment changes have an impact on system tables in both the current database (syssegments and sysindexes) and the master database (sysusages).

SYSSEGMENTS

When you create a segment, the server makes an entry in the syssegments table in the database. The entry consists of a *segment*, *name*, and *status*.

segment   A unique integer value assigned by the system. The maximum value is 31, and there can be no more than 32 segments in a database.

name   A unique name you assign with sp_addsegment.

status   A bit column indicating the default segment.

The following example shows the contents of syssegments. There is one row in syssegments per segment in the database; syssegments is a database-level system table.

```
segment name                            status
-------  -----------------------------  ------
0        system                         0
1        default                        1
2        logsegment                     0
3        indexes                        0
```

SYSUSAGES

Creation of a segment also will have an impact on sysusages. The `segmap` column in sysusages is a bitmap of segments mapped to that device fragment.

Segment Number	0	1	2	3	4
Bitmap Value	1 (2^0)	2 (2^1)	4 (2^2)	8 (2^3)	16 (2^4)
Segment Name	system	default	logsegment	Seg1	index_segment
Value	0	0	0	8	16

The value of `segmap` for the row in sysusages corresponding to `DATA_2` is $(0 + 0 + 0 + 8 + 16) = 24$.

SYSINDEXES

Object placement is recorded in the segment column of sysindexes. `sp_help` displays the segment in which an object is stored.

USING SQL TO QUERY SYSSEGMENTS

To join syssegments to sysusages, you need to select on `dbid` and perform a "bit-wise and" (&) between the segmap column in sysusages and the segment values in the database. Your `where` clause will look like the following:

```
where segmap & power(2, segment) > 0
  and db_id() = dbid
```

For example, to determine the number of fragments and the total megabytes allocated to each segment, execute the following command:

```
select s.name, count(*) "fragments", sum(size)/512 "allocation"
from master..sysusages u, syssegments s
where segmap & power(2, segment) > 0
  and db_id() = dbid
group by s.name
```

Segments are overlapping. In this database, there is a 3MB allocation to `default`, `logsegment`, and `system` on the same device, as shown in the following output:

```
name                             fragments  allocation
-------------------------------- ---------- ----------
default                          1          3
logsegment                       1          3
system                           1          3
```

Thresholds

For any of the segments in your database, you can define a threshold procedure to monitor the free space that is available. Thresholds were new in System 10. The threshold tells the server to monitor a particular segment in a database. Once the threshold is crossed (meaning the space available has fallen below a certain level), a stored procedure that you create will be executed.

This procedure can expand the segment, dump the transaction log, write to the errorlog, or execute a remote procedure call. A remote procedure call could be to an Open Server, enabling you to send electronic mail, or even to page the person responsible for the system. You can define up to 256 thresholds in each database.

Adding a Threshold

You use the `sp_addthreshold` command to add a threshold.

```
sp_addthreshold database_name, segment_name,
    space_left_in_pages, procedure_name
```

Here is an example of this command:

```
sp_addthreshold CustomerDB, "default", 10240, CustDefaultSegWarning
```

Simple Procedure Code: *CustDefaultSegWarning*

Following is a very simple procedure to alert you that you are running out of space in the CustomerDB database:

```
create procedure CustDefaultSegWarning
as
print "WARNING: The default segment in the CustomerDB database"
print "    Add more space to the database ASAP!!!"
go
```

Note

You must be using the database to which you are adding the threshold when executing `sp_addthreshold`. This is redundant, but required.

In the preceding example, when the available space in the default segment of the CustomerDB database falls below 20MB, the server automatically executes the `CustDefaultSegWarning` procedure. (The print messages are directed into the errorlog.) Your daily review of the errorlog would alert you to alter the CustomerDB database.

USER-DEFINED SEGMENTS

Create a threshold or thresholds for every user-defined segment in your database. Reporting on free space for a user-defined segment is not particularly easy. sp_spaceused, often used to report on available space, may indicate you have 1GB of space available in the database. User-defined segments, unlike default, normally only apply to a small portion of the fragments available to your database. Users may receive "no space available" messages and call you to investigate. If you were not aware that the table in question was on a user-defined segment, you might execute sp_spaceused and be confused by the results.

@@THRESH_HYSTERESIS

Once a threshold has been crossed, it will not be executed again until the amount of free space in the segment increases by @@thresh_hysteresis pages (normally 64). Therefore, in the "Example", the amount of free space that must be available before the threshold is crossed and the stored procedure kicks in would be 20MB + 128KB. (The example put a threshold at 10,240 pages, which is 20MB. Given that @@thresh_hysteresis is normally 64 pages, and pages are normally 2KB, the amount of space available would have to vary greater than 128KB from the point of the threshold for the procedure to be re-executed.) This prevents the procedure from executing repeatedly when the free space hovers around the threshold.

Each additional threshold added to a segment must be at least two times @@thresh_hysteresis (2 × 64 = 128 pages, for 2KB pages this total is 256KB) away from other thresholds. This means thresholds must have at least 1/4MB of space (256KB) between them.

MODIFYING THRESHOLDS

Use sp_modifythreshold to change threshold information. You can associate a different stored procedure, change the free space value, or associate the threshold with a different segment. You can drop the threshold and create a new one based on the new information provided.

```
use database_name
go
sp_modifythreshold database_name, segment_name, free_pages
     [, new_procedure [, new_free_space [, new_segment ] ] ]
go
```

The three required parameters (database_name, segment_name, free_pages) identify the threshold, the three optional parameters (new_procedure, new_free_space, new_segment) are used to indicate the change. You can use Null if a parameter does not change (or you can simply provide the previous value). To change the threshold from the previous example to point to the system segment, execute the following code:

```
use CustomerDB
go
sp_modifythreshold CustomerDB, "default", 10240, null, null, "system"
go
```

DROPPING A THRESHOLD

Use sp_dropthreshold to drop an existing threshold; you must provide enough information to identify the threshold:

```
use database_name
go
sp_dropthreshold database_name, segment_name, free_pages
go
use CustomerDB
go
sp_modifythreshold CustomerDB, "system", 10240
go
```

DISPLAYING THRESHOLD INFORMATION

Use sp_helpthreshold to report on all thresholds in a database or the threshold associated with a particular segment:

```
use database_name
go
sp_helpthreshold [segment_name]
go
```

SUMMARY

Databases are the main storage and allocation structure in SQL Server. Databases provide a way for you to logically and physically store data, they provide a way to perform backups and recovery with full transactional integrity, and are a useful security mechanism, as you will see in the next chapter.

Segments improve database performance and control the growth of objects more carefully than a database alone can. Thresholds make segments far more useful because they enable the administrator to monitor the capacity and space availability of each storage unit.

CHAPTER 6

Security and User
Administration

Implementing a security and user administration plan in a Sybase SQL Server is not a terribly difficult task once you have an approach. This chapter offers several approaches, but first you explore some basics to help you implement an approach correctly.

OVERVIEW

To access server data, a user needs to clear four security levels (see Figure 6.1):

◆ The operating system
◆ The Sybase server
◆ The Sybase database
◆ The Sybase object

Think of each level as a door to a room: either the door needs to be unlocked, or you need a key to open it. You can establish a virtually unlimited number of doors that can be set up to secure data within a database. Let's look at each level independently.

Figure 6.1.
SQL Server security
consists of four access
levels.

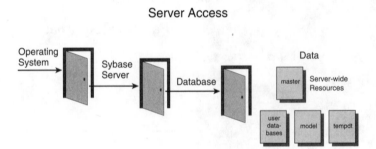

OPERATING SYSTEM SECURITY ISSUES

A user may require some access to several operating systems to run a typical client/server application:

◆ A client workstation and its file, disk, and presentation resources
◆ A network operating system for the client/server application (as well as mail, file, and print services)
◆ The SQL Server host operating system where SQL Server is running

Normally, each of these processes—client, network, SQL Server—runs on a distinct system; in some cases, however, the client application actually runs on the same host system as the SQL Server process (this is far more common in the UNIX and Open VMS environments than on other SQL Server systems).

A user does not require a login on the host machine where the Sybase SQL Server is running unless the user's client process is also hosted by the same system. To enable database access without requiring operating system logins, the SQL Server is network-port addressable. The client can connect directly to the SQL Server without logging into the database server hardware first. (See Chapter 3, "SQL Server Installation and Connectivity," for a detailed discussion of network port addresses.)

You require an operating system login for a `sybase` user. This login owns the directories where SQL Server is installed and all the disk or file resources used by the dataserver process. You need to log in to the host as `sybase` to restart the server manually and to run maintenance programs such as `buildmaster`. The `sybase` login also is required to perform all upgrades.

Note

> Remember, this is the operating system process that is actually running the SQL Server.

Operating system security is the responsibility of the OS administrator and varies dramatically between environments, so further discussion is beyond the scope of this book.

Note

> In SQL Server for Windows NT, there is a closer integration between OS security and SQL Server security. By default, OS administrators have administrative access to SQL Server. Users can inherit privileges to the server through their Windows NT login or group. (The documentation refers to this as integrated or mixed security.)
>
> This integration between host and server security is not standard to SQL Server implementations. If you are staging your development or test systems on NT but planning to migrate to a Sybase SQL Server for production, build your security around the standard Sybase security mechanisms to avoid problems in portability.

SYBASE SQL SERVER SECURITY: LOGINS

Access to a SQL Server is controlled through a server login and password. (Logins are discussed later in this chapter in "Sybase SQL Server Logins.")

Once a user has entered the server door (gained access to the server), there are a variety of database doors available.

The door to the master database is always unlocked, and a person will end up in that room if you don't specify a different default when setting up the login, or if the user's default database is unavailable. (We'll get into this in detail later on.)

However, there are several other doors, including other system databases and any user databases that have been created.

SYBASE DATABASE SECURITY: USERS

After you create a user login, you provide access to a Sybase database in one of the following ways:

- ◆ Adding a user to a database (giving the user a key)
- ◆ Telling the database to treat a user as some other valid user (an alias— giving the user a copy of someone else's key)
- ◆ Creating a guest user (unlocking the door and propping it open)
- ◆ Making that login the owner of the database

Once in a database, a user is able to see definitions for the objects contained in that database. This is because definitions are stored in the system tables, which any user of a database has select access to (except for certain sensitive columns). The user still needs permission to access each database object. (Database users are discussed in the "Database Access" section later in this chapter.)

OBJECT-LEVEL SECURITY: PERMISSIONS

When you create an object (a table, procedure, or view), SQL Server automatically assigns ownership to you. Object ownership confers complete control over the object—its access, integrity, and administration. By default, only the object owner may select from a table until access is granted to others.

Object-level security is the last level of security. To provide access to an object, you must grant the user permission to use it. For example, a user can select from a table once the owner has granted the select permission. If that person does not have the necessary permission, access will be denied.

Although this is the last main level in your security scheme, object security can contain several sublevels. (The "Permission Approaches" section, later in this chapter, shows how the use of dependent objects can tighten the security in your system.)

For example, you can grant permission to a view, but not to its underlying (base) tables. This enables an administrator to deny direct access to tables, but allow access to the data through the view. This same concept applies to stored procedures and triggers.

Sybase offers a variety of ways to control access to data. SQL Server login and database user approaches affect the way in which a permissions strategy is implemented.

At the object level, most sites grant broad permissions and then limit or grant specific access as needed to minimize the administrative overhead in implementing a permissions plan. This usually involves granting to public or a user-defined group, then revoking or granting specific permissions to a user-defined group or a specific user.

SYBASE SQL SERVER LOGINS

A SQL Server login provides access to the SQL Server. Logins are usually the first line of defense for the DBA in a security plan. (Remember: OS passwords are usually the responsibility of the OS administrator.) When you grant a login, the user can connect to the server and can use the master database (you learn why later).

A SQL Server login usually requires a password, although there are exceptions. For example, upon initial installation, the sa login has no password. On pre–System 10 servers, you can add new logins without a password (password is null). We urge you to require passwords on all servers, even on a pre–System 10 server. Without passwords, it is difficult to implement any meaningful security on SQL Server.

Add logins with sp_addlogin:

```
sp_addlogin login_name, password [ , defdb [ , deflanguage  [ , fullname ] ] ]
sp_addlogin rbrown, shake#crown
```

In versions prior to System 10, sp_addlogin reports login added. In System 10 and later, you get these messages:

```
Password correctly set.
Account unlocked.
New login created.
```

The next example shows the contents of syslogins after running sp_addlogin (adding a row to the syslogins table in the master database):

```
select suid, name from syslogins

suid   name
------ ------------------------------
1      sa
2      probe
3      mon_user
```

```
4        testuser1
5        jeff
6        rbrown
```

Let's take a look at each of the parameters of sp_addlogin. You pass parameters to stored procedures by name or by position. Passing by position is more common, especially when dealing with system procedures such as sp_addlogin.

When passing by position, you provide each parameter in order. To specify a parameter that falls late in the list (fullname in the example), you must specify all the others that precede it. Use null to specify no value; in that case, the stored procedure usually provides a default value. In this example, the login of joe gets the default values for defdb and deflanguage:

```
sp_addlogin joe, "secret", null, null, "Joe Smith"
```

When passing by name, you can specify any parameters you choose, in any order. To retrieve the names of the parameters, use sp_help:

```
sp_help sp_addlogin
go
```

The other method of displaying proper syntax for stored procedures (and all other SQL statements) is to use the sp_syntax procedure (System 10 only):

```
sp_syntax {command ¦ fragment} [, modulename [, language]]
```

The parameters of sp_syntax define the syntax requests. command or fragment is the command (or portion of a command) for which you require syntax. modulename is the name or partial name of the module or utility to which the syntax applies. language is any valid installed language on your server. (The sybsyntax database is loaded from an installation script that—in all likelihood—hasn't been run on your server.) For more information, see Chapter 3.

Use sp_syntax with no parameter to list installed modules.

Once you have the full syntax for the command, including the names of all parameters, you can run the procedure, passing parameters by name instead of position. Here's the same example, this time passing by name:

```
sp_addlogin @fullname = "Joe Smith", @loginame = "joe", @passwd = "secret"
```

The unspecified parameters (defdb and deflanguage) get a default value.

You also can mix parameter-passing methods, but once you start naming parameters, you cannot stop. In the following example, name and password are passed by position, but fullname is passed by name:

```
sp_addlogin joe, secret, @fullname = "J. Smith"
```

In System 10, only `login_name` and `password` are required; previous to System 10, the password is also optional. `login_name` must be unique for the server and must not be more than 30 characters long. Passwords must be between 6 and 30 characters long.

You can define a default database for each login. The default database does not grant any inherent privilege to use a database: it merely tells SQL Server to attempt to use the defined database at login time. If the login does not yet have access to the default database, the server issues an error message; the user is logged in and the current database is the master database. A login that does not have a default database specified will also default to the master database.

Tip

It's important to assign a default database and provide access to that database for each login in your system.

In a well-secured system, a user can't really do any damage to the master database—rattle around, select from the system tables, make a general nuisance of himself, maybe, but not do any real damage without the sa password.

To be safe, don't leave users in master. Set valid default databases for users so they don't end up defaulting to master.

"WHY CAN'T I USE THE DATABASE?"

There are circumstances where you have done everything right, but users still end up pointed to the master database when they log in. Here are a few things to look for, starting with the obvious and moving toward the obscure.

Each of the specific error messages you receive is followed by this general error message:

```
Error 4001: Cannot open default database 'testdb'.
```

The following are common errors, their diagnoses, and the actions you should take.

Error received:

```
Message 916: Server user id 6 is not a valid user in database 'testdb'.
```

Diagnosis:

The login has not been added as a user to this database.

Action required:

Add the user to the database with `sp_adduser`, `sp_addalias`, or `sp_changedbowner`, or add the guest user to the database.

Error received:

```
Error 930: Database 'testdb2' cannot be opened because either an earlier
system termination left LOAD DATABASE incomplete or the database is
created with 'for load' option. Load the database or contact a user with
System Administrator
(SA) role.
```

Diagnosis:

The database cannot be used until a restore from backup is complete.

Action required:

Restore the database from backup. The user must wait until the restore is completed.

Error received:

```
Error 905: Unable to allocate a DBTABLE descriptor to open database
'testdb'. Another database must be closed or dropped before opening
this one.
```

Diagnosis:

Your system configuration settings need to enable more concurrently open databases.

Action required:

Increase the `open databases` setting with `sp_configure`. Meanwhile, a database needs to be closed before this database is available.

The default language option (`deflanguage`) is used at sites that have loaded other character sets besides `us_english` (the language that is always available to the server). If this parameter is provided, the user receives all system messages in the language selected.

The *fullname* parameter (System 10 and later only) provides the capability of associating a user's full name with the login name.

Note that the optional parameters (`defdb`, `deflanguage`, and `fullname`) can be updated later using the `sp_modifylogin` (System 10 and later) or `sp_defaultdb` (pre-System 10) procedures, which are described later in this chapter.

Of course, your users may ask whether they can change their own default database or password. A user can change his or her password using sp_password. Passwords should be changed frequently—about once every month is appropriate. Also, users can change their default database with the sp_modifylogin or the sp_defaultdb command.

SPECIAL LOGINS

There are two special logins that are created as part of the installation of the SQL Server. These two logins are sa and probe.

SA

The sa login is a special login that is created as part of the installation process. The sa login owns the server, although you can use roles to transfer sa authority to other logins. The sa login owns the system databases (master, model, tempdb, sybsystemprocs, and any others installed by the sa). The sa login is the database owner (dbo) within those databases because it is the login that literally is mapped to the dbo user (more on dbo later in this chapter). (When an individual—a login—creates a database, the server records the suid column from the server's row in syslogins as the database owner in sysdatabases.) Regardless of actual database ownership, the sa is seen as the dbo of any user database. It is important to note that in System 10 and later, the sa login has its capabilities as a result of roles that have automatically been granted to the login as part of an installation. The roles granted to the sa are sa_role and sso_role. See the section titled "Roles" later in this chapter for more information.

PROBE

There also is a probe login that is provided as part of installation. This login is used between servers to manage two-phase commit activities.

GENERIC LOGINS

Some sites add a general login, such as templogin or sybguest, to be used by temporary users of a server for in-house training or self-study. Often the logins have no password, or the password is the same as the login name. Of course, many administrators prefer an individual login for each user of a server; this provides better control and does permit auditing of work by individual when that is necessary.

HOW LOGINS WORK

When a new login is created, a row is added to a system table in master called syslogins. Each login is assigned a unique system user ID (suid), an integer that identifies that user uniquely in the server. During login, the server matches the name passed in the login structure against the name column in the syslogins table. If a match is found and the password matches, the suid is stored in the memory allocated for the new connection.

The login name is not stored in any table except syslogins. The suid is the key used in all other tables that relate to a person's login, including system tables assigning roles and those relating server access to database access.

Tip

To retrieve a list of suids and login names:

```
select suid, name from syslogins
```

Although you can select the password column if you are the sa, the values are encrypted in System 10 and above. Prior to System 10, the password column is plainly readable by the sa:

```
select suid, name, password from syslogins
```

The system functions suser_name() and suser_id() convert login IDs to names and vice versa. For example:

```
select suser_name(2)
```

returns the value probe (because probe is always the second user inserted in the syslogins table). Conversely, the following:

```
select suser_id("probe")
```

returns the value 2. When the functions are used without arguments, they return the login name or ID for the current user.

Note

These system functions are most useful in accessing data from system tables, where they enable you to decode a name or ID without needing to specify a join, as in this following example. These system functions are also frequently used in the Sybase provided system-stored procedures.

```
use master
go
select spid, suid, suser_name(suid) "name"
```

```
from sysprocesses
order by suser_name(suid)
go

spid    suid    name
-----   ------  ------------------------------
2       0
3       0
4       0
5       0
6       6       rbrown
1       1       sa
```

You also should notice the rows in sysprocesses with an suid of 0 and no name: these processes are system processes in charge of mirror, network, and checkpoint handling. In System 10 and later, an additional handler—a shutdown handler—has been added.

MODIFYING LOGIN INFORMATION

Again, don't worry if you don't have all the login information at the time a login is added. It always can be changed using sp_modifylogin (System 10 and later) or sp_defaultdb (pre-System 10):

sp_modifylogin *login_name*, *option*, *value*

The options are defdb (default database), deflanguage (default language), and fullname (user's full name):

sp_defaultdb *login_name*, *default_db*

DISPLAYING LOGIN INFORMATION

Login information can be displayed using the sp_displaylogin procedure. sp_displaylogin reports information on a login's suid, the system login name (login name), the full name, any roles that have been configured for that login, an indication of whether the account is locked, and the date of the last password change. The syntax for sp_displaylogin is the following:

sp_displaylogin [*login_name*]

Only users that have been granted the sa_role or the sso_role can provide a login name as an argument. For all other users, the procedure must be executed without a login name. For those users who execute sp_displaylogin without providing login names, the login information for their logins is displayed.

PASSWORDS

A password is used to verify the authenticity of a login. Previous to System 10, passwords were not required, but they must be provided for System 10 versions and greater. Passwords must be at least six characters long. There is no minimum password length prior to System 10. Passwords can include any printable characters, including A–Z, a–z, 0–9, or any symbols.

Tip

Add symbols or mix the case to make it difficult to guess a password.

CHANGING PASSWORDS

Passwords can be changed by the user or by the site security officer (a login with the sso_role, known hereafter in this book as sso). Change passwords with sp_password:

```
sp_password caller_password, new_password [ , login_name ]
```

To change a password, a user passes the current password and the new password. If a user without the sso_role passes a login_name to sp_password, the system returns an error message.

An sso changing another user's password passes the sso password, the new user password, and the login name. If the sso omits the login name, the sso password will be changed!

PASSWORD EXPIRATION

Periodic changes to passwords improve system security. Users have a nasty habit of sharing their passwords with others rather than encouraging their colleagues to get proper permission from the system administrator. When passwords change, the residual security breach caused by shared passwords is reduced.

By setting the configuration option password expiration interval (unfortunately, System 10 and later only), you can set passwords to expire periodically. The server warns users of a pending password expiration; if a user fails to modify the password before it expires, the sso needs to change the password and let the user know the new value. This example reconfigures the server to set the password expiration for three weeks:

```
/* configure password expiration for three weeks */
sp_configure "password expiration interval", 21
reconfigure
```

The default value, 0, indicates no password expiration. Possible values range from 0 to 32767 days, although a reasonable time is probably 45 to 60 days.

You can determine the day your password will expire, which is found by adding the password expiration interval to the pwdate column in syslogins (the date the password was originally set). Find the number of days to expiration (expiration date minus current date).

Find the ratio of days until expiration (days to expiration divided by password expiration interval).

If the ratio is less than 25 percent or days to expiration is less than 7, the system notifies the user that the password will expire in [ ] days. (Error 4023: Your password will expire in 5.0 days.)

If your password has expired, you may connect to the server, but the only command you can execute is sp_password. All other actions receive this error message:

```
Error 7742: You must change your password using the sp_password system stored
procedure before you can continue.
```

Note

The decision to implement password expiration is usually based on organizational security regulations. We have seen SQL Server sites where password expiration is not implemented because the application developers would need to build a password change subsystem, and there's no budget for it. Naturally, that is not the best reason for not forcing password changes, but it is often the excuse.

If possible, password expiration should be configured to make your site as secure as possible.

DATABASE ACCESS

After server login security, the next level of security is database access. You manage database access by establishing a link between logins (stored at the server level) and users (stored at the database level). User access to a database is required to use the database (change your current context to the database); it also is required to access any object stored in the database.

> *Note*
>
> This information is also added to the memory structure set up for a connection or process, and a review of sysprocesses (built dynamically) shows the uid and database ID (dbid) for a process.
>
> The uid is used to identify ownership of objects within a database. Although the ID assigned to an object is used to relate that object with other tables, there is a unique index on the combination of an object name and a uid (database user ID). This is why more than one user can have an object with the same name and is very important when determining a development approach.

ADDING USERS

You grant access to a database by adding a user to the database. Use sp_adduser to add users; it adds an entry in the database-level sysusers table. Here is the syntax of sp_adduser:

sp_adduser *login_name* [, *name_in_db* [, *grpname*]]

To add rbrown to the testdb database, use the following:

```
use testdb
go
sp_adduser rbrown
go
```

At the completion of the sp_adduser procedure, a row is placed in the sysusers table in the database where the user was added. The following example shows the contents of the database-level table, sysusers, after rbrown has been added to the database testdb:

```
use testdb
go
select suid, uid, name
from sysusers
go

suid    uid    name
------  ------ -----------------------------
-16389  16389  replication_role
-16388  16388  navigator_role
-16387  16387  sybase_ts_role
-16386  16386  oper_role
-16385  16385  sso_role
-16384  16384  sa_role
-2      0      public
1       1      dbo
4       3      testuser1
6       4      rbrown
```

Note

The six roles are defined in the sysusers table, in addition to the users and logins defined by the dbo. These roles were new to System 10. See the section titled "Roles" later in this chapter for more information.

The only required parameter is *login_name*, which is checked against the name column in master..syslogins. (The login name must already exist in the syslogins table.) *login_name* is used to derive the suid to be placed into the sysusers table.

The *name_in_db* parameter is infrequently used in real life, and its purpose is not to be confused with true aliasing (sp_addalias). This parameter is inserted in the name column in the sysusers table.

Tip

Normally, the default value for this parameter is the string specified for the *login_name*, and—unless you have a very good reason—you should always keep them the same. It makes the matching of database users to server users much simpler. In fact, if a value is not specified or a value of null is provided, it defaults to the *login_name*.

The *grpname* parameter defines the group for the user. By default, a user is placed in the group public, which has a group ID (gid) of 0, although the word public can be specified for this parameter. Groups are discussed later in this section.

Use sp_helpuser to get a list of users in a database or to see specific information about a single user, as in this example:

```
Users_name      ID_in_db Group_name    Login_name       Default_db
------------     -------- ----------    ----------       ----------
dbo             1        public        sa               master
rbrown          4        public        rbrown           testdb2
testuser1       3        public        testuser1        master
```

SPECIAL USERS

There are two special users that can exist in a Sybase database, dbo and guest.

DBO

The dbo is the database owner. dbo is added to the model database as part of installation (and cannot be dropped); hence the dbo exists in all databases in a server. The dbo can never be dropped from a database and always has a database user ID (uid) of 1.

Note

It is unusual for the user ID (uid in sysusers) and the login ID (suid in master..syslogins) to have the same value. The values are predictably the same only for the sa, who is dbo in all databases.

GUEST

The guest user is provided to grant database access to anyone who logs into the server. The guest user must be explicitly added to a database using sp_adduser (or added to the model database before a subsequent database creation).

The presence of a guest user means that anyone logged in to the server can access the database. This is a catch-all to enable access to a database when the login has not been explicitly added as a user of the database (or aliased to another user—see the next section). The guest user always has a uid of 2. Guest permissions default to the permissions granted to the group public.

Tip

Be careful about adding the guest user to the model database, because this means the guest user will exist in any new database that is created. This could weaken your security strategy.

ADDING ALIASES (ALTERNATES)

To use a database, a user does not necessarily have to be added explicitly as a separate user of the database. Sybase provides the capability of relating a login to another login who is already a user of the database.

For example, every database has a user dbo, whose name can be found in the name column in the sysusers table. The sysusers row for dbo includes an suid, and a database uid (which is always 1 for dbo). The value specified in the suid column for dbo determines the login ID of the actual database owner—the individual who has all administrative privileges within that database. You can provide database access to additional users as dbo by defining aliases within the database for each such user.

Tip

The most common user privilege to be shared with aliases is `dbo`, which enables several logins to divide the responsibility for database implementation, evolution, and maintenance. This is most common in a development environment, where several users share responsibility for object creation and maintenance.

`sp_addalias` adds an entry to the sysalternates table, enabling an additional login to access a database as that user:

```
sp_addalias login_name, name_in_db
```

In the next example, `mwhite` is added as an alias to `rbrown` in the `testdb` database: now `mwhite` receives all the access and permissions granted to `rbrown` within this database:

```
sp_addalias mwhite, rbrown
```

Both *login_name* and *name_in_db* are required. *login_name* must be a valid entry in syslogins with no `suid` entry in sysusers or sysalternates in the current database. *name_in_db* must be a valid user name within the database.

`sp_addalias` adds a row to the sysalternates table. The login ID of *login_name* is stored in the `suid` column. The login ID of the actual login mapped to *name_in_db* is stored in the `altsuid` column.

Note

I'd like to meet the comedian who decided that aliases should be added with `sp_addalias` but stored in the sysalternates table!

Execute `sp_helpuser` with a user name to get detailed information about a user, including aliases, as in this example:

```
sp_helpuser rbrown

Users_name        ID_in_db Group_name       Login_name          Default_db
----------------  -------- ---------------- ------------------  --------------
rbrown            4        public           rbrown              testdb2

Users aliased to user.
Login_name
-----------------------------
mwhite
```

If you examine the contents of the three system tables (syslogins, sysusers, and sysalternates) after adding an alias, you can understand the mapping of logins, users, and aliases.

Syslogins and sysusers join on suid. Syslogins and sysalternates also join on suid. Sysusers and sysalternates join on suid and altsuid, respectively (see Figure 6.2).

Figure 6.2.
The relationship
between the login, user,
and alias entities is
built on a system user
ID (suid) column in the
syslogins tables.

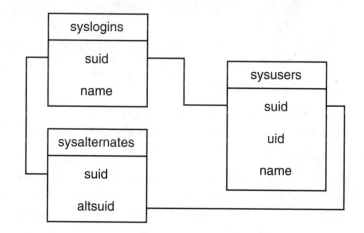

The values from sample versions of sysusers, sysalternates, and master..sysobjects show the correspondence between suid, uid, and altsuid among the tables:

```
select suid, uid, name
from sysusers
where uid > 0
select *
from sysalternates
select suid, name
from master..syslogins

sysusers
suid    uid     name
------  ------  --------------------------------
1       1       dbo
4       3       testuser1
6       4       rbrown
( 10 rows affected)

sysalternates
suid    altsuid
------  -------
7       6
( 1 row affected)
```

```
master..syslogins
suid    name
------  ----------------------------
1       sa
2       probe
3       mon_user
4       testuser1
5       jeff
6       rbrown
7       mwhite
( 7 rows affected)
```

Here are some features to notice about the contents of these tables:

- The dbo of the database is the sa (suid of the dbo in sysusers = 1).

- Besides dbo, there are two users of the database—rbrown (suid 6 in syslogins corresponds to suid 6 in sysusers) and testuser1.

- mwhite (suid 7) is aliased to rbrown (suid 6) in this database.

How Database Access Works

So what does the server do when trying to determine access to a database? When a person tries to use a database, the server looks for an entry in sysusers and sysalternates to decide whether to grant access. It first looks in the sysusers table to see whether a match can be made on the suid.

A row will be found in sysusers for an suid if the following conditions exist:

- The user has been added through the sp_adduser procedure (normal user addition).

- The user created the database (suid matches with uid of 1, the dbo).

- Ownership of the database has been transferred to the user.

After trying to find a match for the suid in the sysusers table, the server then tries to match the suid column in the sysalternates table.

If a match is found for the suid column in sysalternates, the server then determines the suid that is found in the altsuid column. This value is then matched against the suid column in the sysusers table, as you did previously. Then the uid that corresponds to that suid is used by the user for activities conducted in the database.

If a match is not found in sysalternates, the server then looks at the sysusers table again to see whether the special user guest has been added. If it has, the person assumes the uid of guest within that database.

The database access validation procedure is outlined in Figure 6.3. If none of these matches can be made, the person is denied access.

Figure 6.3.
SQL Server database permissions depend on user mappings or the presence of a guest user in the database.

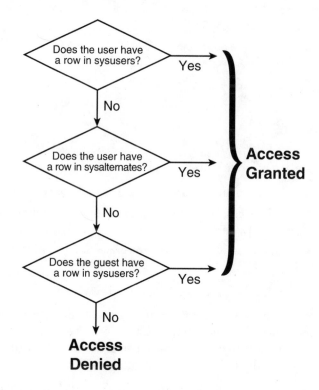

GROUPS

Groups can be used as part of an effective database security strategy. Object and command permission are granted to users, groups, or roles. A user who is a member of a group inherits all the permissions granted to the group.

You can assign a user name to a group with sp_adduser (discussed earlier) or sp_changegroup. Assigning users to groups is a dbo responsibility. There is a detailed discussion of how to implement groups into your permission strategy in the "Permissions" section later in this chapter.

Note

SQL Server allows a user to belong to only one group. (This isn't strictly true: a user may belong to one group in addition to public.)

The interesting question is why that limitation exists. It's clear that the structure of the system tables plays a role in that requirement— after all, a user's group membership is recorded in the gid column in sysusers. Permissions are granted to entries in sysusers. Because groups are stored in sysusers alongside users, all permissions checks require that only two tables be read: sysprotects and sysusers.

In order to enable multiple group memberships, SQL Server needs to have a separate associative table where the many-to-many relationship between users and groups would be resolved. Needing to join a third table during permissions checks hurts performance. (Remember that every attempt to access a database object requires a permissions check.) One guess is that Sybase kept this part of the system simple to improve performance.

PUBLIC GROUP

Every user in a database is a member of the public group.

Warning

Don't forget that if you add a guest user to a database, any person that has a valid server login can use that database. The guest user will, of course, be able to perform any functions that have been granted to public.

It is common for an administrator to grant permissions to the public group rather than to each individual user. For example, if you have 500 users of a database, and all users need to select from the customer table, an administrator could execute a grant statement once for each user (500 statements) or a single select permission to the public group.

The public group is found in the sysusers table in each database with a uid of 0, and you cannot delete it.

Warning

Prior to System 10, revoking permissions from the public group also revokes the object owner's permission.

ADDING GROUPS

Although the public group is a convenient way to grant universal access to database objects, it is inappropriate to use public when you need to grant different permissions to discrete sets of users. You may need to create additional groups to represent different permissions requirements. Add groups with sp_addgroup:

```
sp_addgroup groupname
```

For example, to add a group, marketing, to the current database, use the following:

```
sp_addgroup marketing
```

This procedure adds a row to the sysusers table with a uid of –16384 or less.

Note

> As part of the implementation of roles in System 10 and later, each role actually takes up a row in sysusers as a group, so new groups are usually added with a uid of 16390 or less.

DETERMINING GROUPS IN A DATABASE: *SP_HELPGROUP*

To determine the groups that exist in a database, or for more information about an individual group within a database, use sp_helpgroup:

```
sp_helpgroup [ groupname ]
```

Without any parameters, this procedure reports on all groups in a database. sp_helpgroup reports all groups in the database. Note that in System 10 and later each of the roles is recorded as a group in the sysusers table:

```
sp_helpgroup
```

Group_name	Group_id
marketing_group	16390
navigator_role	16388
oper_role	16386
public	0
replication_role	16389
sa_role	16384
sso_role	16385
sybase_ts_role	16387

There already are entries for each of the systemwide roles (sa_role, sso_role, oper_role, navigator_role, replication_role, sybase_ts_role), public, and the new group, marketing_group. Pass the *groupname* as a parameter to list all users in a group:

```
sp_helpgroup marketing_group
```

Group_name	Group_id	Users_in_group	Userid
marketing_group	16390	rbrown	4
marketing_group	16390	testuser1	3

Drop groups with sp_dropgroup, but only if that group does not contain any users:

```
sp_dropgroup groupname
sp_dropgroup marketing_group
```

Use sp_changegroup to change a user's group membership. Only the dbo may execute sp_changegroup:

```
sp_changegroup groupname, name_in_database
sp_changegroup marketing_group, rbrown
```

How Groups Work

sp_addgroup adds a row to the sysusers table. The uid and group ID (gid) are assigned the same value (16834 or greater). When you add users to a database without specifying a group name, the group ID of 0 (public) is assigned to that person. When you specify a group (either as a parameter in sp_adduser or with sp_changegroup), the gid of that group is placed in the gid column for that user.

Note

After you assign a user to a group, the user is no longer explicitly assigned to the public group. Nevertheless, any permissions assigned to public will apply to that user. The public group always encompasses all people.

Login Approach

There are several approaches to security in Sybase systems; the following are the major ones:

◆ Sybase login equals the Operating System/Application (OS/App) login.

◆ Sybase login is independent of the OS/App login.

◆ A single login for all users of an application or user type.

Sybase Login = OS/App Login

This is a fairly maintainable approach to logins. A user is given a login to the operating system. (The operating system could be the client workstation login, network login, or the user login to the server, if the client application runs on the server.) The operating system sets environment variables for the user name (and possibly the password) during its login process. Applications read the environment information when logging into SQL Server.

For example, SQL Server facilities such as ISQL and bcp look for the environment variables USER and PASSWORD when connecting to the server. When the user does not need to specify the -U option for ISQL, the application passes the user name from the environment when connecting to the server.

Administering OS/SQL Server logins is easier because you can develop (administrative or automated) procedures to maintain these user (login) names and passwords in sync.

Tip

Ensure that maintenance procedures such as this will work in your environment. Otherwise, maintaining synchronized names and passwords will drive you nuts.

One drawback of this approach is that users do occasionally need to access an application with a different SQL Server login. Applications still must provide a facility for a different login name and password from the one stored at the operating system level.

SYBASE LOGIN INDEPENDENT OF OS/APP LOGIN

To enable separate OS and SQL Server login IDs, applications must include a login function. (Often, when there is some correspondence between Sybase and OS login IDs, applications automatically populate the login screen with information drawn from the environment.)

This approach is more difficult to administer and maintain than the previous one, but it can provide additional security.

SINGLE SYBASE LOGIN

The single Sybase login approach is often used by sites that want a single point of control for logins to the SQL Server. It is simple, but its simplicity has drawbacks.

Only one login exists for an entire application or for each major application piece. When a person invokes the application, the application connects to the server using hardcoded values for the login name and password. This approach has some benefits:

- ◆ Users do not need to log into the server explicitly.
- ◆ A password changing routine does not have to be written into the application to accommodate password changes. (Applications that use individual logins with the capability of changing passwords often integrate a password

changing application to shield users from having to connect to the server by using another interface to change their passwords.)

♦ The administration activity required to manage logins and passwords is extremely low.

However, drawbacks to this approach include the following:

♦ A database administrator often executes sp_who to see who is logged into the SQL Server. Part of the output from this command is the login name. If all users log into the SQL Server with same name, the output of sp_who will contain numerous processes with the same login name. If a problem is encountered, determining the actual user associated with a process becomes almost impossible. (To overcome this problem, applications pass the OS login ID as a hostname value when logging in to SQL Server. Hostname values are also included in the sp_who display.)

♦ Auditing user activity is meaningless. Because every person would be the same application user, you can track only application activities and not individual user activities.

♦ If an outside source is able to determine the application login and password, they have free rein of the server. As mentioned previously, auditing cannot be used to target suspects. The application has to change its password, which may require recompilation of the application—not always a desirable thing to do in production.

This approach is not recommended due to these drawbacks. It can be used, however, if it is determined that the reduction in flexibility is worth the reduction in administrative activity.

SEPARATE LOGIN IDs FOR APPLICATION WORK VERSUS AD HOC QUERY

Users often require access to a system through an ad hoc query generator or other front-end tool, in addition to their regular access through an application. If you allow the user to use an application login when running an ad hoc tool, you may find the user updating tables or running stored procedures without the protection or validation normally ensured by the application.

For example, a user who normally uses the application to delete a row from the ten-billion-row sales_history table by retrieving it and pressing a delete button (complete with are you sure? messages!) may be surprised when the delete sales_history statement removes every row from the table.

Unfortunately, you can't restrict most tools from enabling updates to tables or executing stored procedures. Worse, SQL Server never knows whether the user requesting a deletion is running a carefully written application in PowerBuilder or is using ISQL after taking a one-day video course on SQL.

What's the solution?

You could try removing all the neat and interesting front-end products, but you bought SQL Server to enable those products to run.

You could try not to tell anyone how to insert, update, or delete, but that usually doesn't work.

You could require that all updates, inserts, and deletes use a stored procedure (related objects and permissions are discussed later in this chapter), but even that isn't foolproof; if the user can run the proc from the application, it can be run from a command-line interface such as ISQL as well.

One approach is to have two sets of logins: one for users running neat and interesting front-end tools, the other for using applications that are permitted to perform updates. The first set of logins and passwords is known to the users; the second set is based on the user name, but known only to the updating applications.

For example, a user mdoe with a password littlelamb would have an application user name mdoe_app and a password littlelamb_00946. The login names for the application are visible from sp_who, so the passwords need to be difficult to guess. (You may want the password to be derived from the user password and some hashed version of the uid. Keeping your password derivation method secret is critical here.)

This approach to logins and passwords is not easy. To make it work, you prevent users from running sp_password, so password administration becomes your problem. But with perseverance you can have a system that is safe from the errors of a persistent and uneducated user.

PASSWORD APPROACH

There are several standards that companies use when identifying a password administration plan. These usually fall into one of three categories:

- Password same as login
- General application login and password
- Password independent of login

Whether you use a login approach of "Sybase Login = Application Login" or not, you still must determine whether the password for that login will be dependent or independent of the login.

PASSWORD = LOGIN

At many sites, passwords are identical to logins. Realistically, this is as close to having no password as you can get—the password for a user is the same as the login name. Therefore, a login for user1 has a password of user1. In this approach, it is very easy for a person to find a way to access the server because only a login name must be determined. Many sites also use a standard for naming logins to a system—for example, market01 through market99, with passwords of market01 through market99, respectively. This is the least secure approach to a user password administration (second only to null password, which is not permitted in System 10 and later). It is also one of the least flexible, because login name and password must remain the same, denying the capability of using password expiration (System 10 and later).

Note

When you talk to hackers about methods they use to guess passwords and break into systems, they invariably tell you that the first password to guess is the login name. (After that come the literal words, "password" and "secret.")

GENERAL APPLICATION LOGIN AND PASSWORD

There are other sites that use a general application login for all users of an application. This means that users access an application, and when the application is connected to the database, it does so as a single general user—regardless of the number of connections it opens. This approach results in a severe reduction in the capability of linking activities to users. When sp_who is executed, for example, all user names are the same. This makes it very difficult to track down who executed a certain command. Fortunately, this approach often enables changing the general user password, depending on whether the application reads its password information from a configuration file or is hardcoded in the application itself.

PASSWORD INDEPENDENT OF LOGIN

This approach is the most secure. Each user has a distinct password not related to the login name in any way. The user can change the password periodically, and the use of the "password expiration interval" forces the issue. This approach is normally selected at sites that have regulations (Federal) regarding their applications or at sites that are most worried about unauthorized access to the database.

Because each user has a password and the capability of changing it, access to sp_password is required. Unfortunately, many sites want to keep users shielded from database operations because they are not usually accustomed to dealing directly with a database. Because of this, a command-line interface (ISQL) is not an acceptable alternative. This normally results in the creation of a user administration module for users to change passwords. This does increase overall application complexity somewhat, but is done to continue to shield users from the database.

This is naturally the preferred approach by secure sites, and is recommended if your environment is structured to handle the administrative complexities.

PERMISSIONS

Permissions are used to control access within a database. This is accomplished through the use of the grant and revoke statements. Any permission that can be granted can also be revoked, so when the word "grant" is used within this section, it can be thought of in the broader sense of controlling access (granting or revoking).

The granting of permissions results in the addition of rows to the sysprotects system table. Each database contains the sysprotects table, which means that permissions are database-specific. Because permissions are granted to database users, not server logins, there is no way to grant general access to a login (except through the use of roles).

USERS

Permissions are used to control access by users of a database. In this context, a user is essentially any uid that exists in the sysusers table. The sysusers table initially contains rows for the database owner (dbo), the public group (public), and the six roles that can exist within a SQL Server (sa_role, sso_role, oper_role, navigator_role, replication_role, and sybase_ts_role). Additional users of a database are added with sp_adduser, and additional groups in a database are added with sp_addgroup. Therefore, the list of users that permissions can be granted to actually contains users, groups, and roles.

OBJECT PERMISSIONS

Granting of permissions on objects is performed using the grant command syntax:

```
grant  {all [ privileges] ¦ permission_list }
  on { table_name [ ( column_list ) ]
  ¦ view_name [ ( column_list ) ]
  ¦ stored_procedure_name }
  to{ group_name ¦ user_name ¦ role_name}
[ { , {next_user_group_role } } ...]
  [ with grant option ]
```

Revoking of permissions on objects is performed using the revoke command syntax:

```
revoke [ grant option for ]
  {all [ privileges] ¦ permission_list }
  on { table_name [ ( column_list ) ]
  ¦ view_name [ ( column_list ) ]
  ¦ stored_procedure_name }
  to{ group_name ¦ user_name ¦ role_name}
[ { , {next_user_group_role } } ...]
  [cascade ]
```

READING SYSPROTECTS

When you grant or revoke permissions on a table, SQL Server records that information in a database-level table, sysprotects. Every database includes explicit lines granting permission to system tables to public. (As of this writing, there were 17 rows of default system table permissions in the most recent version.)

Let's add some permissions and see how they affect sysprotects. The following command adds permissions entries:

```
grant all on marketing_table to public
```

Look at the contents of sysprotects after the grant statement:

```
select id, uid, action, grantor
from sysprotects
where id = object_id("marketing_table")
go

id          uid    action grantor
----------- ------ ------ -------
144003544   0      151    1
144003544   0      193    1
144003544   0      195    1
144003544   0      196    1
144003544   0      197    1
```

The id column identifies the table in the database.

The uid column indicates the user (or group) ID to whom permission is granted.

The action column specifies the type of action affected by the permission. You can decode the action value by referring to the spt_values table in the master database. Permissions actions are identified with the type "T." The output that follows lists all the permission action codes as of System 10:

```
use master
go
select name, number, type
from spt_values
where type = "T"
and number > 0
order by 2
go
```

```
name                            number      type
----------------------------    ----------- ----
References                      151         T
Select                          193         T
Insert                          195         T
Delete                          196         T
Update                          197         T
Create Table                    198         T
Create Database                 203         T
Grant                           205         T
Revoke                          206         T
Create View                     207         T
Create Procedure                222         T
Execute                         224         T
Dump Database                   228         T
Create Default                  233         T
Dump Transaction                235         T
Create Rule                     236         T
```

The grantor records the ID of the user who executed the grant statement.

The object owner grants or revokes permissions on objects to control access to objects within a database. These objects include tables, views, and stored procedures. Permissions default to the object owner, which is why a user who creates an object does not have to grant permissions to himself. However, any other user of the system, except for users with the sa_role, would have to be granted permission on an object.

Note

sa object permissions are not checked. You do not need to grant object permissions to users with the sa_role. Ever.

The types of permissions that can be granted/revoked to these objects include select, update, insert, delete, references, and execute. Select and update can have a column list specified (to control access at the column level), references applies only to tables (and can contain a column list), and execute applies only to procedures. Table 6.1 summarizes how object permissions can be granted.

TABLE 6.1. OBJECT PERMISSIONS.

Permission	Specify Columns?	Can Grant On
Select	Yes	Tables, views
Update	Yes	Tables, views
Insert	No	Tables, views
Delete	No	Tables, views
References	Yes	Tables
Execute	N/A	Stored procedures

Select, insert, update, and delete are pretty straightforward. They indicate whether a user can issue that type of command with a table or view listed in the from clause (a normal select or an insert, delete, or update with a join clause) or as the object of the action (update table or view, insert table or view, or delete table or view).

Note

Text and image columns enable use of the `readtext` and `writetext` commands:

◆ The capability of using the `writetext` command is transferred through update permission.

◆ The capability of using the `readtext` command is transferred through select permission.

Execute permission is granted on a stored procedure to enable a user to execute the procedure. This can have very powerful implications because a system can be implemented when access is granted completely to procedures and not the underlying tables or views.

The references permission is part of System 10, and later, systems and applies to the capability of using declarative referential integrity. When implementing declarative referential integrity, the `create table` or `alter table` statement can include a references clause to indicate the relationship between tables. This permission needs to be granted only when objects owned by two different users have referential integrity considerations (a user that owns both objects automatically has references permission). It is not likely that references permission would have to be granted in a production system, because most production systems have all objects owned by the same user name (dbo).

A permission list can contain a comma-delimited list of permissions or the word all (or all privileges). If all is specified, only the permissions that apply to the type of object the permission is being granted on is actually granted.

The with grant option (System 10 and later only) enables the capability of granting permission to be transferred to another user. For example, if select permission is granted on table customer to jsmith with the with grant option, jsmith then can grant select permission on customer to other users in the database. This option has ramifications, however, because exclusive control of permissions on an object is no longer in effect.

To revoke permissions on an object to a user, the revoke command is used. If an object owner wants to deny further granting of permissions on an object to a user that was granted access with the with grant option, the revoke command is used with the grant option for. When the revoke grant option for ... command is used, it tells the server to deny the specified user(s) the capability of granting the specified permissions. For example, user1 can execute this statement:

```
grant select on table from user1 with grant option
```

The user then can revoke the capability of granting select on all columns by revoking the capability of granting on selected columns. This is accomplished by executing this statement:

```
revoke grant option for select on table(column2) from user1
```

To revoke all permissions from the user and all users who were granted permission, add the keyword cascade. Here is an example of this statement:

```
revoke select on table from user1 cascade
```

COMMAND PERMISSIONS

By default, the dbo is the only user who may create objects and perform backups. In some environments, users are granted access to these commands. These are called command permissions.

Note

It's important to differentiate between command and object permissions. Command permissions enable users to create objects themselves. This is rarely granted. Object permissions enable users to access objects that already exist. This permission must be granted to enable a system to operate.

Command permissions are granted to users by executing the following grant syntax:

```
grant  {all [ privileges] ¦ command_list }
  to{ group_name ¦ user_name ¦ role_name}
[ { , {next_user_group_role } } ...]
```

Here is the syntax for revoking those command permissions:

```
revoke  {all [ privileges] ¦ command_list }
  on { table_name [ ( column_list ) ]
  ¦ view_name [ ( column_list ) ]
  ¦ stored_procedure_name }
  from{ group_name ¦ user_name ¦ role_name}
[ { , {next_user_group_role } } ...]
```

Command permissions are granted and revoked to users to control access to certain commands within a database. These commands include the following:

- ◆ create database (master database only)
- ◆ create default
- ◆ create procedure
- ◆ create rule
- ◆ create table
- ◆ create view

These permissions are most often granted in a development environment to enable developers to create objects in the course of developing a system. In a production environment, these permissions are not usually needed.

Warning

Usually, you should not grant the create database permission to users. Create database authority should be reserved for those logins with the sa_role.

If you really need to grant the create database permission, don't give it to the guest user in the master database! Add the login as a new user in the master database, then grant create database to that new user.

A command list can contain a comma-delimited list of commands or the word all (or all privileges). If all is specified, only those commands that can be executed in that database are granted. This is only an issue with create database; you may grant permission to create database only within the master database. Note the following about command permissions:

♦ The creation of databases usually is performed by the system administrator (or person with the sa_role) and normally is not granted.

♦ The creation of temporary tables is permitted by any user of the server and does not need to be specifically granted.

PERMISSION APPROACHES

You should establish the access requirements of tables, views, and stored procedures during the design phase of a system. As each object is identified, the documentation should contain notes on what types of users need what types of access. It is easier to develop an effective permissions plan if you start gathering this information early.

First, define the users of a system. Try to group them logically based on job description, department, or responsibility (for example, managers, clerks, marketing personnel, billing personnel, and so forth). Often, you will develop systems knowing only the broad user classifications; you will fill in names of users later on. In any case, determine what logical groups will be using a database and define what access is needed to which tables, views, and procedures by each group and the entire database user community as a whole.

Note

As you can see, any approach to permissions is deeply associated with a specific login and user approach. Permissions are granted to either users, groups, or roles. Granting permissions to roles does not usually play a part in production systems, except wherein objects are created for use by logins with a certain role. Most permission plans focus on controlling access to users.

It generally is easiest to grant broad permissions and then limit access to specified users. The easiest way to implement broad permissions is to grant them to groups. Users assigned to a group automatically have the permissions granted to that group. Recall that a group can be any group that is specifically added to a database or the system group public (which includes all users of a database).

PUBLIC

The public group is a special group that all belong to even when they are specifically added to a user-defined group. It is important to remember that the guest user is, of course, also a member of the public group. If you grant permissions to public, you are allowing anyone who has access to the database to receive the permissions specified to public.

If individual users are added to a database (not guest), you have substantial security at the database level. If you are satisfied with database level security, granting to public allows all the users in the database to perform those functions specified. Using public is a good approach even when you have several user-defined groups in a database.

Often, several groups exist requiring special access to a select number of tables. Most other tables are available to all users of a database.

Take the example of a database with 100 tables and 10 user-defined groups. If you want to grant select permission on all the tables to all users, granting to each user-defined group requires 10 grant statements for each table. If all groups need select access to all tables, it is easiest to grant select permission to public for each table. This requires only one grant statement per table. If one group needs insert, update, and delete access to a table, additional permission can be granted on that table to only that group.

PUBLIC AND GUEST

As indicated previously, the public group contains all users, even the guest user. Combining the addition of a guest user to a database and using to public as a means for defining permissions should only be used by those sites that are extremely confident with the security enforced at the server level. Once a person gains access to the server, that user then has access to any database that has a guest user defined and consequently can perform any activities granted to public.

Addition of the guest user invalidates control of access at the database level. However, you can grant permissions to public and revoke permissions from guest to curb the activities the guest user can perform.

Warning

Do this in the correct order, please! Sybase permissions obey one simple rule: Whatever happened last takes effect.

If you revoke from guest and then grant to public, guest receives the permission because guest is a member of public. There is no hierarchy of permissions. That is, user permissions do not take priority over group permissions, or vice versa.

The safest way to manage permissions is to maintain a script of all the permissions for a particular database. Every time you need to make a change, insert the permission statement into the correct part of the script and re-execute the entire script. In this way, you can avoid unexpected consequences from grant and revoke statements.

Be careful! You probably shouldn't run your big permissions script when users are online. You may end up revoking permissions while users are processing. The only safe way to implement this approach during active hours is to run the script in a transaction or set of transactions, with begin tran and commit tran. However, this can really slow processing dramatically because of locks placed on the system tables.

GRANTING TO USER-DEFINED GROUPS

Beyond the use of the public group, granting permissions to user-defined groups is the next easiest way to implement a permission strategy. Of course, this approach is often combined with granting to public or to specific users. The approach is to define logically the access that applies only to a specific group and then grant or revoke permissions to that group.

For example, if only the marketing group needs to be able to perform select, insert, update, and delete on marketing tables, you can add a marketing group and execute this command:

```
grant all on market_table to marketing
```

for each of the marketing tables. If you have billing tables that only billing personnel needed all permissions to, you add a billing group and execute the following for each of the billing tables:

```
grant all on billing_table to billing
```

What if billing personnel need to select from marketing tables and marketing personnel need to select from billing tables? You can grant select permission on each table to the appropriate group or use the public group by granting select permission on each table in a database to public:

```
grant select on billing_table to public
grant select on marketing_table to public
```

Granting to Specific Users

Granting permissions to specific users requires the most administration but offers the greatest control. Normally, it is not used exclusively in a permission strategy because the addition of each new user requires executing individual grant statements for each object wherein access is needed. Granting and revoking to users is most commonly used in combination with granting to public or user-specified groups.

For example, all marketing users can select, insert, and delete on all marketing tables, but only the user super_market_user can update information in the database. In this case, you execute these commands:

```
grant select, insert, delete on market_table to marketing
grant update on market_table to super_market_user
```

(This assumes that the super_market_user is also a member of the marketing group.)

Object Dependencies

Many organizations use dependent objects (views, procedures, and triggers) to implement advanced security structure. Recall from Chapter 1, "A Brief Introduction to Client/Server and Sybase," the following points:

- ◆ Views can restrict access to specific rows and columns of data.
- ◆ Procedures can restrict and validate all data modifications.
- ◆ Triggers can perform related updates or update substantive audit records.

In each of these cases, users need access to the dependent object, but should not have comparable access to a dependent object.

If object ownership is distributed among several database users, implementing any of these types of advanced security is fruitless. For example, in Figure 6.4, John wants to select from a view owned by Bob, but Mary owns the base table.

Figure 6.4.
When the owner of an
object and a dependent
object are different,
permissions must be
granted explicitly on
both objects.

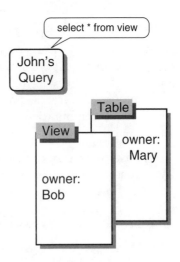

The permissions required for this scheme include the following:

```
[Mary:]grant select on basetable to bob
[Bob:]grant select on viewname to john
[Mary:]grant select on basetable to john
```

The final grant statement, in which Mary permits John to read the table directly, undermines the effect of a view intended to enforce security.

If both the base and dependent object are owned by a single user, the user needs to grant permission to the user only for the dependent object. Because there is no change in ownership between the dependent and base objects, permissions are not checked.

In Figure 6.5, Mary owns both objects, and John wants access to the view.

Figure 6.5.
When the owner of an
object and a dependent
object are the same,
permissions on the base
object are not checked.

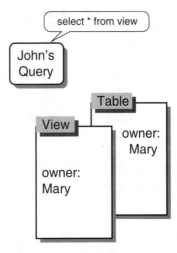

This scheme requires only a single permission statement:

```
[Mary:]grant select on viewname to john
```

Because Mary owns both objects, John's permissions are checked only at the view level but not at the table level. With no change in ownership, permissions are not checked.

ROLES

Roles were introduced in System 10 to enable Sybase sites the capabilities of distributing certain activities and identifying the users performing these actions. Although there are six roles defined for a Sybase SQL Server, only three are used heavily. These three roles are sa_role, sso_role, and oper_role.

SYSTEM ADMINISTRATOR (SA_ROLE)

The sa_role was introduced to enable the activities historically conducted by the system administrator (sa) login to be executed by people who access the server with login names other than sa.

Warning

As noted before, the sa login can perform system administration functions only because that login has been granted the sa_role (and sso_role) upon server installation. A system administrator is essentially above the law, because the sa operates outside of normal command and permission checking. This is an important capability for a system administrator to have in order to maintain absolute control of the system and be able to perform almost any function in the system at any time.

The sa_role should not be granted without carefully considering the extreme capabilities a system administrator has. Types of activities that can be conducted by the system administrator include the following:

◆ Installing SQL Server and/or specific SQL Server modules.

◆ Managing allocation of physical storage to the server.

◆ Tuning configuration variables such as memory and connections.

◆ Creating user databases and transferring ownership.

◆ Performing any activities as the database owner of any database the system administrator uses.

It is obvious that controlling system administrative functions is paramount to the function of a SQL Server. Anyone who is granted the sa_role is seen as the system administrator and has any capabilities associated with that role.

Historically, if several users needed the capability of performing system administration functions, they all logged into the SQL Server using the sa login. People familiar with pre–System 10 servers can attest to the annoyance of executing sp_who and seeing five or 10 processes with a login of sa.

By using roles, each of these processes appears in sp_who with the login used to access the server. If a problem develops wherein a process needs to be killed, you can easily determine who owns the specific process. This accountability is important in graceful administration of processes on the server. If auditing is installed, one can audit commands that require the sa_role to provide an audit history of which system administrators performed a certain activity.

About the only difference between the capabilities of the sa login in pre–System 10 servers and System 10 and later users with the sa_role is that users with the sa_role are not able to add or manage logins to the server. This activity has been distributed to the sso_role, described later. A person with the sa_role can grant the sa_role to other logins in the system, but is unable to grant any of the other roles available to the server.

The server will not enable the revocation of the sa_role from the last login that possesses its capabilities. This ensures that at least one login is active that can function as the system administrator at all times. The server will, however, enable a user with the sa_role to revoke the sa_role from the sa login! This is odd, but in System 10 and later, the sa can be made to look like any other user by the revocation of certain roles (sa_role and sso_role).

You shouldn't strip sa of all powers. If the intent is to require system administrators to log into the server as a user other than sa, the recommended approach is to lock the sa login (using sp_locklogin) once the necessary logins have been granted the sa_role.

Site Security Officer (*SSO_ROLE*)

The site security officer (sso) role is used to give a specific login the capability of performing functions associated with adding logins and auditing a SQL Server. The sso_role was introduced to satisfy the needs of many large corporations in which the addition of logins to operating systems and databases is centralized in a group separate from database administration. A user that has been granted the sso_role has the capability of performing functions such as the following:

- ◆ Adding logins to the server
- ◆ Administrating passwords
- ◆ Configuring password expiration intervals
- ◆ Managing the audit system
- ◆ Granting all roles except the `sa_role`

The server will not enable the revocation of the `sso_role` from the last login that possesses its capabilities. This ensures that at least one login will be active at all times that can add new logins to the system and manage the audit system, if installed.

Note

> Oddly, the `sso_role` does not have the ability to add or drop users to or from a database which, in essence, forces the DBA to perform security functions. Many sites modify the default `sp_adduser` and `sp_dropuser` system stored procedures to enable the `sso_role` role user (centralized security group) full capability to manage security.

It should also be noted that the `sa` login has the capability of performing site security officer functions only because that login has been granted the `sso_role` upon installation. The `sso_role` can be revoked from the `sa` login.

OPERATOR (*OPER_ROLE*)

The operator (`oper`) role is used to give a specific login the capability of managing the backup and recovery system. The operator role was introduced to satisfy corporations in which the backup and recovery function is performed by a group other than database administration or by a select group within database administration that doesn't need the capabilities defined by database ownership (`dbo`).

Historically, a user was aliased to the `dbo` in a database to be able to dump and load a database. (Prior to System 10, the `dump database` command was transferable by the `dbo`, the `load database` command was not.) Therefore, that user had far-reaching capabilities in a database, which resulted in potential exposure to sabotage and/or accidental modifications in a database.

A user that has been granted the `oper_role` can perform only the following commands:

- ◆ Dump transaction
- ◆ Dump database

◆ Load transaction

◆ Load database

Therefore, a user with the oper_role can perform backup and recovery on any database in a server without having to have more capabilities than needed to perform the tasks.

OTHER ROLES

It can be seen in the system tables that a navigator_role, replication_role, and sybase_ts_role can also be granted using the sp_role procedure.

The navigator_role is granted to users who manage the navigation server, and the replication_role is granted to users who manage the replication server.

The Sybase technical support role (sybase_ts_role) is a role whose use may not be readily apparent. The sybase_ts_role must be granted to execute certain dbcc (database consistency checker) commands that are considered outside the realm of normal system administration tasks. An example of dbcc commands that may require the sybase_ts_role include dbcc help, dbcc page, and dbcc traceon. However, as newer versions of the server are introduced, additional dbcc commands might be executed by users that have only the sa_role. The command dbcc page falls into this category. In version 10.0 of the server, that command could be executed only by a person with the sybase_ts_role, but in version 10.0.1, a person with only the sa_role is able to execute that command.

When executing nondocumented dbcc commands (not strongly recommended, unless you know what you are doing), it is often a good idea to have the sybase_ts_role granted to your login. The other roles can be granted only by a user possessing the sso_role.

GRANTING AND REVOKING ROLES: *SP_ROLE*

Roles are granted to (and revoked from) users through the sp_role system procedure:

```
sp_role { "grant" | "revoke" } ,
{ sa_role | sso_role | oper_role
| sybase_ts_role | replication_role | navigator_role } ,
login_name
```

You can grant a role only to an active login account (an account that is available for login). If the user executes the sp_displaylogin procedure, it reflects the newly granted role as part of the Configured Authorization, but the select show_role() command will not show that role as active. An active login that has been granted a role is able to perform in that role only if the set role command is used.

A role can be revoked, however, only if the specified login name is not currently active. This means that if you want to revoke a role from a person, that user must log off before you can revoke that role. (Of course, you can always kill the user's process, if you're in a bad mood.)

Turning Roles On and Off: *SET ROLE*

The set role command is used to turn a role on or off for an active login:

```
set role "role_name" { on ¦ off }
```

where *role_name* is sa_role, sso_role, oper_role, sybase_ts_role, navigation_role, or replication_role.

Roles can be set on at any time, but the capability of setting a role off depends on the capability of existing within a database without that role. For example, if you have a database called testdb in your server, a person that has been granted the sa_role can use that database and consequently is seen as the database owner with a uid of 1 (system administrators become the dbo user in any database they use). If the person is using that database and tries to execute this command:

```
set role "sa_role" off
```

the server displays an error, because that user would not be able to use the database if it were not for the sa_role (assuming there is not a guest user).

Displaying Configured Role Information: *SP_DISPLAYLOGIN*

The roles configured for a login are reported by sp_displaylogin. This command reports a variety of information, including a list under Configured Authorization of the roles that have been configured for a specified login. Note that this is different from the show_role() function, which reports on active roles for a specified login (based on an individual connection). The syntax for sp_displaylogin is the following:

```
sp_displaylogin [ login_name ]
```

The output from sp_displaylogin is not set up as a table of result values:

```
sp_displaylogin jeff

Suid: 5

Loginame: jeff
Fullname:
Configured Authorization: sa_role sso_role
Locked: NO
Date of Last Password Change: Nov  8 1994  1:28PM
```

Only users that have been granted the sa_role or the sso_role can provide a login name as an argument. For all other users, the procedure must be executed without a login name. For users who execute sp_displaylogin without providing a login name, the login information for their login is displayed.

DISPLAYING ACTIVE ROLE INFORMATION: *SHOW_ROLE*

The function show_role() displays the active current roles for the login associated with a specific process. The syntax for this statement is the following:

```
select show_role( )
```

This command produces a list of the active roles for the login associated with a specific process. This is an important point, because a single login that is configured for the sa_role, sso_role, and oper_role roles could have three separate connections to the server. For each of the connections, the user can turn off any role that has been configured for the login. Therefore, one process may return sa_role, a second process may return sso_role, and a third process may show oper_role and sa_role as output to the command select show_role().

On the other hand, the execution of the sp_displaylogin procedure reports on configured roles for a login and returns identical information for each process. The Configured Authorization is "sa_role, sso_role, and oper_role," because sp_displaylogin reports on the actual login, and the select show_role() statement reports the roles active for a specific connection.

ROLES AND STORED PROCEDURES: *PROC_ROLE*

Although the permission to execute a certain procedure can be granted to a specific role, a user that does not have a specified role may also execute that procedure. If an extra level of checking is needed, the stored procedure can be created to check for a certain role before enabling execution of the code contained within the stored procedure. This is accomplished by using the proc_role function. The syntax for this function is the following:

```
proc_role ( "role_name" )
```

where role_name can be any of the roles configured for a server.

Consider a situation where you have a table called archive_database_info. This table contains information about customers that have been archived from the active customer database to an archive database. You want to create a procedure called get_archive_names to retrieve the information from this table. However, you only want operators (users granted the oper_role) to be able to execute the code contained in this procedure. You could use the proc_role function to test whether the person executing this code has the appropriate role. Here is an example of how this function might be used in a procedure:

```
create proc get_archive_names
(@name char(30) = null )
as
if ( proc_role ( "oper_role" ) = 1 )
begin
select name, tape_location
from archive_database_info
where name = @name
return 0
end
else
begin
print "You are not a user with the Operator Role !!!"
return - 1
end
```

Note

If a user has a specified role, the value 1 is returned. If the user does not have a specified role, a value of 0 is returned. This seems backwards, because most functions in Sybase return a value of 0 when execution is successful and a non-zero return code when there is a problem.

APPROACHES

It is conceivable that a site can continue to operate a System 10 and later server in the same manner as a pre–System 10 server. Essentially, all activities can be conducted by the single sa login, with no accountability for the actions by that user.

However, you should use roles as they were intended. This means that users that need to perform system administration functions are granted the sa_role, users that need to add logins to the system are granted the sso_role, and users that will be performing backup and recovery operations are granted the oper_role. A recommended checklist for setting up roles includes the following tasks:

1. Identify each individual user that needs to perform system administration functions.
2. Grant each user the sa_role by the sa login.
3. Identify each individual user that is responsible for adding logins, managing password administration, and managing of the auditing system (if installed).

4. Grant each user the `sso_role` by the sa login.

5. Identify each individual user that needs to be able to dump and load any database in the server.

6. Grant each user the `oper_role` by the sa login.

7. Enable the sa login to be locked by one of the other users with the `sa_role`.

At this point, any system administration activities have to be performed by a login other that the sa login, and the activities of that user can be audited.

SUMMARY

SQL Server security is implemented in four layers: the operating system, the Sybase server, the Sybase database, and the Sybase object. Each allows greater or lesser control, depending on your requirements.

Sybase offers a variety of ways to control access to data. Server login and database user approaches affect the way in which a permissions strategy is implemented.

At the object level, most sites grant broad permissions and then limit or grant specific access as needed to minimize the administrative overhead in implementing a permissions plan. This usually involves granting to `public` or a user-defined group, then revoking or granting specific permissions to a user-defined group or a specific user.

Roles in System 10 and later added important capabilities, especially for large organizations that distribute the traditional sa tasks between several groups. Through roles, you can identify real logins by using `sp_who`, and an administrator's activities can be audited when the audit system is enabled. With roles in place, individual logins can be limited to the access they need to perform expected tasks.

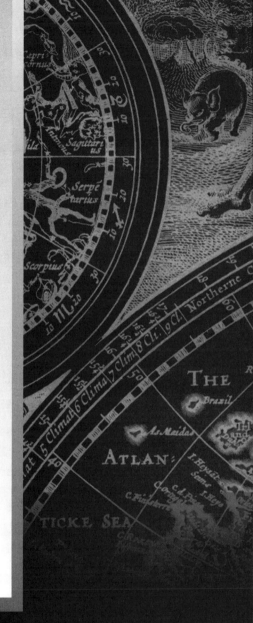

- What Is a
  Transaction?

- What Is the
  Transaction Log?

CHAPTER 7

Database Logging and
Recovery

Sybase uses a write-ahead log and automatic forward recovery to maintain up-to-the-transaction data integrity, even in the case of erratic or unexpected server shutdowns. This chapter explores how the Sybase transaction log works, and how it manages recovery. You'll understand commits and checkpoints, and how the server manages data integrity through various server events.

Sybase's use of terms may differ from your prior experience with computer systems. For example, you may think of recovery or disaster recovery as the administrative process of getting back to work after a catastrophe, but it means something quite different in the SQL Server world. You need to understand the following crucial Sybase terms first:

♦ A *transaction* is a unit of work. Transactions can be long or short, and they can involve changes to millions of rows of data or only one. SQL Server promises that every transaction, no matter how long or complex, will run to completion or will be completely reversed if it cannot be completed for any reason. The transaction log is the component of the system responsible for transactional data integrity.

♦ *Recovery* is the automatic process of reconciling the log and the data. Recovery occurs when the server is started. We will examine the recovery process in detail in this chapter.

♦ A *backup* is a physical copy of the database or transaction log. The Sybase term for a backup is a "dump," and dump is the Transact-SQL command used to initiate backups.

♦ *Restoration* is the process of taking a backup of the database from storage and copying it back onto the server (restore).

Backup and restoration are the topic of Chapter 8, "Backing Up and Restoring the Database and Transaction Logs."

WHAT IS A TRANSACTION?

A *transaction* is a set of operations to be completed at one time, as though they were a single operation. A transaction must be fully completed, or not performed at all. Standard examples of transactions include bank transfers (withdraw $500 from checking, add $500 to savings) and order entry systems (write an order for five widgets, remove five widgets from inventory).

All SQL statements are inherently transactions, from grant and create statements to the data modification statements, insert, update, and delete. Consider the following update example:

```
update titles
set price = price * 1.02
```

This statement modifies all rows in the titles table. SQL Server guarantees that, regardless of the size of the titles table, all rows will be processed or no rows will be processed at all. What if half of the rows are modified and the server fails? When the server comes back up (but before the database is available for use) it rolls back the incomplete transaction, removing all evidence that it ever began. That's part of the recovery process, which is discussed later in this chapter.

SQL Server also includes transaction control syntax to group sets of SQL statements together into single logical work units:

begin transaction	Starts a unit of work.
commit transaction	Completes a unit of work.
rollback transaction	Cancels a unit of work.

The following example enters an order and depletes inventory in a single transaction:

```
begin transaction
   update inventory
      set in_stock = in_stock - 5
      where item_num = "14141"
   insert orders (cust_num, item_num, qty)
      values ("ABC151", "14141", 5)
commit transaction
```

SQL Server guarantees that the inventory will not change unless the order also is entered.

Here is the same example, but it uses the rollback transaction statement instead of commit:

```
begin transaction
   update inventory
      set in_stock = in_stock - 5
      where item_num = "14141"
   insert orders (cust_num, item_num, qty)
      values ("ABC151", "14141", 5)
rollback transaction
```

When the server encounters the rollback statement, it discards all changes in the transaction and returns the data to the state it was in before work began.

This chapter examines the mechanism used by SQL Server to manage data integrity (both rollback and commit) in transactions.

WHAT IS THE TRANSACTION LOG?

The transaction log is the database-level system table, called syslogs. The syslogs table contains a sequential list of all modifications to every object in the database, as well as any information required to maintain data integrity.

7

DATABASE LOGGING AND RECOVERY

The transaction log is

◆ Shared by all users of a database.

◆ Modified in cache, and only flushed to disk at commit time.

◆ Written first (a write-ahead log).

The log is not

◆ Usefully manipulated or read with SQL.

◆ Readable in any useful format.

Note

There are now third-party utilities that do access the log, enabling some direct interaction with the log and providing some measure of "undo" functions. However, nothing in the standard SQL Server suite will enable you to interact directly with the log.

A WRITE-AHEAD LOG

Write-ahead means that the log is written first, before the data itself, any time that a query modifies data.

Note

In addition to standard SQL data modification statements (insert, update, delete), all create statements, permissions statements (grant and revoke), and many system stored procedures (for example, sp_adduser, sp_bindrule) change the contents of *system* tables. The server logs each of these data modifications as well.

When modifying data, the server takes the following steps:

1. Write a begin tran record in the log (in cache).

2. Record the modification in the log (in cache).

3. Perform the modification to the data (in cache).

4. Write a commit tran record to the log (in cache).

5. Flush all "dirty" (modified) log pages to disk.

COMMITS

A *commit* flushes all "dirty" (modified) log pages for that database from cache to disk. Figure 7.1 shows the state of the data after the transaction is complete and the commit has taken place.

Figure 7.1.
The commit process
only writes log changes
to disk.

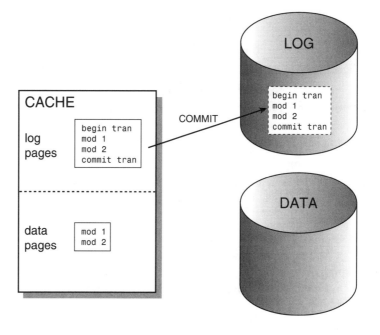

The server does all the work in RAM first, before making changes to disk, to improve processing speed. When the process is complete, the only work written to disk is any change to the log. However, RAM is volatile. If the server goes down unexpectedly, or if someone pulls the plug out of the wall, the changes to data that are stored only in memory are lost, right? That's where the transaction log earns its keep.

Remember, each modification has been recorded in the log. At recovery time (after the server goes down and is restarted), committed transactions that have not been written to the data area are rolled forward into the data. This is *forward recovery*, or *roll forward*. If the commit tran has been executed and the write to the log has been made to disk, the server guarantees that the data can be recovered if the server goes down.

Note

It is interesting to note here that the log is really the part of the database that matters when it comes to recovery and restore. If the disk on which the data is stored catches fire, you can use the information in the log, in combination with your backups, to restore the system up to the last complete transaction. On the other hand, if the log disk gets wet while you are putting out the fire, you will only be able to restore up to the time of the last backup.

Moral of the story: Let the data disk burn to a crisp, but save the log disk (and keep your backups safe).

Serious moral of the story: If you have to choose between mirroring logs and mirroring data, mirror the logs.

At recovery time, uncommitted transactions (begin tran markers without a commit tran) are rolled back. All data modifications associated with the transaction are undone. This is rollback. But how do uncommitted transactions get into the log in the first place?

Frequently, when transactions overlap, the commit tran will flush uncommitted, as well as committed, work to disk. Uncommitted work can be identified by a begin tran entry in the log with no corresponding commit tran. Figure 7.2 illustrates a commit that writes both committed and uncommitted work to the log.

Figure 7.2.
The commit process
writes all dirty log
pages for the database
to disk, including those
with incomplete
transactions.

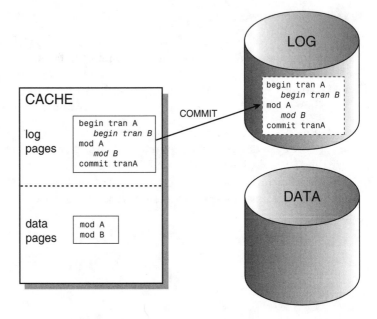

Note

Why write both committed and uncommitted work with every commit? Keep in mind that Sybase always performs I/O at the page level or higher. Entries in syslogs are ordered by a consecutive timestamp value, so transactions that are processing concurrently will be intermingled on a single page.

Remember, also, that the commit process is the crucial bottleneck for an on-line system. The user is waiting and pages are locked until the commit is complete. By writing out commits at the page level without first weeding out any uncommitted work, the server can streamline commits. If the uncommitted work is subsequently rolled back, the server can record that fact in a later row in syslogs.

CHECKPOINTS

The log is the part of the database that keeps track of data integrity, transaction control, and recoverability. For the server to guarantee data integrity, it needs only to make certain that the log is written to disk. However, if enough transactions pile up in the log without being recorded on the data disk as well, after the server goes down it will take weeks for it to recover all of the committed transactions. When does the data get updated while the server is running? During a checkpoint.

A *checkpoint* writes all dirty pages for the database from cache to disk, starting with the log (see Figure 7.3). A checkpoint reduces the amount of work the server needs to do at recovery time.

A checkpoint occurs under three different circumstances:

◆ The dbo issues the checkpoint command.

◆ The server needs additional cache space.

◆ The server recovery interval has been exceeded.

Before the checkpoint starts, the server first notes in the log that a checkpoint has been performed in the database. The checkpoint marker enables the server to assume that all committed work recorded in the log prior to the checkpoint marker is reflected in the data.

If long-running transactions are underway when the checkpoint begins, uncommitted work may be written not only to the log, but also to the data (see Figure 7.4). The recovery process uses the checkpoint marker in the log to identify work in incomplete transactions that has been written to the data disk by a checkpoint.

Figure 7.3.
The checkpoint process
writes all dirty pages
for the database,
starting with the log.

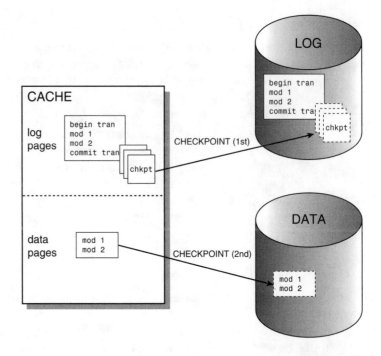

Figure 7.4.
The checkpoint marker
indicates where the last
update to the data took
place. Recovery will roll
back incomplete work
written by a checkpoint
and will recover
transactions that
completed after the
checkpoint began.

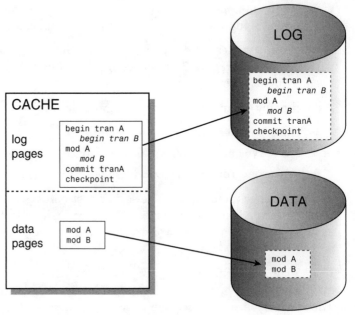

RECOVERY

Recovery is an automatic process that verifies that completed transactions are in the data and that incomplete transactions are removed from the data. Recovery guarantees that any completed transaction is reflected in the data. During the recovery process, the server does the following:

◆ Checks syslogs for each database, backing out incomplete transactions and rolling forward completed transactions not in the data.

◆ Checkpoints the database.

◆ Drops and re-creates tempdb.

RECOVERY INTERVAL

With the `recovery interval` configuration option, the sa can set the approximate amount of time per database to wait for the SQL Server to start up. For example, to set the server recovery interval to 12 minutes per database, use the following:

```
sp_configure "recovery interval", 12
reconfigure
```

This option is a dynamic configuration setting, so the new value will take effect as soon as you issue the `reconfigure` statement. Here's how it works. Once a minute, one of the system processes listed in `sp_who` (you have seen it listed there: it always seems to be stuck on `checkpointsleep`) wakes up and examines each database in turn. Based on the amount of work recorded in the log for each database, the process determines whether it will take longer than the recovery interval to restore the database. If so, the system process issues an automatic checkpoint. Finally, if the database is set for `truncate log on checkpoint`, the system process truncates the log.

The length of time it will take your server to recover completely after an unexpected shutdown depends on your recovery interval and the number of databases on the server. The worst-case answer is that it could take (recovery interval × number of databases) minutes. (In other words, 12-minute recovery interval × 20 databases = 4 hours!)

You will seldom encounter the worst case, but even if you do, you can access your own database as soon as recovery is complete. (Databases are recovered in order by `dbid`.)

Note

> Don't forget that the `shutdown` statement includes an automatic checkpoint on every database. If you issue `shutdown with nowait`, the system skips the checkpoint and shuts down immediately. Server recovery is much faster after a `shutdown` than after a `shutdown with nowait`.

It's tempting to set the recovery interval low to ensure a quick recovery after any shutdown, but the checkpoint process creates overhead when you are running a high volume of transactions through the server. Set the configuration setting to the highest tolerable value.

RECOVERY FLAGS

Use the `recovery flags` setting with `sp_configure` to display the names of transactions during recovery. If you use transaction names in SQL code, the names will be displayed in the error log if the transaction is rolled back or brought forward during recovery.

```
sp_configure "recovery flags", 1
reconfigure
```

Note

> Restart the server after this option to have the recovery flags take effect. During the first restart, transaction names will not be listed. Subsequent restarts will display transaction names as they are processed.

Setting recovery flags enables you to determine exactly which work actually made it into the server before a shutdown. To make good use of the errorlog information, there needs to be a correlation between SQL Server transaction names and batch or work unit identifiers in the manual process. For example, if the batch number is 17403, the transaction name might be B_17403. Pass the transaction name to the server with the `begin tran` statement, as follows:

```
begin tran B_17403
    ...
commit tran
```

WHEN THE TRANSACTION LOG FILLS UP

If the transaction log fills for any reason, all data modifications to the database will fail immediately. Most standard maintenance measures (dump the log, resize the log) will fail as well. The only reliable way to clear the log is to issue the statement, `dump tran ... with no_log`, and dump the entire database.

THRESHOLDS AND THE TRANSACTION LOG

A "last-chance" threshold is provided for the logsegment for any database that has the log on a separate device. This is to prevent the log from completely filling up. The amount of free space available when the last chance threshold is reached is approximately the space needed to write the log records necessary to dump the transaction log.

If the threshold is reached, the server executes `sp_thresholdaction`, which is written by you.

CREATING SP_THRESHOLDACTION

The last-chance threshold procedure can be extremely simple (print a notification message in the log) or very complex (create a temporary dump device and dump the transaction, or send a pager notification through open server). Normally, you should create a dump device to use for emergencies, or code the procedure to dump to the device you would normally use for the database. The type of device depends on your environment. If you have automatic tape facilities, you could dump to your normal devices without worry. If it is possible that the tape drive is unavailable, use a disk device.

Note

Unless you add a notification process, it is up to you to read the error log and discover that `sp_thresholdaction` was executed on the database. If you backed up the data to a disk during your threshold procedure, copy the data to a tape as soon as you realize what has happened.

Remember, this is emergency processing. The database is essentially locked for updates and will remain that way until space in the log is available.

You need to decide whether you will have a single threshold procedure for all databases, or specific procedures for databases with special characteristics. You should certainly create one `sp_thresholdaction` in sybsystemprocs for all databases. Later, you can create specific procedures in individual databases. When the last-chance threshold is crossed in a database, the server first looks for `sp_thresholdaction` in that database. It only looks for the procedure in sybsystemprocs if the procedure is not found in the database itself.

The server always includes four parameters when it calls a threshold procedure:

- ◆ @dbname (varchar(30)) is the name of the database.
- ◆ @segmentname (varchar(30)) is the name of the segment. In the last-chance threshold, this value is always "logsegment."
- ◆ @space_left (int) is the number of pages available.
- ◆ @status (int) indicates whether this is a last-chance threshold (1) or not (0).

Here is an example of a simple last-chance threshold procedure that performs a backup to an emergency backup device and prints a warning message in the transaction log. For this procedure to work, the Emergency_Device must already exist (set it up with sp_addumpdevice).

```
create procedure sp_thresholdaction
    @database_name varchar(30),
    @segment_name varchar(30),
    @free_space_in_pages int,
    @status int
as
dump transaction @dbname to Emergency_Device
print "WARNING: Last Chance Threshold crossed!"
print "Transaction log for the %1! segment in the %2! database ", @segment, @database
print " was dumped to the Emergency_Device!!!"
go
```

SUSPENDED TRANSACTIONS

Once the last-chance threshold is crossed, processes that add rows to the log will either abort or suspend, depending on how you have configured the database. (By default, the processes will be suspended. You can verify that processes are suspended with sp_who.)

sp_thresholdaction normally dumps or expands the transaction log, freeing up space for the suspended transactions. The suspended transactions will awaken and should execute normally. If a process does not awaken on its own, use lct_admin to unsuspend all suspended processes for a database, as in the following example:

```
select lct_admin ("unsuspend", db_id)
```

You should call Sybase Technical Support before using this facility, because all processes should wake up when space is made available in the log.

ABORTING PROCESSES

If you have not written `sp_thresholdaction`, configure the database to abort trans-actions when the log is full. Otherwise user processes will appear to hang until you realize that the log is full. You must be in the master database to issue the `sp_dboption` command and change this value, as in the following example:

```
use master
go
sp_dboption database_name, "abort tran on log full", true
go
```

ADDITIONAL LOG THRESHOLDS

It's a good idea to create several additional thresholds in your database log to allow you the time to act proactively. Thresholds are defined by the percentage of remaining space in the segment. Create thresholds so that you are warned periodically before log space is in crisis, such as at 50 percent available, 25 percent available, 10 percent available, and 2 percent available, depending on the size of the log.

SUMMARY

Transactions ensure consistency of database integrity to manage simultaneous updates and to ensure recovery after a server shutdown. All SQL statements are transactions themselves, and many SQL statements can be combined into a larger transaction.

You need to manage the transaction log, either with thresholds or by regularly monitoring the amount of available space in the log.

7

DATABASE LOGGING AND RECOVERY

- Why Back Up?

- Roles and
  Responsibilities

- Types of Backups

- Dump Devices

- Backup Server

- Dumping and Loading

- Additional
  Considerations

- Transaction Logging

- Developing Your
  Backup and Recovery
  Plan

CHAPTER 8

Backing Up and
Restoring the Database
and Transaction Logs

Backup is common to any database environment. A backup is a copy of a database (or portion of a database) stored on some type of media (tape, disk, and so forth). A restore is the process used to return a database to a point in time. In Sybase, a backup is normally referred to as a dump and a restore is normally referred to as a load, because these are the names of the commands to back up and restore, respectively.

It takes work to define an effective backup and recovery plan. This is especially true in very large database (VLDB) environments because the complexity of administrative activities is magnified. Timing of activities quickly becomes an issue. For large tables and databases, consistency checks (dbcc), updating index statistics, and index creation can take several hours to *days*. Plans for automating backups must consider the impact of these activities as well as application activities.

The backup media you choose also can affect your plan. Dumping to tape devices means the physical tapes have to be managed. This must be considered in your plan. Additionally, when a tape is full, a subsequent backup would fail, which could affect your entire backup and recovery process. When dumping to file devices, you must consider the organization of the directory structure as well as management of the backup files.

WHY BACK UP?

Backups are a hassle. Why bother? (Why do you have car insurance?) Backups are the easiest and most foolproof way of ensuring you can recover a database. Without a backup, all data may be lost and would have to be re-created from the source. This is normally an option only for Decision Support Systems (DSS), because its data normally originates in some other system. For OnLine Transaction Processing (OLTP) systems, the majority of data originates on the server. *The lost data may not be reproducible.*

Backups can guard against table or database corruption, media failure, or user error. They should be performed as frequently as necessary for effective data administration. SQL Server backups can be performed while the database is in use, but generally it is more effective to back up during nonpeak activity periods.

ROLES AND RESPONSIBILITIES

The capability of executing the dump and load commands defaults to the dbo of the database. The dbo could be the login who created the database, anyone aliased to the dbo in the database, or the sa login (the sa becomes dbo in any database the sa uses).

Logins granted the oper_role have the capability of dumping and loading *any* database in the server.

Note

Sybase added the concept of roles in System 10—a good idea! As with many of the enhancements in System 10, roles address the needs of large organizations.

For most sites using versions previous to System 10, backups were normally performed by the sa. In small organizations, this approach was adequate because the DBA was responsible for *all* activities on the server.

Larger organizations often distribute database administration functions. Separate groups usually exist to manage logins, conduct backups, and configure and administer the server. Operators logging in as sa had inappropriate server access for executing simple backups and restores, but it was the only practical way to access those features.

The oper_role solves these problems.

You should identify who is responsible for performing backups in your organization. For each of these individuals, create a login and grant the operator role:

```
sp_role "grant", oper_role, login_name
```

As always, the sa or dbo has the capability of dumping and loading the database.

TYPES OF BACKUPS

There are two types of backups: full and incremental. A full backup is a copy of all the allocated pages in your database, including all system tables (see Figure 8.1). The system tables include syslogs, normally referred to as the transaction log. The transaction log is also dumped to ensure that all transactions have been included in the backup.

Figure 8.1.
A database backup
(dump database acctg_db)
copies the entire
database, including log
and data.

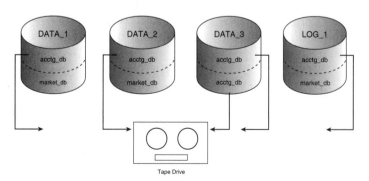

Tape Drive

Warning

Full backups do not truncate the transaction log, which often is confusing and sometimes disastrous for new DBAs. Even if all your backups are complete backups, you must run the incremental backup process periodically to clear the transaction log. Otherwise, you will certainly fill up your log, and processing on that database will halt until you clear the log. (See "Dumping Database Logs" later in this chapter.)

An incremental backup is simply a copy of the transaction log (see Figure 8.2). The transaction log contains the transactions that have occurred since the last dump transaction command. This is similar to incremental backups of file systems, where only the files that have changed are backed up. Dumping the transaction log truncates the log, unless the with no_truncate option is specified.

Figure 8.2.
An incremental backup
(dump transaction
acctg_db) copies only the
transaction log.

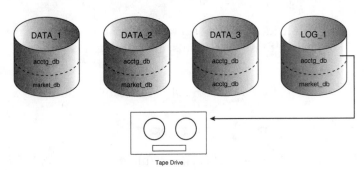

DUMP DEVICES

A dump device is created for the exclusive use of the dump and load commands. When dumping a database or transaction log, you must tell it where to create the backup. Creating a dump device enables you to associate a logical name with the physical backup media. The two most common types of media are tape devices and disk devices.

TAPE DEVICES

A tape device records backups to removable tapes. Tape drives can be used alone, or several can be used at one time in parallel. Purchase as many drives as you can afford, based on the needs of your backup and recovery strategy. Tape devices are inherently more secure than disk devices because the media (tape) is removable and portable. Tape capacity has increased dramatically over the last five years. In 1990, standard 1/4-inch cartridges held only 150MB of data. Now, smaller cartridges

(4mm or 8mm are common sizes) hold over 50 times the amount of data (8GB). The size and compactness of tapes will almost certainly continue to progress.

Tape devices are used by most production sites. Tape devices provide a removable source of backup media that can easily be moved offsite for additional security. A tape device adapts to changing database size much more gracefully than disk devices. Dumping a 50MB database to disk can be easily managed by your file system. As the database grows to 50GB, however, a disk dump probably will prove impossible, because most sites do not have that amount of free space in the file system. Additionally, to move the dump offsite, you must back up the dump files *to tape*.

Disk Devices

A disk device is just a file in a directory, usually stored in the file system of your database server. Dumping to a disk device is faster than dumping to a tape device. When you dump to a disk device, you actually can see the file grow if you check the file size at intervals during the dump.

Note

One important fact to remember is that a dump to a disk device overwrites an existing file unless you specify a number of days to retain the file as part of the dump command. This is an important distinction between dumping to tape devices and dumping to file devices—overwrites are automatic.

A dump to a tape device will not overwrite any other dumps on the tape *unless you tell it to (*with the init option*)*. A dump to a disk device has one of three results:

◆ The dump to the device creates a brand new file. This is the ideal situation.

◆ The dump to the device replaces or overwrites an existing file. This is potentially disastrous, because the "good" dump file from last night easily could be overwritten by a corrupt dump. *Make sure you specify the* with retaindays = #_of_days *option to avoid overwriting a dump.*

◆ The dump to the device fails. This may cause an interrupt in your backup and recovery schedule. Database backup scripts rarely—if ever—perform a retry if a dump fails (normally, a retry also will fail anyway). What if you can back up only once a week? This essentially means an entire backup may be missing from your backup schedule. This is not an ideal situation for most environments.

If you assume a file will be created (new, or replacing an existing file), you must ensure that any file created as part of a production dump will not be overwritten until a copy can be made of the file. This normally results in writing automation scripts to dump a database to a file and is immediately followed by one of the following:

- Moving that file to a different filename, clearing the way for the next dump
- Backing up that file to a tape drive, which means the existing file could be overwritten without worry

For these reasons, many people will tell you, "Don't use disk drives for backups!" This is another one of those "rules of thumb," which has several exceptions.

There are situations wherein disk devices are appropriate. One normal environment in which you might back up to disk drives is a development environment, where backups often are conducted by developers. There is a major production system in the United States wherein disk devices are used in production because the dump can be completely automated, requiring no user intervention. Another reason has to do with the added baggage from tapes. Tapes must be managed. It is likely you will need to hire an operator or make a significant purchase (a tape silo) to manage the process.

ADDING DUMP DEVICES

Use `sp_addumpdevice` to add a new dump device to a SQL Server.

SYNTAX

```
sp_addumpdevice "tape", logicalname, physical_name, size
sp_addumpdevice "disk", logical_name, physical_name
```

Tip

In System 10 and later, you don't have to add dump devices with `sp_addumpdevice`. The physical name can be provided as part of the `dump` syntax.

I learned this the hard way by misspelling the logical name of a dump device in the `dump` command:

```
dump tran my_db to dumpdev1
```

It should have been `dump_dev1`. Imagine my surprise to find a file, dumpdev1, in the /home/sybase/install directory!

LOGICAL NAME

After executing this command, you can use the logical name for all dumps and loads; a good practice is to choose the logical name based on the type of device being added.

For tape devices, use a general name for the tape (Tape1, Tape2, and so forth). For disk devices, use a logical name indicating the database and dump type (`CustomerDB_dump` or `CustomerDB_tran`, for example).

PHYSICAL NAME

The physical name is normally predefined for tape devices. Tape devices should be specified as dictated by your hardware. A common example of the physical name is /dev/nrst0. (Check the documentation for your specific hardware environment.) The following example adds a nonrewinding "`/dev/n...`" tape device called "`Tape1`" with a capacity of 8GB. This device will recognize any ANSI tape labels:

```
sp_addumpdevice "tape", "Tape1", "/dev/nrmt0", 8000
```

For file devices, it is a good idea to organize a directory structure for all your databases. For example, the root directory may be called /dbdump. Each database in your server would be a subdirectory. The CustomerDB subdirectory would be /dbdump/CustomerDB. The filename created is based on the dump type. Therefore, the two dump devices for the CustomerDB database would be created in the following manner:

```
sp_addumpdevice "disk", "CustomerDB_dump",
    "/dbdump/CustomerDB/CustomerDB_dump", 2

sp_addumpdevice "disk", "CustomerDB_tran",
    "/dbdump/CustomerDB/CustomerDB_tran", 2
```

By standardizing your structure, you can now write scripts that accept a database name as a parameter. The entire `dump` command can be created dynamically. The location of the dump is also known, enabling you to move the dump file immediately to a different name to avoid having it overwritten.

SIZE

The `size` parameter is used to specify the tape capacity in number of megabytes. Use the maximum size allowable for your tape device.

Do not be stingy with the number of dump devices added. Using dump devices helps standardize your dump approach, especially for disk devices.

BACKUP SERVER

Backups for System 10 and later releases require backup server, an open server process that directly queries the controller and is approximately seven times faster than pre-System 10 technology. The SQL Server instructs the backup server, via remote procedure calls, to back up a specific database. The backup server handles

I/O, rather than using SQL Server resources. The use of the backup server has several advantages:

◆ Backups can be striped (portioned), enabling you to specify up to 32 separate devices for dumping or loading a database. The backup server breaks the database into approximately equal portions and dumps those portions in parallel.

◆ Backups can be performed remotely, enabling you to dump your database or a portion (stripe) of your database to a device on hardware *other* than the hardware where your SQL Server resides.

◆ Backups can be dumped to multiple tapes without using the console program.

◆ Several backups can be recorded on the same tape. A subsequent reload locates only the file it needs to recover.

◆ Tape options are expanded.

◆ Messages can be sent to the session initiating the dump or load, or to an operator console.

Backup server is a separate server process from your SQL Server and therefore requires remote access to be enabled before commands can be issued. A "local" backup server *must* be available on the same hardware as your SQL Server. The local backup server listens on a different port number from the SQL Server. (You can easily confirm this by viewing your interfaces file.) You can dump to your local backup server, a remote backup server, or both.

REMOTE BACKUP SERVER

The SQL Server can instruct a backup server, located on separate hardware from your SQL Server, to back up a specific database using remote procedure calls. In order to perform dumps with System 10 and later, you must have a local backup server process running on the same physical server as SQL Server. The local backup server sends the necessary packets of data across the network to the remote backup server, which stores the data to a dump device (see Figure 8.3).

There are special instances in which a remote backup is appropriate. In most circumstances, the increased load on the network, the poor performance of the dump itself over the network, and the logistics of managing multiple-server backups remotely all imply that a local backup is more effective.

However, all these problems can be overcome if the specific business case warrants the time and money to be invested. Certainly, remote backup is feasible; it is just more complex.

Figure 8.3.
The local backup server can perform backups itself, or it can communicate over the network with other backup servers on other equipment to perform remote dumps.

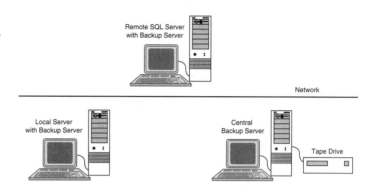

ADDING A SERVER

Sybase looks for an entry for the backup server name in the interfaces file. The backup server is named SYB_BACKUP by default. The entry for the backup server is added to the interfaces file and to the SQL Server with `sybinit`. You must make remote backup servers known to your SQL Server by using the `sp_addserver` command.

SYNTAX

```
sp_addserver remote_backup_name, null, network_name
```

The *network_name* can be copied from your interfaces file.

STARTING A BACKUP SERVER

Start a backup server with `startserver`. `startserver` is passed a startup script that invokes `backupserver`. This is similar to starting a SQL Server, except the startup script invokes `dataserver`. The startup script is automatically created by the sybinit procedure, and is named SYB_BACKUP by default. At the operating system command line, you execute the following:

```
startserver -f SYB_BACKUP
```

If you want to shut down a backup server, you can provide the name of the backup server to the `shutdown` command (backup server is normally shut down using `isql`):

```
shutdown [backup_servername] [ with {wait ¦ nowait} ]
```

Here is an example:

```
shutdown SYB_BACKUP with nowait
```

The `with wait` option is the default. It brings down the backup server gracefully by enabling all current dumps or loads to complete. No new backup or dump requests are honored. The `with nowait` option immediately shuts down the backup server, even if a dump or load is in progress. *Do not specify the* with nowait *option unless it is really necessary.*

Dumping and Loading

Now that the basics have been defined, you need to take a close look at the dump and load commands. At this point, you should have backup server up and running and your dump devices should be identified. Let's look at the dump and load options for both the entire database and for the transaction log.

Dumping the Database

Use dump database to make a full copy of your database. The simplified syntax for the dump database command is the following:

```
dump database databasename to devicename
```

This command is valid in all environments. In System 10 and later, however, the backup is handled by a backup server that has several other options, including remote backup, striped backups, and tape handling specifications. Here is the full format for the dump database command:

```
dump database databasename
    to stripe_device [ at backup_server_name ]
        [ density = density_value,
          blocksize = number_of_bytes,
          capacity = number_of_KB,
          dumpvolume = volume_name ]
    [ stripe on stripe_device ...]
    [ with {
          [ dismount ¦ nodismount ],
          [ nounload ¦ unload ],
          retaindays = number_of_days,
          [ noinit ¦ init ],
          file = file_name,
          [ notify = { client ¦ operator_console } ]
          }
    ]
```

Table 8.1 presents detailed descriptions of each parameter of dump database.

TABLE 8.1. dump database PARAMETERS.

Parameter	Description
databasename	This is the name of the database you are attempting to dump.
stripe_device	When dumping locally, this is either the logical or physical name of the dump device. When dumping remotely, you must specify the *physical* name.

Parameter	Description
backup_server_name	Use this option when specifying a remote dump device.
density blocksize capacity	These parameters relate to the physical characteristics of the tape device you are using. Assume the defaults unless instructed otherwise.
retaindays = #_of_days	This is a UNIX option that can be used for any type of dump device. It does not allow the dump to be overwritten until the number of days specified has passed. This is an important option for any production backup strategy.

There are several other options that focus on how the dump is to be conducted, irrespective of the physical device characteristics. Several of these options should be incorporated into your backup strategy.

The options in the next six sections apply only to tape devices.

DUMPVOLUME

The option Specify dumpvolume for production dumps labels your dump, which then can be specified during a load. For example, specify a dumpvolume of your database name and the date (CustomerDB_Jan07). Then, if you have dumps for January 7th through 10th on a single tape, you can easily reload the January 7th dump by specifying dumpvolume as part of the load.

DISMOUNT ¦ NODISMOUNT

The dismount ¦ nodismount option is valid only on platforms that support logical dismounts (OpenVMS). It determines whether the tape will be available for future dumps. By default, the dismount option is used. Specify nodismount to enable the tape to be used for subsequent dumps.

NOUNLOAD ¦ UNLOAD

Th nounload ¦ unload option controls the rewinding of the tape. nounload should be used unless this is the last dump you wish to have on the tape.

NOINIT ¦ INIT

The noinit ¦ init option determines whether the dump will be appended to the tape or reinitializes the entire tape volume. Use init when dumping to a tape for the first time or to reuse an old tape. You might use noinit to allow for multiple dumps to a single tape.

FILE = FILE_NAME

Use the file = file_name option to specify a filename of up to 17 characters in length. This option normally is not specified. By default, backup server names the file by concatenating the last seven characters from the database name, the two-digit year, the Julian day (1 through 366), and a hex representation of the time.

NOTIFY = {CLIENT ¦ OPERATOR_CONSOLE}

Volume change messages are sent, by default, to the operator console if available. If not, the messages are sent to the client initiating the request. You need to specify this parameter only if the default function is not desired. In UNIX systems, the messages are sent to the client. Specify operator_console to route the messages to the terminal on which backup server is running. For OpenVMS, the messages are sent to the operator console. Specify client to send the messages to the client where the dump was initiated.

The following is an example of striped dumps:

```
# Dump the CustomerDB database across 4 dump devices (Tape1-4).
# Name each volume, initialize the tapes, do not rewind,
# prevent other dumps from overwriting this dump for 2 weeks,
# and send the messages to the client terminal.
dump database CustomerDB to Tape1 dumpvolume = Volume1
     stripe on Tape2 dumpvolume = Volume2
     stripe on Tape3 dumpvolume = Volume3
     stripe on Tape4 dumpvolume = Volume4
     with init, nounload, retaindays=14, notify=client
```

This is an example of remote dumps:

```
# Dump the CustomerDB database across 2 remote devices on two
# different backup servers. Append to the tapes, do not rewind,
# prevent other dumps from overwriting this dump for 1 week
dump database CustomerDB to "/dev/nrmt0" at REMOTE_BACKUP1
     stripe on "/dev/nrmt0" at REMOTE_BACKUP2
     with noinit, nounload, retaindays=7
```

Here is an example of multiple dumps to a single tape:

```
# Dump the CustomerDB, ProductDB, and SecurityDB to Tape1
# For the first dump, initialize the tape but do not rewind.
# Dump the second database after the first.
# After the third database is dumped, rewind the tape.
```

```
# (Send the messages to the client terminal.)
dump database CustomerDB to Tape1 dumpvolume = CustVol1
    with init notify=client
dump database ProductDB to Tape1 dumpvolume = ProdVol1
    with notify=client      /* no unload is the default */
dump database SecurityDB to Tape1 dumpvolume = SecVol1
    with unload, notify=client
```

You can dump a database while the server is in use. It impacts performance to some degree. Striping dumps decreases the total amount of time required to execute the dump, decreasing the duration of the impact. Benchmark user response times with and without a dump process running to determine the impact on your system.

Dumping Database Logs

Use `dump transaction` to make a copy of the transactions that have occurred against your database since the last transaction log dump. This is the simplified syntax for the `dump transaction` command:

```
dump transaction databasename to devicename
```

This command is valid in all environments. In System 10, however, the options available to the `dump database` command are also available to the `dump transaction` command. Transaction log dumps can occur remotely, be striped across several devices, and have the same tape handling facilities. `dump transaction` also has a few other options used for special purposes. Here is the full format for the `dump transaction` command:

```
dump tran[saction] databasename
    {with { truncate_only ¦ no_log } ¦
    to stripe_device [ at backup_server_name ]
        [ density = density_value,
          blocksize = number_of_bytes,
          capacity = number_of_KB,
          dumpvolume = volume_name ]
    [ stripe on stripe_device ...]
    [ with {
        [ dismount ¦ nodismount ],
        [ nounload ¦ unload ],
        retaindays = number_of_days,
        [ noinit ¦ init ],
        file = file_name,
        no_truncate,
        [ notify = { client ¦ operator_console } ]
        }
    ]
    }
```

The special-purpose options are in bold letters. These options are `truncate_only`, `no_log`, and `no_truncate`.

TRUNCATE_ONLY AND NO_LOG

The truncate_only and no_log options are used to prune the transaction log without making a copy of it. As you can see from the format of the command, you either specify one of these options or indicate a device to which to dump the transaction log. Use truncate_only to truncate the log gracefully. It checkpoints the database before truncating the log. Use no_log when your transaction log is completely full. no_log does not checkpoint the database before dumping the log.

Either of these options throws away the log. Once the command has been executed, you are exposed. If a disaster occurs before you can dump the database, you will not be able to recover *any* data that has been added since the last dump. The frequency of dumping transaction logs determines the scope of your exposure.

Any database that does not have its transaction log on a separate device cannot dump the transaction. Every system has a database meeting this characteristic. This usually is discovered when the transaction log for the master database fills up.

Because master must fully reside on the master device, the database space is shared between data and log, negating the capability of dumping the transaction log.

To avoid this problem, periodically prune the transaction log with truncate_only (or no_log, if completely full). Make sure you dump the database after logged operations (database creation, user addition, and so forth). For databases that do not require up-to-the-minute recovery, and for databases with no separate log segment, set the trunc log on chkpt option on for the database and dump frequently.

NO_TRUNCATE

The no_truncate option is exactly opposite of the previous two options. no_truncate makes a copy of your transaction log, but *does not prune it*. Use this option when you have a media failure of a device being used by your database. *The master database must be available.* This option enables the server to dump the transaction log, but does not try to touch the database in any way. (In a normal dump tran, a checkpoint is executed. If a database device is unavailable, the checkpoint process cannot write the dirty pages. no_truncate simply backs up the transaction log, without checkpointing.)

Dumping the transaction log is disabled after nonlogged operations such as writetext, select into, and fast bcp. You can dump a transaction log while the server is in use. The impact on performance should be minimal. It is common to dump transaction logs even during normal business hours.

LOADING THE DATABASE

Use `load database` to load a backup into an existing database. The database can be the database used to create the dump, but this is definitely not a requirement. The simplified syntax for the `load database` command is the following:

```
load database databasename from devicename
```

This command is valid in all environments. Most options available to the `dump` command can be used in the `load`. This is the full format for the `load database` command:

```
load database databasename
    from stripe_device [ at backup_server_name ]
        [ density = density_value,
          blocksize = number_of_bytes,
          dumpvolume = volume_name ]
    [ stripe on stripe_device ...]
    [ with {
        [ dismount | nodismount ],
        [ nounload | unload ],
        file = file_name,
        listonly [ = full ],
        headeronly,
        [ notify = { client | operator_console } ]
        }
    ]
```

All options listed are identical to the `dump` command *except* for the `listonly` and `headeronly` options. If you specify either of these options, information is displayed but no data is loaded. Use these options *immediately after* a database dump to verify that the load process can read the dump. It can be used for tape or file devices.

LISTONLY

Use `listonly` to obtain a listing of all dump files on a tape volume. The output contains database name, device name, and date and time of the dump. The `= full` option provides additional information.

HEADERONLY

Use `headeronly` to display information about a single dump file. If the device specified is a tape device, information about only the first file on the dump is displayed, unless you specify the `file` parameter.

Note

No one can use the database while `load` is being executed, including the person executing the `load` command.

Here are some loading examples. The first shows striped loads:

```
# Load the CustomerDB database across 4 dump devices (Tape1-4).
# Indicate each volume, rewind the tape after the load, and notify
# the client terminal
load database CustomerDB from Tape1 dumpvolume = Volume1
    stripe on Tape2 dumpvolume = Volume2
    stripe on Tape3 dumpvolume = Volume3
    stripe on Tape4 dumpvolume = Volume4
    with unload, notify=client
```

The following is an example of using fewer devices to load:

```
# Load the CustomerDB database which was dumped across 4 devices
# with only 3 dump devices (Tape1-3).
# Indicate each volume, rewind the tape after the load, and notify
# the client terminal
load database CustomerDB from Tape1 dumpvolume = Volume1
    stripe on Tape2 dumpvolume = Volume2
    stripe on Tape3 dumpvolume = Volume3
    with unload, notify=client
```

Once the first three stripes have loaded, a message will be sent to the operator to load the fourth. After placing the fourth tape in the Tape2 device, execute:

```
load database CustomerDB from Tape1 dumpvolume = Volume4
    with unload, notify=client
```

The following is an example of striped remote loads:

```
# Load the CustomerDB database from 2 remote devices on two
# different backup servers. Rewind the tape upon completion.
load database CustomerDB from "/dev/nrmt0" at REMOTE_BACKUP1
    stripe on "/dev/nrmt0" at REMOTE_BACKUP2
    with unload
```

The load database command loads all used pages from the dump into the target database and runs recovery of syslogs to ensure consistency. Any unused pages are initialized by the load process. (This is the primary reason why a load can take significantly longer than a dump. The time required to dump a database is proportional to the used pages in the database; the time required to load a database is proportional to the overall number of pages in the database. Therefore, a 50GB database with 20MB of data may take only a few minutes to dump, but the load could take several hours or days.)

Dumps are conducted to be able to restore a database to a point in time. A load is executed to restore a database, normally after a corruption or user error occurs. If you are loading for a reason other than a disaster, the current database structure can be used to load the database dump. This does not require any extra work other than ensuring tapes are loaded (or files are in the correct locations).

RESTORING AFTER A DISASTER

If the load is a result of a disaster, the database must first be dropped. The `drop database` may not execute in the case of a corruption. For corrupt databases, use the `dbcc dbrepair` command:

```
dbcc dbrepair(database_name, dropdb)
```

A new structure must now be created. If you are creating a database for the exclusive purpose of loading, use the `for load` option to `create database`.

CREATING FOR LOAD

Creating a database for load allocates the structure but does not initialize the pages. Using this option takes *significantly* less time than a normal create. The database will not be usable except for running a `load`. The database must be created in the same fashion as the dumped database. For example, if you initially created the CustomerDB database with 1GB for data and 100MB for log and subsequently altered the database by 500MB for data, execute the following commands:

```
use master
go
create database CustomerDB on DataDevice1 = 1000,
    log on LogDevice1 = 200
    for load
go
alter database CustomerDB on DataDevice2 = 500 for load
go
load database CustomerDB from CustomerDB_dump
go
```

The easiest way to ensure the correct order is to save each `create` or `alter` command in a single create script as the commands are executed. If you have not saved your scripts, you can retrieve this information from the sysusages table in the master database:

```
select segmap, "Size in MB"=size/512
from sysusages
where dbid = db_id ("database_name")

segmap     Size in MB
3          1000
4          200
3          500
```

The `segmap` column refers to the segments defined in your database. Initially, there are three segments in your database: system, default, and logsegment. If you convert the segmap number to binary, you can determine how the segmap relates to segment names:

2^0 = system segment
2^1 = default segment

2^2 = logsegment
2^3 = first user-defined segment
2^4 = second user-defined segment

The segment mapping for the example database is the following:

```
              log   data  sys
segmap 2^3    2^2   2^1   2^0    size
3      0      0     1     1      1000
4      0      1     0     0      200
3      0      0     1     1      500
```

Therefore, a segmap of 3 indicates a data device (default + system), and a segmap of 4 indicates log only.

If you have added user-defined segments (and possibly dropped the default and system segments from a fragment), there are indicators in the 2^3 column and greater. These fragments should be created as data fragments. Because segments are database-specific, the database system tables containing the user-defined segment definitions are loaded in the load process, which resolves the segment mapping within the database.

Note

If you created your database with the log on a separate device, the log fragments should have a 1 in the log column (2^2) only.

LOADING INTO A DIFFERENT DATABASE

Occasionally, you may want to create an exact copy of a database in your system. First, dump the existing database. Then create a new database to load with this dump. The database does not have to be the same size as the original. The only requirement is that the destination database must be at least as large as the dumped database and have the same beginning fragments as the original database. For example, consider loading the dump from the previous database into a database of 3GB. The command to create this database might be the following:

```
use master
go
create database NewCustomerDB on DataDevice2 = 1000
     log on LogDevice2 = 200
     for load
go
alter database NewCustomerDB on DataDevice2 = 500 for load
go
alter database NewCustomerDB on DataDevice3 = 300 for load
go
alter database NewCustomerDB on DataDevice4 = 1000 for load
go
load database NewCustomerDB from CustomerDB_dump
go
```

Note

I've been told that the `create database ... for load` command will not work in System 10 under NetWare but have not tried it myself. It's always worth a try when you are restoring a database. At worst, the command will not work in your environment, meaning you will need to drop the new, corrupt database and try again.

Loading a Transaction

Use `load transaction` to load a transaction log backup. Transaction logs must be loaded in the order they were dumped. During a `load database`, the data in the dump is copied over the database. After the `load` is complete, the database contains all the data in the database at the time of the dump. The loading of a transaction log is different than loading a database. The transaction log load copies the contents of the dump over the current syslogs definition. Once the log has been loaded, a recovery takes place. The server marches through the log applying changes in the log that are not reflected in the database (normally, all records in the log are new transactions). The simplified syntax for the load database command is the following:

```
load transaction <databasename> from <devicename>
```

This command is valid in all environments. Most options available to the `dump` command can be used in the `load`. The full format for `load transaction` is:

```
load tran[saction] <databasename>
    from <stripe_device> [ at <backup_server_name> ]
        [ density = <density_value>,
          blocksize = <number_of_bytes<,
          dumpvolume = <volume_name> ]
    [ stripe on <stripe_device> ...]
    [ with {
        [ dismount ¦ nodismount ],
        [ nounload ¦ unload ],
        file = <file_name>,
        listonly [ = full ],
        headeronly,
        [ notify = { client ¦ operator_console } ]
        }
    ]
```

Most options listed are explained in the section titled "Dumping the Database" except for the `listonly` and `headeronly` options, which are explained in the section titled "Loading the Database."

Loading a transaction log dump requires significantly less time than loading a database because the log is normally much smaller than the database itself. No modifications can be made to the database between a `load database` and a `load transaction` (or between transaction log loads).

ADDITIONAL CONSIDERATIONS

The pieces of the puzzle are starting to fall in place. You have defined the groundwork necessary to begin development of your backup and recovery approach. Now you must consider several issues that can impact your plan.

AUTOMATIC BACKUPS

Sybase does not provide any facilities to automate the backup (or recovery) of your databases. Recovery is not usually automated due to the nature of recovery. You hope that recoveries are something you never have to perform. Recovery is normally performed when a catastrophe has occurred, and the setup necessary to begin a restoration *should* involve DBA interaction. Procedures should be developed to address recovery, but *do not* automate this procedure.

Backups, however, should be planned and scheduled. Investigate third-party tools once you have developed your backup plan. Off-the-shelf tools can automate backups, but may not address all the elements in your plan. If the tool does not have scripting extensions, it is to your advantage to develop your own facility.

Write my own facility? It is not as daunting as it sounds. Virtually all operating systems have scripting languages, and most have scheduling facilities (that is, UNIX crontab) or these facilities can be purchased. Scripts can range from simple (10 or 20 lines of code) to complex (1000+ lines of code). The scope varies based on the functionality, error checking, and reporting requirements. Consider the following simple UNIX script:

```
[text file - custdump.sql]
use master
go
select "Start Time"=getdate()
go
dump database CustomerDB to CustomerDB_dump
go
select "End Time"=getdate()
go

[shell script - custdump.ksh]
#!/usr/bin/ksh
isql -U oper_login -P oper_password -e < custdump.sql > custdump.out
[crontab entry]
# Dump the customer database every day at 10 PM
# Format is minutes, hour, year, month, day, script
# See your manual page for more information
# Minutes - 0 (on the hour)
# Hour - 22 (10 PM, military time)
# Year - * (every year)
# Month - * (every month)
# Day - * (every day)
# Script (full path) - /home/dba/scripts/custdump.ksh
0 10 * * * /home/dba/scripts/custdump.ksh
```

FREQUENCY OF DUMPS

As mentioned previously, dumps should be executed as frequently as necessary for effective database administration. This is intentionally vague, because the frequency of dumps varies based on your requirements. The true driver is *the duration of time your business can afford for the database to be unavailable after a disaster.*

The total time to restore a database is the sum of database load time plus the transaction log load time. The database load is atomic; it happens only once during a recovery of a database. The transaction log loads, however, are dynamic. The time to load transaction logs is based on the amount of activity since the database dump.

Consider the difference between a database dumped yearly versus a database dumped weekly, with transaction logs dumped every day between dumps for both. The yearly dump scenario has 364 transaction log dumps between database dumps; the weekly dump scenario has six transaction log dumps. If a disaster occurs on January 4, the time to recover in both cases is identical. Each scenario has a database load (January 1 database dump) and three transaction log loads (January 2, 3, and 4 transaction log dumps). Consider the worst case scenario, however. A yearly dump approach could result in having to load a full year's worth of activity, one day at a time. The weekly dump approach would have a maximum of only a week's worth of activity to load.

Therefore, dump your database as often as possible. Ideally, database dumps should occur with no activity on the system. Although this is not a requirement, it assures you that the dump contains the state of your database before *and after* your dump. If this is not possible, execute your dumps when activity is as light as possible.

Dumps can be executed during normal business hours, but will have an effect on the performance of your system. Database dumps in System 10 and later are much less devastating to performance than in earlier versions. This is due to code changes in the implementation of the database dump and increased speed of the process, the capability of striping dumps, and the implementation of backup server as a separate process from SQL Server.

Transaction log dumps are often scheduled during normal business hours, but low (or no) activity periods are obviously preferred. Dumping a transaction log takes significantly less time than a database dump, and the time required is based solely on the amount of data in the log (which is based on modifications since the last dump transaction). A backup plan for a production system should include transaction log dumps to provide up-to-the-minute recovery. Development environments normally do not dump transaction logs because this type of recovery is not needed. Fairly frequent database dumps usually suffice.

STRIPING DUMPS

Dumps can be striped across as many as 32 parallel devices in System 10 and later. This can significantly reduce the time required to dump or load your database or transaction logs.

In spite of the performance improvement, try to avoid striping. Each stripe can be considered a possible point of failure. If one of the stripes cannot be read, the load will fail. Consider striping when you decide the time required to dump to a single device is too great to fit the activity in your administration window.

LOCKING

The dump process locks pages differently in version 4.x than it does in later releases. In version 4.x, you cannot modify pages not yet read by the dump process. It is like a virtual shared lock on these pages—users can read but cannot write (insert, update, or delete).

Starting with System 10, the dump process consists of three distinct phases. During the first two portions, the dump process dumps all the used pages in your database (log first, data second). The third phase dumps the new log pages created by modifications during the first two phases. Any modifications that take place during this last activity are not reflected in the dump. This is a significant improvement over the version 4.x process because the dump process does not require a single, locked, consistent version of the database while running.

Note

Many administrators using version 4.x of SQL Server need a database dump that includes transactions occurring during the dump itself (like System 10 and 11 database dumps provide automatically). To do that, dump the transaction log immediately after the database dump is complete.

CAPTURING STATISTICS

Capture as many statistics as possible about the dump and load processes. It will be invaluable in estimating durations and give you real statistics about the performance of your system. Here are important statistics to gather:

- ◆ Total database size (`sp_helpdb`)
- ◆ Total number of used pages (for information about `sp_spaceused`, see Chapter 5, "Defining, Altering, and Maintaining Databases and Logs")
- ◆ Total execution time (wrap the `dump` or `load` command with `select getdate()`)

For dumps, the time to execute is fairly linear based on used pages. For loads, the time to execute is based on total database size and used pages.

You need to understand and monitor database size and usage when planning backup regimens for databases that have not leveled off in size. During the early stages of a system, data volume can be low. Data is added over time. This increase levels off once your purge and archive criteria kick in.

For example, a 15GB database may be created to support your production system. Initially, it may be loaded with only 2GB of base information (used pages). If your application adds 5GB of data each year and data is purged when it is two years old, the database size levels off at 12GB. Your statistics may show that the 2GB database dumps in one hour. If you have a four-hour dump window, you have to start investigating alternative approaches once your database reaches 8GB. By capturing statistics, you would be able to forecast this problem *a full year* in advance.

CONFIGURING TAPE EXPIRATION

The `retaindays` option to the `dump` command is not the only way to prevent your tapes from being overwritten. Use the `tape retention` configuration option to set a default retention value:

```
/* Configure the default retention to 3 weeks */
use master
go
sp_configure "tape retention", 21
go
reconfigure
go
```

This value is initially set to 0, which enables tapes to be overwritten by default. Note that the `retaindays` option to the `dump` command overrides the configuration value.

TRANSACTION LOGGING

It is important to prevent the transaction log from running out of space. When the transaction log fills, no other logged operations can be executed until space is available in the log. This is disastrous in production systems. In version 4.x, however, it was a fairly common experience. The DBA was forced to pay close attention to the available space in the log, executing a `dump transaction` before the log ran out of space.

Over time, database activity stabilizes and can be estimated. You should know the amount of time your system can be active, under normal conditions, before the transaction log completely fills. Based on the amount, schedule transaction log dumps often enough to prevent this situation from occurring. (Dump transaction logs when they are about one-half to three-quarters full.)

Even though you may have the `dump transaction` activities scheduled, the system may experience peak activities (end of quarter, fiscal year end, and so forth) that cause the log to fill at a greatly accelerated rate. Version 4.*x* users are still forced to monitor the log to be proactive. System 10 users can use the threshold facility to set an indicator to automate the monitoring of available space.

MONITORING AVAILABLE LOG SPACE

Sybase offers the following two tools to monitor space availability. Use either to get a report on the syslogs table.

- ◆ sp_spaceused
- ◆ dbcc checktable

sp_spaceused checks the reserved column to see how many pages are in use. Relate this to your overall log size to determine availability.

dbcc checktable checks each page in a table and provides an accurate reporting of the number of data pages used. As with sp_spaceused, relate this value to overall log size to determine availability. If your log is on a separate device, the output is easier to analyze. It reports statistics regarding space used and space free in megabytes as well as percentage:

```
dbcc checktable (syslogs)
```

Thresholds are an excellent facility that should be exploited. Make sure you create sp_thresholdaction to minimize the possibility of completely filling the log. Always create a threshold on the default segment. The default segment can (by default) use any nonlog fragment in the database. Therefore, a default threshold reports on available database space in most cases. If you use user-defined segments, thresholds are also a must. Stage your thresholds to provide increasingly harsh messages and review your errorlog daily. By following these suggestions, you may never run out of space again!

DEVELOPING YOUR BACKUP AND RECOVERY PLAN

Consider *all* your databases when developing the backup and recovery plan. System databases have different requirements than user databases.

SYSTEM DATABASES

There are four system databases created as part of server installation: master, model, tempdb, and sybsystemprocs (three for version 4.*x*—no sybsystemprocs).

tempdb is temporary and by definition is exempt from backups. All other system databases should be backed up, however.

THREATS

There are two things to watch out for with system databases:

◆ Database or table corruption

◆ Damage to the master device

If a corruption occurs, follow the steps to rebuild that individual database. If the master device is damaged, it has to be reinitialized. This affects the master, model, tempdb, and possibly the sybsystemprocs databases (which can exist on the master device or an alternate device).

MASTER

The master database is not a high-activity database. It is fairly small and is created on the master device with a default allocation of about 18MB. This size is adequate for most small installations, but the requirements of larger installations quickly mandate an increase in size. Because it is on a single device, data and log compete for available space and the transaction log cannot be dumped. It cannot grow beyond the confines of the master device.

The following activities result in the insertion or modification of rows in various system tables:

◆ Creating, altering, or dropping the database

◆ Using `disk init`

◆ Adding or dropping logins or users

◆ Adding or dropping dump devices

◆ Adding servers

Because master controls the server, a database corruption or the loss of the master device can be devastating. The server is unavailable until the master database is repaired. Not having a current backup of master can be fatal (or at least quite painful). *Back up the master database whenever commands are executed that insert, update, or delete rows in the system tables*. It cannot be stressed enough how important the backup of this database is. Trying to re-create master from scratch can be extremely difficult, especially if you have not saved the data from the system tables.

Note

The master database has no separate log segment, so all backups are full database dumps.

DETECTING THE PROBLEM

If you lose the master device, the server goes down alerting you to the problem. The normal method of detecting corruption in any database is the suite of dbcc commands. If a corruption does occur in master, the system likely will be affected instantaneously. Often, the server goes down and does not come up, or major errors appear in the errorlog (page faults, I/O errors, and so forth).

Tip

If a dbcc detects corruption in master, log a call to Sybase Technical Support. Corruption in model or sybsystemprocs may not be as serious on the surface, but could be indicative of a problem with the underlying master device. If you are confident you can solve the problem yourself, start executing the steps in the recovery process.

You must be proactive to avoid a painful recovery. First of all, avoid striping the master database dumps, even if it is a standard for your user databases. Make sure all the master dump can fit on a single tape or in an operating system file. (Based on the normal size of the master database, this should not be a problem.) SQL Server must be started in single-user mode to start the recovery process. If the load requires a volume change, you cannot open another connection to tell backup server that the new tape is in place.

MITIGATING THE RISK

Master should be dumped regularly, probably on the same schedule as your user databases. If you make a change and you don't want to wait for the backup scripts to run, execute it by hand. As always, you should have scripts saved for every activity that modifies master. To be extra safe, bulk copy the data from the following files:

- sysdatabases
- sysdevices
- sysusages
- syslogins
- sysloginroles

You may have to reinitialize master using `buildmaster -m`. (See Chapter 16, "Tools for Sybase Administrators," for detailed information about this command.) At the completion of this command, you will have the vanilla master created when you install SQL Server. At this point, master has no knowledge of any user databases in your system, including sybsystemprocs. You have to execute one of the following:

- Loading your *current* master backup (preferred)
- Transferring the data, using `isql` or `bcp`
- Re-creating items from DDL scripts

You should have all the resources to undertake any of these approaches at any time. It is the only way to ensure that the master database (and the server) will be available when you need it.

MODEL

The model database is copied into any database created with `create database`. It houses those items you want available across all databases (rules, defaults, user-defined datatypes, and users). If you have made any modifications to model, save all DDL files and back up the database after changes are made.

If you detect corruption only in the model database, re-create it using the `-x` option to `buildmaster` (make sure you shut down the SQL Server first). The end result is the vanilla model database. Run `dbccs` to ensure the corruption no longer exists. If you still find corruption after re-creating model, call Sybase Technical Support. It likely is a problem with the master device. If model is free of corruption and you have not made any changes, the recovery process is complete. If you have made modifications to model, reload it from backup or rerun your DDL scripts.

SYBSYSTEMPROCS

If sybsystemprocs exists, check to see whether you can execute system stored procedures (run `sp_who`). If you are unable to use it, drop the database and re-create the structure (at least 10MB). After the structure is in place, load the backup (if you have one) or run `installmaster`:

```
isql -Usa -P < installmaster
```

This loads the Sybase-provided system stored procedures. If you have created any of your own, reload the DDL files.

USER DATABASES

Your business requirements define whether a database should be backed up. Backups are normally a requirement for production systems. Your approach should define the following:

- *Who?* Identify the person or group responsible for backup and recovery.
- *Name?* Outline your naming standards for database names and dump devices.
- *Which databases?* Identify the databases in your system to be backed up.
- *Types of dumps?* Identify whether you will dump the database only or whether you also will dump the transaction log.
- *How?* Identify whether dumps will use disk or file devices and whether the dump is a single process or striped.
- *Frequency?* Identify the schedule for dumping the database and the transaction logs.
- *Execution?* Determine whether dumps will be initiated by hand or automated. If automated, detail whether it is conducted by an off-the-shelf tool or custom developed. Include all code (dump script and scheduler, if applicable) and make sure it is commented extremely well.

For database recovery, detail the procedures involved in loading each database. If using a tool, outline its use.

VLDB CONSIDERATIONS

When developing a backup and recovery plan for VLDB environments, several items must be considered. The challenge of a VLDB is its sheer size—everything is larger. Tables are measured in gigabytes, and databases are measured in tens or hundreds of gigabytes. The fact that several Sybase VLDBs exist in industry today gives credence to the product's capability of handling vast amounts of data. VLDBs are not easy to implement, however, for a variety of reasons. Here are the top 10 VLDB issues:

1. Impact of corruption
2. Time for recovery
3. Time of backups
4. Time to perform initial load of data
5. Time to update statistics of indexes
6. Time to perform database consistency checks
7. Time to create indexes

8. Impact of incremental batch data loading routines

9. Impact of online activity

10. Backup media capacity and backup facilities

Based on these items, you need to make several database architecture choices. These choices include the following:

◆ Physically implementing a single logical database as several smaller physical databases

◆ Segmenting tables horizontally and/or vertically

◆ Table or index placement

◆ Log size and placement

◆ tempdb size and placement

Let's consider the issues list in regard to your choices. The time required to perform database dumps, loads, update of statistics, and creation of indexes increases linearly with size. Follow these steps:

1. First, consider the amount of time you are willing to be "down" while performing a recovery (impact of corruption). If you need a database to be recovered within eight hours, determine the size of a database that can be recovered in that amount of time. Note that the load process is much slower than the dump process. Assume that 4GB is the maximum database size that can be reloaded in the defined window.

2. Taking 4GB as a baseline, analyze table estimates for your database. If you have a 40GB logical database, you may need to implement 10 4GB databases. Are any tables greater than 4GB? How many tables can you fit in a database? Are any tables candidates for segmentation based on this determination alone?

3. Develop your utopian administration schedule. For every day during a month, determine what periods of time can be dedicated to administrative activities. Weekends might be available, but this is not always the case. If you determine that you have five hours per night to perform administrative activities, you then need to determine what activities need to be completed and whether they can be distributed over your available administration time.

4. Determine the rate of the dump process. Take into consideration backup media capacity, speed, and number. Benchmark several scenarios. Create a database and load with about 2GB of data. Perform several database dumps, a varying number of dump devices (striped dumps), and a number of dump processes that can occur in parallel.

5. Determine periodic activity timings for each of your tables. This should be a matrix with table names down one axis and activities (dbcc, update statistics, index creation) across the other axis. Once you develop a baseline for these activities, you easily can group tables together to determine the total amount of administration time needed for a certain combination of tables.

6. Determine which activities must take place in a batch window. If you want to perform database consistency checks immediately prior to dumping a database, the time required to perform both activities can be determined from your timings. Assume a dump takes three hours and a dbcc takes two hours. Although this fits in your five-hour window, it does not consider the fact that you have 10 of these to complete during the course of a week. Perform activities in parallel to determine concurrent processing times. Can you dbcc and dump two databases in a five-hour period?

7. Finalize your schedule and document accordingly.

SUMMARY

Development of a backup and recovery approach is not a trivial process. You must consider internal and external forces and determine their impact. In the end, you should document your approach so it is clear how you plan to handle these activities. Make sure to gather statistics on all activities, and use those statistics to predict future performance.

Although building a good backup and recovery plan seems like a tremendous amount of work, it is worth it in the long run. Project plans must allocate time to create the plan and it should be in place *before* you make your production database available.

- Using sp_configure in System 10 and Earlier

- System 11 Configuration Changes

- SQL Server Configuration Options

- Configuration Variables That Require Substantial Memory

CHAPTER 9

Configuring and Tuning the SQL Server

SQL Server contains a number of user-definable configuration parameters that control its behavior. In this chapter, you will look at these configuration parameters and examine the aspects of SQL Server that they control, their defaults, and the range of values for which they can be configured. Chapter 10, "Optimizing SQL Server Configuration Options," looks more in depth at those configuration parameters that have the greatest impact on performance and provides guidelines for tuning them to optimize SQL Server performance.

USING *SP_CONFIGURE* IN SYSTEM 10 AND EARLIER

You can view the configuration settings and change the SQL Server configuration with the sp_configure stored procedure. The syntax for sp_configure for SQL Server version 10.*x* and earlier is as follows:

```
sp_configure [option [, value]]
```

The sp_configure stored procedure, when executed without any parameters, lists all options for the current version of SQL Server. For example, the following sp_configure output is from a System 10 SQL Server running on Windows NT:

```
sp_configure
go
```

name	minimum	maximum	config_value	run_value
recovery interval	1	32767	0	5
allow updates	0	1	0	0
user connections	5	2147483647	0	25
memory	3850	2147483647	0	4096
open databases	5	2147483647	0	12
locks	5000	2147483647	0	5000
open objects	100	2147483647	0	500
procedure cache	1	99	0	20
fill factor	0	100	0	0
time slice	50	1000	0	100
database size	2	10000	0	2
tape retention	0	365	0	0
recovery flags	0	1	0	0
nested triggers	0	1	1	1
devices	4	256	0	10
remote access	0	1	1	1
remote logins	0	2147483647	0	20
remote sites	0	2147483647	0	10
remote connections	0	2147483647	0	20
pre-read packets	0	2147483647	0	3
upgrade version	0	2147483647	1002	1002
default sortorder id	0	255	40	40
default language	0	2147483647	0	0
language in cache	3	100	3	3
max online engines	1	32	1	1

parameter name	minimum	maximum	config_value	run_value
min online engines	1	32	1	1
engine adjust interval	1	32	0	0
cpu flush	1	2147483647	200	200
i/o flush	1	2147483647	1000	1000
default character set id	0	255	2	2
stack size	20480	2147483647	0	28672
password expiration interval	0	32767	0	0
audit queue size	1	65535	100	100
additional netmem	0	2147483647	0	0
default network packet size	512	524288	0	512
maximum network packet size	512	524288	0	512
extent i/o buffers	0	2147483647	0	0
identity burning set factor	1	9999999	5000	5000

(38 rows affected)

To see the setting for a specific configuration parameter, pass the name of the parameter, or a substring of the name that can uniquely identify the parameter, to sp_configure. For example, to see the current setting for additional netmem, you can issue either this command:

```
sp_configure "additional netmem"
```

or this:

```
sp_configure "netmem"
```

The descriptions of the columns in the output are as follows:

- ◆ parameter name is the description of the variable.
- ◆ minimum is the minimum allowable configuration setting.
- ◆ maximum is the theoretical maximum value to which the configuration option can be set. Note that the actual maximum value is going to be dependent on the platform and resources available to SQL Server.
- ◆ config_value reflects the value in the sysconfigures table.
- ◆ run_value reflects the value in the syscurconfigs table.

THE SYSCONFIGURES AND SYSCURCONFIGS TABLES

The sysconfigures and syscurconfigs tables store the configuration parameters. When the server comes up, the values in the permanent table, sysconfigures, are copied into the memory-only table, syscurconfigs. Note that not all the values are necessarily going to be the same between sysconfigures and syscurconfigs. The sysconfigures table stores the current configuration settings as set by sp_configure. The syscurconfigs table stores the values with which the SQL Server is currently running.

A list of all configuration options, with their maximum and minimum values, are stored in spt_values, a lookup table in the master database. Rows related to configuration values in spt_values are marked with a type of 'C'.

SETTING CONFIGURATION VALUES

To set a configuration option with sp_configure, provide both the option name and the value to which you want to set it. You must be a system administrator to modify configuration settings. A user with the sso_role can execute sp_configure to modify security-related options such as password expiration and audit queue size.

The following example sets the recovery interval to seven minutes:

```
sp_configure "recovery interval", 7
```

To make the configuration options take effect, you need to run the reconfigure command, which performs a sanity check on the modifications to the configuration settings and installs the changes. The syntax is as follows:

```
reconfigure [with override]
```

The with override option is necessary if you want to force the SQL Server to accept configuration options it deems invalid (such as configuring more user connections than you have available memory to support) or when you want to force the SQL Server to enable updates to the system tables.

If for some reason, you manage to change the configuration options in such a way that the SQL Server will not start up anymore, you have to run the buildmaster command (at the operating system level) with the -r option. This resets the configuration parameters to the defaults.

SYSTEM 11 CONFIGURATION CHANGES

Sybase has made a number of improvements for managing the SQL Server configuration in System 11. To begin with, there are a number of additional configuration parameters available to better fine-tune the behavior and performance of SQL Server. The configuration options are also now grouped into logically related sets to make it easier to manage and view configuration options.

You no longer need to issue the reconfigure command when you run sp_configure to change configuration settings. sp_configure itself validates and installs configuration changes. The reconfigure command still exists for compatibility with pre-System 11 script files, but performs no action.

The primary change in System 11 is that now the configuration settings are stored in an external ASCII text file. This provides a number of benefits, as you shall soon see.

VIEWING CONFIGURATION SETTINGS IN SYSTEM 11

The sp_configure command is still used in System 11 to view and change configuration settings. When executed without any parameters, sp_configure displays all current configuration settings:

Group: Configuration Options

Group: Backup/Recovery

Parameter Name	Default	Memory Used	Config Value	Run Value
allow remote access	1	0	1	1
print recovery information	0	0	0	0
recovery interval in minutes	5	0	5	5
tape retention in days	0	0	0	0

Group: Cache Manager

Parameter Name	Default	Memory Used	Config Value	Run Value
memory alignment boundary	2048	0	2048	2048
number of index trips	0	0	0	0
number of oam trips	0	0	2	2
procedure cache percent	20	19958	5	5
total data cache size	0	365616	0	365616
total memory	7500	409600	204800	204800

Group: Disk I/O

Parameter Name	Default	Memory Used	Config Value	Run Value
allow sql server async i/o	1	0	1	1
disk i/o structures	256	33	256	256
number of devices	10	#30	75	75
page utilization percent	95	0	95	95

Group: General Information

Parameter Name	Default	Memory Used	Config Value	Run Value
configuration file	0	0	0	/sybase/SYB

Group: Languages

Parameter Name	Default	Memory Used	Config Value	Run Value
default character set id	1	0	1	1
default language id	0	0	0	0
default sortorder id	50	0	50	50
number of languages in cache	3	4	3	3

Group: Lock Manager

Parameter Name	Default	Memory Used	Config Value	Run Value
address lock spinlock ratio	100	0	100	100
deadlock checking period	500	0	1000	1000
freelock transfer block size	30	0	30	30
max engine freelocks	10	0	10	10
number of locks	5000	4688	50000	50000
page lock spinlock ratio	100	0	100	100
table lock spinlock ratio	20	0	20	20

Group: Memory Use

Parameter Name	Default	Memory Used	Config Value	Run Value
additional network memory	0	150	153600	153600
audit queue size	100	42	100	100
default network packet size	512	#248	512	512
disk i/o structures	256	33	256	256
event buffers per engine	100	#1172	3000	3000
executable codesize + overhead	0	4919	0	4919
max number network listeners	15	1202	15	15
max online engines	1	1661	4	4
number of alarms	40	1	40	40
number of devices	10	#30	75	75
number of extent i/o buffers	0	1605	100	100
number of languages in cache	3	4	3	3
number of locks	5000	4688	50000	50000
number of mailboxes	30	1	30	30
number of messages	64	1	64	64
number of open databases	12	395	12	12
number of open objects	500	512	500	500
number of remote connections	20	33	20	20
number of remote logins	20	22	20	20
number of remote sites	10	801	10	10
number of user connections	25	7989	100	100
partition groups	1024	21	1024	1024
permission cache entries	15	#63	15	15
procedure cache percent	20	19958	5	5
remote server pre-read packets	3	#32	3	3
stack guard size	4096	#568	4096	4096
stack size	36864	#5113	36864	36864
total data cache size	0	365616	0	365616
total memory	7500	409600	204800	204800

Group: Network Communication

Parameter Name	Default	Memory Used	Config Value	Run Value
additional network memory	0	150	153600	153600
allow remote access	1	0	1	1
default network packet size	512	#248	512	512
max network packet size	512	0	4096	4096
max number network listeners	15	1202	15	15

number of remote connections	20	33	20	20
number of remote logins	20	22	20	20
number of remote sites	10	801	10	10
remote server pre-read packets	3	#32	3	3
tcp no delay	0	0	0	0

Group: O/S Resources

Parameter Name	Default	Memory Used	Config Value	Run Value
max async i/os per engine	2147483647	0	2147483647	2147483647
max async i/os per server	2147483647	0	2147483647	2147483647
o/s asynch i/o enabled	0	0	0	0
o/s file descriptors	0	0	0	2000
tcp no delay	0	0	0	0

Group: Physical Resources

Group: Physical Memory

Parameter Name	Default	Memory Used	Config Value	Run Value
additional network memory	0	150	153600	153600
lock shared memory	0	0	0	0
shared memory starting address	0	0	0	0
total memory	7500	409600	204800	204800

Group: Processors

Parameter Name	Default	Memory Used	Config Value	Run Value
max online engines	1	1661	4	4
min online engines	1	0	1	1

Group: SQL Server Administration

Parameter Name	Default	Memory Used	Config Value	Run Value
allow nested triggers	1	0	1	1
allow updates to system tables	0	0	1	1
audit queue size	100	42	100	100
cpu accounting flush interval	200	0	200	200
cpu grace time	500	0	500	500
deadlock retries	5	0	5	5
default database size	2	0	2	2
default fill factor percent	0	0	0	0
event buffers per engine	100	#1172	3000	3000
housekeeper free write percent	1	0	1	1
i/o accounting flush interval	1000	0	1000	1000
i/o polling process count	10	0	10	10
identity burning set factor	5000	0	5000	5000
identity grab size	1	0	1	1
lock promotion HWM	200	0	200	200

```
lock promotion LWM              200        0      200      200
lock promotion PCT              100        0      100      100
number of alarms                40        1       40       40
number of extent i/o buffers     0     1605      100      100
number of mailboxes             30        1       30       30
number of messages              64        1       64       64
number of open databases        12      395       12       12
number of open objects         500      512      500      500
number of pre-allocated extent   2        0        2        2
number of sort buffers           0        0      800      800
partition groups              1024       21     1024     1024
partition spinlock ratio        10        0       10       10
print deadlock information       0        0        0        0
runnable process search count    3        0        3        3
size of auto identity column    10        0       10       10
sort page count                  0        0      160      160
sql server clock tick length 100000       0   100000   100000
time slice                     100        0      100      100
upgrade version               1100        0     1100     1100
```

Group: User Environment

PARAMETER Name	Default	Memory Used	Config Value	Run Value
default network packet size	512	#248	512	512
number of pre-allocated extent	2	0	2	2
number of user connections	25	7989	100	100
permission cache entries	15	#63	15	15
stack guard size	4096	#568	4096	4096
stack size	36864	#5113	36864	36864
systemwide password expiration	0	0	0	0
user log cache size	2048	0	2048	2048
user log cache spinlock ratio	20	0	20	20

The descriptions of the columns in the output are as follows:

◆ Parameter Name is the description of the variable.

◆ Default is the default configuration value.

◆ Memory Used displays the amount of memory (in kilobytes) required by the parameter at its current setting.

◆ Config Value reflects the value in the sysconfigures table—the most recent value to which the option has been set.

◆ Run Value reflects the value in the syscurconfigs table—the value with which the SQL Server is currently running.

Notice how the output is now displayed in logical groups. The sp_configure command will still take a single parameter name to view the settings, or optionally, you can specify a group name to display all the configuration settings for a group. For example, to see all configuration settings related to "user environment", execute the following:

```
sp_configure "user environment"
```

When viewing configuration settings, you can set the level of detail that SQL Server displays by using the sp_displaylevel command. There are three levels of display: basic, intermediate, or comprehensive. The default level is comprehensive, which displays all configuration options. basic shows just the most basic configuration options, those appropriate for general server tuning. The syntax for sp_displaylevel is as follows:

```
sp_displaylevel login_name [,"basic" ¦ "intermediate" ¦ "comprehensive"]
```

CHANGING CONFIGURATION SETTINGS

There are two ways to modify configuration settings in System 11. You can use the sp_configure command as in previous releases, or you can edit the configuration file directly by using your favorite text editor.

When you run sp_configure in System 11, it now updates sysconfigures and syscur-configs if it is a dynamic option and writes the change to the configuration file. The configuration file is typically located in the Sybase home directory. Each time you make a modification with sp_configure, a new copy of the configuration file is generated. The configuration file with the suffix of .cfg is the file that SQL Server will use on startup. Previous versions are stored using the naming convention of *filename.001*, *filename.002*, and so forth.

The advantages of having an external configuration file include the following:

◆ The ability to replicate standard configurations across multiple servers by simply copying the configuration file.

◆ The ability to create multiple configuration files and switch between them on SQL Server startup as your resource needs change (for example, DSS versus OLTP).

◆ If SQL Server won't start, you can modify the offending option in the configuration file and try again.

◆ The ability to set up a sample configuration in a configuration file and use sp_configure to validate it without having to set the values in SQL Server.

USING CONFIGURATION FILES WITH *SP_CONFIGURE*

The syntax for using configuration files with sp_configure is as follows:

```
sp_configure "configuration file", 0, "action", "filename"
```

The "configuration file" parameter specifies that sp_configure is to take an action on a configuration file. The 0 is included for backward compatibility with sp_configure (it's the position of the value parameter for the normal option setting). The "filename" parameter specifies the full pathname of the configuration file on which you want to take one of the following four actions:

◆ `verify` performs a validation check on the configuration file.

◆ `read` performs a validation check on parameters in the file and loads those that pass validation into SQL Server.

◆ `write` creates a configuration file, using the specified filename, based on the currently running values. If the file already exists, a message is written to the error log and the existing file is renamed.

◆ `restore` creates a new file with the values in the sysconfigures table.

The following example verifies the configuration file called test.cfg:

```
sp_configure "configuration file", 0, "verify", "$SYBASE/test.cfg"
```

EDITING CONFIGURATION FILES DIRECTLY

The configuration file is an ASCII file that can be edited by using any text editor that can save the file in ASCII format. The format for each parameter in the file is the following:

```
parameter_name={value ¦ default}
```

If `default` is specified, SQL Server applies the default configuration setting for that parameter.

When hand-editing a configuration file, there is no way to validate the settings until you restart the SQL Server. It is recommended that you use the `sp_configure` command to verify changes to a configuration file prior to shutting down SQL Server.

The following shows an example of the contents of a configuration file:

```
##########################################################################
#
#             Configuration File for the Sybase SQL Server
#
#             Please read the System Administration Guide (SAG)
#             before changing any of the values in this file.
#
##########################################################################

[Configuration Options]

[General Information]

[Backup/Recovery]
        recovery interval in minutes = DEFAULT
        print recovery information = DEFAULT
        tape retention in days = DEFAULT
```

```
[Cache Manager]
        number of oam trips = 2
        number of index trips = DEFAULT
        procedure cache percent = 5
        memory alignment boundary = DEFAULT

[Named Cache:default data cache]
        cache size = DEFAULT
        cache status = default data cache

[16K I/O Buffer Pool]
        pool size = 100.0000M
        wash size = DEFAULT

[Named Cache:lookup_01]
        cache size = 2M
        cache status = mixed cache

[Named Cache:syslog_01]
        cache size = 2.00M
        cache status = log only

[4K I/O Buffer Pool]
        pool size = 512.0000K
        wash size = DEFAULT

[Named Cache:system_tables_01]
        cache size = 1.00M
        cache status = log only

[Named Cache:temp_db]
        cache size = 50M
        cache status = log only

[Disk I/O]
        allow sql server async i/o = DEFAULT
        disk i/o structures = DEFAULT
        page utilization percent = DEFAULT
        number of devices = 75

[Network Communication]
        default network packet size = DEFAULT
        max network packet size = 4096
        remote server pre-read packets = DEFAULT
        number of remote connections = DEFAULT
        allow remote access = DEFAULT
        number of remote logins = DEFAULT
        number of remote sites = DEFAULT
        max number network listeners = DEFAULT
        tcp no delay = DEFAULT

[O/S Resources]
        max async i/os per engine = DEFAULT
        max async i/os per server = DEFAULT

[Physical Resources]
```

```
[Physical Memory]
        total memory = 204800
        additional network memory = 153600
        lock shared memory = DEFAULT
        shared memory starting address = DEFAULT

[Processors]
        max online engines = 4
        min online engines = DEFAULT

[SQL Server Administration]
        number of open objects = DEFAULT
        number of open databases = DEFAULT
        audit queue size = DEFAULT
        default database size = DEFAULT
        identity burning set factor = DEFAULT
        allow nested triggers = DEFAULT
        allow updates to system tables = 1
        print deadlock information = DEFAULT
        default fill factor percent = DEFAULT
        number of mailboxes = DEFAULT
        number of messages = DEFAULT
        number of alarms = DEFAULT
        number of pre-allocated extents = DEFAULT
        event buffers per engine = 3000
        cpu accounting flush interval = DEFAULT
        i/o accounting flush interval = DEFAULT
        sql server clock tick length = DEFAULT
        runnable process search count = DEFAULT
        i/o polling process count = DEFAULT
        time slice = DEFAULT
        deadlock retries = DEFAULT
        cpu grace time = DEFAULT
        number of sort buffers = 800
        sort page count = 160
        number of extent i/o buffers = 100
        size of auto identity column = DEFAULT
        identity grab size = DEFAULT
        lock promotion HWM = DEFAULT
        lock promotion LWM = DEFAULT
        lock promotion PCT = DEFAULT
        housekeeper free write percent = DEFAULT
        partition groups = DEFAULT
        partition spinlock ratio = DEFAULT

[User Environment]
        number of user connections = 100
        stack size = DEFAULT
        stack guard size = DEFAULT
        systemwide password expiration = DEFAULT
        permission cache entries = DEFAULT
        user log cache size = DEFAULT
        user log cache spinlock ratio = DEFAULT

[Lock Manager]
        number of locks = 50000
        deadlock checking period = 1000
        freelock transfer block size = DEFAULT
```

```
max engine freelocks = DEFAULT
address lock spinlock ratio = DEFAULT
page lock spinlock ratio = DEFAULT
table lock spinlock ratio = DEFAULT
```

SQL SERVER CONFIGURATION OPTIONS

There are two kinds of configurable values, dynamic and nondynamic. *Dynamic values* are those parameters that, when modified, take effect immediately. Some examples are `recovery interval`, `password expiration interval`, and `default language`. Any variables that are not explicitly dynamic will not take effect until the server is cycled (shut down and started up again). In the following review of the configuration settings, the dynamic variables are flagged with asterisks (*).

Note

Don't forget! You need to shut down and restart the SQL Server for nondynamic options (those without an asterisk) to take effect.

The configuration options in this section are grouped the same way that SQL Server groups them in System 11. Configuration options that are only available in System 11 will be noted. Also, many of the configuration options in System 11 and previous versions are the same, but the names have changed. For the sake of simplicity, and because the new names are more descriptive, we will use the configuration option names as they appear in System 11. For versions prior to System 11, refer to Table 9.1 to match the old names with the new.

TABLE 9.1. SYSTEM 10 CONFIGURATION OPTION NAMES VERSUS SYSTEM 11 CONFIGURATION OPTION NAMES.

System 10 Option Name	System 11 Option Name
recovery interval	recovery interval in minutes
allow updates	allow updates to system tables
user connections	number of user connections
memory	total memory
open databases	number of open databases
locks	number of locks
open objects	number of open objects
procedure cache	procedure cache percent
fill factor	default fill factor percent

continues

TABLE 9.1. CONTINUED

System 10 Option Name	System 11 Option Name
time slice	time slice
database size	default database size
tape retention	tape retention in days
recovery flags	print recovery information
nested triggers	allow nested triggers
devices	number of devices
remote access	allow remote access
remote logins	number of remote logins
remote sites	number of remote sites
remote connections	number of remote connections
pre-read packets	remote server pre-read packets
upgrade version	upgrade version
default sortorder id	default sortorder id
default language	default language id
language in cache	number of languages in cache
max online engines	max online engines
min online engines	min online engines
engine adjust interval	N/A
cpu flush	cpu accounting flush interval
i/o flush	i/o accounting flush interval
default character set id	default character set id
stack size	stack size
password expiration interval	systemwide password expiration
audit queue size	audit queue size
additional netmem	additional network memory
default network packet size	default network packet size
maximum network packet size	max network packet size
extent i/o buffers	number of extent i/o buffers
identity burning set factor	identity burning set factor

BACKUP AND RECOVERY GROUP

This set of parameters affects the operation of the dump and restore processes, as well as the way memory is configured.

ALLOW REMOTE ACCESS*

Units: 0 or 1 (flag)

Default: 1 (yes)

The `allow remote access` variable determines whether this server can communicate with another one. With System 10, it is imperative that you have this option turned on. The backup server is another server, so you cannot perform a backup without remote access. Only a login with the `sa_role` can modify `remote access` values. This option is only dynamic in System 10 and later versions.

PRINT RECOVERY INFORMATION

Units: 0 or 1 (flag)

Default: 0 (no)

If this option is turned on, at startup time the server will list in the error log detailed information on each individual transaction that is rolled forward or backward during the recovery process. If the option is off, only the database name and quantity of transactions rolled forward or backward are listed. Turning this option on can be helpful to determine which transactions may have been rolled back following a system crash.

RECOVERY INTERVAL IN MINUTES*

Units: Integer number of minutes

Default: 5

`recovery interval in minutes` is the maximum number of minutes per database that the server will take during the recovery process. This value affects how often the SQL Server checkpoints databases.

On SQL Server startup, the recovery process examines the transaction log to determine the oldest active transaction since the last time a checkpoint occurred in the database. A checkpoint synchronizes changes in the transaction log with the database on disk. The greater the number of records since the last checkpoint, the more transaction records that need to be processed by the recovery process to bring the log and database in sync before users can access the database.

It is a common misconception that the recovery interval is the number of minutes between checkpoints. This is simply not true. Rather, it is an estimate of the number of minutes recovery will take based on the number of records since the last checkpoint. SQL Server estimates it takes about one minute to recover 6,000 rows in the transaction log. Therefore, if the recovery interval remains set to the default value of five minutes, SQL Server will checkpoint the database when there are 30,000 records in the transaction log since the last checkpoint.

Notice that SQL Server doesn't take into consideration the type of transaction records in the log when estimating recovery time, only the number. Different types of transactions in the log could cause the recovery process to take substantially more or less time to complete recovery than that specified by the recovery interval in minutes setting.

Note

The checkpoint process "wakes up" approximately once a minute to examine the transaction log for each database to determine whether a checkpoint is required. If you have the trunc. log on chkpt. option on for a database, the checkpoint process automatically performs a checkpoint and truncates the log for that database each time it comes around to check the log.

TAPE RETENTION IN DAYS

Units: Integer days

Default: 0

When you attempt to overwrite a database or transaction log dump, the backup server checks to see how long ago this was dumped. The tape retention in days parameter is a safety feature that prevents you from overwriting your dumps prematurely. Operators may then manually override the retention time when they are prompted that there is a violation of the tape retention period, or by specifying the with init option when executing the dump command. You can also change the tape retention period for a particular dump by using the retaindays option on the dump command.

CACHE MANAGER GROUP

New for System 11, there exists more advanced configuration options for defining attributes for data and procedure cache.

MEMORY ALIGNMENT BOUNDARY

Units: Bytes in multiples of 2048

Default: 2048

memory alignment boundary sets the alignment boundaries for data caches. This parameter should be left alone unless you know that your machine performs I/O more efficiently on other boundaries. It should not be modified unless recommended by Sybase Technical Support.

NUMBER OF INDEX TRIPS*

Units: Integer number of trips

Default: 0

This is the number of times an index page traverses the MRU/LRU chain before it is considered for swapping out to make room available in cache for other pages. If you increase this value, index pages will stay in cache longer. You may want to adjust this value upward in DSS systems to increase the likelihood of finding index pages in cache.

Warning

Do not set this too high if your cache space is relatively small, because it may cause processes to time out waiting for cache space to become available. If you set it too low, index pages will be written to disk too often, which may result in poor performance.

NUMBER OF OAM TRIPS*

Units: Integer number of trips

Default: 0

This is the number of times OAM pages will traverse the MRU/LRU chain before being considered for aging out. OAM pages are used for controlling page allocation for tables and indexes. In systems that incur a significant amount of allocations (for example, large bulk copy operations), keeping OAM pages in cache longer will improve performance.

Warning

Do not set this too high if your cache space is relatively small, because it may cause processes to time out waiting for cache space to become available.

PROCEDURE CACHE PERCENT

Units: Integer percentage

Default: 20

Compiled stored procedure execution plans are stored in an area of memory called *procedure cache*. The balance of server memory, less that used by the server for its internal kernel and other variable elements, will be used by the server for data and procedure cache. The procedure cache percent configuration setting is the percentage of cache set aside for procedures. The larger the procedure cache, the more compiled plans can reside in memory.

At any given time, each user who executes a stored procedure needs his own executable procedure in cache. To establish an initial value for procedure cache, start by leaving enough room in cache to store at least one copy of your largest stored procedure for each concurrent user, plus a fudge factor. Here is an example:

100 concurrent users × 60KB (the largest stored procedure) = 6MB × 1.25 (fudge factor) = 8MB

Now you know how large to make the procedure cache, but the procedure cache percent setting doesn't require the size of the procedure cache; you need to indicate what percentage of cache should be set aside for procedures. If you have 50MB available for cache (run dbcc memusage to get available cache and procedure sizes), 8/50 = 16%. Note that if you use procedures heavily, you may want to increase cache capacity and also the percentage for procedures. For more information on configuring procedure cache for performance, see Chapter 10.

 ### *TOTAL DATA CACHE SIZE*

Units: N/A

Default: N/A

This is a calculated value that is not user-configurable. It represents the total amount of memory, based on the current configuration, that is available for data, index, and log pages.

TOTAL MEMORY

Units: Integer number of 2KB pages

Default: Varies depending on SQL Server platform

This is the most important configuration parameter you will tune. When the SQL Server comes up, it will request this amount of memory to be allocated from the operating system to SQL Server. If the allocation fails, the server will not come up, and an error is recorded in the error log.

The server needs this memory to manage devices, users, locks, databases, and objects. All the rest of the memory is used for cache. You can see how memory is used in dbcc memusage. Properly configuring memory to support SQL Server requirements and have enough available for sufficient data and procedure cache can have a large impact on performance. See Chapter 10 for a discussion on how to optimize your memory configuration.

DISK I/O GROUP

This section defines parameters that affect SQL Server's disk I/O behavior. Many parameters that were not easily accessible prior to System 11 can now be tuned. Modify these parameters cautiously.

ALLOW SQL SERVER ASYNC I/O

Units: Flag

Default: 1

This option enables SQL Server to run with asynchronous I/O. Both SQL Server and your operating system must have asynchronous I/O enabled.

Asynchronous I/O is almost always faster than synchronous I/O, unless you set up devices on block-oriented I/O operating system files. Using block I/O is *not* recommended, because SQL Server cannot guarantee data integrity in the event of a system crash.

DISK I/O STRUCTURES

Units: Control blocks

Default: 256

This is the number of disk I/O structures allocated on startup. This should be configured as high as your operating system allows to minimize the chance of running out of disk I/O structures (see your operating system documentation). Each user process will require its own disk I/O control block for SQL Server to initiate I/O request for that process.

NUMBER OF DEVICES

Units: Integer quantity less than 256

Default: 10

This is the number of database devices that may be initialized with the `disk init` command. Virtual device numbers must be unique and must be less than the configured value. Devices require 512 bytes each. The master device uses `vdevno` of `0`.

Warning

Do not set this value less than the number of defined devices. On restart, SQL Server will be unable to initiate I/O to any devices with device numbers higher than `number of devices`, and any databases on those devices will be marked suspect and made inaccessible.

System 11 ▶ *PAGE UTILIZATION PERCENT**

Units: Integer percentage

Default: 95

SQL Server compares the percentage of used-to-reserved (used plus unused) pages for a table, and if the `page utilization percent` setting is lower than the actual ratio, the Server allocates a new extent automatically instead of searching the OAM for free pages. A value of `100` instructs the server always to scan for free pages before allocating new extents. A lower `page utilization percent` setting will result in more unused pages. A high `page utilization percent` setting will result in slower page allocations for large tables.

Note

This parameter is ignored by `bcp`. `bcp` always allocates new extents until there are no more extents available in the database before it scans for free pages.

General Information Group

This group contains parameters that are not related to any specific behavior of SQL Server, and it currently contains only one configuration value.

CONFIGURATION FILE*

This parameter specifies the location of the configuration file currently in use.

◀ *System 11*

Languages Group

This section lists the parameters that enable you to define the default language, sort order, and character set for SQL Server.

DEFAULT CHARACTER SET ID

Units: Integer character set ID

Default: Varies depending on platform

This is the number of the default character set specified at installation time. This can be changed by the SQL Server installation utility.

DEFAULT LANGUAGE ID*

Units: Integer language ID

Default: 0 (us_english)

This is the default language in which messages will be displayed, unless you override the default when you add logins with sp_addlogin or change the default language with sp_modifylogin.

DEFAULT SORTORDER ID

Units: Integer sort order ID

Default: 50 (binary)

This displays the current sort order, but you cannot change this value with sp_configure. Your install utility provides a method for changing the server sort order. If you change your sort order, you will need to rebuild all indexes on the server manually, which is not necessarily a fast process.

The default value (50) provides the best performance for sorting and indexing data. Changing the sort order from binary causes approximately 10 percent overhead at sort/index creation times.

NUMBER OF LANGUAGES IN CACHE

Units: Integer quantity

Default: 3

This is the maximum number of languages that may be held in cache simultaneously.

LOCK MANAGER GROUP

This section contains the parameters that modify SQL Server locking behavior.

 ### ADDRESS LOCK SPINLOCK RATIO

Units: Integer ratio

Default: 100

This value specifies the number of rows in the address locks hash table (*hash buckets*) protected by one spinlock for SQL Servers running with multiple engines. A single-engine SQL Server uses only a single spinlock, because only that one engine can access the address locks hash table.

A spinlock is an internal locking mechanism that prevents a process from accessing a resource currently in use by another process (all processes must wait, or "spin," until the lock on the resource is released).

SQL Server manages the acquiring and releasing of address locks using an internal hash table. There are a maximum of 1,031 hash buckets, or rows, in this hash table. The default value for address lock spinlock ratio of 100 rows indicates that a maximum of 11 (1031/100) spinlocks can concurrently be held on the address locks hash table.

Theoretically, the lower this setting, the better performance should be, because it will allow more spinlocks and, therefore, less contention. However, the default value is appropriate for most systems.

 ### DEADLOCK CHECKING PERIOD*

Units: Integer number of milliseconds

Default: 500

This parameter specifies the number of milliseconds SQL Server waits to initiate a check for deadlocks for a process waiting for a lock to be released. Deadlock checking is a time-consuming process.

If you set this value higher, the deadlock checking overhead can be avoided if the lock request is granted before the waiting period expires. If you expect your applications will deadlock infrequently, you may see better performance by setting this value higher and avoiding the deadlock checking overhead for most processes. For more information on deadlocks and locking performance, see Chapter 13, "Basic Application Performance and Tuning."

FREELOCK TRANSFER BLOCK SIZE*

Units: Integer Number of Locks

Default: 30

This parameter specifies the number of locks moved from the global freelock list to an engine's freelock list when an engine runs out of locks.

On a multi-engine SQL Server, each engine has its own freelock list to satisfy lock requests. If the engine freelock list runs out of locks, SQL Server will move locks from the global freelock list to the engine freelock list. When the number of locks in the engine freelock list exceeds its maximum (see the next parameter, `max engine freelocks`), SQL Server will move locks from the engine freelock list back to the global freelock list to make them available to other engines.

Setting this value higher will reduce the number of transfers between engine freelock lists and the global freelock list, thereby minimizing contention for the global freelock list. A higher value, though, will result in a process accessing more lock structures than it needs. The default setting should be sufficient for most systems.

MAX ENGINE FREELOCKS*

Units: Integer percentage

Default: 10

This parameter sets the maximum number of locks available to the engine freelock lists as a percentage of total number of locks. The greater the number of freelocks available to an engine, the fewer times it needs to access the global freelock list.

Setting this value too high could result in having insufficient freelocks available in the global freelock list. If an engine cannot acquire freelocks because they are all being held by other engines, you may see error message 1279, which indicates that an engine ran out of available locks. When you see this message, you may need to decrease `max engine freelocks` or to increase `number of locks`.

NUMBER OF LOCKS

Units: Integer quantity

Default: 5000

This is the number of concurrent open locks that may be in simultaneous use. If you begin getting error messages that locks are unavailable, you may need to bump up the number of available locks by a thousand or two—the memory cost is very low (72 bytes per lock). However, before arbitrarily increasing the number of locks, you may first want to determine why your user processes are acquiring so many locks and see whether they can be rewritten to minimize locks.

PAGE LOCK SPINLOCK RATIO

Units: Ratio

Default: 100

This value specifies the number of rows in the page locks hash table (hash buckets) protected by one spinlock for SQL Servers running with multiple engines. A single-engine SQL Server uses only a single spinlock, because only that one engine can access the page locks hash table.

A spinlock is an internal locking mechanism that prevents a process from accessing a resource currently in use by another process (all processes must wait, or "spin," until the lock on the resource is released).

SQL Server manages the acquiring and releasing of page locks using an internal hash table. There are a maximum of 1,031 hash buckets, or rows, in this hash table. The default value for page lock address spinlock ratio of 100 rows indicates that a maximum of 11 (1031/100) spinlocks can concurrently be held on the page locks hash table.

Theoretically, the lower this setting, the better performance should be, because it will allow more spinlocks and, therefore, less contention on the page locks hash table. However, the default value is appropriate for most systems.

TABLE LOCK SPINLOCK RATIO

Units: Integer Ratio

Default: 20

This value specifies the number of rows in the table locks hash table (hash buckets) protected by one spinlock for SQL Servers running with multiple engines. A single-engine SQL Server uses only a single spinlock because only that one engine can access the table locks hash table.

A spinlock is an internal locking mechanism that prevents a process from accessing a resource currently in use by another process (all processes must wait, or "spin," until the lock on the resource is released).

SQL Server manages the acquiring and releasing of table locks using an internal hash table. There are a maximum of 101 hash buckets, or rows, in this hash table. The default value for `table lock spinlock ratio` of 20 rows indicates that a maximum of six (101/20) spinlocks can concurrently be held on the table locks hash table.

Theoretically, the lower this setting, the better performance should be, because it will enable more spinlocks and, therefore, less contention on the table locks hash table. However, the default value is appropriate for most systems.

MEMORY USE GROUP

This section of configuration parameters lets you set how SQL Server uses memory internally.

ADDITIONAL NETWORK MEMORY

Units: Bytes (should be in multiples of 2048)

Default: 0

When large network packets are being shipped, the client application can use a larger packet size than the default packet size of 512 bytes if the SQL Server is configured to allow using larger packet sizes. Larger packets will require additional memory for each user connection using the larger packets than is available in the standard user connection. This additional memory used for the larger network packets is taken from a separate pool of memory, allocated by `additional network memory`.

Each user connection uses three buffers within the SQL Server: a read buffer, a write buffer, and a read overflow buffer. Each buffer will be the size of the requested network packet size. To estimate the amount of additional network memory to configure, determine the number of concurrent processes that will use the larger packet sizes and multiply that value times the largest packet size times three buffers. Finally, factor in two percent overhead to manage the network buffers and round it up to the nearest multiple of 2048.

The additional network memory required by 10 concurrent user processes using a 2KB packet size is the following:

3 (buffers/user) × 2048 (packet size) × 10 (connections) × 1.02 (overhead)
= 62668.8

The total is rounded up to the nearest multiple of 2048 (65536).

Note

Before any process can use the additional network memory, you first must configure the max network packet size allowed to be higher than the default of 512. (See the description of max network packet size in the "Network Communication Group" discussed later in this chapter.)

AUDIT QUEUE SIZE

Units: Integer quantity of audit records

Default: 100

This is an option, configurable by a user with the sso_role, that instructs the server to retain a specific number of audit records in memory before they are written physically to the sysaudits table in the sybsecurity database. The larger this value is, the better your performance will be, because fewer physical writes occur and audited user processes will not be forced to sleep until space becomes available in the audit queue. Unfortunately, if the server is brought down unexpectedly, audit records stored in cache are lost permanently. audit queue size also affects memory, because the audit queue will set aside 424 bytes per configured record in the server kernel.

DEFAULT NETWORK PACKET SIZE

Units: Bytes (should be a multiple of 512)

Default: 512

This parameter determines the default packet size used by user connections that do not request a larger packet size. The default packet size is 512 bytes.

Each SQL server connection uses a read buffer, a write buffer, and a read overflow buffer, each of which requires a packet in memory. The memory allocated for a configured user connection includes three 512-byte buffers. If you increase the default network packet size, this will increase the memory requirements per configured user connection as follows:

$3 \times$ default network packet size (DNPS) $\times$ # user connections.

For example, if the default network packet size is configured to 1024, and you configure for 100 user connections, you would use the following equation to determine how much memory will be required for network packets:

$3 \times 1024 \times 100 = 305,200$ bytes

If you increase the DNPS, you also must increase maximum network packet size to the same or higher value.

Tip

> If you have any application programs or third-party products that were developed with earlier versions (prior to System 10) of Open Client and that use only 512-byte network packets, do not increase the default network packet size beyond 512 or these applications will not be able to connect to the SQL Server.
>
> To support larger packet sizes for applications that can take advantage of them, set max network packet size appropriately and have the applications request larger packets.

DISK I/O STRUCTURES

(See the description of disk i/o structures in the section "Disk I/O Group" earlier in this chapter.)

EVENT BUFFERS PER ENGINE

Units: Integer number of events

Default: 100

This specifies the number of events per SQL Server engine that can be monitored simultaneously. Monitor Server makes use of the events for monitoring SQL Server activity. The number of event buffers recommended is dependent on the number of engines in the SQL Server, the level of activity, and the types of applications. Setting it too low can result in a loss of event information. Consider setting it to 2000 and above for most environments. The higher the value, the less Monitor Server will degrade SQL Server performance.

Each event buffer per engine consumes 100 bytes of memory. Multiply the configuration value by the number of SQL Server engines to determine the total memory requirements. If you are not going to be using Monitor Server, set event buffers to 1 to make memory available for other uses within SQL Server

EXECUTABLE CODE SIZE + OVERHEAD

Units: Number of bytes

Default: N/A

This is the size of the SQL Server executable code and kernel structures for the current platform. It is not configurable.

MAX NUMBER NETWORK LISTENERS

Units: Integer

Default: 15

Each master port defined in the SQL Server interface file requires a network listener. If your SQL Server defines multiple master ports to support multiple network interfaces, configure max number network listeners accordingly.

MAX ONLINE ENGINES

Units: Integer quantity

Default: 1

This is the number of engines you want the SQL Server to use in a Symmetric Multiprocessing (SMP) environment. An engine does not necessarily correspond with a physical CPU. It corresponds with the amount of work that would be performed by a physical CPU.

Tip

For the best performance, and to best utilize all resources, the number of engines should not exceed the number of available physical CPUs minus 1.

NUMBER OF ALARMS

Units: Integer number of alarm structures

Default: 40

This is the number of preallocated alarm structures used by the server for event handling. Each configured alarm structure requires 20 bytes. Alarms are used by processes executing the waitfor command. If you have a large number of processes using waitfor, you may need to increase this value.

NUMBER OF DEVICES

See the description of number of devices in the section "Disk I/O Group" earlier in this chapter.

NUMBER OF EXTENT I/O BUFFERS

Units: Integer quantity of eight-page extents

Default: 0

Index creation takes a huge amount of CPU and I/O resources. To reduce the load on the server during index creation, you can allocate additional memory in eight-page extents (16KB on most platforms) for the `create index` command to use.

The first `create index` command you issue will use all the defined extent I/O buffers allocated. Other simultaneous index creations will use standard I/O (reading and writing individual pages for intermediate sort results and index pages).

Tip

You may want to use a larger value here at initial load time so that when indexes are created they can take advantage of the extent I/O buffers. Then, reduce the value to 0 when you go to production and allow the memory to be used for cache instead.

You have to experiment to find the optimal setting for your system. Most people have found that values between 40 and 60 provide optimum performance gains.

Do not set the value higher than 100 or you will see performance degrade.

NUMBER OF LANGUAGES IN CACHE

Units: Integer quantity

Default: 3

This is the maximum number of languages that may be held in cache simultaneously.

NUMBER OF LOCKS

See the description of `number of locks` in the section "Lock Manager Group" earlier in this chapter.

NUMBER OF MAILBOXES

System 11

Units: Integer

Default: 30

These are structures used by the kernel for internal communication. This is a parameter that was occasionally changed using the `buildmaster -ycnmbox` command. Do not modify this parameter unless instructed to do so by Sybase Technical Support.

System 11 ▶ *NUMBER OF MESSAGES*

Units: Integer

Default: 64

This is used, along with mailbox structures, by the kernel. Do not modify this parameter unless instructed to do so by Sybase Technical Support.

NUMBER OF OPEN DATABASES

Units: Integer number of open databases

Default: 12

This is the total number of databases for which SQL Server will build internal pointers in its kernel, and for which it can maintain simultaneous connections. This includes master, model, tempdb, sybsystemprocs, sybsyntax, sybsecurity, and any user databases that might be used concurrently.

Tip

> If the process tries to exceed the configured number, you will typically get messages in the error log describing the incident. Unfortunately, the message reported to the user is fairly confusing. Avoid this problem by configuring the variable to equal the number of created databases within the SQL Server, and then forget about it. The amount of memory taken up is effectively insignificant.

NUMBER OF OPEN OBJECTS

Units: Integer Quantity

Default: 500

This is the number of concurrent open objects that may be in simultaneous use. If you begin getting error messages that object connections are unavailable, increase this number. The memory cost is low (40 bytes).

NUMBER OF REMOTE CONNECTIONS

Units: Integer quantity

Default: 20

This is the total number of remote connections both to and from this SQL Server. For example, if this is set to 20 (the default), and there are 10 remote logins currently, only 10 outgoing connections may be made.

NUMBER OF REMOTE LOGINS

Units: Integer quantity

Default: 20

This is the total number of concurrent connections that can be made from this SQL server to other servers. This value should be set equal to or less than number of remote connections.

NUMBER OF REMOTE SITES

Units: Integer quantity

Default: 10

This parameter controls the number of remote sites that simultaneously connect to SQL Server. SQL Server invokes a site handler for each site connecting to SQL Server. All access to SQL Server from a remote site is handled with a single-site handler.

NUMBER OF USER CONNECTIONS

Units: Integer quantity

Default: 25

The user connections variable determines the number of concurrent connections that may be made to SQL Server at any given time. Every time a user logs in, it requires a single connection. (A single user could have dozens of connections at one time.)

The user connections variable has the most dramatic effect on configured memory. You need approximately 51KB of memory per user connection (this is higher if the stack size or default packet size is increased). In addition to actual users who are logged into the server, the server consumes user connections for the following:

◆ One per master network listener (each line for the master device in the interfaces file)

◆ One for standard output

◆ One for the error log

- One for internal use (if you are running on the VMS platform)
- One for each data device
- One for each mirror device
- One for the backup server
- One per active site handler
- One per remote server

The global variable @@max_connections is set to the absolute maximum server connections; the actual number of user connections allowed equals @@max_connections less the system connections in the preceding list.

Determining the number of user connections required depends on the number of concurrent users and the number of connections per user.

To determine how many connections are currently in use, execute sp_who.

 PARTITION GROUPS

Units: Integer Quantity

Default: 1024

When you partition a heap table, SQL Server needs internal memory structures to control access to individual partitions of the table. Each partition group will manage up to 16 partition caches, one for each table partition. If a table has more than 16 partitions, it will require more than one partition group.

The number of partition groups determines the number of open partitioned tables. If there are 64 partition groups, SQL Server is limited to 1,024 (16 × 64). If either of these values is exceeded, attempts to partition a table or access a table partition will fail.

 PERMISSION CACHE ENTRIES*

Units: Number of 28-byte cache protectors

Default: 15

This parameter specifies the amount of permission cache used before the server has to check the sysprotects tables.

Information on user permissions is held in the permission cache. SQL Server checks the permission cache first when checking permissions before looking in the sysprotects table.

The permission cache gets wiped out with each grant and revoke. Don't spend a lot of time tuning this parameter, because the performance gains are negligible.

PROCEDURE CACHE PERCENT

See the discussion of procedure cache percent in the section "Cache Manager Group" earlier in this chapter.

REMOTE SERVER PRE-READ PACKETS

Units: Integer quantity

Default: 3

This is the number of packets the site handler may pre-read from a remote site. Because a site handler may be handling multiple users from a single remote site, the site handler can pre-read and keep track of data packets for each user process before it is ready to receive it. The default value is usually appropriate. Increasing it will increase memory requirements. Decreasing it may slow network traffic between servers.

*STACK GUARD SIZE**

Units: Bytes, in an even multiple of your server's page size (usually 2KB)

Default: 4096 (multiple of 2KB)

The stack guard size is the size of the overflow stack area at the end of each stack. This area is used to monitor whether a transaction exceeds its available stack space. The stack guard helps avoid having a stack overflow overwrite other memory areas.

Typically the default size is appropriate. If you are having problems with stack overflow, you may be better served by increasing stack size.

Increasing stack guard size will increase the memory requirements per configured user connection accordingly.

STACK SIZE

Units: Bytes, in an even multiple of your server's page size (usually 2KB)

Default: Varies depending on platform

Stack size is the capacity of the server's execution/argument stack. If you have queries with large numbers of arguments in the where clause or long select lists, or deeply nested stored procedures, you may get an error that says stack overflow or stack size exceeded. This is your clue to add a few kilobytes to this variable, or to break these large queries into smaller queries.

Increasing stack size will increase the memory requirements per configured user connection accordingly.

TOTAL DATA CACHE SIZE

See the discussion of total data cache size in the section "Cache Manager Group" earlier in this chapter.

TOTAL MEMORY

See the discussion of total memory in the section "Cache Manager Group" earlier in this chapter.

NETWORK COMMUNICATION GROUP

This section identifies parameters that affect network communications for SQL Server.

ADDITIONAL NETWORK MEMORY

See the discussion of additional network memory in the section "Memory Use Group" earlier in this chapter.

DEFAULT NETWORK PACKET SIZE

See the discussion of default network packet size in the section "Memory Use Group" earlier in this chapter.

MAX NETWORK PACKET SIZE

Units: Bytes (should be a multiple of 512)

Default: 512

Some applications need to send large quantities of data across the network lines (bcp, for example). These applications can request larger packet sizes through client-library requests. When these requests are made, memory is allocated from the fragment acquired in the additional netmem variable. If no memory is available here, packet size will not increase.

If an application does not request the larger packet size, it uses the size specified in default network packet size (DNPS). The maximum network packet size should be at least as large as DNPS. If you increase max network packet size higher than DNPS, you will need to configure additional network memory to support the larger packets.

MAX NUMBER NETWORK LISTENERS

Units: Integer

Default: 15

Each master port defined in the SQL Server interface file requires a network listener. If your SQL Server defines multiple master ports to support multiple network interfaces, configure `max number network listeners` accordingly.

NUMBER OF REMOTE CONNECTIONS

Units: Integer quantity

Default: 20

This is the total number of remote connections both to and from this SQL Server. For example, if this is set to 20 (the default), and there are 10 remote logins currently, only 10 outgoing connections may be made.

NUMBER OF REMOTE LOGINS

Units: Integer quantity

Default: 20

This is the total number of concurrent connections that can be made from this SQL server to other servers. This value should be set equal to or less than `number of remote connections`.

NUMBER OF REMOTE SITES

Units: Integer quantity

Default: 10

This parameter controls the number of remote sites that simultaneously connect to SQL Server. SQL Server invokes a site handler for each site connecting to SQL Server. All access to SQL Server from a remote site is handled with a single-site handler.

REMOTE SERVER PRE-READ PACKETS

Units: Integer quantity

Default: 3

This is the number of packets the site handler may pre-read from a remote site. Because a site handler may be handling multiple users from a single remote site, the site handler can pre-read and keep track of data packets for each user process before it is ready to receive it. The default value is usually appropriate. Increasing it will increase memory requirements. Decreasing it may slow network traffic between servers.

TCP NO DELAY

Units: Flag

Default: 0

By default, TCP bundles smaller logical packets into larger physical ones to improve network performance. Disabling this setting (which is the default) will enable packets to be sent regardless of size. This increases network traffic, but may improve performance in low-volume applications with small packet sizes.

O/S RESOURCES GROUP

This section lists configuration parameters that affect operating system parameters.

 MAX ASYNCH I/OS PER ENGINE

Units: I/O quantity

Default: 2147483647

This parameter sets the maximum number of asynchronous disk I/O requests that may be outstanding for an engine. This should be set to your operating system limitation for maximum concurrent asynchronous I/O requests to avoid having the O/S reject SQL server requests. If an engine issues an asynchronous I/O request and either max asynch i/os per engine or max asynch i/os per server has been reached, SQL Server will delay sending the I/O request until enough outstanding I/O has completed to fall below the limit exceeded.

 MAX ASYNCH I/OS PER SERVER

Units: I/O quantity

Default: 2147483647

This parameter sets the maximum number of asynchronous disk I/O requests that may be outstanding for a SQL Server, regardless of the number of engines. This should be set to your operating system limitation for maximum concurrent asynchronous I/O requests to avoid having the O/S reject SQL server requests.

 O/S ASYNCH I/O ENABLED

Units: N/A

Default: N/A

Indicates whether asynchronous I/O has been enabled at the operating system level. This is a read-only parameter and cannot be changed.

O/S FILE DESCRIPTORS

System 11

Units: N/A

Default: N/A

Displays the maximum number of file descriptors available per process as configured for the operating system. This is a read-only parameter and cannot be changed.

TCP NO DELAY

System 11

See the discussion of `tcp no delay` in the section "Network Communication Group" earlier in this chapter.

PHYSICAL MEMORY GROUP

This section contains parameters that affect physical memory resources for SQL Server.

ADDITIONAL NETWORK MEMORY

See the discussion of `additional network memory` in the section "Memory Use Group" earlier in this chapter.

LOCK SHARED MEMORY

System 11

Units: Flag

Default: 0 (off)

This parameter allows or disallows swapping of SQL Server pages to disk, and allows the O/S kernel to avoid the SQL Server's internal page locking code. This can reduce disk I/O.

Not all operating systems allow locking of shared memory.

SHARED MEMORY STARTING ADDRESS

System 11

Units: Physical address

Default: 0

This parameter identifies the location in memory where SQL Server starts its shared memory region. This is typically not modified unless Sybase Technical Support recommends it.

TOTAL MEMORY

See the discussion of total memory in the section "Cache Manager Group" earlier in this chapter.

PROCESSORS GROUP

This section lists parameters for configuring processors in an SMP environment.

MAX ONLINE ENGINES

See the discussion of max online engines in the section "Memory Use Group" earlier in this chapter.

MIN ONLINE ENGINES

Units: Integer number of engines

Default: 1

Specifies the minimum number of SQL Server engines that should be online in a multiprocessor environment.

SQL SERVER ADMINISTRATION GROUP

This group lists parameters that relate to general SQL Server Administration.

ALLOW NESTED TRIGGERS*

Units: 0 or 1 (flag)

Default: 1 (on)

If a trigger modifies a table that has a trigger, the trigger on the second table will fire if allow nested triggers is on (the value equals 1). Otherwise, it will not.

ALLOW UPDATES TO SYSTEM TABLES*

Units: 0 or 1 (flag)

Default: 0 (no)

The allow updates option is a flag that directs the server to allow the dbo to modify system tables directly (that is, without using supplied system stored procedures).

Warning

Turning on `allow updates` is a bad idea! The first few times I tried this, I permanently crashed the server. Do not do this without the safety net of having Sybase Technical Support on the telephone directing you to do so.

If you do attempt to modify system tables, always back up the database first, and perform all system table modifications in a transaction. That way, if you really mess things up, you can issue a `rollback tran` command and get back to where you started.

Note

One reasonable time to `allow updates` is after inadvertent device failure. If a device is not available to the server (the power is down, for example) when the server comes up, any databases using that device will be recorded in sysdatabases as suspect. If you update the sysdatabases table (changing the SUSPECT bit), you may be able to bring the server down, power up the offending device, and reconnect to your database. The following shows the `update` statement you might issue to retry connecting to all suspect databases:

```
update sysdatabases
set status = status - 256
where status & 256 = 256
```

After you use the `allow updates` option, be sure you turn it off.

AUDIT QUEUE SIZE

See the discussion of `audit queue size` in the section "Memory Use Group" earlier in this chapter.

CPU ACCOUNTING FLUSH INTERVAL*

System 11

Units: Machine clock ticks

Default: 200

This is the frequency with which you want CPU usage accounting information dumped from sysprocesses to syslogins. This information can be gathered by using the `sp_reportstats` stored procedure and can be used for chargeback accounting. This information accumulates in syslogins until you use the `sp_clearstats` stored procedure.

How you set this option depends on how often you plan on running usage reports. Set it higher if you are running reports infrequently—for example, on a monthly basis. However, if you are doing periodic queries against syslogins to monitor CPU usage by process, set this lower to update the totcpu column in syslogins more frequently.

CPU GRACE TIME

Units: Milliseconds

Default: 500

This parameter sets the maximum amount of CPU time a process can use before the SQL Server aborts the process with a time-slice error. This feature, which can stop runaway processes, creates "Infected" processes.

DEADLOCK RETRIES

Units: Integer number of retries

Default: 5

Specifies the number of times a transaction will attempt to acquire a lock after it has been designated the deadlock victim. After failing the configured number of retries, the transaction is rolled back.

DEFAULT DATABASE SIZE

Units: Megabytes

Default: 2

This is the size a database will be if you do not specify the size in the create database statement. This tends to be an infrequently adjusted variable, because you will almost always specify the size of your database during creation.

DEFAULT FILL FACTOR PERCENT

Units: Integer percentage

Default: 0

fill factor is the extent to which index pages should be filled (excluding the root) as indexes are created. This includes the data pages of clustered indexes. Note that this is a performance tool.

Note

The `fill factor` required by `sp_configure` is two words, but the `create index` statement keyword `fillfactor` is a single word.

Low fill factors cause index pages to be partially full, which in turn will create more index levels. The performance benefit comes at insert and update time, when row additions will be less likely to cause page splits. (Lots of page splits during updates are bad for performance.)

Note

A fill factor of 0 does not mean that pages will be empty. This is a special case. Clustered index data pages and nonclustered index leaf pages are 100 percent full, and some space is left in the intermediate levels (typically 75 percent full).

High fill factors fill the pages as much as possible. This reduces index levels and increases query performance.

Note

Fill factors are not maintained after index creation. To re-create indexes with the fill factors intact, you must drop and re-create the index. Some shops with intensive update applications do this on a nightly basis.

Maintaining fill factors is typically the only reason you might periodically drop and re-create indexes, because Sybase indexes tend to be self-maintaining and self-balancing.

EVENT BUFFERS PER ENGINE

See the discussion of `event buffers per engine` in the section "Memory Use Group" earlier in this chapter.

HOUSEKEEPER FREE WRITE PERCENT

Units: Integer percentage

Default: 1

This parameter sets the maximum percentage by which the housekeeper task can increase database writes over normal database writes. When the frequency is set to 20, the housekeeper task can make the I/O only up to 20 percent busier by writing changed pages to disk.

When SQL Server has no tasks to process, the housekeeper task begins writing "dirty" pages from cache to disk. This helps improve CPU utilization and decreases the need for buffer washing during transaction processing.

The housekeeper task can be disabled by setting housekeeper free write percent to 0, or it can be made continuous by setting housekeeper free write percent to 100.

System 11 ▶ I/O ACCOUNTING FLUSH INTERVAL*

Units: Machine clock ticks

Default: 1000

This is the frequency with which you want I/O statistics information dumped from sysprocesses to syslogins. This information can be gathered by using the sp_reportstats stored procedure and can be used for chargeback accounting. This information accumulates in syslogins until you use the sp_clearstats stored procedure.

How you set this option depends on how often you plan on running usage reports. Set it higher if you are running reports infrequently—for example, on a monthly basis. However, if you are doing periodic queries against syslogins to monitor I/O statistics by process, set this lower to update the totio column in syslogins more frequently.

System 11 ▶ I/O POLLING PROCESS COUNT

Units: Number of processes

Default: 10

This parameter defines the maximum number of SQL Server processes that run before the SQL Server scheduler checks to see whether disk and/or network I/O tasks have completed. Tuning this will affect response time and throughput.

Increasing this value may increase throughput for applications with high disk/network I/O activity.

IDENTITY BURNING SET FACTOR

Units: Percentage in decimal form × 10 million

Default: 5000 (represents .05 percent)

When you define a column as `identity` in a table (new for System 10), the server will automatically assign a unique, sequential number for that column in the table at row insertion time. To avoid excessive I/O, the Sybase SQL Server keeps blocks of numbers available in memory, and writes `"Next available block"` information only to the database, rather than to each individual row. This is a performance enhancement.

The number of values in the block of information is controlled by the `identity burning set factor` variable. Note the units that are specified: `5000` means that .05 percent of the numbers will be made available. Because identity columns must be a numeric data type with a predefined precision, the server uses the possible range of values to determine which numbers are reserved with each available block. If the server is brought down unexpectedly, all numbers in the burning set memory block will be lost to each table that has an identity column. An orderly shutdown will not cause identity values to be burned.

For example, an identity column is defined as `numeric(7,0)` (values range from `1` to `9,999,999`). The burning set factor is the default value of `5000`, so .05 percent of the values is made available at a time. The worst case is that all the values in the available block are lost when the server shuts down, with a loss of 9,999,999 (max identity value) × .05% (burning factor) = 500 values.

Tip

If the server is going through an erratic phase (going up and down frequently and unexpectedly), which may happen in testing or early production before stability has been reached, or after a version upgrade, large sets of numbers may be used up. This moves you toward your maximum column value more quickly than you might have expected. Until things stabilize, set your burning factor lower, even if it means that performance takes a hit.

IDENTITY GRAB SIZE

Units: Number of values

Default: `1`

This is the number of identity values that each process may preallocate for its own use. The higher this value, the more potential gaps you will have in column values. The lower this value, the more often a process has to request identity values.

LOCK PROMOTION *HWM***

    Units: Integer number of locks

    Default: 200

    Prior to System 11, lock escalation from page level locking to table level locking happened automatically at the 200-page lock level. Now, you can set a high water mark, which instructs the server not to escalate from page locking to table locking until this number of locks is obtained on a table.

 LOCK PROMOTION *LWM***

    Units: Integer number of locks

    Default: 200

    The server will never attempt to escalate locking when the number of table locks is below this level (low water mark).

 LOCK PROMOTION PCT**

    Units: Integer percentage

    Default: 100

    If the number of locks is between the HWM and the LWN, this is the percentage of page locks permitted before lock escalation.

 NUMBER OF ALARMS

    Units: Integer

    Default: 40

    This is the number of preallocated alarm structures used by the server for event handling.

NUMBER OF EXTENT I/O BUFFERS

    See the discussion of extent i/o buffers in the section "Memory Use Group" earlier in this chapter.

 NUMBER OF MAILBOXES

    Units: Integer

    Default: 30

These are structures used by the kernel for internal communication. This is a parameter that was occasionally changed using the `buildmaster -ycnmbox` command. This is not one to play with.

NUMBER OF MESSAGES

Units: Integer

Default: 64

This is used, along with mailbox structures, by the kernel.

OPEN DATABASES

See the discussion of `open databases` in the section "Memory Use Group" earlier in this chapter.

OPEN OBJECTS

See the discussion of `open objects` in the section "Memory Use Group" earlier in this chapter.

NUMBER OF PREALLOCATED EXTENTS

Units: Integer Quantity

Default: 2

This is the number of extents that `bcp` will preallocate during a single trip to the page manager. For `bcp` processes using large batches, a higher value will improve performance by reducing the number of allocation records that will be written to the log. However, if you are using small batches with `bcp`, a high value may result in the allocation of more pages than needed.

NUMBER OF SORT BUFFERS*

Units: Integer Quantity

Default: 0

This is the number of pre-reserved buffers used to hold pages read from the input buffer. When tuning the number of sort buffers in conjunction with `extent i/o buffers`, `number of sort buffers` should be set to eight times the value of `extent i/o buffers`. You should run benchmark tests to determine the optimal setting for this parameter. Be aware that setting sort buffers too high may result in slower performance.

PARTITION GROUPS

See the discussion of partition groups in the section "Memory Use Group" earlier in this chapter.

PARTITION SPINLOCK RATIO

Units: Integer Quantity

Default: 10

A spinlock is a simple mechanism to lock a partition cache in use by another process. This parameter specifies the ratio of spinlocks to internal caches.

> Although a 1:1 ratio of spinlocks-to-partitions might provide the least contention, the recommended ratio is 10 percent of the number of partitions in use.

PRINT DEADLOCK INFORMATION

Units: Flag

Default: 0 (off)

This parameter instructs the server to print deadlock information to the error log for purposes of tracking down deadlocks. This is the information that was displayed in earlier releases of SQL Server using the dbcc traceon(1204) command (see Appendix A, "The Database Consistency Checker (dbcc)," for information on how to use and interpret this output).

Warning

> Setting this option on can seriously degrade SQL server performance. Only use this option when attempting to debug the cause of deadlocks within a database. Do not leave it on all the time.

RUNNABLE PROCESS SEARCH COUNT

Units: Integer quantity

Default: 3

This parameter determines the number of times an engine loops looking for a runnable task before relinquishing a CPU.

Tip

> On single-processor systems, you should consider setting this parameter to 1. On multiprocessor systems, increasing the runnable process search count to 750-1250 may improve performance for CPU intensive applications; 50-200 may improve performance for I/O intensive applications.

SIZE OF AUTO IDENTITY COLUMN

Units: Bytes

Default: 10

If the database option auto identity is on, the server automatically appends an identity column to every table at creation time. This parameter specifies the default width of that column.

SORT PAGE COUNT*

Units: Integer

Default: 0

This parameter specifies the maximum amount of memory a sort operation can use.

Because sorts require about 50 bytes per row while processing the input table, an optimal value for sort page count can be estimated by the following:

(# of sort buffers * rows per data page) / 50

This gives you a good starting point. You'll need to benchmark your applications with different settings to find the best value.

Warning

> Changing this parameter can cause dump incompatibilities between systems with different sort page count settings if a create index command is contained in the transaction log dump. To minimize this risk, always dump a database after creating indexes with large values configured for sort page count or number of sort buffers.

SQL SERVER CLOCK TICK LENGTH

Units: Microseconds

Default: `100000`

This parameter enables you to specify the duration of the SQL Server's clock tick in microseconds.

Tip

In mixed-mode environments, decreasing this number can help performance for I/O-bound tasks. A recommended value is `20000`. A lower clock tick length causes CPU-bound tasks to context switch more frequently, giving other processes more access to the CPU.

If your applications are CPU-bound, a higher clock tick length may improve performance by enabling CPU tasks to process longer between context switches.

TIME SLICE

Units: Milliseconds

Default: `100`

The time slice is theoretically the number of milliseconds the server allocates to each user process as the server does its own internal multithreading. In practice, the server uses `time slice` as a guideline, and may increase or decrease it (transparent to the configuration setting) if processes are taking too long to swap in and out.

If set too low, SQL Server may spend too much time switching between processes, which will hurt performance because context switching is expensive.

If set too high, CPU-intensive processes may monopolize the CPU, resulting in longer response times.

Tip

Leave the `time slice` alone, unless otherwise directed by Sybase Technical Support.

UPGRADE VERSION*

Units: N/A

Default: N/A

This is the version of the upgrade, automatically set by the installation software (and also the upgrade software). If you don't believe the number, try running the following to get a detailed report on your current version of Sybase:

```
select @@version
```

USER ENVIRONMENT GROUP

This group lists parameters that modify the user environments.

DEFAULT NETWORK PACKET SIZE

See the discussion of default network packet size in the section "Memory Use Group" earlier in this chapter.

NUMBER OF PREALLOCATED EXTENTS

See the discussion of number of preallocated extents in the section "SQL Server Administration Group" earlier in this chapter.

NUMBER OF USER CONNECTIONS

See the discussion of number of user connections in the section "Memory Use Group" earlier in this chapter.

PERMISSION CACHE ENTRIES*

See the discussion of permission cache entries in the section "Memory Use Group" earlier in this chapter.

STACK GUARD SIZE

See the discussion of stack guard size in the section "Memory Use Group" earlier in this chapter.

STACK SIZE

See the discussion of stack size in the section "Memory Use Group" earlier in this chapter.

SYSTEMWIDE PASSWORD EXPIRATION*

Units: Integer number of days

Default: 0 (indicating that passwords do not expire)

Only a user with the sso_role can set this option, which dictates how often a login must change the current password. When the time interval is within 25 percent of the interval (or seven days, whichever is greater), users will get warning messages indicating they need to change the password. If a password has expired, a user can still log in to the server, but cannot execute any commands except sp_password (to change the password) until the password is modified.

 ### USER LOG CACHE SIZE

Units: Bytes

Default: 2048

This parameter specifies the default size for user log caches.

There is one log cache for each configured user connection. SQL Server uses the log cache to hold transaction information for a single transaction for a single user. When a transaction commits, the contents of the log cache for that user are written to disk. By buffering each user's transaction records until the transaction completes, contention is reduced between multiple processes writing to the log.

> It is a waste of resources to allocate more space for this value than your maximum server transaction length, because it is flushed on each commit.

USER LOG CACHE SPINLOCK RATIO

Units: Ratio

Default: 20

This specifies the ratio of user log caches per user log cache spinlock. SQL Server needs to use spinlocks to protect user log caches, because multiple processes can access the contents of a user log cache.

If you have a single-processor CPU, there will be only one log cache spinlock, regardless of the number of user connections.

CONFIGURATION VARIABLES THAT REQUIRE SUBSTANTIAL MEMORY

Several variables use a substantial amount of SQL Server memory. They are summarized in Table 9.2.

Table 9.2. Variables that use substantial memory.

Parameter	Bytes of Memory per Unit
user connections	Approximately 51KB (this is platform-specific)
devices	.5KB
open databases	17KB
open objects	40 bytes
locks	72 bytes
audit queue size	424 bytes
default network packet size	$3 \times$ the number of user connections $\times$ DNPS (total, not per unit)
extent i/o buffers	8 pages (16KB on most platforms)
procedure cache	Percentage of remainder of cache

SUMMARY

SQL Server System 11 provides a number of configuration options for defining SQL Server behavior and tuning SQL Server performance. In the next chapter, you examine in more detail the configuration options that have the greatest impact on SQL Server performance and explore examples and guidelines for tuning them.

CHAPTER 10

Optimizing SQL Server Configuration Options

There are a number of configuration options within SQL Server that affect SQL Server performance. These include memory configuration, CPU configuration, network configuration, and lock configuration. The most important of these configuration variables in relation to performance is memory.

SQL Server 11 introduces an array of new configuration options that directly impact the performance of SQL Server. SQL Server 11 allows much finer control over memory configuration, lock resources and escalation, and I/O. Used properly, these configuration options can offer worthwhile increases in server performance. Used poorly, they can turn SQL Server into a performance dog just as quickly. Understanding what these configuration options define is just as important as understanding how to change them.

MEMORY UTILIZATION

Figure 10.1 represents physical memory on your server box. In this figure, all physical memory except for that set aside for the O/S kernel is allocated to SQL Server. The amount of memory allocated to SQL Server is configurable within SQL Server and should always be less than all available memory.

Figure 10.1.
Physical memory allocated to the SQL Server is configurable, as is the distribution of cache between the procedure cache and data cache.

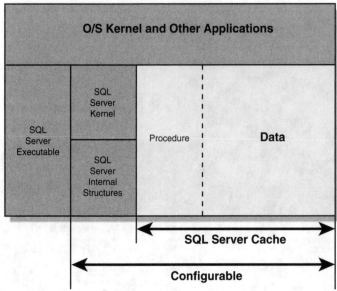

The first chunk of memory in physical memory is used by the operating system kernel. The amount of memory required by the O/S is typically defined by the operating system administrator (who is often not the SQL Server system administrator). It contains information about what can be done with memory, caching, connections, I/O, and other OS-specific activities. Occasionally at installation time, you may need to reconfigure the OS kernel to accommodate SQL Server memory and I/O needs. Don't forget to leave additional memory set aside within the O/S for other applications that may be running on the same server box (for example, Backup Server, Monitor Server, bcp, batch jobs, and so forth).

When the SQL Server starts up, it refers to a system configuration setting, memory, to determine the number of pages (remember, SQL Server pages are 2KB unless you are running on a Stratus system that uses 4KB pages) of real memory that the SQL server requests from the operating system when it comes up.

Warning

If the server does not have enough memory to start properly, it will not start at all. (There is no partial server execution.) Prior to System 11, if you have misconfigured and the server is unable to get enough memory to start, you have to use buildmaster with the -r option to reconfigure all the memory settings to their default values (discussed later in this section). If that doesn't work, it is time to call Sybase Technical Support and probably have them rebuild the master for you one variable at a time (using the -y option of buildmaster).

In System 11, you can simply edit the SQL Server configuration file and modify the offending configuration parameter, then try to start SQL Server again.

Within the block of memory allocated to SQL Server, the first chunk of memory is set aside for the SQL Server executable. SQL Server is software, which is executed within the operating system. The amount of memory needed for the SQL Server executable varies from about 1MB to about 4MB, based on the software version and the platform on which it is running.

The next block of memory is set aside for SQL Server's own internal kernel, the memory structures for managing user connections, open databases, open objects, locks, and so forth. How you configure kernel-related items determines how much memory the kernel requires. Whatever memory is left over at this point is available for data and procedure cache. For example, if you allocate 5,000 pages for memory and use 500 pages for the executable and 2,000 pages for kernel, there are 2,500 pages available for data and procedure cache.

Cache enables the server to read information repeatedly from memory rather than disk. Because memory is always much faster than disk, sufficient cache size is a critical element in server performance. Cache is effectively divided between data cache, which stores data pages being read or modified, and procedure cache, which stores the optimized, executable stored procedures.

DBCC MEMUSAGE

The Database Consistency Checker command (dbcc) can detail the current memory allocations within SQL Server, which will help you make the best use of memory resources. In order to see the dbcc memusage output, you need to direct the output to your terminal by using dbcc trace functions (trace flags). Several dbcc trace flags are talked about in this book; two very common values are 3604 and 3605.

Here are the important dbcc commands related to memory usage and what they do:

dbcc traceon (3604)	Sends subsequent dbcc output to the local session
dbcc traceon (3605)	Sends subsequent dbcc output to the error log
dbcc traceoff (3604 ¦ 3605)	Terminates output to specified destination
dbcc memusage	Must be used with dbcc traceon (3604) if you want to see the output on your screen

Tip

On some platforms or releases of the server, dbcc traceon (3604) must be in its own batch to take effect for the subsequent dbcc memusage command:

```
dbcc traceon (3604)
go
dbcc memusage
go
```

Warning

If you are running SQL Server in an SMP environment with multiple engines configured, running dbcc memusage can cause other processes within the SQL Server to time out and die. Do not run dbcc memusage while other processes are active in a multi-engine environment.

MEMORY UTILIZATION

You can use dbcc memusage to determine how memory is being used within SQL server and whether your memory allocations are appropriate. It provides extremely useful information about overall memory size, cache size, and the actual objects stored in the cache. This is the memory usage section of dbcc memusage:

```
Memory Usage:

                            Meg.        2K Blks          Bytes

        Configured Memory:400.0000      204800        419430400

              Code size:  3.4259          1755          3592296
        Kernel Structures:  5.9769        3061          6267212
        Server Structures: 13.9494       7143         14627040
             Cache Memory:357.0625      182816        374407168
             Proc Buffers:  0.6974        358           731272
             Proc Headers: 18.8848       9669         19802112
```

The first section of the output is the server kernel information. The following are things you want to look at and consider:

Configured Memory	This should be the same as what you configured for total memory using sp_configure. Here, it is reported in megabytes (400.0000) as well as in 2KB blocks (204800).
Code Size	This is the amount of memory required for the SQL Server executable.
Kernel Structures	These represent the memory requirements for Server Structures, the fixed overhead and configurable options (for example, user connections).
Cache Memory	This is the amount of memory available for data cache.

Note

In System 11, you also can use sp_configure to determine the amount of memory available for data cache. This is reported in the Memory Use group as total data cache size (see Chapter 9, "Configuring and Tuning the SQL Server").

Proc Buffers Proc Headers	This is the total amount of memory available as procedure cache. Proc Buffers represents the size of the memory structures set aside for managing compiled objects in procedure cache. Proc Headers is the actual amount of procedure cache space available.

Note

The amount of memory available for procedure cache also can be determined by viewing the SQL Server error log (this is discussed shortly).

DATA CACHE USAGE

The second part of dbcc memusage is a list of the 20 objects (tables and indexes) using the largest number of pages in data cache:

```
Buffer Cache Memory, Top 20:
```

Cache	Buf Pool	DB Id	Object Id	Index Id	Meg.
default data ca		5	400004456	0	1.8926
	2K	5	400004456	0	1.8926
default data ca		5	400004456	2	0.5000
	16K	5	400004456	2	0.5000
default data ca		5	48003202	0	0.1777
	2K	5	48003202	0	0.0059
	16K	5	48003202	0	0.1719
default data ca		1	36	0	0.0469
	16K	1	36	0	0.0469
default data ca		1	37	0	0.0156
	16K	1	37	0	0.0156
default data ca		1	2	0	0.0059
	2K	1	2	0	0.0059
default data ca		5	2	0	0.0039
	2K	5	2	0	0.0039
default data ca		1	2	1	0.0020
	2K	1	2	1	0.0020
default data ca		1	8	0	0.0020
	2K	1	8	0	0.0020
default data ca		1	30	0	0.0020
	2K	1	30	0	0.0020
default data ca		1	30	2	0.0020
	2K	1	30	2	0.0020
default data ca		1	33	0	0.0020
	2K	1	33	0	0.0020
default data ca		1	33	1	0.0020
	2K	1	33	1	0.0020
default data ca		2	2	0	0.0020
	2K	2	2	0	0.0020
default data ca		2	8	0	0.0020
	2K	2	8	0	0.0020
default data ca		2	14	0	0.0020
	2K	2	14	0	0.0020
default data ca		2	99	0	0.0020
	2K	2	99	0	0.0020
default data ca		3	8	0	0.0020
	2K	3	8	0	0.0020

```
default data ca       5           2           1           0.0020
          2K          5           2           1           0.0020
default data ca       5           8           0           0.0020
          2K          5           8           0           0.0020
```

The output shows not only the largest objects in cache, but also the named cache they belong to and the buffer pool within the cache they are using for I/O.

Unfortunately, the output only provides the IDs of the databases, tables and indexes. You need to translate these to the names of the databases and tables you are familiar with by using the following steps:

1. To determine the name of the database, use the db_name() function to convert a database ID to a name:

```
select db_name(5)
go


- - - - - - - - - - - - - - - - - - - - - - - - -
perftune
```

2. Use the object_name() function to convert the object ID to an object name. The object_name() function takes the object ID and the database ID as parameters. For example, find out which table is the largest one in the cache:

```
select object_name(400004456, 5)
go


- - - - - - - - - - - - - - - - - - - - - - - - -
perftab
```

3. Using the index ID and the following table, you can determine what component of a table is cached:

Index ID	Component of Table
0	Table itself
1	Clustered index
2 to 250	Nonclustered index
255	Text/image chain

To determine which nonclustered index is cached when the index ID is greater than 1, use the following select statement from sysindexes:

```
select name
from sysindexes
where id = 400004456 /* object id from memusage */
and indid = 2 /* index id from memusage */
go

name
- - - - - - - - - - - - - - - - - - - - - - - - -
idx1
```

PROCEDURE CACHE UTILIZATION

The last part of dbcc memusage is a list of the 20 (or less if there are not 20 procedures currently in cache) largest stored procedures in cache, along with the size and number of compiled plans that are in memory for that procedure. An example of the third section is shown in the following output:

```
Procedure Cache, Top 8:

Database Id: 1
Object Id: 640005311
Object Name: sp_configure
Version: 1
Uid: 1
Type: stored procedure
Number of trees: 0
Size of trees: 0.000000 Mb, 0.000000 bytes, 0 pages
Bytes lost for alignment 0 (Percentage of total: 0.000000)
Number of plans: 4
Size of plans: 0.645847 Mb, 677220.000000 bytes, 332 pages
Bytes lost for alignment 10032 (Percentage of total: 1.481350)

    . . . .
Database Id: 4
Object Id: 1232007420
Object Name: sp_helpdb
Version: 1
Uid: 1
Type: stored procedure
Number of trees: 0
Size of trees: 0.000000 Mb, 0.000000 bytes, 0 pages
Bytes lost for alignment 0 (Percentage of total: 0.000000)
Number of plans: 1
Size of plans: 0.163151 Mb, 171076.000000 bytes, 84 pages
Bytes lost for alignment 2988 (Percentage of total: 1.746592)

    . . . .
Database Id: 4
Object Id: 1376007933
Object Name: sp_help
Version: 1
Uid: 1
Type: stored procedure
Number of trees: 0
Size of trees: 0.000000 Mb, 0.000000 bytes, 0 pages
Bytes lost for alignment 0 (Percentage of total: 0.000000)
Number of plans: 1
Size of plans: 0.156525 Mb, 164128.000000 bytes, 81 pages
Bytes lost for alignment 1633 (Percentage of total: 0.994955)

    . . . .
Database Id: 4
Object Id: 240003886
Object Name: sp_helpuser
Version: 1
Uid: 1
Type: stored procedure
```

```
Number of trees: 0
Size of trees: 0.000000 Mb, 0.000000 bytes, 0 pages
Bytes lost for alignment 0 (Percentage of total: 0.000000)
Number of plans: 1
Size of plans: 0.123927 Mb, 129947.000000 bytes, 64 pages
Bytes lost for alignment 363 (Percentage of total: 0.279345)


- - - -
Database Id: 4
Object Id: 28527135
Object Name: sp_cacheconfig
Version: 1
Uid: 1
Type: stored procedure
Number of trees: 0
Size of trees: 0.000000 Mb, 0.000000 bytes, 0 pages
Bytes lost for alignment 0 (Percentage of total: 0.000000)
Number of plans: 1
Size of plans: 0.119993 Mb, 125822.000000 bytes, 62 pages
Bytes lost for alignment 2131 (Percentage of total: 1.693662)


- - - -
Database Id: 4
Object Id: 1440008161
Object Name: sp_lock
Version: 1
Uid: 1
Type: stored procedure
Number of trees: 0
Size of trees: 0.000000 Mb, 0.000000 bytes, 0 pages
Bytes lost for alignment 0 (Percentage of total: 0.000000)
Number of plans: 1
Size of plans: 0.036139 Mb, 37895.000000 bytes, 19 pages
Bytes lost for alignment 412 (Percentage of total: 1.087215)


- - - -
Database Id: 1
Object Id: 624005254
Object Name: sp_getmessage
Version: 1
Uid: 1
Type: stored procedure
Number of trees: 0
Size of trees: 0.000000 Mb, 0.000000 bytes, 0 pages
Bytes lost for alignment 0 (Percentage of total: 0.000000)
Number of plans: 1
Size of plans: 0.027714 Mb, 29060.000000 bytes, 15 pages
Bytes lost for alignment 54 (Percentage of total: 0.185822)


- - - -
Database Id: 4
Object Id: 1872009700
Object Name: sp_who
Version: 1
Uid: 1
Type: stored procedure
Number of trees: 0
Size of trees: 0.000000 Mb, 0.000000 bytes, 0 pages
```

10

OPTIMIZING CONFIGURATION OPTIONS

```
Bytes lost for alignment 0 (Percentage of total: 0.000000)
Number of plans: 1
Size of plans: 0.023154 Mb, 24279.000000 bytes, 12 pages
Bytes lost for alignment 175 (Percentage of total: 0.720788)

....

DBCC execution completed. If DBCC printed error messages, contact a user with
System Administrator (SA) role.
```

Note

SQL Server's stored procedures are recursive and reusable, but not reentrant. If many processes want to run a procedure at one time, the server creates a new query plan for each concurrent execution. The size shown by dbcc memusage is the cumulative size for all plans. The size of an individual plan is the Size of plans/Number of plans. For example, in the previous output, the sp_configure procedure has 4 copies in cache using 332 pages. The size of a single plan therefore is 332/4 or 83 pages.

The procedure size statistics reported in dbcc memusage refer to the largest plans in cache, but not necessarily the most frequently used. To find out which are the most frequently used, you can implement auditing to track procedure execution.

USING *DBCC MEMUSAGE* INFORMATION

Run dbcc memusage regularly to understand how memory is being used in your server. Pay special attention to these issues:

♦ Look at the overall memory figures to make certain that you have as much data cache as you expected.

♦ Look at data cache to see whether any particular object is monopolizing the cache at the expense of other objects, because it may be appropriate to take other tuning steps on that object.

♦ Look at how large stored procedures are, because smaller procedures compile and execute faster.

OTHER METHODS FOR VIEWING MEMORY UTILIZATION

There are two methods other than dbcc memusage that are used to examine the memory utilization within SQL Server: sp_configure and the SQL Server error log.

USING *SP_CONFIGURE*

In addition to providing a means for changing your SQL Server configuration, sp_configure also provides some reports on memory utilization within SQL Server.

An information-only configuration option, total data cache size, is available to view the total data cache memory available:

```
sp_configure "total data cache size"
go
```

Parameter Name	Default	Memory Used	Config Value	Run Value
total data cache size	0	365616	0	365616

For other memory-related configuration options—such as procedure cache percent, number of user connections, and number of devices—SQL Server reports in the Memory Used column the amount of memory required for the currently running configuration value.

USING THE ERROR LOG

Another place to determine the amount of data and procedure cache available within SQL Server is the SQL Server error log. Scan the messages generated the last time the SQL Server was rebooted and look for lines similar to the following:

```
00:96/01/22 00:49:22.88 server   Number of proc buffers allocated: 709.
00:96/01/22 00:49:23.00 server   Number of blocks left for proc headers: 855.
00:96/01/22 00:49:24.60 server   Memory allocated for the default data cache cache:
                                 2494 Kb
00:96/01/22 00:49:24.93 server   Size of the 2K memory pool: 1982 Kb
00:96/01/22 00:49:24.95 server   Size of the 16K memory pool: 512 Kb
00:96/01/22 00:49:24.97 server   Memory allocated for the perftune_cache cache:
                                 5120 Kb
00:96/01/22 00:49:24.98 server   Size of the 2K memory pool: 5120 Kb
```

The Number of blocks left for proc headers value indicates the number of pages set aside for the procedure cache. Number of proc buffers allocated represents to the maximum number of compiled objects that can reside in procedure cache at one time—in this case, 709.

The data cache space is broken out by named data cache. For example, the default data cache is 2494 Kb in size and the perftune_cache is 5120 Kb. The total data cache is the sum of these two values, 7614KB. You will explore the meaning of memory pools later in this chapter.

CONFIGURING THE PROCEDURE CACHE

Compiled stored procedure execution plans are stored in an area of memory called procedure cache. The balance of server memory, less that used by the server for its internal kernel and other variable elements, will be used by the server for data and procedure cache. The procedure cache configuration setting determines the amount of procedure cache set aside for procedures, triggers, and SQL batch executions. The larger the procedure cache, the more query plans that can reside in memory.

Stored procedure query plans in procedure cache are reusable, but not reentrant. This means that if more than one user executes a stored procedure or trigger simultaneously, multiple copies of the query plan are created in the procedure cache.

Query plans for stored procedures and triggers remain in cache after execution for subsequent execution by the same or other SQL Server users, providing there is sufficient cache space available for the query plan to remain in cache. If space needs to be made available, the oldest query plans in cache not in use are flushed out of cache to make room. If the stored procedure query plan is larger than available space in the procedure cache (for example, all query plans are in use) and there is insufficient space to load another query tree or plan into procedure cache, the user will see the following error message:

```
Message 701: "There is not enough procedure cache to run this procedure,
trigger, or SQL batch. Retry later, or ask your SA to reconfigure SQL Server
with more procedure cache."
```

To avoid this error condition, and to have enough procedure cache space to avoid having frequently used query plans flushed from cache, make sure you configure procedure cache large enough. A good starting point for sufficient procedure cache space is to configure it large enough to store at least one copy of your largest stored procedure for each concurrent user, plus a fudge factor to accommodate other uses of procedure cache (trigger, rules, and so forth).

To derive this estimate, multiply the number of concurrent users executing stored procedures times the size of the largest stored procedure they will execute. You can determine the stored procedure size by using dbcc memusage, if the stored procedure is one of the 20 largest currently in procedure cache. Otherwise, you can get a rough estimate of the size of a procedure query plan by using the following select statement:

```
select (count(*) / 8) + 1
   from sysprocedures
where id = object_id("proc_name")
```

To get a report for all procedures and triggers in a database ordered by size, execute the following:

```
select o.name, "size in pages" = ((count(*)/8)+1)
from sysprocedures p, sysobjects o
where p.id = o.id
and o.type in ("TR", "P")
```

```
group by o.name
order by 2 desc
go

name                          size in pages
- - - - - - - - - - - - - - - - - - - - - - -    - - - - - - - - - - - -
storename_proc                4
totalsales_trig               4
deltitle                      3
title_proc                    3
history_proc                  3
storeid_proc                  3
titleid_proc                  3
insert_salesdetail_proc       3
byroyalty                     2
discount_proc                 2
insert_sales_proc             2
```

Assume there are 100 concurrent users, the largest stored procedure query plan is 60KB (30 2KB pages), and you need an additional 25 percent for other uses of procedure cache. The amount of memory then is calculated as follows:

100 concurrent users × 60KB (the largest stored procedure) = 6MB × 1.25 (fudge factor) = 8MB

This indicates that procedure cache needs to be at least 8MB. However, the procedure cache setting specifies the percentage of available cache memory to be set aside for the procedure cache.

The amount of memory available as cache space is the total memory configured for SQL Server minus the amount of memory required for the SQL Server executable and kernel and server structures. Use dbcc memusage to determine the amount of memory used for these purposes and subtract it from the total memory configured. If you have 50MB available for data and procedure cache, 8MB is 16 percent of that (8/50 = 16 percent).

Note that this is the minimum amount of memory you need for procedure cache to avoid an out-of-memory condition. If you use procedures heavily in your applications or use nested procedures, you may need to increase the procedure cache percentage to keep procedures in cache. Be careful not to overconfigure the procedure cache beyond what is needed because that wastes cache memory that can better be used as data cache.

TUNING THE DATA CACHE

For versions of SQL Server prior to System 11, tuning the memory configuration is fairly straightforward. You estimate your overall memory requirements for SQL Server executable, SQL Server Kernel, and other SQL Server structures (user connections, devices, open databases, locks, and so forth), and the amount of memory for procedure cache. Whatever is left is the amount of memory used for data cache. This data cache is used by all tables and indexes accessed.

In System 11, you estimate your total memory requirements in the same way, but the data cache management scheme is much improved. Rather than a single data cache shared by all databases, tables, and indexes, you can now partition the data cache into multiple buckets, or *named caches*, and bind databases and tables to specific cache areas. In this section, you learn how to configure and use named caches and the performance benefits.

Estimating Total Memory Requirements

To estimate the total memory requirements, you first need to estimate how much data you want to keep in cache. Preferably, if you can keep an entire database in cache memory, your performance will be ideal. However, with most databases, this is simply not feasible. You need to size memory to improve your cache hit ratio. The cache hit ratio is the ratio of logical reads to physical reads, or in other words, the likelihood that a requested page will be found in data cache rather than having to be read from disk. For best performance, you want the cache hit ratio for your frequently used tables and indexes to be high.

Note

To determine your cache hit ratio, you can use the set statistics io option. This command displays the number of logical and physical page reads incurred when processing a statement against a table. Because every physical read incurs a corresponding logical read, the cache hit ratio is calculated as follows:

logical reads – (physical reads × pages per I/O) / logical reads

Prior to System 11, the number of "pages per I/O" was always a single page. In System 11, depending on how the cache buffers are configured within a named cache, SQL Server can perform reads on up to 8 pages at a time (16KB using 2KB pages). Therefore, if SQL Server uses 16KB reads for a query, and statistics io reports 20 physical reads, it actually reads 160 (20 × 8) pages. To determine the I/O method used by a query, you also turn on the showplan output:

```
select count(*) from pt_tx_CIid
go

QUERY PLAN FOR STATEMENT 1 (at line 1).
```

```
STEP 1
    The type of query is SELECT.
    Evaluate Ungrouped COUNT AGGREGATE.

    FROM TABLE
        pt_tx_CIid
    Nested iteration.
    Index : idx2
    Ascending scan.
    Positioning at index start.
    Index contains all needed columns. Base table will not be read.
    Using I/O Size 16 Kbytes.
    With LRU Buffer Replacement Strategy.

STEP 2
    The type of query is SELECT.
```

Table: pt_tx_CIid   scan count 1,   logical reads: 40,   physical reads: 3

From this output, you see that SQL Server performed 3 physical reads, using 16KB I/O and 40 logical reads. The cache hit ratio is the following:

(40 - (3 * 8)) / 40 = 16 / 40 = 40%.

In other words, 16 pages, or 40 percent of the table, was found in cache.

Remember, the first time you access a table, the cache hit ratio will be zero because none of the table will be in cache memory.

To improve the cache hit ratio for your frequently accessed tables and indexes, determine which tables and indexes you wish to fit in cache and size your data cache accordingly.

Assume that you determine you need at least 100MB of data cache to hold your frequently accessed tables and indexes. How much total memory do you need to configure SQL Server for?

First, you need to figure out how much memory you need for the SQL Server executable and kernel and the server structures. This can be determined from the dbcc memusage output. If you don't have a SQL Server up and running yet, you'll have to estimate your memory requirements.

At the end of Chapter 9, there is a table of values indicating how much memory is required by certain SQL Server configuration values. The most important of these is user connections. At 51KB per configured user connection, this configuration variable requires the greatest amount of memory. The rest of the configuration parameter memory requirements are minimal in comparison.

Start adding things up with the assumption that you need 2MB for the SQL Server executable and 8MB for the procedure cache:

2MB (SQL Server executable)

+5.1MB (100 users × 51KB / user connection)

+5MB (rough estimate of other server and kernel memory requirements)

+8MB (procedure cache requirements)

=20.1MB

To have roughly 100MB of memory available for data cache, you therefore need to configure SQL Server for 120MB of memory. If you need 8MB set aside for procedure cache, calculate the procedure cache percentage as follows:

120MB

–12MB

=108MB for data and procedure cache

8MB / 108MB = 8%

Therefore, procedure cache should be set to 8.

Note

If, in the future, you need to increase your memory allocation to increase data cache size, don't forget to adjust the procedure cache setting to accommodate. For example, if you are adding another 100MB to increase the data cache to 200MB and get more tables and indexes to remain in cache, you set the total memory configuration to 220MB.

However, if your procedure cache setting is 8%, you would have 17MB set aside for procedure cache. Your requirements for procedure cache are the same as before—only 8MB—because you haven't increased the number of users on the system or increased stored procedure sizes. You would waste 9MB of memory that might better be used for data cache (9MB could be enough memory for an entire table to remain in memory). After configuring total memory to 220MB, set the procedure cache setting down to 4% to make that 9MB of memory available to the data cache.

Warning

Do not overconfigure the total memory parameter for SQL Server. If set too high—either more than the available physical memory or the available free memory within the O/S—the SQL Server will either not start at all or, if it does, may end up using virtual memory within the O/S. The paging in and out of virtual memory seriously degrades SQL Server performance.

Buffer Management in SQL Server

After you install System 11 SQL Server, it contains a single data cache called the `default data cache` that will be used for all tables, indexes, and logs. This is similar to pre-System 11 SQL Server, which also had a single global data cache.

A pre-System 11 SQL Server data cache consists of a single MRU/LRU (most recently used/least recently used) buffer chain (see Figure 10.2). As pages age out of cache, they move toward the wash marker. The wash marker ensures that pages past the marker at the LRU end of the chain are either clean (not modified) or are in the process of being written to disk. Clean pages are used for requested data pages not in cache and are moved to the MRU end of the chain as they are needed.

Figure 10.2.
Pre-System 11 Data
Cache MRU/LRU
chain.

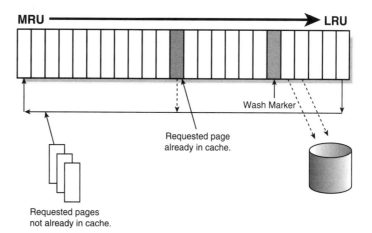

The MRU/LRU chain is a doubly linked list of 2KB pages. As cache space is needed and new data pages are read in, the least recently used pages are moved toward the wash marker. As a page crosses the wash marker, it is written to disk if it contains any data modifications not already written out previously. This is referred to as a "dirty" page. Once it is written out, it is then marked as clean and cycled back to the MRU end of the chain as new data pages are read in from disk to cache.

If a page already in cache is accessed again, it is moved back to the MRU end of the chain. This has the effect of keeping your frequently accessed data in cache memory.

Indexes in the Data Cache

Indexes are treated slightly differently from data pages in the data cache in an effort to keep them in cache longer. Index pages can make multiple trips through the MRU/LRU chain. By default, the number of trips for an index page is 0, which results in index pages making only a single trip through the MRU/LRU chain. This can be modified by using the sp_configure command to change the setting for number of index trips. To keep index pages in cache longer, increase the number of index trips; reduce it to have them flush out sooner.

Warning

Do not set the number of index trips too high. In a high-transaction environment, the cache can flood with index pages that do not age out. This can cause processes to time out waiting for cache space to become available.

Conversely, setting it too low causes index pages to age out too frequently, possibly resulting in poor performance if physical I/O is required too often to read index pages into cache.

Pre-System 11 Buffer Management Performance

One shortcoming of a single data cache in SQL Server prior to System 11 is that all databases and user processes share the same data cache reading all data into the MRU end of the cache chain. This makes it difficult to ensure that frequently used tables will remain in cache, especially with queries on very large tables. If a process performs a table scan on a table that is larger than available cache space, the table can easily fill up the data cache, flushing other data and index pages out of the data cache. There is no way to prevent this from happening because there is no way to partition the cache or to modify how tables are read into cache.

This cache strategy can have an adverse impact on performance as smaller, frequently accessed tables that can easily fit in cache need to be read from disk again. In addition, it can increase the frequency of writes as modified pages get flushed out of cache by a large table scan.

System 11 Enhancements to Buffer Management

System 11 offers you a number of enhancements to the buffer management scheme in SQL Server:

- The ability to partition the data cache into multiple caches—each with its own MRU/LRU chain—and bind databases, tables, and indexes to specific caches

- The ability to configure multiple buffer pools within a data cache to support large I/Os

- The ability to use different cache replacement strategies for data that does not need to remain in cache

The rest of this section looks at ways of configuring and tuning SQL Server to take advantage of these improvements.

Note

The ability to create multiple data caches should not be seen as a substitute for proper indexing and optimizing queries using normal query optimization techniques. Splitting the data cache into multiple smaller caches can actually degrade performance if not configured wisely. For example, restricting a data cache area to a single table that is not accessed frequently takes away valuable data cache space for other objects that could have used that memory.

CONFIGURING NAMED DATA CACHES IN SYSTEM 11

One of the biggest enhancements System 11 offers is the ability to partition the data cache into multiple named data caches and binding databases or database objects to specific data caches. Named data caches can help improve performance in a number of ways:

- Multiple data caches can minimize data cache contention in an SMP environment. With a single data cache, there is contention between multiple processes attempting to access the cache concurrently. SQL Server places a "spinlock" on the cache when one process makes changes to the cache, which can cause contention in a high-transaction environment, even though the spinlocks are held for a very short duration. With multiple caches, each has its own spinlock, which can increase concurrency if user processes are accessing objects in different caches.

- You can configure a named cache and bind critical tables and indexes to it to keep them in cache.

- Tables in a VLDB environment can be assigned to data caches configured to support large I/Os to improve table scan and large query performance. This also prevents large table scans from flushing other pages required by OLTP applications out of cache.

◆ Active tables can be assigned to a different cache than its indexes to in-crease concurrency.

◆ Transaction logs can be bound to separate cache from the data to reduce contention for cache space between the data and the log.

◆ tempdb can be bound to its own cache area to minimize contention for cache space between tempdb and user databases. If configured large enough, physical I/O in tempdb can be avoided completely, greatly improving tempdb performance.

CREATING NAMED DATA CACHES

Before setting up named data caches, you should try to configure SQL Server with as much memory as possible. Use dbcc memusage or examine the value reported for total data cache size by sp_configure to determine the amount of memory left in your SQL Server configuration for data cache. As you create additional named data caches, you will be reducing the size of the default data cache that will be used by databases and tables not bound to a specific cache.

To create a named cache, use the sp_cacheconfig stored procedure.

SYNTAX

```
sp_cacheconfig [cachename, [cachesize[P¦K¦M¦G] [, logoonly ¦ mixed]]]
```

PARAMETERS

Table 10.1 defines the parameters for sp_cacheconfig.

TABLE 10.1. sp_cacheconfig PARAMETERS.

Parameter	Description
cachename	The name you want to assign to the data cache. It must be unique within the SQL Server.
cachesize	Specifies the size of the named cache in Pages, Kilobytes, Megabytes, or Gigabytes.
logonly or mixed	Indicates whether the cache can be used for only log pages or data and log pages, respectively.

NOTES

Without any parameters, sp_cacheconfig reports on all configured caches within SQL Server. Specifying only cachename will report on the configuration of the specified cache.

Changes made by using sp_cacheconfig will not take effect until SQL Server is restarted. At that time, the size of the default data cache will be decreased accordingly to accommodate the new named cache.

EXAMPLES

Create a 5MB cache called perftune_cache.

```
sp_cacheconfig "perftune_cache", "5M"
go
```

```
. . . . . . . . . . .
0
The change is completed. The SQL Server must be rebooted for the change to take
effect.
```

Before restarting, examine what the cache configuration looks like:

```
sp_cacheconfig
go
```

Cache Name	Status	Type	IO Sz	Wash Sz	Config Value	Run Value
default data cache	Active	Default			0.00 Mb	7.48 Mb
default data cache	Active	Default	2 Kb	512 Kb	0.00 Mb	6.98 Mb
default data cache	Active	Default	16 Kb	160 Kb	0.50 Mb	0.50 Mb
perftune_cache	Pend/Act	Mixed			5.00 Mb	0.00 Mb
				Total	5.00 Mb	7.48 Mb

Note the difference between the Config Value and the Run Value as well as the current size of the default data cache. Cache configuration changes that are not in effect yet have a status of Pend/Act. Now restart the SQL Server and execute sp_cacheconfig again:

```
sp_cacheconfig
go
```

Cache Name	Status	Type	IO Sz	Wash Sz	Config Value	Run Value
default data cache	Active	Default			0.00 Mb	2.44 Mb
default data cache	Active	Default	2 Kb	512 Kb	0.00 Mb	1.94 Mb
default data cache	Active	Default	16 Kb	160 Kb	0.50 Mb	0.50 Mb
perftune_cache	Active	Mixed			5.00 Mb	5.00 Mb
perftune_cache	Active	Mixed	2 Kb	512 Kb	0.00 Mb	5.00 Mb
				Total	5.00 Mb	7.44 Mb

Note that the perftune_cache is now active and its type is mixed. It is currently configured only for 2KB I/Os (IO Sz) and its wash marker (Wash Sz) is 256 pages (512KB) from the LRU end of the page chain. Notice also how the default data cache has been reduced in size to allocate the 5MB to the perftune_cache. Currently, all the space is assigned to the 2KB buffer pool. You'll see how to change the buffer pool configuration shortly.

If you want to set a minimum size for the default data cache, use sp_cacheconfig and specify a size. For example, to ensure that the default data cache is always at least 10MB in size, execute the following:

```
sp_cacheconfig "default data cache", "10M"
```

Note

The default data cache is the only cache space used during SQL Server recovery. The smaller the default data cache, the longer it can potentially take for recovery to complete. If you have a high-transaction-rate environment, make sure the default data cache is large enough for recovery to occur in a reasonable period of time.

USING THE CONFIGURATION FILE TO CONFIGURE NAMED CACHES

In addition to using sp_cacheconfig to set up named caches, you can also set up named caches in the configuration file that will take effect the next time SQL Server is restarted. The configuration file syntax is as follows:

```
[Named Cache:cachename]
    cache size = {size[P¦K¦M¦G] ¦ DEFAULT}
    cache status = {mixed cache ¦ log only ¦ default data cache}
```

Warning

Unlike when using sp_cacheconfig, editing the configuration file directly doesn't verify the cache settings. If you configure a named cache larger than you have available cache space, SQL Server will not restart. You have to modify the configuration file to reduce the named cache size(s) or increase the total memory configuration variable. For this reason, it is recommended that you use the sp_cacheconfig procedure when setting up named caches.

DEFINING BUFFER POOLS

By default, SQL Server performs 2KB I/Os (the size of a data page) when retrieving data from disk into cache. A named cache is initially set up with a 2KB buffer pool to perform 2KB I/O only. If you want to support larger I/Os within the named cache, you need to configure additional buffer pools within the cache. This includes the default data cache as well.

The benefit of large I/Os is better read performance for queries retrieving large amounts of contiguous data. Types of queries that can benefit from large I/Os include table scans, large range retrievals using a clustered index, nonclustered index leaf level scans, text/image retrievals, bulk copy operations on heap tables, and update statistics. If 16KB I/O is supported in a named cache, eight pages can be read per I/O request, significantly reducing the amount of read requests required.

Buffer pool configuration within a cache is dynamic. You can create buffer pools or modify buffer pools without having to restart SQL Server.

Creating buffer pools divides the memory within a cache area into multiple slices, one for each I/O size. To set up buffer pools, use the sp_poolconfig procedure.

SYNTAX

sp_poolconfig cachename [, "memsize[P¦K¦M¦G]", "poolK" [, "affectedpoolK"]]

PARAMETERS

Table 10.2 defines the parameters for sp_poolconfig.

TABLE 10.2. sp_poolconfig PARAMETERS.

Parameter	Description
cachename	The name of the data cache for which you are configuring a buffer pool.
memsize	The amount of memory within the cache to allocate to the specified buffer pool.
poolK	Specifies the buffer pool being configured.
affectedpoolK (optional)	The buffer pool that space will be taken from for the poolK buffer (the default is the 2KB buffer pool). Note that the 2KB buffer pool cannot be reduced smaller than 512KB.

EXAMPLE

Set up a 16KB buffer pool in the perftune_cache that's 3MB:

```
sp_poolconfig "perftune_cache", "3M", "16K"
go

sp_cacheconfig "perftune_cache"
go

Procedure  sp_cacheconfig
```

Cache Name	Status	Type	IO Sz	Wash Sz	Config Value	Run Value
perftune_cache	Active	Mixed			5.00 Mb	5.00 Mb
perftune_cache	Active	Mixed	2 Kb	512 Kb	0.00 Mb	2.00 Mb
perftune_cache	Active	Mixed	16 Kb	608 Kb	3.00 Mb	3.00 Mb
				Total	5.00 Mb	5.00 Mb

You now have a 3MB 16KB buffer pool configured that can be used for large I/O operations such as a table scan.

USING BUFFER POOLS

When the optimizer optimizes a query, it knows whether the table or index is bound to a named cache, the size of the named cache, and whether any buffer pools in the named cache are configured for large I/Os. If the optimizer determines that large I/Os would improve performance for the method used to access the table and there are cache buffers available in the named cache to support large I/Os, it will attempt to use large I/Os as long as there are sufficient buffers available within the pool.

If the optimizer attempts to perform 16KB I/O and there are no 16KB buffers available, SQL Server attempts to use the next available smaller I/O size to process the query.

In addition to the optimizer automatically choosing to use large I/Os, the user can force a specific I/O size by using the `prefetch` clause in a query.

CHANGING THE WASH AREA FOR A NAMED CACHE

The *wash area* is an area in the buffer pool where once dirty pages cross the wash marker, SQL Server will write the pages out to disk. Once the write completes, the page is marked as clean and is made available in the LRU end of the cache chain. This process ensures that queries that need clean pages in the data cache will find them at the LRU end of the memory pool.

In most cases, the default size of the wash area will provide the best performance. Tune all other aspects of the system before you play around with the wash area. If you set the wash area too high, pages will reach the wash marker too quickly, causing it to be written to disk. This will increase the number of writes for the database, especially if the page remains in the wash area and is modified again and needs to be written to disk. Setting the wash size too low may result in insufficient clean pages being available. This may result in a process requiring a clean page to have to wait until a dirty page is written to disk. This can significantly degrade performance.

To change a pool's wash size, use `sp_poolconfig`:

```
sp_poolconfig cache_name, "io_size", "wash=size[P¦K¦M¦G]"
```

For example, to set the wash size for the 2KB buffer pool in the `perftune_cache` at 400KB from the end of the LRU chain, execute the following:

```
sp_poolconfig perftune_cache, "2K", "wash=400K"
```

BINDING DATABASES AND OBJECTS TO NAMED CACHES

Once you have the named caches configured, the next step is to bind databases and database objects to the named caches to make use of them. Databases and objects can be bound to a named cache by using the `sp_bindcache` procedure.

SYNTAX

```
sp_bindcache "cachename", dbname [, "tablename[.indexname]" [, text]
```

PARAMETERS

Table 10.3 defines the parameters for `sp_bindcache`.

TABLE 10.3. `sp_bindcache` PARAMETERS.

Parameter	Description
cachename	Specifies the named cache to which you want to bind the database or object.
dbname	Specifies the database or the database the object belongs to that you are binding to the cache.
tablename	Specifies the table you are binding, unless *indexname* is also specified.
indexname	Specifies the name of the index for the specified table being bound to the named cache.
text	Allows binding of the text/image data for a table to the named cache.

When binding a database to a named cache, you must be in the master database. To bind tables or indexes, you must be in the database where they are stored.

Examples

First, bind the pubs2 database to the `perftune_cache`:

```
sp_bindcache "perftune_cache", pubs2
```

Next, bind the pt_tx table to the `perftune_cache`:

```
sp_bindcache "perftune_cache", perftune, pt_tx
```

Finally, bind the NCamount2 index for the pt_tx_NCamount table to the `perftune_cache` as well:

```
sp_bindcache "perftune_cache", perftune, "pt_tx_NCamount.NCamount"
```

If you ran a query against the pt_tx table requiring a table scan, it should now use the 16KB memory pool in the `perftune_cache`. You can confirm this with the `set showplan on` option:

```
set showplan on
go
select count(*) from pt_tx
go


QUERY PLAN FOR STATEMENT 1 (at line 1).


    STEP 1
        The type of query is SELECT.
        Evaluate Ungrouped COUNT AGGREGATE.

        FROM TABLE
            pt_tx
        Nested iteration.
        Index : idx2
        Ascending scan.
        Positioning at index start.
        Index contains all needed columns. Base table will not be read.
        Using I/O Size 16 Kbytes.
        With LRU Buffer Replacement Strategy.

    STEP 2
        The type of query is SELECT.


- - - - - - - - - - -
7282
```

Dropping Cache Bindings

To drop a binding of a table from a named cache, use the `sp_unbindcache` procedure:

```
Sp_unbindcache dbname [, tablename[.indexname] [, text]
```

To remove all bound databases and objects from the data cache, use sp_unbindcache_all:

```
sp_unbindcache_all "cachename"
```

> ### Note
>
> When you unbind an object from a cache, all pages for that object are flushed from cache. This can be a useful technique when you want to test physical I/O performance of your SQL Server (for example, comparing the performance difference using 2KB or 16KB I/Os). The first time you access the table, its pages are read into cache. The next time you run your test you will perform logical I/O. To force physical I/Os, unbind the table from its named cache and then rebind it. This causes the table to be flushed from cache so that SQL Server will perform physical I/O on the next test.

GETTING INFORMATION ON NAMED CACHE BINDINGS

You saw earlier in this chapter how you can get basic size information on named caches by using the sp_configure and sp_cacheconfig stored procedures. To determine which objects are bound to a named cache, use the sp_helpcache procedure.

SYNTAX

```
sp_helpcache ["cachename"]
```

EXAMPLE

```
sp_helpcache "perftune_cache"
go
```

Cache Name	Config Size	Run Size	Overhead
perftune_cache	5.00 Mb	5.00 Mb	0.27 Mb

```
----------------- Cache Binding Information: -----------------
```

Cache Name	Entity Name	Type	Index Name
perftune_cache	perftune	database	
perftune_cache	pubs2	database	
perftune_cache	perftune.dbo.pt_tx_NCamount	index	NCamount2
perftune_cache	perftune.dbo.pt_tx	table	

TUNING THE PRIVATE LOG CACHE

Another cache-related enhancement in System 11 is the introduction of the Private Log Cache (PLC). The PLC provides a separate user log cache for each user process. The user log cache is where log records are cached for a user's transaction before they are written to disk. The PLC is automatically enabled for all user connections within the SQL Server.

Prior to version 11, significant contention could occur between multiple user processes trying to write their log records to the end of the syslogs table. With the advent of a private log cache for each user in System 11, the log records for a given process are cached in their own private log space first, rather than being written to the log immediately. This minimizes contention for log writes, especially in multi-processor environments where greater contention for the log tends to occur.

Another advantage of the PLC is that if the begin tran for a long running or open transaction is in the PLC rather than the transaction log, the log can still be truncated.

The PLC is flushed to the transaction log whenever any one of the following events occurs:

- The next log record won't fit in the PLC.
- The transaction commits or aborts.
- The transaction modifies an object in another database (that is, internal two-phase commit).
- A modified data page must be written to disk (log records must always be written to disk before data pages).
- A checkpoint occurs.
- A trigger is executed for the transaction (the PLC is flushed to the transaction log before the trigger).

The default and minimum size of the PLC is 2048 bytes. You can configure the size of the user log cache by using the sp_configure stored procedure:

```
sp_configure "user log cache size", 4096
```

This example sets the user log cache to 4096 bytes. Be careful not to configure the user log cache size greater than the maximum amount of log information written by an application's largest transaction. Because the SQL Server flushes the user log cache when the transaction completes, any additional memory not used within the user log cache will be wasted. Don't configure the user log cache for large, long-running transactions because it is more likely for one of the other system events to occur before the transaction completes (see the previous list). This flushes the cache early and wastes user log cache memory.

Avoid setting the user log cache too small for your transactions. This causes the user log cache to be written to disk more than once per transaction, increasing the contention for the transaction log.

ESTIMATING TRANSACTION SIZE

How do you estimate the transaction size? One way to do this is to add up the size of the rows modified by the transaction plus the log overhead (54 bytes per row). Inserts and deletes log a single transaction record for each row inserted or deleted. An update generates an insert and a delete record for each row modified (unless an update in place occurs). Use the following formula to estimate transaction size:

Number of inserts $\times$ (row size + 54)

+Number of deletes $\times$ (row size + 54)

+Number of updates $\times\ 2 \times$ (row size + 54)

For example, if a transaction inserts 3 rows 50 bytes wide, updates a 200-byte row, and deletes 10 100-byte rows, the following is an estimate of the transaction size:

(3×104)

$+(10 \times 154)$

$+(1 \times 2 \times 254)$

$=2360$ bytes

In this example, if this is the largest transaction, and it is not a long-running transaction, you may want to bump up your user log cache size to 2500 bytes to fit this transaction in user log cache.

An alternative method is to use the `dbcc log` command (see Appendix A, "The Database Consistency Checker (`dbcc`)," for full syntax and description of `dbcc log`) and view the log records for your transactions. One of the fields displayed for each log record is the length of the log record (`len=#`). Match all the records for a transaction (those where `sessionid` is the same) and add up the lengths of each record to determine the transaction size. For example, examine the following records from a transaction log:

```
BEGINXACT     (3652,0)
attcnt=1 rno=0 op=0 padlen=2 sessionid = (3652,0) len=60 status=0x0000
masterxsid=(empty)
xstat=XBEG_ENDXACT,
spid=1 suid=1 uid=1 masterdbid=0 mastersite=0
name=$ins   time=Jan 17 1996 12:37PM

INSERT     (3652,1)
attcnt=1 rno=1 op=4 padlen=2 sessionid = (3652,0) len=72 status=0x0000
oampg=2360 pageno=2419 offset=1660 status=0x00 cid=0
old ts=0x0001 0x0000426d   new ts=0x0001 0x00004273
```

```
   xrow:
2094808c:   004a0100 00000100 00000100 00000789   .J..............
2094809c:   0000f320 d000                          ... ...

   ENDXACT     (3652,2)
   attcnt=1 rno=2 op=30 padlen=0 sessionid = (3652,0) len=28 status=0x0000
   endstat=COMMIT time=Jan 17 1996 12:37PM
```

Adding up the `len=` values shows this transaction is 160 bytes in size.

GUIDELINES FOR CACHE CONFIGURATION IN SYSTEM 11

To configure named caches in SQL Server properly, analyze your databases, database objects, I/O patterns, and queries to determine whether there are situations that will benefit from named caches and cache binding. Consider the following items:

- ◆ The size of any frequently accessed tables you want to keep entirely in cache.

- ◆ If tempdb is heavily used, determine the size of cache needed for tempdb and consider placing tempdb into a separate named cache.

- ◆ On multi-CPU systems, consider spreading your busiest tables and indexes across multiple caches to minimize cache contention.

- ◆ Make sure you leave a large enough default data cache for activity on unbound tables and indexes. In addition, the recovery process uses only the 2KB buffer pool in the default data cache. If this is too small, recovery will run slowly.

- ◆ Don't try to micromanage the data caches for every index and table. You'll probably end up wasting cache space and hurting performance rather than helping it.

- ◆ Overpartitioning the cache space can result in no cache large enough to keep moderately sized tables in cache. This can cause poor performance.

When setting up buffer pools, follow these guidelines when deciding whether to configure for large I/Os to improve performance:

- ◆ Determine whether you have queries that can benefit from large I/Os such as table scans on large tables that are scanned frequently, scans of large nonclustered indexes whose leaf level is scanned frequently, and range queries on clustered indexes that retrieve a large number of rows.

- ◆ Be careful not to leave too little space for the 2KB buffer pool. Many queries and types of data do not need large I/O (for example, single-row retrievals using an index). In addition, some tasks use only 2KB I/Os (for example, `disk init`, certain `dbcc` commands, and `drop table`).

- Consider reconfiguring buffer pools to match workload requirements. For example, increase the smaller buffer pools (that is, 2KB and 4KB pools) during the day when performing OLTP activities. Reconfigure them for a larger 16KB buffer pool for DSS activities run at night. (Remember, you do not need to reboot the SQL Server to change buffer pool configuration.)

- Consider the syslogs table and the amount of update activity. In addition, the I/O size for transaction logs is 4KB by default. To get the best log performance, make sure that the data cache the log is bound to has a 4KB buffer pool.

Note

Over time, with inserts and updates and the corresponding page splits, a table that initially took advantage of large I/Os to minimize the number of I/O requirements, may lose some of its performance gains as the table becomes more fragmented. Large I/Os provide the greatest benefit when the pages are sequential—that is, each page in the page chain points to the next physical page in the extent. If the page pointers cross extent boundaries, it could take up to 40 separate reads, rather than five 16KB reads, to read in 40 pages.

To correct this situation, you can drop and re-create the clustered index on the table. This makes the data pages contiguous again. If you use a low fillfactor when creating the index, you make the table larger than it needs to be at first, but it helps slow down fragmentation by leaving available space on the data pages for new data rows.

If you don't have room to create the clustered index with the data in the table, bcp the data out in sorted order and drop and re-create the clustered index. Then load the data into the table in the clustered index order and the data should be relatively sequential.

LOCK ESCALATION CONFIGURATION

SQL Server performs locking at two different levels for query processing. A single query can lock individual data pages within a table, or it can lock the entire table, depending on the number of pages being read. The "magic number" for lock escalation prior to System 11 was always 200 pages. In other words, any query was allowed to allocate 200 page locks on a table. As soon as that query attempted to allocate page lock 201, SQL Server's locking scheme would attempt to upgrade from 200+ individual page locks to a single table lock.

Although this mechanism introduced efficiency into the algorithms of the locking manager, its impact on query performance, particularly with large numbers of users, is not quite so obvious. The figure of 200 pages is unyielding. Whether a table has 400 or 4,000,000 pages, a single query acquiring 200 locks will attempt to escalate to a table level lock. As a result, a single query reading 250 pages (500KB of data) from a table containing 5,000,000 pages (a 10MB table), would lock the entire table. This is even more problematic in very large databases where individual table sizes can be measured in gigabytes.

With SQL Server 11, there are now three configuration options available that enable an administrator to adjust the thresholds for lock escalation. These options can be set globally at the SQL Server level or at the database or table level. The following are the three lock promotion thresholds that can be set in System 11:

◆ `lock promotion HWM` (high water mark)

◆ `lock promotion LWM` (low water mark)

◆ `lock promotion PCT` (percentage)

The `lock promotion LWM` configuration option sets the minimum number of page locks that SQL Server must acquire on a table before it will consider the option of upgrading to a table lock. In effect, it is the "on switch" for lock escalation.

The `lock promotion HWM` configuration option sets the maximum number of page locks a query can acquire before it is escalated to a table lock. The `lock promotion HWM` value is absolute and does not change based on activity or query size. As a result, this value may mean that smaller tables never receive table locks when needed, and very large tables may incur substantial blocking as table locks are applied where they shouldn't be.

The problem of relating lock escalation to table size is solved by using `lock promotion PCT`. The `lock promotion PCT` sets the number of page locks based on a percentage of the overall table size at which SQL Server will attempt to escalate page level locks to a table level lock. The `lock promotion PCT` value is checked when the number of locks on a table is between the LWM and HWM. Setting PCT lower increases the likelihood of a process escalating to a table level lock. This percentage is calculated as the following:

(PCT × number of rows in table) / 100

Setting PCT higher decreases the likelihood of a process acquiring a table level lock, causing it to use more page level locks for the duration of the transaction. This could lead to the process exhausting the available locks on the server.

The decision hierarchy that SQL Server uses to define the actual point of lock escalation is as follows:

1. If the `lock promotion LWM` value is never reached—that is, a table scan operation does not generate *at least* the `lock promotion LWM` number of page locks—SQL Server will not escalate to a table lock.

2. If the LWM threshold is reached, SQL Server upgrades page locks to a table lock based on which of the remaining configuration options is encountered *first*:

   If the high water mark is encountered before the percentage, page locks are escalated to table locks.

   If the percentage is encountered before the high water mark, page locks are escalated to a table lock.

SETTING LOCK THRESHOLDS AT THE SQL SERVER LEVEL

The default value for both `lock promotion LWM` and `lock promotion HWM` is 200 pages, and the default for `lock promotion PCT` is 100 percent. This mimics the lock escalation behavior of versions of SQL Server prior to System 11.

There are two ways to set the default lock escalation thresholds for all tables in the SQL Server: `sp_configure` (see Chapter 9) and the `sp_setpglockpromote` stored procedures. The lock thresholds are dynamic options that take effect immediately.

SYNTAX

```
sp_configure "{lock promotion HWM ¦ lock promotion LWM ¦ lock promotion PCT}",
             value
sp_setpglockpromote "server", NULL, new_LWM, new_HWM, newPCT
```

EXAMPLES

To set the high water mark for the entire server to 500 by using `sp_configure`, execute the following:

```
sp_configure "lock promotion HWM", 500
```

To set the server defaults by using the `sp_setpglockpromote` procedure, specify the `"server"` option as the first parameter. The following command sets the default HWM value to 1000 pages, the LWM to 200 pages, and the PCT to 75:

```
sp_setpglockpromote "server", null, 200, 1000, 75
```

SETTING LOCK THRESHOLDS AT THE DATABASE OR TABLE LEVEL

The server level lock promotion thresholds may not be appropriate for all databases or tables in the server. For a finer level of control over lock escalation at the database or table level, you can configure them specifically by using sp_setpglockpromote.

For example, if you have only a few large tables in your SQL Server, you may wish to leave the server level lock thresholds at the default settings and increase the thresholds, specifically for the database containing those tables or the tables themselves. Any settings at the table level will override the database and server settings.

To remove table or database lock promotion settings, use the sp_droplockpromote stored procedure.

SYNTAX

```
sp_setpglockpromote "{database | table}", {dbname | tablename},
                    new_LWM, new_HWM, newPCT
```

EXAMPLES

The following two commands set the previous server level options at the database and table levels, respectively:

```
sp_setpglockpromote "database", pubs2, 200, 1000, 75
sp_setpglockpromote "table", titles, 200, 1000, 75
```

TUNING NETWORK I/O FOR PERFORMANCE

In a client/server environment, the network must always be treated as a potential bottleneck. In order to minimize the bottleneck, you want to move as little information across the network as possible. This typically means avoiding performing large batch work (backups, bcp) across the network, especially when other users are working, or using stored procedures to minimize the SQL transmitted to the SQL Server.

In this section, you will examine some configuration options available in SQL Server to improve network performance. However, although the options discussed here will help to improve performance on the network, the real key to removing the network as a bottleneck is to minimize the amount of network traffic as much as possible.

SQL Server and the Network

All communication between SQL Server and clients occurs via the network. Requests for data from clients, and data and responses to those requests, are sent via packets. On the client and server side, the information is first put into Tabular Data Streams (TDS) packets. TDS packets are a network-independent protocol for passing information between a client and a server. This is what gives SQL Server its network independence. It is the Net-Library's responsibility in the client and server applications to wrap the necessary network-specific information around the TDS packets to route them on the network to the proper destination (see Figure 10.3).

Figure 10.3.
Communication
between SQL Server
and an Open Client
application is done via
Tabular Data Streams
(TDS) packets.

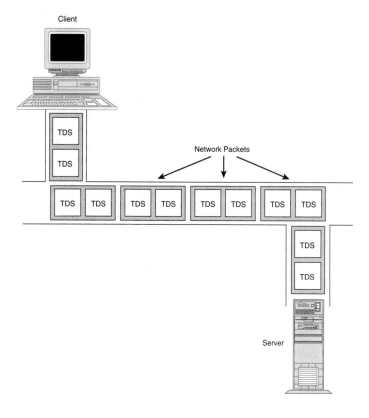

Sybase SQL Server was built on a network based client/server architecture and, as such, was designed to minimize network traffic as much as possible. However, it still uses the network exclusively for communication with clients, and the more optimally you can tune the network, the better the performance will be.

CONFIGURING NETWORK PACKET SIZE

By default, SQL Server uses a packet size of 512 bytes. This is appropriate for OLTP type environments where most transactions are short queries with small result sets. Many OLTP processes rarely even fill a packet. In DSS environments, however, queries typically return much larger result sets. In addition, both environments often have special processing requirements for large data loads or text processing. These types of processes can benefit from using larger packets to reduce the number of server reads and writes to the network by making each read or write more efficient.

You also may be able to improve performance by matching the TDS packet size to the network packet size, reclaiming unused space in the underlying networks.

Using larger packets also helps to improve network performance by reducing the number of packets sent between the client and the server. In most cases, the number of packets is more important than the size of the packets. The overhead to process the packets will typically affect performance the most.

In System 10, Sybase introduced the ability to configure the network packet sizes as a way to improve network performance. You can increase the default network packet size and/or configure additional network memory and the maximum network packet size to be used by applications requiring larger network packets for best performance.

Note

For details on how to configure and size the network configuration variables, refer to Chapter 9.

DEFAULT NETWORK PACKET SIZE (DNPS)

default network packet size specifies the smallest packet size all clients will use to communicate with the SQL Server. By default, this is 512 bytes. If you increase the default packet size, remember to also increase the maximum packet size accordingly.

Each user connection structure includes three buffers, each the size of default network packet size, to support network communications between the client and the server. Increasing default network packet size increases the memory requirements for each configured user connection accordingly. If not all applications need the larger packet sizes, you are wasting memory. You may choose to leave default network packet size at 512 and configure max network packet size and additional network memory to enable applications that can better take advantage of the larger packet sizes to request them (for example, `bcp` can specify larger network packet sizes using the `-A` option).

Warning

If you increase `default network packet size` above 512, older applications using pre-System 10 Open Client libraries will not be able to connect to SQL Server. Until it is definite that third-party applications are using System-10-or-later Open Client libraries, leave `default network packet size` at 512. Configure `max network packet size` and `additional network memory` to enable those applications that can use large packet sizes to request them.

MAX NETWORK PACKET SIZE (MNPS)

Some applications have special needs for sending large quantities of data across the network lines (`bcp`, for example). Setting `max network packet size` enables these applications to request larger packet sizes up to `max network packet size` as needed via client-library requests. Memory for larger network packets does not come from the three buffers set aside for each configured user connection, however. Memory for using the larger packets is allocated from the fragment acquired in the `additional network memory` variable. If sufficient memory is not available here, the requested packet size will not be granted. Instead, the largest network packet size that can be supported by `available network memory` will be used.

ADDITIONAL NETWORK MEMORY

The additional memory used for the larger network packets is taken from a separate pool of memory outside the memory allocated to SQL Server by the `total memory` parameter.

TCP NO DELAY

In TCP/IP networks, by default, SQL Server performs packet batching, briefly delaying sending partially full logical packets over the network by batching them into single larger physical packets. The purpose is to improve network throughput for terminal emulation environments. Disabling `tcp no delay` by setting this configuration variable on may help improve performance for applications that send and receive small TDS packets, enabling them to be sent immediately regardless of size. However, this will increase your network traffic volumes.

10

OPTIMIZING CONFIGURATION OPTIONS

NETWORK PERFORMANCE TIPS

Although larger packet sizes can improve performance for applications performing large data transfers, there is eventually a point of diminishing returns. Unfortunately, there is no reliable method for predicting where this point is. The best method is to vary the network packet size and benchmark the I/O rates. Plot them until you find the point where performance is optimal.

Although you may see performance improvement for some applications using larger packet sizes, the greatest performance gains will come from optimizing network communications. Some optimization methods to consider include the following:

- Use stored procedures to reduce overall network traffic.
- Filter data at the server rather than the client to avoid sending unnecessary data across the network.
- Minimize the impact of other network-intensive activities (for example, network backups, bcp loads) by running them on a separate network or running them during periods when user activity is at a minimum.

SPEEDING UP INDEX CREATION

System 10 SQL Server introduced the number of extent i/o buffers variable, which allows you to set aside an area of memory exclusively for index creation. Extent I/O buffers enable SQL Server to use eight-page (16KB) buffers for reading and writing intermediate and final results when creating indexes.

Only one user process can take advantage of the extent i/o buffers when creating an index. Other simultaneous index creations use standard I/O (reading and writing individual pages for intermediate sort results and index pages).

The optimal setting for number of extent i/o buffers appears to vary depending on your system and the size of your tables. Many have found that values between 40 and 60 provide optimal performance. You may want to experiment with different settings to find the optimal setting for your environment. Do not set it too high, however. Setting number of extent i/o buffers over 100 has been found to degrade index creation performance, possibly due to the additional overhead of managing the buffers.

You may want to use a large value for number of extent i/o buffers at initial load time, so when indexes are initially created on your system they can take advantage of the extent I/O buffers to minimize index creation time. Once the system is loaded and indexes created, reduce the value to zero to make the memory available for data cache instead.

If you have ample memory available and frequently re-create indexes, you may want to set number of extent i/o buffers permanently. Otherwise, you can reconfigure the SQL Server during off-hours to use extent I/O buffers and run your index creates then.

TUNING AN SMP CONFIGURATION

The SQL Server Symmetric Multiprocessing (SMP) architecture is a Virtual Server Architecture running 1 to 32 cooperating SQL Server processes in parallel. Each process is referred to as an engine. There is no master processor.

The SQL Server SMP architecture is a "shared everything" architecture. The engines share the same SQL Server resources (memory, disk, and so forth). SQL Server performs its own task management, scheduling SQL Server tasks onto available engines. Tasks are not bound to a specific engine. When a SQL Server engine requires CPU resources, the operating system schedules the engine onto an available CPU. Engines are not bound to CPUs keeping the processing load symmetrically balanced.

Figure 10.4 demonstrates the scheduling of the following tasks within SQL Server:

1. As a client login request is received, SQL Server initially handles the request on engine 0, then passes it to the engine handling the fewest number of user connections (Note that in System 11, network traffic can be handled by all engines, not just engine 0.)

2. The task is then put to sleep in the sleep queue waiting for the client process to send a request.

3. When a request is received, the task is then put at the end of the runnable queue.

4. When the task reaches the front of the queue, it gets scheduled on the next available engine.

5. The SQL Server engine then requests CPU cycles from the operating system, and the operating system assigns it to an available CPU.

6. The task processes on the engine until it blocks on disk I/O or a lock request, or exceeds its time slice.

7. If the task is blocked waiting on a resource, it goes into the sleep queue where it remains until the request is satisfied.

8. The process then moves back to the end of the runnable queue.

9. When the task reaches the front of the queue, it gets scheduled on the next available engine and the process continues until the task finishes.

10. The task is then put onto the sleep queue waiting for a client request.

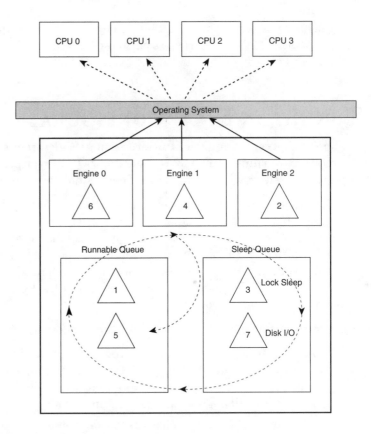

Figure 10.4.
SQL Server SMP task
management.

CONFIGURING MULTIPLE ENGINES

SQL Server is initially configured for a single engine. If current performance is not up-to-par and you determine that the SQL Server is CPU-bound, you may want to increase the number of engines if you have additional CPUs available. Use a tool such as Sybase SQL Monitor or an operating system utility to monitor CPU utilization. Generally, if the average CPU utilization is greater than 85 percent, adding an additional engine may improve performance.

Tip

When measuring CPU performance, you may want to disable the housekeeping task within SQL Server to prevent its operations from skewing the CPU measurements. You can disable the housekeeper task with the following command:

```
sp_configure "housekeeping free write percent", 0
```

You can reconfigure the number of available engines with the `sp_configure` command:

```
sp_configure "max online engines", 3
```

This is not a dynamic configuration value. A reboot of SQL Server is necessary for it to take effect.

Engine Tuning Guidelines

Consider the following guidelines when configuring `max online engines`:

◆ Never have more engines than usable CPUs (if a CPU fails, remember to reconfigure the number of engines within SQL Server).

◆ Have only as many engines as usable CPUs. If there is a lot of processing by another application within the O/S, one engine per CPU is excessive. Leave at least one CPU available for the O/S and other applications.

◆ Start with what you think will be the minimum number of engines required, then monitor CPU usage and increase the number of engines slowly until CPU utilization falls to the desired level.

Application Design Issues in an SMP Environment

As you increase the number of engines, the number of concurrent activities increases as well because more than one process can run simultaneously. This may increase contention for locks, I/O, network, and other SQL Server resources. To reduce contention in an SMP environment, follow these application development guidelines:

◆ Minimize the number of indexes on the tables. The greater the number of indexes, the greater overhead and the number of locks held during updates, increasing potential for contention.

◆ Spread your disk I/O across multiple databases to reduce I/O contention between the multiple concurrent processes.

◆ Use a lower fillfactor when creating indexes. This minimizes page splits temporarily and improves insert performance, thereby minimizing page and locking contention. The effect of fillfactor, however, will be lost as data is inserted and updated.

◆ Set the `max_rows_per_page` attribute on heavily accessed tables as a permanent means to spread rows out across multiple pages and to minimize page contention.

◆ Consider using heap table partitioning to set up multiple page chains to minimize locking and I/O contention on heap tables with concurrent insert activity.

◆ Keep transactions short and as concise as possible so that locks are held for as short a period as possible.

SUMMARY

The main configuration parameter that affects SQL Server performance is the memory configuration. SQL Server 11 introduces some new options for fine-tuning the memory configuration. Other configuration options can be tuned to improve SQL Server performance as well.

SQL Server 11 implements more varied and flexible configuration options than previous releases. This gives an administrator finer control over the SQL Server performance, but also the ability to configure incorrectly and possibly make the performance worse. Be careful when playing around with configuration options you don't fully understand.

Finally, keep in mind that although you may see performance improvement by tweaking the SQL Server configuration, the greatest performance gains are typically realized through proper database and index design, and writing efficient SQL code. For example, you may see a 10 percent performance improvement by tuning your network configuration, but a 100 percent or better performance improvement through proper index design.

- Database Design
  Issues

- What Is Logical
  Design?

- Denormalizing the
  Database

CHAPTER 11

Database Design and
Performance

The purpose of a logical database design is to understand and describe your data.

Logical database designers are very good at drawing diagrams explaining the relationship of the data within an organization and even explaining the diagrams in front of a group. Usually, they can even take the logical design to the next few steps, most notably assigning attributes to their entities (that is, identifying which columns go into which tables).

Many shops swear by this design, and require this logical design to be the physical design, simply because it is easy to understand.

This is not a good approach. A logical design does not have the same purpose as a physical design. The primary purpose of a physical design is performance.

Designing databases for performance, however, requires an understanding of the underlying DBMS. You have learned much from the preceding chapters in this book. This chapter explores physical database design techniques for improving SQL Server performance.

DATABASE DESIGN ISSUES

There are three primary design issues to consider when developing a physical database design:

♦ Data integrity
♦ Ease of use
♦ Performance

When developing a physical database design, you want the design to support your data consistency and *referential integrity* (RI) requirements easily. If a data element is represented exactly once within a database, it is easier to track and maintain than if it is represented multiple times. Referential integrity must also be maintained and, if possible, enforced at the server level.

Tip

One of the more frequently asked questions is whether to handle integrity checking (of all sorts) at the client level or at the server level. The ideal answer is to check in both places. Check at the client level because it is cheaper and faster; check at the server level to guarantee database integrity across all applications uniformly, including those that might not perform integrity checks.

A DBA also should consider ease of comprehension in a physical database design. Tables should be browsable so that end users can easily find the data they need and know what data a table contains.

Finally, the DBA typically wants to make database access and modification fast. Speed of data retrieval and update is usually the yardstick used to measure the success of a physical database design. Often, designing a database for access speed or to improve update performance requires modifying the physical design of the database—for example, duplicating or partitioning frequently used data from infrequently used data.

Unfortunately, it is often impossible to design for all three criteria (data integrity, ease of use, and performance) because they tend to be mutually exclusive. For example, breaking up a table to improve access speed makes it harder to browse and pull data together for the end users. During physical database design, decisions need to be made regarding balancing these objectives.

What Is Logical Design?

Logical database design is the process of defining end users' data needs and grouping elements into logical units (for example, tables in an RDBMS). This design should be independent of the final physical implementation. The actual physical layout of the tables, access paths, and indexes is provided at physical design time. Database design tradeoffs have ramifications in physical design and performance because an RDBMS cannot detect a poorly designed database and compensate accordingly.

Logical design is intended to reduce (eliminate) redundant data and thereby minimize row size. This has the effect of increasing the number of joins required to pull related data elements together. The ultimate goal of logical design is to make it easy for a user to grasp a gestalt of his data and for the DBA to design the physical database.

Normalization Conditions

In order to understand how to change the database in the physical design to suit your performance needs, you first need to understand relational database *normalization*, which is the end result of logical database design. Here's a review of the basic terminology and conditions of normalization:

◆ An *entity* (table) consists of *attributes* (columns) that define *properties* about each *instance* (row) of the entity.

◆ Each instance of data refers to a single event.

- There is a way of uniquely identifying each row, which we call a *primary key*. The primary key enables you to decide which row you want to reference.
- The primary key can be a single column or multiple columns (a *compound* or *composite key*).
- Primary keys cannot be null (if there is no way of uniquely identifying a row, it does not belong in a relational database).

NORMAL FORMS

There are up to five levels of normalization, or five *normal forms*, in the logical design process. The idea behind normalization is to provide data and keys to find the data and to ensure that the data exists in only one place. In this book, third normal form is considered a normalized database because it is pretty much the level the industry considers a normalized database.

FIRST NORMAL FORM

In order for a database to be in *first normal form*, all repeating groups have to have been moved into separate tables; one column contains exactly one value.

This example is not in first normal form because it has a repeating group of titles; there are many titles for the single Publisher row:

```
Publisher           Title1           Title2           Title3

Smith Publishing    The Tale of...   Cooking with...  Computer and ...
```

The following example is in first normal form. There are now several rows for Publisher, one for each Title:

```
Publisher           Title

Smith Publishing    The Tale of...
Smith Publishing    Cooking with...
Smith Publishing    Computer and...
```

SECOND NORMAL FORM

When *second normal form* is met, nonkey fields must depend on the entire primary key. A database without compound primary keys is automatically in second normal form (if first normal form is met).

This example is not in second normal form because the key is Publisher and Title, but Publisher Address relates only to one part of the key field (Publisher) but not to Title:

Publisher	Title	Publisher Address
Smith Publishing	The Tale of...	New York, NY
Smith Publishing	Cooking with...	New York, NY
Smith Publishing	Computer and...	New York, NY

To correct the example, break the table into two parts. Publisher-specific information belongs in the Publisher table:

Publisher	Publisher Address
Smith Publishing	New York, NY

Title-specific information belongs in the Title table:

Publisher	Title
Smith Publishing	The Tale of...
Smith Publishing	Cooking with...
Smith Publishing	Computer and...

THIRD NORMAL FORM

Third normal form dictates that nonkey fields must not depend on other nonkey fields.

This example table is not in third normal form because the Location column depends on the department, not the employee, even though Employee is the key field:

Employee	Dept	Location
Smith	10	Bldg C
Jones	10	Bldg C
Thomas	10	Bldg C
Alders	8	Bldg D

To bring the table into third normal form, break it into two parts, one for Employee that indicates the department:

Employee	Dept
Smith	10
Jones	10
Thomas	10
Alders	8

and the other for Dept, indicating the location:

Dept	Location
10	Bldg C
8	Bldg D

BENEFITS OF NORMALIZATION

A normalized database reduces redundancy and, therefore, storage requirements in the database. Data integrity also is easier to maintain in an environment where you have to look in only one place for the data, where each entity is represented only once.

In addition, when the database is normalized, the rows tend to get narrower. This enables more rows per data page within SQL Server, which can speed up table scanning and queries that return more than one row, improving query performance for single tables.

DRAWBACKS OF NORMALIZATION

There are some drawbacks to a normalized database design, however, mostly related to performance. Typically, in a normalized database, more joins are required to pull information together from multiple tables (for example, to get employees along with their current location requires a join between the Employee table and the Dept table).

Joins require additional I/O to process, and are therefore more expensive from a performance standpoint than single-table lookups.

Additionally, a normalized database often incurs additional CPU processing. CPU resources are required to perform join logic and to maintain data and referential integrity. A normalized database contains no summary data, because summary data violates normalization in two ways: it is redundant information and it has no independent business meaning. To calculate summary values requires aggregating multiple rows of data, which incurs both greater CPU processing and more I/O.

NORMALIZATION AND THE DATABASE DESIGN PICTURE

Normalization provides a good place to start a physical database design because data is logically grouped and consistent. (I once had a student request to put those first seven words in writing and sign my name. Apparently, his shop didn't understand the difference between the purposes of the two designs.) Third normal form should always be applied to all database design, at least initially. Denormalization is something that is done intentionally—and with malice and forethought—for the purpose of performance.

Remember, however, *normalization can cause substantially more I/O than a denormalized database*. Redundancy can reduce physical I/O, which might be judged to be more expensive than storage costs. Redundancy, however, incurs additional cost at update time.

DENORMALIZING THE DATABASE

Denormalizing is the process of taking a normalized logical design and intentionally disobeying the rules for the purpose of increasing performance. To denormalize effectively, you must understand the bias of the data that is to be loaded into the database and how the data will be accessed.

ADVANTAGES OF DENORMALIZATION

Denormalization can help minimize joins and foreign keys and help resolve aggregates. Because these are resolved within the database design, you might be able to reduce the number of indexes and even tables to process them.

GUIDELINES

Here are some basic guidelines to enable you to determine whether it is time to denormalize your database design:

◆ Balance the frequency of use of the data items in question, the cost of additional storage to duplicate the data, and the acquisition time of the join.

◆ Understand how much data is involved in the typical query; this affects the amount of redundancy and additional storage requirements.

◆ Remember that redundant data is a performance benefit at query time, but is a performance liability at update time because each copy of the data needs to be kept up to date. You typically write triggers to maintain the integrity of the duplicated data.

BASIC DENORMALIZATION TECHNIQUES

Be aware that denormalization is a technique for tuning a database for a specific application, and as such tends to be a last resort when tuning performance. Adding indexes to a table is a tuning method that is transparent to your end users and applications; modifying the database schema is not. If you change the database design, your application code that accesses that database needs to be modified as well.

A variety of denormalization methods can be used to modify the physical database design in an effort to improve performance:

◆ Adding redundant data by duplicating columns or defining summary data

◆ Changing your column definitions by combining columns or shortening existing columns

◆ Redefining your tables by combining tables, duplicating entire tables or portions of a table, and partitioning tables into multiple tables

REDUNDANT DATA

Redundant data helps performance by reducing joins, or computations, which in turn reduces I/O and CPU processing, respectively. It tends to be either an exact copy of the data or summary data.

Duplicate data should be of exactly the same name, type, and domain, and have the same integrity checking as the original data. Triggers should be used to maintain integrity between the original and the duplicate data. Note that the more volatile the data, the more often you will incur overhead to maintain the duplicate data. You need to balance frequency of use and the cost of the acquisition join against the frequency of modification and the cost of the extra update.

It is occasionally a good idea to duplicate static data to avoid joins. In Figure 11.1, moving the title to the salesdetail table saves you from having to perform a lookup when you need that data for, perhaps, a report on sales by title. Is this a good candidate for duplication? The advantage is that it will improve performance, and the title is a *nonvolatile* data attribute (that is, it won't change much). The disadvantage is it might make the salesdetail table a lot larger.

Figure 11.1.
Duplicating the title
column from the titles
table in the salesdetail
table.

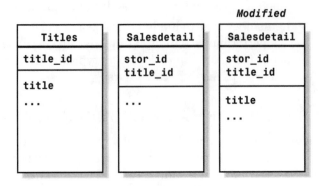

Why is this denormalized? Because there is redundant data and title does not depend on the entire key (stor_id, title_id) of the salesdetail table.

FOREIGN KEY DUPLICATION

Another candidate column for duplication is a foreign key to reduce the number of joins required to retrieve related information.

Figure 11.2 shows a normalized version of a database, requiring a three-table join to retrieve the name of the primary author for a title. If you want to be able to know the primary author for a book 80 percent of the time you retrieve the title, how can you reduce the joins? The easiest way is to add the author ID or author name for the primary author to the titles table. (See Figure 11.3.) Author name or author ID is a good candidate for duplication because it is unlikely to change very often.

Figure 11.2.
In a normalized version
of this database, a
three-table join is
required to retrieve the
name of the primary
author.

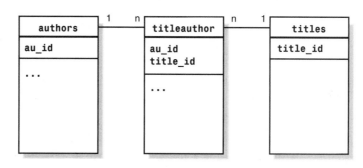

Figure 11.3.
Duplicating the
primary au_id value in
the titles table reduces
that to a two-table join
for better performance.

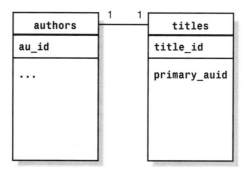

DERIVED OR SUMMARY COLUMNS

Derived columns contain data that is duplicated for the purpose of avoiding repeated calculations. This is called *summary data*.

In any environment, application designers have recognized that certain summary values need to be maintained and available constantly in order to speed their retrieval. If you store frequently accessed sums, averages, and running tallies, reports and queries can run substantially faster, but data modification is slowed somewhat.

Figure 11.4 shows the titles table with a derived column, total_sales, which contains a sum of the qty column from the salesdetail table for the rows related to that title. The total_sales is updated automatically every time a qty is inserted or modified in the salesdetail table. This speeds data retrieval, but adds overhead to modifications on salesdetail.

Figure 11.4.
Storing a derived value
in the titles table,
total_sales, which is the
sum of qty for the
corresponding rows in
the salesdetail table.

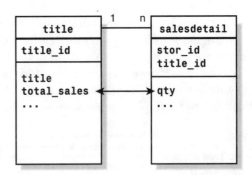

In this example, it is less expensive to maintain a running total_sales column than it is to calculate the total sales every time it is needed. This decision is based on comparing the frequency of the request for the quantity information with the additional cost of the update on salesdetail.

When defining summary data, triggers should be used on the detail tables to maintain the integrity of the summary data, and the summary data needs to be used often enough to justify the update-time overhead created by the triggers.

CHANGING COLUMN DEFINITION

You've seen that adding redundant columns and derived columns can enhance performance. You also can see an improvement in performance when you shorten critical columns by using two strategies:

◆ Contrived columns

◆ Shortening long columns

When the columns get narrower, a narrower index enables more keys to be searched with fewer I/O operations. The corresponding data rows also can wind up being smaller, enabling more rows per data page, which minimizes the number of I/Os required to scan the data.

CONTRIVED COLUMNS

A *contrived* column is typically a substitute for a long key; it has no business use of its own.

In Figure 11.5, is there enough information in the customer table to make rows unique? Is Name unique enough? City? State? Zip? Address? Maybe not. George Foreman presumably lives with each of his five sons, all named George, making six George Foremans (Foremen?) at one residence. How about Social Security Number?

Some people don't have one. Some people lie. Sometimes the Social Security Administration makes a mistake and issues a duplicate number. What do you do? What makes sense for a foreign key in the order table? Unfortunately, not necessarily any of the existing columns do.

Figure 11.5.
The customer table has
no easily identifiable
primary key for the
order table to reference.
A contrived key can be
used as both primary
key in customer and
foreign key in order.

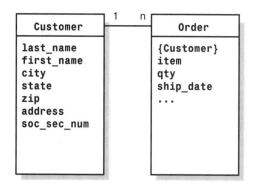

To use a contrived column, add the contrived key to the table and treat it as the primary key for all purposes. Use it as a foreign key in all related tables. This is most helpful in long or multicolumn key situations. You will save storage in the short *and* long run. Using a contrived column will result in a much shorter key than trying to decide how many columns guarantee uniqueness and using all those columns as the foreign keys.

Access performance also improves because index columns are narrower, speeding up individual lookups and joins. In addition, a contrived key is a column that generally doesn't change, so you don't have to worry as much about maintaining the foreign key values. If the customer name is part of the key and is used as a foreign key, any name change has to be cascaded to all foreign key entries as well, increasing the overhead on updates to customer. With a contrived key, you can update customer information without affecting the primary and foreign keys.

REDEFINING TABLES

Creating duplicate tables tends not to be the only solution, and it is frequently not the best solution. It is, however, a viable method of reducing I/O and search speed for specific types of queries.

There are two basic methods of duplicating tables: subsets and partitioning.

Subsets are duplicates of the original data—by row, column, or both. (Note that the replication server can do this across SQL Servers automatically!)

DATA PARTITIONING

Data *partitioning* takes on two basic varieties:

- ◆ Vertically, by separating infrequently used columns
- ◆ Horizontally, by separating infrequently used rows

Not all data are good candidates for duplication or partitioning.

If the data is fairly stable, it might be useful to consider duplicating or partitioning a table; volatile data is less likely to work well. The more volatile the data, the more you have to double your work. Triggers are necessary for maintaining data consistency and integrity of duplicate data, which incurs additional overhead on data modifications. In addition, if both tables of a partition must be checked to satisfy a query, additional code must be written (either a union or a join) to bring the results together into a single result set.

Duplicate data also means that you will incur an additional storage expense. On the other hand, you might need to scan less data to derive the same results. In addition, your joins will be faster (because the tables are smaller), and you might gain a benefit by archiving some of your historical, infrequently accessed data.

Although the potential benefits of duplication and partitioning might be large, the amount of extra maintenance might be correspondingly large.

VERTICAL PARTITIONING

Vertical partitioning is a denormalization technique by which you split a table, by columns, into two or more tables. This technique is typically used to minimize the size of the primary table, or to move infrequently accessed columns to a separate table. Consider the following situation:

> "Our invoicing job will not fit in the overnight batch window. We need to reduce join time between orders and items."

In Figure 11.6, a table with several descriptive columns can be partitioned vertically. The information needed for the active processing is all in the Item_Active table; less-used information is stored in the Item_Inactive table. The Item_Active table is considerably smaller and has a higher row density (rows per page). Given this implementation, order-entry operators can still look at descriptions, take orders, and so forth by performing a simple join between Item_Active and Item_Inactive. Because these are point queries, retrieving one row at a time, the additional cost of the join is negligible. However, the nightly batch process that needs to scan a large number of item numbers and prices at a time speeds up significantly.

Figure 11.6.
Vertically partitioning
a table creates an active
set of data with
substantially higher
row density.

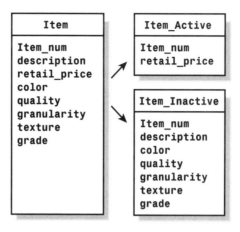

The advantage, if you choose to partition columns, is that the number of locks held on tables might be reduced, and table scans might be faster. However, if excessive joining takes place between vertically partitioned tables, and it adversely impacts performance, you might need to reevaluate your decision.

HORIZONTAL PARTITIONING

Table scan time grows proportionally with table size. When activity is limited to a subset of the entire table, it makes sense to isolate that subset. This is useful not only for production, but for test tables. Horizontal partitioning is a method of splitting a table at the row level into two or more tables.

The method used to partition the rows horizontally varies depending on how the data is used. The most common method used is by date, partitioning the most current, active data from the historical, inactive data. Other partitioning options include partitioning by activity, department, business unit, geographical location, or a random hash value.

Consider the following two situations:

> "98 percent of the time we are using 5 percent of the rows; the rest of the rows are getting in our way."

> "The most recent 15 percent of the data is being used 85 percent of the time. Why perform statistics updates on the whole 200,000,000 rows when only a part of the table is volatile?"

Figure 11.7 illustrates an orders table partitioned horizontally, with active rows in one table and inactive rows in another.

11

DATABASE DESIGN AND PERFORMANCE

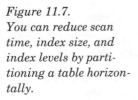

Figure 11.7.
You can reduce scan
time, index size, and
index levels by parti-
tioning a table horizon-
tally.

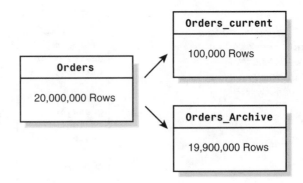

One of the main drawbacks to consider when horizontally partitioning tables is that retrieving data from more than one table as a single result set requires the use of the UNION statement. If you use a random hashing scheme to partition the data, it also is harder for end users to determine where the data resides, making the database less browsable.

VIEWS AS A PARTITIONING TOOL

One advantage of vertical partitioning over horizontal partitioning is that the vertical partitioning can be hidden from the end user or application developer through the use of views. If you split a table by columns, a view can be created that joins the two table partitions. Users can then select from the view as if it were a single table.

Views cannot be used to hide horizontal partitioning from end users or applications, because in the current releases of SQL Server, the UNION statement is not permitted in views.

SUMMARY

A fully normalized database, although easier to maintain, does not necessarily lend itself to optimal performance. To determine whether the database design needs to be modified to improve query performance, identify the problem queries and look at the base tables on which the queries rely. Identify any potential join problems due to column widths and types or due to the large quantity of rows that need to be accessed. Then consider modifying columns or creating derived, summary, or contrived columns where they might be helpful. Additionally, identify any potential scanning problems in the base tables and consider partitioning tables if there are no alternatives. Due to the impact on end users and application developers, the first choice for query optimization tends to be adding additional indexes, rather than modifying the physical database design.

CHAPTER 12

Remote Server Management

This chapter presents the definition and management of remote servers, privileges, and security.

As your systems grow in size, complexity, or geographic distribution, you may find it necessary to enable your servers to communicate with each other directly. Remote server access in a multiserver environment enables applications to share data (in a limited way) and to access data and functions on other SQL Servers and Open Servers (see Figure 12.1).

Figure 12.1.
Remote servers include
SQL Servers and Open
Servers such as Net
Gateway, OmniSQL
Gateway, and others.
Open Server processes
require the same remote
server administration
as SQL Servers.

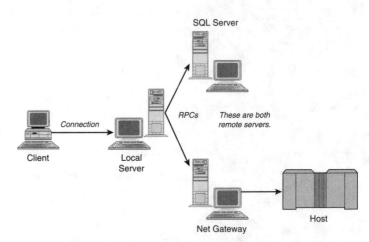

Because the remote server interface can access Open Servers, it also is the mechanism for connecting heterogeneous data sources, including mainframe databases from DB/2 to IMS to VSAM flat files, other non-Sybase databases, and nontraditional data sources. The most interesting applications involve the integration of real-time devices (stock tickers, news sources, and data-collection devices).

By definition, a remote server is a server you access as part of a client process without opening a distinct, direct client connection. Sybase SQL Server manages communications between servers using remote procedure calls (RPCs). You call a remote procedure the same way you call a local procedure; the only difference is that you need to fully qualify the name of the procedure with the name of the server. Here is the syntax:

```
execute remote_server_name.db_name.owner_name.procedure_name
```

You've already used this syntax, with the exception of the `remote_server_name`.

No matter what type of external data source you want to access, you need to implement remote servers. Now, with System 10, all servers require remote access because the backup server (your backup technique) is accessed via RPC.

DEFINITIONS

For the purposes of this discussion, consider the case in which a client is directly connected to a SQL Server, but needs to send and retrieve periodic information to a remote server using an RPC (see Figure 12.2).

Figure 12.2.
The remote server is accessed through the local server, and the client maintains only a single connection to the local server.

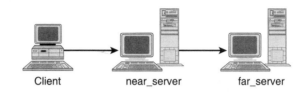

Client   near_server   far_server

First, refresh your memory with a few definitions:

◆ A local server is the server you have logged in to.

◆ A remote server is another server to which you would like to connect from the local server.

◆ Remote access means connecting to a remote server.

To illustrate the configuration of remote servers, Figure 12.3 presents an example of two servers: a local server (near_server) and a remote server (far_server).

Figure 12.3.
In this example, the name of the local server is near_server. The remote server is named far_server.

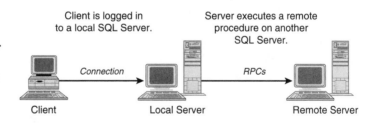

Client is logged in to a local SQL Server.

Server executes a remote procedure on another SQL Server.

Client   Connection   Local Server   RPCs   Remote Server

Ensuring remote access is not complicated, but it is complex. There are several steps to get just right:

1. Name the local and remote servers on both servers.
2. Configure each server for remote access.
3. Add all servers to the local interfaces file.
4. On the remote server, define the method for mapping logins and users to its own logins and users.
5. Set remote options, if necessary.

Let's go through each step in detail. Step 1 names the servers on each server. Until you start working with remote access, server names seem pretty arbitrary. For example, although you specify a named server when logging in, that server name is transformed into an address and port (or an address and named pipe) long before a packet goes out on the network. The server name you use on your local workstation does not need to correspond to the name in the interfaces file at the server.

With remote servers, the names are relevant to the communication; the names of servers must be defined consistently on each server or communication will not work properly.

Use sp_addserver to add a server name to the sysservers table in the master database. Prior to System 10, this is an sa-only task. With System 10, this becomes an sso-only task because it involves system access. You need to execute sp_addserver once for the local server name and once for each of the remote servers, as in the following example:

```
sp_addserver local_server_name , local
sp_addserver remote_server_name
```

Note that the local flag distinguishes the name of the local server.

For an example, on the local server (near_server), execute the following:

```
exec sp_addserver near_server, local
exec sp_addserver far_server
```

On the remote server (far_server), execute this:

```
exec sp_addserver far_server, local
exec sp_addserver near_server
```

Step 2 configures each server for remote access. The syntax is the following:

```
sp_configure 'remote access', 1
reconfigure
```

Note

As of System 10, this setting is the default at server installation. If you are not currently configured for remote access, and need to execute this step, you have to cycle your server (bring it down and back up) so that memory is reallocated for the remote connections. (See Chapter 9, "Configuring and Tuning the SQL Server," for a full discussion of memory allocation.)

For an example, on the local server (near_server), execute the following:

```
sp_configure 'remote access', 1
reconfigure
```

On the remote server (`far_server`), execute this:

```
sp_configure 'remote access', 1
reconfigure
```

Don't forget to shut down and restart each server.

Step 3 updates the interfaces file on the local machine to reflect the names and addresses of all servers to be accessed.

Tip

It is a good idea to have a single interfaces file with complete references for every server and propagate it throughout your network.

This is probably an sa task. At the operating system level (where the interfaces file resides), only the sybase user can modify the file. For more on the interfaces file, see Chapter 3, "SQL Server Installation and Connectivity."

For an example, on each server, add both servers to the interfaces table:

```
near_server
      query tli sun-ether near_box ...
far_server
      query tli sun-ether far_box ...
```

Step 4, on the remote server, maps remote logins and users to the local environment. Here is the syntax:

```
sp_addremotelogin remote_server_name [, local_name [, remote_name]]
```

For an example, on the remote server (`far_server`), execute this:

```
sp_addremotelogin near_server
```

Step 5 sets remote options as necessary. Here is the syntax:

```
sp_remoteoption far_server, login_name, remote_name, option_name, {true ¦ false}
```

For an example, on the remote server (`far_server`), execute this procedure to set up logins without requiring synchronized passwords between servers:

```
sp_remoteoption near_server, near_server_login, null, trusted, true
```

ADDING SERVERS WITH *SP_ADDSERVER*

Use the `sp_addserver` procedure to populate the sysservers table. The names in the sysservers table are mapped to the names in the interfaces file. Here is the syntax:

```
sp_addserver server_name [ { local ¦ null } [, network ]]
```

The local keyword identifies the name of the server into which you are signed. (There can be only one local server.) You can verify this by selecting the @@servername global variable. Note that this does not take effect until the server is cycled; until then, RPCs will not work. In this example, you add a local server, near_server, and a remote server, far_server:

```
exec sp_addserver near_server, local
exec sp_addserver far_server
```

The network parameter is the name of the server within the interfaces file, in case you want the names to be different. This permits server name aliasing. The following example adds a remote server, extremely_far_server (listed as such in interfaces), as server17 in sysservers.

```
exec sp_addserver extremely_server17, null, far_server
```

As of System 10, at least one remote server—the backup server—is added automatically at installation time.

To remove a server from the sysservers table, use sp_dropserver. Here is the syntax:

```
exec sp_dropserver server_name [ ,droplogins ]
```

The droplogins keyword also instructs the server to remove all corresponding entries from sysremotelogins (discussed next). The following example removes the entry for server17, created before, and removes all associated logins:

```
sp_dropserver server17, droplogins
```

Adding Remote Logins with
SP_ADDREMOTELOGIN

Remote logins enable you to map requests to a remote server to that server's local set of privileges and authorizations. Remote logins are established on the remote server.

The next three sections explore the methods for mapping remote logins to local logins on the remote server.

Using the Remote ID as the Local ID

Use this syntax to map the remote ID as the local ID:

```
sp_addremotelogin remote_server_name
```

This is the simplest mapping method. It presumes that the logins are the same on both servers, and maps login to login. In the example, the remote server named over_there is set up to log in to the current server.

The following example (executed on `far_server`) requires each remote login on `near_server` to have a corresponding entry in syslogins on `far_server`:

```
sp_addremotelogin near_server
```

Using a Single Local Login for All Remote Logins

If you want a single local login for all remote logins, use this syntax:

```
sp_addremotelogin remote_server_name, local_name
```

This is another straightforward mapping method. Any legitimate user on a server listed in sysservers will be mapped to a single login. In the following example, all logins originating from the server named `near_server` map to login `near_server_user`. (You need to run `sp_addlogin near_server_user` before running `sp_addremotelogin`.)

```
sp_addremotelogin near_server, near_server_user
```

Using a New Local Name for All Remote Users

Here is the syntax for using a new local name for all remote users:

```
sp_addremotelogin remote_server_name, local_name, remote_name
```

The following is an example:

```
sp_addremotelogin near_server, selected_server_user, mdoe
```

In this example, the login named `mdoe` on `near_server` can access `far_server` using the login `selected_server_user`. (You still need to run `sp_addlogin selected_server_user`.)

Removing Logins with *SP_DROPREMOTELOGIN*

To remove a remote login after adding it, use the `sp_dropremotelogin` procedure. Here is the syntax:

```
sp_dropremotelogin remoteserver [, loginname [, remotename ] ]
```

The following drop statements remove the remote logins added previously:

```
sp_dropremotelogin near_server
sp_dropremotelogin near_server, near_server_user
sp_dropremotelogin near_server, selected_server_user, mdoe
```

REMOTE OPTIONS

A variety of options can be set for specific servers, logins, and remote names. These define the way the server deals with the specific logins. Here is the syntax:

```
sp_remoteoption [remote_server [, login_name [, remote_name]], option_name,
                {true | false}]
```

Options are listed in Table 12.1.

TABLE 12.1. OPTIONS AVAILABLE FOR USE WITH `sp_remoteoption`.

Option	Task
trusted	Passwords are not rechecked.
net password encryption	Passwords are encrypted at both ends of the network.
timeouts	The server times out the connection after one minute of inactivity.

In the following example (run on `far_server`), logins from the `near_server` do not need to retransmit passwords:

```
sp_remoteoption near_server, near_server_user, null, trusted, true
```

Note

If the trusted option is not turned on, you need to establish and maintain synchronized passwords between servers. Very few applications include the capability of transmitting a distinct remote password when necessary.

GETTING INFORMATION ON REMOTE SERVERS

To obtain information on remote servers defined for your server, you can use the `sp_helpserver` procedure. This procedure reads and decodes information from the sysservers table in the master database. Here is the syntax:

```
sp_helpserver [server_name]
```

Use `sp_helpserver` without a server name to list all servers defined on your system.

The following example includes two servers: the primary server and the backup server. The backup server is normally installed as part of System 10.

```
sp_helpserver
```

```
name               network_name   status                                    id
---------------    ------------   --------------------------------------    --
SYB_BACKUP         SYBASE_BS      no timeouts, no net password encryption   1
SYB_PRIMARY        SYB_PRIMARY                                              0
```

For information on individual logins for a server, use the `sp_helpremotelogin` command:

```
sp_helpremotelogin [remoteserver [, remote_name] ]
```

For a list of remote logins, execute `sp_helpremotelogin` without a parameter. In the following example, the server has two remote logins for two distinct servers. One remote login maps all logins from SYB_BACKUP to a similarly named login on this server. The second remote login maps all logins from near_server to a single local login, near_server_login.

```
sp_helpremotelogin
```

```
server                 remote_user_name        local_user_name          options
-------------------    --------------------    --------------------    ----------
SYB_BACKUP             ** mapped locally **     ** use local name **     trusted
near_server            ** mapped locally **     near_server_login        -- none --
```

SUMMARY

Making your server accessible to other servers and able to access other servers requires a number of simple steps. Follow the cookbook and remote access should be working.

If you think you followed the cookbook, and remote access is not working, you probably forgot to shut down and subsequently restart the server.

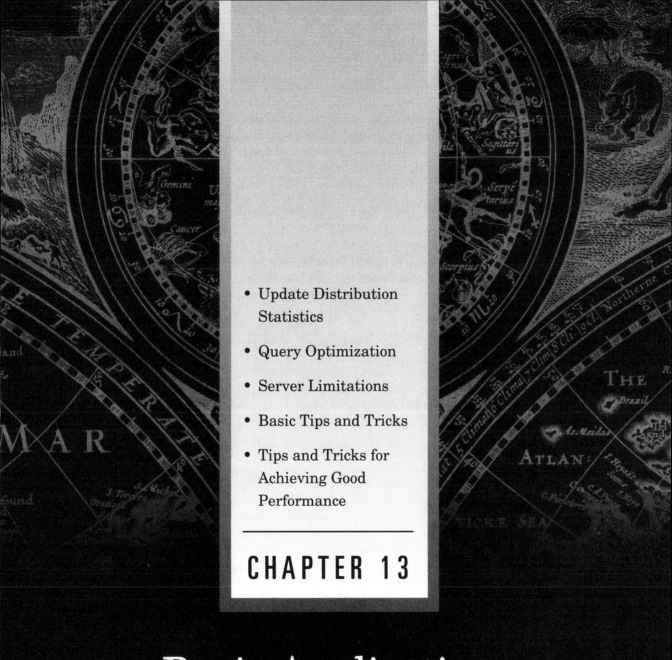

- Update Distribution
  Statistics

- Query Optimization

- Server Limitations

- Basic Tips and Tricks

- Tips and Tricks for
  Achieving Good
  Performance

CHAPTER 13

Basic Application
Performance and Tuning

Sybase has a cost-based optimizer. This means that the server determines before execution how it is going to retrieve the data based on available techniques and join orders for each query. The only thing you need to do periodically is keep the statistics up to date to enable the optimizer to pick the best query path.

Little of what you do on a periodic basis as a System Administrator is directly related to performance; performance is typically a design issue, rather than an administrative issue. Oddly, though, you often are called when there are performance problems. It is important to have a basic understanding of how the optimizer works, so that you can look like a genius whether you have a lot of experience with the server or not. In addition to explaining how the statistics work, this chapter covers the following topics:

◆ Query optimization
◆ Server limitations
◆ Basic tips and tricks

UPDATE DISTRIBUTION STATISTICS

The most important thing that a Sybase database administrator (DBA) can do to ensure consistent, positive query performance is to keep index statistics current.

Note

A government agency that monitors real-time data online using a Sybase SQL Server had a batch job that ran in about 30 minutes. Although it ran overnight so that performance was no particular problem, they wanted it to verify that they did not have other, related problems. It turned out that they had never updated statistics. Once they did update statistics, the batch job ran in under 20 seconds.

Other clients have reported similar performance improvements: One three-hour job ran in one minute after updating statistics.

To understand why statistics have such a dramatic effect on performance, look at the following query:

```
select *
from the_table
where key between 5000000 and 6000000
```

Assume that there are one million rows, with key values randomly distributed between 1 and 10 million. Figure 13.1 shows a representation of such a table.

Figure 13.1.
Statistics have a
dramatic effect on
query performance for
very large tables.

Key	Other Data
1	
...	
1,000,000	
...	
5,000,000	
5,000,001	
7,000,056	
...	
10,000,000	

How many rows will be returned? At first glance, the logic might go like this: 1 million rows, with a range of 1 to 10 million, and the range represents approximately 10 percent of the table. Therefore, you have an expected result of 10 percent of the data, or 100 thousand rows.

The reality, though, is that there may not be any rows within your range, or all of the rows may be within your range. A detailed discussion of index selection and query optimization is beyond the scope of this book because those topics are strictly a physical design/performance and tuning issue, but two things are immediately obvious.

1. If you are looking for a specific row, a random search will require you to scan half of the table to find the row. Therefore, if you want to read a single row, index-based access (comprising perhaps three to five disk accesses or I/Os) will be much faster than scanning half a million rows of data, with several thousand accesses.

2. If you need to retrieve all of the rows, it will be faster to start from the beginning and read every page only once, rather than bouncing in and out of an index structure, reading each page once for each row of data on the page. The ratio of time you save will be proportional to the number of rows that fit on the table, plus the number of pages in the leaf level of the index.

It is easy to see that at some point in between reading one row (always use an index) and reading all the rows (never use an index), you need to make a decision regarding whether or not you should use the index to retrieve the data.

Note

> At what point does the server decide to scan the table instead of using an index? Historically, Sybase has published a figure of 20 percent in literature and classes (that is, the server will scan the table instead of using an index when it expects to retrieve more than 20 percent of the data in a table). Be aware that the line might be closer to 10 percent or to 30 percent, and that the server will calculate this for each query.

To estimate the number of rows to be returned by a particular query, the server refers to a distribution page, stored for each index on each table. (With System 10 and subsequent versions, the distribution page is kept for each column of a compound index.) The distribution page is a list of as many key values as will fit on a Sybase page (again, 2KB on all platforms except Stratus, which has a 4KB page). When preparing the distribution page, the server steps through each page of the leaf level of the index, recording the key values at each distribution step.

For example, if the keys in the above example are integral, and you have a 2KB page, you can fit approximately 500 keys (2KB/4 bytes per integer) on a distribution page. With 1 million rows of data and 500 distribution steps, each step represents 1,000,000/500 = 2,000 values. Therefore, the server records the first value in the index, counts 2,000 rows and records the next value, then repeats this process until the page is filled.

Figure 13.2 shows what the distribution page might look like:

Figure 13.2.
Using an index is more
efficient than scanning
the whole table.

1	5,000,000	7,000,000	7,002,000	7,005,000		
					...	10000000

The steps recorded in the distribution page are 1, 5 million, 7 million, and so forth. The range of values in the query—5 million to 6 million—falls within the distribution step between 5 and 7 million, which means that the query requires a maximum of 2,000 rows (or less than 1/500th of the data). In this case, SQL Server will probably use the index because it is more efficient than scanning the whole table.

Warning

Remember that stored procedures are optimized with the first set of parameters passed, which is when an execution plan is compiled and stored in memory. If the optimization plan calls for use of an index (because few rows are affected the first time it is run), the procedure always will use an index when it executes that copy of the plan from procedure cache.

The second time a procedure is run, when it runs from cache, the stored execution plan will be run anyway *even if the server should scan the table (instead of using an index)*: the index will be used, and the performance of the query probably will be terrible. To avoid this problem, identify procedures where substantially different optimization plans might be required (depending on the parameters) and create those procedures with `recompile`.

How are distribution plans kept up to date? They're not. It would cause too much overhead during each insert, update, and delete. That's why you have to issue the `update statistics table_name [(index_name)]` statement for each table periodically. As the data skews, you must update the statistics.

Note

If you have a lot of tables or your list changes frequently, it is best to use a tool that will create a dynamic list of tables, and update all of the statistics sequentially. You can do this with the Sybase `isql` utility by writing a script that does something like the following:

```
select "update statistics " + name from sysobjects where type = 'U'
```

`U` is the type for user tables in the sysobjects table. S is used for system tables. We ran this query in the pubs2 database to get the following result.

```
update statistics authors
update statistics publishers
update statistics roysched
update statistics sales
update statistics salesdetail
```

```
update statistics titleauthor
update statistics titles
update statistics stores
update statistics discounts
update statistics au_pix
update statistics blurbs
```

Now you can run the output from this script as a script itself.

Query Optimization

When the server resolves your query, first it checks the syntax and verifies the existence of all the referenced objects and columns. The parser creates a query tree that is then passed to the optimizer.

The optimizer parses the query a bit differently. The optimizer looks for clues as to which indexes might be used and which join order might be the most appropriate. Those clues are search arguments (SARGs), join clauses, and or clauses.

Search Arguments (SARGs)

A *SARG* is part of a where clause in the format

```
column operator constant
```

For example,

```
au_lname = 'Smith'
price > $50.
```

Join Clauses

A *join clause* is as clause that relates columns in two separate tables. A join clause is used in the following format:

```
table_one.column_name operator table_two.column_name
```

For example,

```
titles.pub_id = publishers.pub_id
```

Or Clauses

An *or clause* is typically of the format

```
Sarg or Sarg
```

For example,

```
last_name = 'Smith' or city = 'Boston'
```

Once the optimizer has identified SARGs, join clauses, and or clauses, it uses the available indexes to evaluate the cost of acquiring the requested data. Available indexes will include on index for the SARG (per table), one index for the join clause, and one index per element of the or clause. For example, in the following query,

```
select * from titles t, publishers p
where type = 'mod_cook'
and t.pub_id = p.pub_id
and (title like "Sushi%" or advance > $5000.)
```

there is one SARG: `type = 'mod_cook'`. There is one join clause: `t.pub_id = p.pub_id` and one or clause: `(title like "Sushi%" or advance > $5000.)`.

The Sybase SQL Server will be able to evaluate one index per table for the SARG, one for the join, and one for each part of the or clause.

SERVER LIMITATIONS

As the number of tables in a query increases, the amount of work the optimizer needs to do in order to resolve the query increases accordingly. For each table that is added to the query, the number of possible resolutions to the query increases geometrically. At some point, it can become more costly to analyze all possible query options than to run the query. Sybase handles this by limiting the number of solutions it evaluates. Queries involving more than four tables are evaluated in groups of four. Therefore, the Sybase SQL Server usually still picks the right query plan, but occasionally it does not. If this is your problem, it may pay to break the query into many queries.

If there is no SARG, the optimizer will usually not look for an appropriate index. With later versions of the server (including System 10) the server will use an index if there is an aggregate in the select list that might cover the query. (*Index covering* means that the information requested can be retrieved from the leaf level of a nonclustered index, releasing the requirement to go to the data page.)

It is possible to make a SARG not a SARG by mixing types. For example,

```
price = 500
```

is not a SARG if `price` is a money type, because `500` is an integer. You should rewrite the clause as

```
price = $500
```

The optimizer cannot improvise this as a SARG because the conversion from integer to money would require a function call, and that would have to happen at runtime. If the improvisation is syntactical only, however, the optimizer may be able to work with it. For example,

```
price between $5000 and $7500
```

could be rewritten as

```
price >= $5000 and price >=$7500
```

This would be performed automatically (and transparently) by the optimizer.

Also, calculations involving a column invalidate a SARG. For example,

```
where substring(title, 1, 4) = 'Data'
```

is not a SARG, but could easily be rewritten as a SARG:

```
where title like 'Data%'
```

BASIC TIPS AND TRICKS

Ninety percent of all performance problems in typical environments happen because application programmers and users do not know how to present queries correctly. Here are some basic tips that may eliminate the great majority of problem queries, leaving you to work on the last few queries that represent real performance problems.

USE SARGS

Write where clauses that use SARGs. For example, instead of writing this:

```
ytd/12 > 5000
```

write this:

```
ytd > 60000
```

PROVIDE ALL JOIN OPTIONS

You can improve join performance in joins of three or more tables sharing a key by providing all join keys.

The key to fast joins is selecting an efficient join order. (When the server joins, it gets a value from one table, then looks for corresponding values in the other. Which table is first or "outer" and which is second or "inner" determines the amount of work required to answer the query.)

The server uses the information you provide about the tables to define the universe of possible orders. For example, if you write the following:

```
select *
from titles t,salesdetail sd,titleauthor ta
where t.title_id = sd.title_id
and sd.title_id = ta.title_id
```

then you have the following two possible join orders:

titles	←	salesdetail	←	titleauthor
titleauthor	←	salesdetail	←	titles

These two join orders are possible with two join conditions in the query.

Add the third leg of the triangle (t.title_id = ta.title_id, see Figure 13.3) to the query to provide more possible join orders.

Figure 13.3.
By adding the third join clause, you complete a triangle of join tables and give the server complete freedom about the most efficient join order.

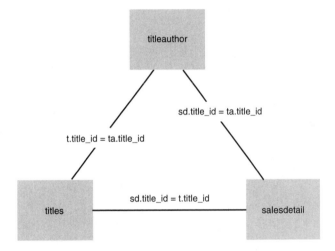

```
select *
from titles t,salesdetail sd,titleauthor ta
where t.title_id = sd.title_id
and sd.title_id = ta.title_id
and t.title_id = ta.title_id
```

Logically you haven't added anything (you will get the same result), but you have provided more possible join orders. There are three join conditions specified, so there are now six possible join conditions:

titles	←	salesdetail	←	titleauthor
titleauthor	←	salesdetail	←	titles
titles	←	titleauthor	←	salesdetail
titleauthor	←	titles	←	salesdetail

	salesdetail	←	titleauthor	←	titles
	salesdetail	←	titles	←	titleauthor

This means that with the additional join clause, you can actually triple your potential number of join orders. You won't necessarily always get a faster result, but you do improve your chances of getting a faster result.

SELECT INDEXES CAUTIOUSLY

Remember that additional indexes may speed up queries, but there is a cost at update time. In an online transaction processing (OLTP) database, be sure to limit indexes to three or four per table.

AVOID *HOLDLOCK* LIKE THE PLAGUE

Using sequential keys incorrectly is a wonderful way to deadlock. The following table is an example of code with `holdlock`, which forces the server to maintain a read lock for the duration of a transaction. (Without holdlock, read locks generated by `select` statements are released immediately after the page is read.) Watch what happens as two users execute the code at the same time.

The Code	user1	user2
`begin tran`	Set `@@trancount` to 1	Set `@@trancount` to 1
`select @local_var = col from key_table holdlock`	Put shared lock on `key_table` for duration of transaction	Also put shared lock on `key_table`
`update key_table set col=col+1`	Escalate read lock to exclusive lock (must wait for user2 to release read lock)	Escalate read lock to exclusive lock (must wait for user1 to release read lock)
`commit tran`	Now what?	Now what?

At the point where each user is waiting for the other to release the lock to go forward, we have created a classic deadlock. The good news is that SQL Server automatically detects the deadlock and chooses a *deadlock victim* (the process with the least amount of accumulated CPU time). The bad news is that the deadlock victim's work is rolled back and the batch is aborted. The server returns an error code of 1205, sets

@@error to 1205, and (if the deadlock occurred in a stored procedure) returns a stored procedure return code of -3. The client application that receives a deadlock error usually just reissues the code.

Deadlocks are expensive. They slow the server and make your applications do twice as much work. Although the server is fairly efficient in removing a deadlock, it still pays to avoid them whenever possible. (Almost any application will encounter deadlocks, regardless of the database design or the application implementation. The key is to avoid them whenever possible.)

Note

> The worst situation about which I have heard was a system where 95 percent of all transactions resulted in deadlocks. By redesigning indexes and data structures and coding without holdlock, we were able to reduce that to 5 percent deadlocks, which resulted in far more acceptable performance.

Using holdlock on a densely used value guarantees deadlocks, as shown in the previous table, especially when holdlock is executed in a stored procedure (where there is frequent execution of the same code by many users). The rule of thumb in transaction processing is *change rows first, read the new value second*. The update action in a transaction places an exclusive lock on the affected pages that lasts for the duration of the transaction, guaranteeing exclusive processing.

For example, examine the following code fragment in a simultaneous two-user environment:

The Code	user1	user2
begin tran	Set @@trancount to 1	Set @@trancount to 1
update key_table set col=col+1	Put exclusive lock on key_table	Wait for exclusive lock on key_table
select @local_var = col from key_table	Lock maintained during select	Wait
commit tran	Release lock, allow user2 access to the value	Proceeds

Tip

> The downside of this approach is that you single-thread all inserts into the main table behind this update lock. If there is a lot of activity on the table, the cost of single-threading may be unbearable. You should certainly try to keep transactions like this short to avoid blocking processes while you do other work.
>
> If you are using System 10 or later, try using an identity key. The system maintains a counter in memory (not on disk), so you don't have to manage the value to ensure uniqueness.

TIPS AND TRICKS FOR ACHIEVING GOOD PERFORMANCE

There are a variety of things that first-time Sybase SQL Server users don't get quite right. The rest of this chapter is a grab bag of topics that you should address when you are trying to get good performance.

New administrators of SQL Server make some incorrect assumptions about the system based on their experience with other database managers. Not all performance problems will be remedied by the steps laid out here, but many of the obvious problems will be solved here and most systems will run well once these issues have been addressed.

The following are the four most common problems we have seen in a new SQL Server shop:

- Response time is four times longer than expected.
- The test environment works correctly but as soon as the number of users exceeds a certain number, everything slows to a crawl.
- Every time a certain activity occurs, the server grinds almost to a halt.
- The server slows, then grinds to a halt at random.

SOME REALLY BASIC STUFF

Sybase is like a formula one race car. If you make a mistake in a Camaro, you will probably survive. In the race car, well ...

Here are some very basic lessons we learned that may help you out.

Lesson 1: Join Keys

When I first got SQL Server, I had a couple of test tables: a list of 10,000 employers and a list of 60,000 transactions for those employers. I created the tables. I got bcp working and loaded the tables, I executed the query

```
select *
from employers, transactions
```

and I waited. About an hour and a half later, I called a Sybase contact and said, "I just issued a query and it's still running. The UNIX server statistics are maxed out and I thought this was a fast database." "What's your join key?", asked Beth. "What's a join key?", I asked. First lesson learned, and I hit the wall hard coming out of the first turn.

Sybase will not assume you are an idiot. If you ask a stupid question (no join keys) it assumes you want a stupid answer (a Cartesian product). It just takes time to return a 600 million row result set (10,000 rows × 60,000 rows).

Lesson 2: Indexes

I learned my lesson and was ready to try again. I issued the query

```
select *
from employers e, transactions t
where e.er_num = t.er_num
```

and I waited. About an hour and a half later, I called a Sybase contact and said, "I just issued the query again and it's still running. The UNIX server statistics are maxed out and I thought this was a fast database." "Tell me about your indexes," asked Beth. "What are indexes?" I asked. Second lesson learned and I hit another wall just as I was getting up to speed.

Sybase will try to help, and if there are no indexes for a join, it might try to help you by *reformatting* the query, which means it will develop a one-time index for you. But that takes a lot of time.

Getting It Right

I put the indexes on the tables, reran the second query, and a result set was ready in about five minutes. Sybase rewards knowledge. I got the checkered flag.

Let's start with a basic assumption, which may or may not be true at your shop: it is possible to resolve the response time problems. Expectations are a key to end-user happiness. For example, somebody writes an ad-hoc query that performs a four-table join on multimillion row tables, the optimizer chooses a poor search plan (that is, a table scan) and these multimillion row tables are all repeatedly table scanned. Or the optimizer is on the ball that day, chooses reformatting, and the query waits for the index creation. In either case, sub-second response time is not going to happen.

You might get sub-second response time if you created the necessary indexes for that query, but that might cause other queries to respond improperly, or severely slow any inserts, updates, or deletes. Tuning is a balancing act, as the name implies. The next few sections spend little time on query tuning, and concentrate for now on quick fixes, not an in-depth explanation of Sybase performance.

Isolate the Bottleneck

When getting good performance is an issue, the first step in resolving response time is to narrow down the problem search scope by isolating the bottleneck. Remember that by definition, when you remove a bottleneck, something else becomes a bottleneck. You are trying to find the widest neck.

You need to know whether the CPU or I/O system is the bottleneck. (There are situations where the bottleneck is something else, like the network, and those require their own solution, but usually, you should start by assuming that you are waiting for CPU or I/O.) One way to identify the bottleneck is to use Sybase's own stored procedure, sp_monitor. Write a quick Transact-SQL program that works something like the following (I actually carry this with me on a floppy as a procedure):

```
create proc do_monitor
(@count int = 60) as
while @count > 0
begin
 select @count = @count - 1
 waitfor delay '00:00:05'
 exec sp_monitor
end
return
```

Every five seconds sp_monitor will be executed for a duration of five seconds * 60 (or five minutes). Execute this with a redirect operator (usually >) into a flat file at a time when the resources are being heavily utilized. Then eyeball the output, looking at two key indicators: CPU busy and I/O busy.

Depending on what you find in the output from sp_monitor, you may need to take specific action. For the purpose of finding a quick fix, define high as greater than 85 percent, low as less than 15 percent. Machines that are running around 70 to 75 percent busy at peak are probably well selected for scale, with a little room for growth or unusual activity in CPU or I/O. Now look at the following table to determine which of the following sections applies to you.

CPU	I/O	Meaning
low	low	If this is happening and there is still a performance problem, Sybase is not the likely cause. Take a look at your network, your overall application design, or perhaps your client workstations.
high	low	See the following section, "CPU Bottleneck."
low	high	See the section "I/O bottleneck," later in the chapter.
high	high	See the section "Server Selection Problem," later in the chapter.

CPU Bottleneck

Your CPU is maxed out but the I/O system is fairly light. The server is working too hard in relation to the disk drives. Likely causes include poor physical design (bad index selection, over-normalization, and so on), badly written queries or procedures (which the optimizer cannot optimize), or just an insufficient pick for CPU size. You also may need to add another processor in an SMP system, but that requires a little more analysis.

I/O Bottleneck

CPU is light, but I/O is maxed out. First, update your statistics. If you are lucky, the optimizer is picking the wrong indices and can be quickly corrected. Otherwise, there may be a problem with queries, but more often it is time to redistribute the data among existing drives.

If you have only one disk drive in your server, you probably need to get another and split log and data activity between the drives. If you already have two or more drives in the server, try to place the database transaction logs on their own drive and controller, particularly in a heavy online transaction processing (OLTP) environment, because they are updated almost constantly. Also, try to place frequently updated indices on their own drives or controllers; index updates can also be heavy, depending on fillfactor, index density (repetitions of the index values, causing frequent page splitting), and the number of indexes.

Limit indexes to four or five per table if you are working online, depending on your cache limits. If you are only doing `select` during real time (an executive information system (EIS) or decision support (DSS) environment), a high number of indexes per table doesn't really matter. It may also be time to invest in a redundant array of inexpensive drives (RAID) device.

> *Note*
>
> If you are operating a DSS or EIS, you can use the `sp_dboption read only` parameter, which theoretically will give you a performance advantage. It's worth a try.

SERVER SELECTION PROBLEM

Your CPU is maxed out. Your I/O system is maxed out. Ouch.

First read the two sections above. Your problem may just be a combination of the factors we listed above. You may eventually need to face the inevitable: the operating system or physical server hardware may not be up to the task. If you disagree (or you are running on the most expensive and highest power super-mini in the world), review your physical database design and your device setup. Remember that Sybase may not necessarily have the same optimal configuration as other relational databases.

CONFIGURATION SETTINGS

System configuration variables that are not modified from the default are usually wrong. Take a look at Chapter 9, "Configuring and Tuning the SQL Server," to learn more about server configuration settings and how they affect performance.

PLATFORM SELECTION

Sybase now runs on VMS, UNIX, OS/2, NLM, and Windows NT. Selecting a platform based solely on cost can be shortsighted. Your platform must be scaleable to whatever size your application may grow. A client chose the NetWare platform very early in its evolution, planning to run on a 486/50, with the expectation that they would be able to replace it with a Pentium chip when it came out (their philosophy was, "don't hope for miracles; rely on them"). This was a pretty gutsy move, considering that they were going to scale a platform for 300 users based on an untested potential platform and operating system.

SET STANDARDS EARLY

Database development and naming standards will not have any effect on performance, but a lack of good standards guarantees many failures, both database side and application side. Take the time up front to set standards for everything from element names to database access. If you don't, you will have an inefficient system and may have to do unnecessary rewrites.

Many SQL Server shops have to do complete rewrites because they started working without standards. Be sure that your standards are appropriate for the new environment. If you must save something from a prior standards investment, save a table of contents. I cringe when I hear somebody say, "Use the DB2 standards." They usually don't make sense for Sybase.

See Chapter 18, "Defining Systems Administration and Naming Standards," for more on this topic.

TRAIN YOUR STAFF

Educating and re-educating your staff is essential to the success of your project. If everybody learns it the hard way, your project will be put together looking and performing that way. Nothing can replace experience, but proper education can help staff avoid making obvious and costly mistakes. Did you ever see the bumper sticker "If you think education is expensive try ignorance?" It was probably written by an MIS manager trying to use mainframe personnel to write client/server.

Education should probably include time to learn and discover (and relearn and rediscover) what was taught in class. Many shops should consider working for three months, experimentally, then throwing everything away (table definitions, procedures, application code, database designs, everything!) and starting over. It is often more efficient than grinding through repeated salvage operations.

CONSIDER DISASTER RECOVERY TIME

When you size your database, you should take into account disaster recovery time. It is good to create a 20GB database, but how are you going to back it up? If it crashes, how long will it take to recover? Are users of other systems isolated from disaster?

It is important to know how long recovery will take. You don't want to find out after you go into production that it is going to take you three days to recover from a catastrophe when your business can only stand to be down for an hour. Remember that there are three types of major disaster:

♦ Hardware failure, which may be addressed via disk mirroring

♦ Software failure (table or database corruption), which may be addressed via database dump and backup

♦ Logical data failure (your user deletes one million rows by mistake), which may be addressed by abuse and ridicule (and database dump and backup)

Decide how each issue will be addressed before the final database design. Incidentally, don't drop a database just because of a table corruption; Sybase can tell you how to drop that table if you can recover it by itself.

PLAN PERIODIC MAINTENANCE

Leave yourself a window for I/O-intensive periodic maintenance. Sybase is a 7 by 24 database (7 days a week, 24 hours a day) that enables you to do backups and other maintenance while users are running queries and performing updates. On the other hand, a full database dump (particularly before System 10) places an immense number of locks on the system. Other required periodic maintenance tasks include running dbcc and update statistics periodically. Creating indexes is also resource-intensive, and is best done when users are sleeping.

Note

Clustered index creation used to place an exclusive update lock in the table; with the latest release of Sybase, it seems as if you are able to select from the table simultaneously anyway. Non-clustered index creation will affect performance, but will not lock out the table.

Along the same lines, define the necessary periodic maintenance and one-time installation tasks are in your organization.

CHOOSE A GOOD PHYSICAL DATABASE DESIGN

Physical database design is partially a matter of creating DDL from a logical design, and choosing Sybase data types for each of the elements. Those tasks do not require excessive experience. All of the rest of the physical design tasks require a solid understanding of how Sybase processes data (that is, how the optimizer works, how cache works, how updates take place, how index structures are maintained, and so on).

KNOW YOUR USERS

If you do not understand your user community's typical queries, you cannot accurately select the most appropriate index (indices) for a table. For example, you could tune the system so that updates to a particular table take less than a second, which is terrific. To do that, you might need to eliminate some indexes that seem to take a long time to update, and you might change the clustered index. The downside is that one query which used to run in a minute takes 15 minutes now.

Here's the problem. That query that used to take a minute and now takes 15 minutes could turn out to be the up-to-the-minute status report for your CEO. If tuning is a balancing act, it's always good to know who's on the other end of the see-saw.

INDEX SELECTION

Poor index selection is a tuning item to take a look at. The following are a few things to keep in mind:

- ◆ Sybase only uses indexes if the first indexed element is in the where clause.
- ◆ The first element in the index should be the most unique (if possible), index order in general should be from most to least unique in a compound key, but remember that selectivity doesn't help if you don't use the first indexed column in your where clause.
- ◆ Understand that choosing the clustered index for the primary key is correct only some of the time. A much more useful application is to choose the column(s) that will be accessed by ranges of data ("Give me all the consumers whose ages are between 25 and 45") or for grouping ("Give me sales by customer").

DENORMALIZE

The best place to start with any database design is with logical design in third normal form (fourth or fifth normal form is even better). This allows you to understand your entire data set and to explore how queries will be resolved.

Then denormalize cautiously. When you denormalize, you combine data in separate tables into a single table to avoid the need to do join work in common queries. Denormalization increases redundancy (and therefore storage overhead) and processing overhead (when the column is updated), but could provide an enormous boost at select time (it reduces the need for a join).

Remember that the storage cost (and effectiveness) of an index is proportional to the width of the index. The narrower, the better. As the index width approaches the size of your row, the index can actually exceed the size of the data itself (at least for non-clustered indices).

If your index keys are wider than your data (as sometimes happens), it may be beneficial to denormalize or create an artificial, shorter key for the data. Physical design is a three-day class; it can't be taught in one long paragraph, but it is crucial to Sybase performance.

TAKE ADVANTAGE OF CLIENT/SERVER

Write true client/server applications. The beauty of client/server is that each box is doing what it is best at. Allow the server to process data, the network to transfer data, and the client to present the data.

The beauty of an open architecture is that it doesn't matter what the client platform(s) are. Let engineering use their UNIX boxes, designers use their Macs, and the rest of the world use their Intel-based Windows boxes (please don't read any personal preferences into the stereotyping). Some application front ends actually cross compile, and do it well.

The following lists several traps you should avoid:

◆ Don't make the server or front end do a disproportionate amount of work (or worse, perform an unsuitable task).

◆ Don't clog your network. A query that returns two million rows to the screen could have been written better. How many times will your user actually press the page down key or click the scroll bar?

◆ Allow the server to limit the number of rows returned. Watch out for front ends that return all of the data, then decide which rows to exclude. I got one call from a client complaining that an index look-up with one row returned was excruciatingly slow; the expectation was a sub-second response. It turned out that the PC-based database product he was using to access the Sybase server actually retrieved all one million rows, and subsequently the table scanned the one million rows on the client side.

Select the Right Tool

Selecting the right tool for the right job is as important in client/server systems as anywhere else. Choose a front end that will meet all of your users' needs, as well as provide a robust development environment. Choose a platform for your back end that will meet your needs both today and in six months. Choose monitoring and administrative tools that will meet all of your needs, not just a select few. If necessary, buy an assortment of tools. For the most part, the third-party utilities I've seen have been very good.

New for System 11

System 11 allows the DBA a great deal of additional tools for widening specific application performance bottlenecks. These include user-defined caches to keep objects in memory; large I/O to allow retrieval of more data per I/O request; separate user logs to reduce log bottlenecks; table partitioning; and a few new tuning options. Most have been discussed in the chapter "Optimizing SQL Server Configuration Options." The others are here.

NEW QUERY TUNING OPTIONS

With the advent of System 11, some old commands have been documented, and some new ones have been added.

`set forceplan on`	This command instructs the server to force the join order to be taken directly from the `from` clause.
`set table count`	This instructs the optimizer to consider a specific number of tables when contemplating join order (it currently uses 4).
`sp_cachestrategy`	Instruct the server to disable or re-enable cache strategies for specific objects.
Setting I/O size for a `select`, `delete`, and `insert`	Use the `prefetch` clause in your `select` statement. For example: `select * from authors (index au_names prefetch 16)`
`au_lname like "Jo%"`	This forces the optimizer to use the `au_names` index and the 16K buffer pool.
`set prefetch`	Setting `prefetch` on or off can force the server to enable or disable the `prefetch` for a session.

You can use any of these options individually or in tandem.

TABLE PARTITIONS

In applications where there is a huge insert rate, particularly where there is no clustered index (and data is being stored in a heap anyway), it is possible to bottleneck on the page being inserted into.

This problem is resolved with System 11 by using partitions. Partitions create multiple page chains, and inserts will be random into the different page chains.

There are three steps to partitioning a table:

1. Create the segment onto which the table is to be partitioned (see "Segments" in Chapter 5, "Defining, Altering, and Maintaining Databases and Logs").

   ```
   sp_addsegment part_seg, vdev3
   ```

2. Create the table on the segment

   ```
   create table part_table (a int, b varchar(12) on part_seg
   ```

   The `on` clause places a specific object on a specific segment.

3. Use the `alter table partition` statement to partition the table.

```
alter table part_table partition 15
```

The number 15 is the number of page chains we are instructing the server to institute on behalf of the table.

SUMMARY

There are a variety of things you can do as a database architect/designer or application programmer to affect performance:

- ◆ Understand how the system works.
- ◆ Educate your programmers and users so they can present efficient queries that make use of indexes.
- ◆ Monitor CPU and I/O utilization and try to remove bottlenecks.
- ◆ Maintain proper server configuration settings.
- ◆ Set standards early and enforce them.
- ◆ Plan periodic maintenance.
- ◆ Choose a good database design.
- ◆ Take advantage of client/server.
- ◆ Select the right tools.

Frankly, many of these items are the topic of another book. The most important thing you can do to keep things running well is to keep statistics current.

CHAPTER 14

Periodic Maintenance for Your SQL Server

One of the main jobs of a production DBA is to make sure that the server is running smoothly, the database(s) are in good working order, and that things will continue to work. The question becomes then "What do we need to do, and how often?" If you want to know the syntax for dbcc checktable, you can look it up. If you want to know how often you need to run it, you're asking a good question.

This chapter divides periodic maintenance tasks into three levels:

◆ Server
◆ Database
◆ Table

SERVER-LEVEL MAINTENANCE

At the server level, you can handle the following tasks:

◆ Monitor CPU- and I/O-busy statistics
◆ Monitor errorlog contents and use
◆ Compare resources allocated with those in use
◆ Keep the software current
◆ Record run-time data

MONITORING BUSY STATISTICS

Most of the server-level maintenance activity involves memory and resource management, including monitoring what is going on in the server from a utilization level, as well as increasing resources before allocated resources are exceeded. This means that you have to identify what appropriate operating levels are for your platform, decide when problems might occur, and act before that threshold is reached.

Sybase provides a system stored procedure called sp_monitor, which is intended to help track server resource utilization. In the following example, the low CPU and I/O utilization rates indicate low server usage since startup:

```
last_run                    current_run               seconds
- - - - - - - - - - - - -   - - - - - - - - - - - - - - - - -  - - - - - - - - - -
Sep 7 1994  3:50PM            Sep 7 1994  3:52PM          99
( 0 rows affected)

cpu_busy                    io_busy                   idle
- - - - - - - - - - - - -   - - - - - - - - - - - - - - -   - - - - - - - - - - - - - - - -
11(0)-0%                     19(0)-0%                  102128(96)-96%
( 0 rows affected)

packets_received            packets_sent              packet_errors
- - - - - - - - - - - - -   - - - - - - - - - - - - -       - - - - - - - - - - - - - - - -
49(6)                        371(7)                    0(0)
( 0 rows affected)

total_read       total_write      total_errors      connections
- - - - - - - - -  - - - - - - - - -  - - - - - - - - - -  - - - - - - - - - - - - - -
496(243)          188(4)           0(0)              6(0)
( 0 rows affected)
```

The output from sp_monitor looks cryptic, but once you understand how the numbers are represented, it is very useful. The first line (last_run...current_run...seconds) indicates the amount of time between runs of sp_monitor (99 seconds). The next line describes CPU and I/O resource utilization. Numbers outside the parentheses represent total seconds since the server came up (11 and 19); numbers inside the parentheses (both 0) indicate CPU seconds since sp_monitor was last run. The percentage is the percentage of total time.

Note

Some documentation reports this as machine ticks, not seconds. Double-check this for your platform and Sybase SQL Server version. If it says machine ticks, it may be in seconds anyway!

CPU %busy + idle %busy should add up to about 100 percent, allowing for rounding. For many versions of the server, they don't come close. This is an undocumented feature.

The next line shows packets received and sent and socket errors. Numbers outside the parentheses (49, 371, and 0) indicate packets sent and received since server startup; numbers inside the parentheses (6, 7, and 0) indicate numbers since sp_monitor was last run.

The final line indicates total reads and writes. This refers to the number of physical disk reads, as opposed to logical requests for a page. Again, numbers outside the parentheses are numbers since server inception; numbers inside the parentheses are since the last time sp_monitor was run. Total errors are read and write errors. At the end of this line is connections, which are login *attempts*.

14

Tip

When server performance is a problem, one of the first things you can do is run a Transact-SQL routine that runs sp_monitor every 10 or 15 seconds for a few minutes while response time is dragging to try to identify what resource is the current bottleneck. (Definition: A bottleneck is a resource that constrains performance. Corollary: Eliminating a bottleneck merely shifts the bottleneck.) For example:

```
declare @loop_var int
select @loop_var =0
while @loop_var < 100
begin
  exec sp_monitor
  select @loop_var = @loop_var + 1
  waitfor delay "00:00:15"
end
```

Look specifically at the CPU and I/O busy numbers. If CPU busy is running at 99 percent, the CPU is getting hit hard. If the I/O busy is running at 99 percent, the disks are getting hit hard. If neither is running at 99 percent, they may be balanced. If both are running low, the bottleneck may be with the network.

Note

Good utilization rates for CPU are 60–70 percent at peak. This indicates a good platform selection with some room for growth. If you are in the 80 percent range, you might start planning a CPU upgrade.

Keep an eye on the minimum, maximum, and average CPU utilization over time. This is your clue as to when it's time to start thinking about a CPU upgrade. (If you're running on an OS/2 or Windows NT platform, it may be time for a platform change—UNIX is more scaleable.)

Warning

These numbers may be misleading if you are running multiple CPU engines and/or multiple virtual devices. If, for example, you are running five CPUs and are 20 percent busy, it may mean that you have one process maxing out one processor, and the other four remaining idle. You need to get a third-party tool so that you can isolate individual engines and virtual devices.

Keep an eye on disk utilization as well. Again, if you have many disks to monitor, the sp_monitor statistics may be misleading. In particular, you want to watch out for the situation wherein one virtual device is being requested for 80 percent of the I/O. This device should be inspected and, where possible, high-activity objects (tables, indices, and so forth) should be migrated to other devices to spread out the I/O. If you can read 1,000 pages per second from one device, you can read nearly 2,000 pages per second from two devices.

Also watch concurrency. The sp_who procedure shows you how many processes are active and which processes are performing what tasks. Sample output from sp_who shows three internal processes and two user connections:

```
spid   status      loginame      hostname    blk dbname     cmd
------ ----------- ------------- ----------- --- ---------- ----------------
1      sleeping    sa                         0  master     MIRROR HANDLER
2      sleeping    sa                         0  master     CHECKPOINT SLEEP
3      sleeping    sa                         0  master     LAZY WRITER UN
4      runnable    sa                         0  perftune   SELECT
5      sleeping    user1                      0  master     WAITFOR
( 1 row affected)
```

The specifics of sp_who are discussed in Chapter 5, "Defining, Altering, and Maintaining Databases and Logs," but note that you can determine what logins are connected, what databases they are using, and what commands are being executed. Remember that sa can configure the maximum number of connections and that each connection uses between 34KB (v4.2) and 50KB (S10) of memory.

Here is an example:

```
sp_configure "user connections", 100
reconfigure
```

The server needs to be cycled before this will take effect.

Tip

If you want to check the current quantity of connections without running sp_who, use the following:

```
select count(*) from master..sysprocesses
```

Locks also consume kernel resources. The sp_lock procedure shows what processes are being locked and by whom.

This example shows lock activity in tables in three databases (note that process 5 holds a blocking lock on a table in the perftune database):

14

PERIODIC MAINTENANCE

spid	locktype	table_id	page	dbname
4	Sh_intent	496004798	0	master
4	Ex_extent	0	40	tempdb
5	Ex_extent	0	128	perftune
5	Ex_extent	0	208	perftune
5	Ex_extent	0	256	perftune
5	Ex_extent	0	264	perftune
5	Ex_extent	0	272	perftune
5	Ex_extent	0	280	perftune
5	Ex_extent	0	496	perftune
5	Ex_table-blk	16003088	0	perftune

The maximum number of locks is configured by the sa (see Chapter 9, "Configuring and Tuning the SQL Server"). The default (and minimum on most platforms) is 5,000 locks. Locks do not take up much memory (40 bytes/lock prior to System 10, 78 bytes/lock with System 10), so it is generally not a problem to configure for 7,000 or 10,000 locks if you are regularly approaching 5,000.

For example, to enable 10,000 concurrent locks:

```
sp_configure "locks", 10000
reconfigure
```

Warning

Always reconfigure after an sp_configure. This accomplishes two purposes. First, it guarantees that the option will take place the next time the server comes up. Second, it ensures that there will be sufficient memory to handle all the server kernel.

When the limit on locks is exceeded, the system errorlog shows a message indicating that no more locks are available, at which time you can reconfigure. (By this time you will also have gotten calls from users with odd error messages.)

Tip

If you don't want all the locking information from sp_lock, and do want to check lock concurrency, you can use the following:

```
select count(*) from master..syslocks
```

Note

For all the serverwide resources, a 60–70 percent utilization at peak should give you some room to grow, as well as some room for utilization spikes. As resources exceed 70 percent, start thinking about allocating more of whatever resource is being heavily used.

MONITORING ERRORLOG CONTENTS AND USE

The system errorlog is an operating-system-level file that is typically kept in the sybase/install directory. You may be able to verify this by running the UNIX or Open VMS command, showserver, and looking at the command line that started at the SQL Server. The startserver option, -e, enables you to specify the name and location of the errorlog (if it isn't fully qualified, it is located in the directory from which Sybase was started up, typically the install directory).

Let's examine the startup information in the log, section by section. The log displayed here is from a version 4.2 server running on Windows NT:

1. Copyright information indicates a server startup. Sample errorlog copy-right information always appears in the errorlog when the server starts up:

```
94/09/06 10:35:37.95 kernel    SQL Server for Windows NT 4.21 (Intel X86)
                               Jan 27 1994 21:47:39
Copyright (c) 1988-1994 Microsoft Corporation;
Copyright Sybase, Inc 1987-1994
94/09/06 10:35:37.95 kernel    Copyright (C) 1988-1993 Microsoft Corporation.
94/09/06 10:35:37.96 kernel    Copyright Sybase, Inc. 1987, 1993
94/09/06 10:35:37.96 kernel    All rights reserved.
94/09/06 10:35:37.98 kernel    Use, duplication, or disclosure by the United
                               States Government is subject
94/09/06 10:35:37.98 kernel    to restrictions set forth in FAR subparagraphs
                               52.227-19(a)-(d) for civilian
94/09/06 10:35:37.99 kernel    agency contracts and DFARS 252.227-
                               7013(c)(1)(ii) for Department of Defense
94/09/06 10:35:38.01 kernel    contracts. Sybase reserves all unpublished
                               rights under the copyright laws of
94/09/06 10:35:38.01 kernel    the United States.
94/09/06 10:35:38.01 kernel    Sybase, Inc. 6475 Christie Avenue, Emeryville,
                               CA 94608, USA.
94/09/06 10:35:38.01 kernel    Logging SQL Server messages in file
                               'C:\SQL\LOG\ERRORLOG'
```

2. Next, the server configures its own kernel (and sometimes prints appropriate messages):

```
94/09/06 10:35:38.08 kernel    initconfig: number of user connections limited
                               to 10
94/09/06 10:35:38.08 server    SQL Server is starting at priority class
                               'normal' with dataserver serialization
                               turned on.
```

Information in this part of the errorlog could tell you why a server won't start up.

3. Virtual devices are initialized (the server verifies that it can access the devices), and the master database is recovered in order to determine the names and physical locations of additional virtual devices. Note that the master device is always virtual device 0 (zero):

```
94/09/06 10:35:38.23 kernel   initializing virtual device 0,
                              C:\SQL\DATA\MASTER.DAT
94/09/06 10:35:38.89 kernel   Opening Master Database ...
94/09/06 10:35:38.95 server   Loading SQL Server's  default sort order and
                              character set
94/09/06 10:35:39.03 server   Recovering Database 'master'
94/09/06 10:35:39.15 server   Recovery dbid 1 ckpt (2627,1) oldest
                              tran=(2627,0)
94/09/06 10:35:39.21 server   1 transactions rolled forward
94/09/06 10:35:39.42 server   Activating disk 'dev1'
94/09/06 10:35:39.43 kernel   initializing virtual device 1, d:\data\dev1.dat
94/09/06 10:35:39.43 server   Activating disk 'dev2'
94/09/06 10:35:39.45 kernel   initializing virtual device 2, d:\data\dev2.dat
94/09/06 10:35:39.60 server   server name is 'NTSERVER'
```

A device problem with a device will be noted in this part of the errorlog. A device failure on the master device is another possible culprit if a server won't come up.

4. Each database is recovered, and information on recovery is displayed. If the sp_configure option recovery flags is set to 0, minimal output is printed (number of transactions rolled forward and backward). If set to 1, names of transactions rolled forward and backward are displayed. This section of the log should end with the words Recovery complete:

```
94/09/06 10:35:39.75 server   Recovering database 'model'
94/09/06 10:35:39.78 server   Recovery dbid 3 ckpt (45,26)
94/09/06 10:35:39.91 server   Clearing temp db
94/09/06 10:35:42.18 kernel   Using 'SQLEVENT.DLL' version '4.21.00'.
94/09/06 10:35:42.27 kernel   Using 'OPENDSNT.DLL' version '4.21.00.02'.
94/09/06 10:35:42.34 kernel   Using 'NTWDBLIB.DLL' version '4.21.00'.
94/09/06 10:35:42.37 ods      Using 'SSNMPNTW.DLL' version '4.21.0.0' to
                              listen on '\\.\pipe\sql\query'.
94/09/06 10:35:44.35 server   Recovering database 'pubs'
94/09/06 10:35:44.38 server   Recovery dbid 4 ckpt (493,10)
94/09/06 10:35:44.80 server   Recovering database 'perftune'
94/09/06 10:35:44.83 server   Recovery dbid 5 ckpt (1981,30)
94/09/06 10:35:45.06 server   Recovering database 'testing'
94/09/06 10:35:45.09 server   Recovery dbid 6 ckpt (997,0)
94/09/06 10:35:45.24 server   Recovery complete.
```

The errorlog contains information for each database as it is recovered.

Note

recovery flags is a nondynamic variable, and it takes effect during the recovery after it is set. (Once you have set the variable and brought the server up and then down, the following recovery has the "noisy" output.)

5. If you are looking to see whether the server is up, the final startup messages are the `default sort order` and `default character set`:

```
94/09/06 10:35:45.28 server    SQL Server's default sort order is:
94/09/06 10:35:45.28 server           'bin_cp850' (ID = 40)
94/09/06 10:35:45.28 server    on top of default character set:
94/09/06 10:35:45.30 server           'cp850' (ID = 2)
```

This is the end of the errorlog information recorded during startup.

Other things to look for include the following:

◆ *Error messages*. These run the gamut from informational messages, such as invalid login attempts, to resource messages, such as insufficient locks.

◆ *SQL Server termination notices*. These tell how and why the server was taken down. This information is particularly useful if the message does not indicate that the server was shut down by request.

The errorlog indicates the reason for a shutdown. A normal shutdown is recorded like this:

```
94/09/06 10:35:26.38 kernel    SQL Server terminating due to 'stop' request from
                               Service Control Manager
```

It is important to check the errorlog regularly. Check it several times a day when an application first goes into production. As you get used to looking at your production errorlog, you will be able to judge the frequency with which you need to check it on a regular basis. Many DBAs who manage multiple servers write utilities to scan the various errorlogs periodically, extracting error information.

Eventually, the errorlog will grow until it takes up the entire partition on which it resides. When it fills up the partition, you will have problems; therefore, you must periodically prune it. A good technique is to move it periodically (biweekly, for example). This has the effect of leaving an archive around temporarily. Trust Murphy's Law: If you simply truncate the errorlog, an odd message will appear and you will wonder whether this is the first time.

Warning

The *wrong* way to archive the log is to write a script that archives to generation datasets every time the server is brought up. (For example, the current is errorlog, next newest is errorlog.01, next newest errorlog.02, and so forth, finally deleting after errorlog.*xx*.) The problem with this approach is that if you run into a situation where the server is bounced up and down (brings itself down suddenly and unexpectedly) a few times in succession, valuable evidence is destroyed— evidence that could help track down the cause of the crashes.

14

COMPARING RESOURCES

You've already learned about monitoring connections and locks. The main reason you monitor resources is that you have a finite amount of memory and disk resources for the use of the server. Connections and locks are not the only resources that use up memory in the Sybase kernel—which could otherwise be used for cache.

Devices use up as much as 43KB per device connection. Is your devices parameter configured for 50 when you are actually using only 5? Sybase, at startup, allocates as much space as is needed for the maximum number of available devices. If you configure for 50 devices, Sybase allocates space for 50 devices.

Tip

> Increment virtual device numbers are assigned at disk init time (see Chapter 4, "Defining Physical and Mirror Devices") sequentially, and do not configure for more than one or two extra devices (so that you can configure for an extra virtual device without cycling the server, yet are not wasting substantial memory).

Most other parameters have a minor effect on memory. (The exception is a remote device, presented in Chapter 9, "Configuring and Tuning the SQL Server.")

One parameter that has a negligible effect on memory but which will drive you crazy when the problem occurs is open databases. If open databases is set at ten and you try to open an eleventh database, you get this message:

```
Unable to allocate a DBTABLE descriptor to open database '[database name]'.
Another database must be closed or dropped before opening this one.
```

(The error is number 905, severity 17.) I have seen experienced programmers get this one, not understand the message, and continue to work in *master* (not good).

KEEPING SOFTWARE CURRENT

Why do you update your software? After all, you finally have it working the way you want. Here are some reasons:

◆ Sybase enhances its optimizer with additional releases.

◆ Bugs and features are fixed in subsequent releases.

◆ After a while, if you are not up to date, Sybase Technical Support will laugh at you if you have a problem.

Additionally, Sybase keeps its software up to date by periodically shipping *Emergency Bug Fixes (EBFs)*. In fact, one of the more frequent results of a call to Sybase Technical Support might be, "We fixed that in the last EBF. Give me your customer number, and we'll ship a new tape."

As a result, you are frequently called upon to upgrade your current software. This is nontrivial, because you will occasionally upgrade software and find that a bug has been introduced that is worse than your original problem.

Warning

Sybase currently does not have in place any way of "unapplying" an EBF. This means that if an EBF causes worse problems than no EBF, you need a way of getting back to where you were. This is an exception condition, but it has happened.

Solution: When applying an EBF, do it in an alternate directory, and start up from the new directory. In case the EBF affects the database, back the database up, and also have the old install tape available.

Warning

With version upgrades—for example, the upgrade to System 10—system tables may be modified or added. This makes backing off the upgrade impossible unless everything is backed up, especially `master`. If you install System 10 and discover that the new "features" make your application stop working, you have to go to some trouble to resume operations in a prior release.

Here are some general recommendations:

1. Don't be the first DBA on your block to install either EBFs or version upgrades. Wait a while, ask around at your user's group, find out what other people's problems have been, and learn from them.

2. Install first on your development server and run a system test. Install next on your QA server and run a user acceptance test.

3. Finally, install with great care on your development server (during a lull in activity) and be fully prepared to back off in a hurry if necessary.

4. Balance these two statements: If it isn't broken, don't fix it; and, if you tell Technical Support you are running version 2, they will die laughing before you ever get your answer.

In all seriousness, it is increasingly difficult to get useful technical support as your version gets more ancient. What was once common knowledge among Technical Support staff now requires a visit to the guru—someone who actually worked for Sybase two years ago.

Note

There are a couple of Sybase sites running version 2! (That's earlier than our experience with SQL Server!) A major financial services DP shop in Manhattan is running 4.01, afraid to upgrade even to 4.2, much less 4.8, 4.9, or System 10. Why? They are running a 24-hour, 7-day-a-week shop and have calculated that, if they are down for a minute, it will cost them $1 million.

RECORDING RUN-TIME DATA

From a disaster-recovery standpoint, it is useful to be able to recreate your environment from scratch. Toward this end, you need to record all the parameters you have set so that you can rebuild with the benefit of all the decisions that you have successfully implemented. Specifically, run the `sp_configure` stored procedure without parameters to display run-time data, and store the results. This example:

```
buildmaster -yall
```

isn't the southern "Hi y'all!" The buildmaster program is an operating-system-level utility that is intended to do just what it says: build the master database. However, it has an additional function. A variety of variables can be set, adjusted, and tweaked for performance reasons.

Warning

None of these are parameters you should adjust without advice from Sybase Technical Support.

Some of these variables seem to be self-adjusting (or perhaps are adjusted by EBFs). Whether they are, or Sybase Technical support asks you to change them, it is important to store the variable values in a safe place.

This example lists all variables:

```
buildmaster -d master_device -yall
```

This example changes the variable `cstacsize` to 32767:

```
buildmaster -d master_device -ycstacsize=32767
```

Database-Level Maintenance

At the database level, you can execute the following:

- Run preventive dbcc commands
- Dump databases
- Dump transaction logs
- Ensure that you can load from backup
- Monitor space utilization of data and log
- Maintain all your object creation lists

Running Preventive *dbcc* Commands

Originally, the database consistency checker (dbcc) was a way of trying to detect a problem in a database that was acting odd, and of checking the database after upgrades.

The next step in dbcc evolution was its use in verifying databases prior to dumping. Why? Because bad data snowballs, and you don't want to start snowballing from the database you just restored from tape. This happens to be the stage dbcc is in today; it is used by database administrators to verify that the database and the data in it are consistent, that pages allocated should be allocated, and that no orphaned data exists.

There are problems in the current iteration of dbcc. Primarily, DBAs are so reliant on it that many will not dump a database without running it (or risk ulcers). That in itself would not be a problem if database verification ran in a timely way. Unfortunately, dbcc on a 2GB database could take hours. In addition, some of the dbcc commands require the database to be in single-user mode or put exclusive locks on tables (users just love that!). As databases grow, and production requirements push to 7 days/24 hours, running dbcc with any frequency becomes impossible.

Tip

If you can't run dbcc before all your dumps, at least find a time slot to run it before aging out your dump tapes. Some DBAs dump the database, load it to another server, and run dbcc there. Not a bad idea if there is no other choice, but extreme.

Table 11.1 summarizes the dbcc commands used in preventive maintenance. For a more detailed discussion of dbcc commands, see Appendix A, "The Database Consistency Checker (dbcc)."

TABLE 11.1. PREVENTIVE MAINTENANCE dbcc COMMANDS.

Command	Task
	TABLE CONSISTENCY
dbcc checktable	Checks a specific table's consistency
dbcc checkdb*	Checks all tables for a database
dbcc checkcatalog*	Checks system tables
	PAGE CONSISTENCY
dbcc checkalloc*	Checks page allocations
dbcc tablealloc	Checks table allocation pointers
dbcc indexalloc	Checks index page pointers
dbcc fix_al	Fixes allocation pages reported by checkalloc

*Run at least these three dbcc commands before performing backups.

Note

checkalloc was replaced by newalloc with version 4.8, which was subsequently moved into checkalloc with version 4.9. If you have a current release of the server, don't worry about it. checkalloc also does the work of both newalloc and tablealloc.

TABLE CONSISTENCY COMMANDS

dbcc checktable actually reads each of the data pages and checks rows in the table. dbcc checkdb does the same for each table in a database. Note that sysindexes tracks information on rows and pages used by the tables. dbcc checktable actually updates that information if it is inaccurate.

Note

These inaccuracies are what caused sp_spaceused to be nicknamed "sp_spaceuseless" for so long.

If there is a problem in the table consistency check, you usually get a message with very specific instructions about how to proceed. You may need to run another dbcc command, or you may need to drop a table, an index, or even a database and restore from backup.

The following output is from `dbcc checktable` for a relatively small table, `pt_tx`:

```
Checking pt_tx
The total number of data pages in this table is 88.
Table has 7282 data rows.
DBCC execution completed. If DBCC printed error messages, see your System
                           Administrator.
```

PAGE CONSISTENCY COMMANDS

Use `dbcc checkalloc` to find *object allocation map (OAM)* problems. Here is sample output from this command:

```
Checking perftune
Database 'perftune' is not in single user mode - may find spurious allocation
                                          problems due to transactions in
                                          progress.
Alloc page 0 (# of extent=31 used pages=58 ref pages=58)
Alloc page 256 (# of extent=4 used pages=24 ref pages=24)
Alloc page 512 (# of extent=32 used pages=236 ref pages=236)
Alloc page 768 (# of extent=32 used pages=256 ref pages=256)
Alloc page 1024 (# of extent=32 used pages=246 ref pages=246)
Alloc page 1280 (# of extent=32 used pages=251 ref pages=251)
Alloc page 1536 (# of extent=32 used pages=256 ref pages=256)
Alloc page 1792 (# of extent=32 used pages=234 ref pages=232)
Alloc page 2048 (# of extent=32 used pages=248 ref pages=248)
Alloc page 2304 (# of extent=32 used pages=256 ref pages=256)
Alloc page 2560 (# of extent=32 used pages=256 ref pages=256)
Alloc page 2816 (# of extent=32 used pages=256 ref pages=256)
Alloc page 3072 (# of extent=11 used pages=87 ref pages=87)
Alloc page 3328 (# of extent=1 used pages=0 ref pages=0)
Alloc page 3584 (# of extent=1 used pages=0 ref pages=0)
Alloc page 3840 (# of extent=1 used pages=0 ref pages=0)
Alloc page 4096 (# of extent=1 used pages=0 ref pages=0)
...
Alloc page 13568 (# of extent=1 used pages=0 ref pages=0)
Alloc page 13824 (# of extent=1 used pages=0 ref pages=0)
Alloc page 14080 (# of extent=1 used pages=0 ref pages=0)
Total (# of extent=409 used pages=2664 ref pages=2662) in this database DBCC
execution completed. If DBCC printed error messages, see your System Administrator.
```

OAM problems seemed most prevalent after the upgrade from version 4.9.1 to early versions of 4.9.2. They would crop up for no apparent reason, and drive DBAs batty. Eventually, Sybase fixed whatever error was causing the problems, and they are once again unusual—but still annoying when they crop up.

If an OAM page error does crop up, you have to run `dbcc fix_al` while the database is in single-user mode. This is annoying and time-consuming, because `dbcc fix_al` on a 2GB database costs about eight hours.

RUN *DBCC MEMUSAGE* REGULARLY

Read Chapter 9, "Configuring and Tuning the SQL Server," for detailed information about `dbcc memusage`. Run it regularly to understand how memory is being used in your server:

- Look at the overall memory figures to make certain that you have as much data cache as you expected.
- Look at the data cache to see whether any particular object is monopolizing the cache at the expense of other objects, because it may be appropriate to take other tuning steps on that object.
- Look at how large your stored procedures are, because smaller procedures compile and execute faster.

DUMPING DATABASES

This and the following sections are included for the sake of completeness, so that a DBA who has skipped the rest of the book for the purpose of finding out what is needed on a regular basis will have a complete list. For a detailed discussion of backup and recovery, see Chapter 7, "Database Logging and Recovery."

The idea behind a database dump is disaster recovery. You, as a DBA, need to create a realistic plan that will bring you from any conceivable problem back to a solid production environment. Disasters do not happen every day, but there are a wide variety of disasters that require you to load the database from a backup copy.

Warning

It is important to back up *all* databases except tempdb. This especially means master, the one database that will cause you the most agony should it need reconstruction.

If you do lose the master database after creating or altering a database, that database is *lost* and cannot be recovered. After every create database or alter database, you *must* perform a backup of master.

DUMPING TRANSACTION LOGS

The only way to prune a log (keep it from filling up) in a production environment is to dump it.

Note

It is possible to keep the logs from filling up quickly by setting the `truncate log on checkpoint` option in the database:

```
sp_dboption db_name, "truncate log on checkpoint", true
```

This is a *bad idea* except in environments where you don't care about recovery, because it renders log recovery (recovering transactions between a prior dump and data device crash) impossible.

When you get a message along the lines of "Unable to allocate space on segment logsegment," you have run out of space in the log. Typically, it means that you haven't been dumping it often enough, or that you had an unexpected quantity of transactions in the database.

Tip

Prior to System 10, use `sp_spaceused` and/or `dbcc checktable` on syslogs to see how activity in the database affects the log size at production times just prior to the dump. This should be as big as it gets, and you should be certain that there is at least 25 percent free space left in the log.

Tip

With System 10 and later, use thresholds to avoid the "Segment full" errors.

ENSURING BACKUP LOADING

You have carefully planned for the worst possible contingencies; you are ready to shine and bring the database up pronto. What is the worst possible thing that could happen?

How about the database not loading from tape? Things happen. If you have never restored from a backup, you really don't know what will happen when you try. Even if you tested the restore a year ago, tapes get old. (Cycle your tapes, and discard them after a year or so, to avoid this problem—similar to mainframe generation data sets.)

Note

There was a weird problem with an old version of the server where a 250MB tape was an inch short, and neither the controller nor Sybase reported the discrepancy. Nothing would load, because any data would be suspect.

MONITORING SPACE UTILIZATION

If you have System 10, you can use thresholds (and should, unless performance is so tight you can't afford it). This helps you monitor and report space issues. You should typically have about 25 percent free space in your data in order to leave room for growth and for the server to have some room to shuffle information (create indices and so forth). Be sure you understand your data growth patterns, so that there are no surprises. If there are surprises, it means something has gone wrong and you need to investigate.

Note

On the other end of the spectrum, what happens if you allocate 2GB for a database and find you are only using 100MB?

Sybase does not have any way of shrinking databases. You have to unload the data, drop and recreate the database (smaller), and recreate the objects and reload the data.

Remember that you cannot dump the 100MB of actual data from the 2GB database, and reload it into a 200MB database. Why not? A database backup is a record of every written page in the database and its location. During recovery, the server first makes certain that every *possible* page in the original database could be written to the new database *in its original location*. There are potential locations in a 2GB database that are not available in the smaller allocation, so the restore fails immediately.

Perhaps Sybase will allow restores into a smaller database at some future date, but frankly, data needs tend to increase, not decrease. It's probably low on Sybase's list of enhancements.

When in doubt, start with a smaller database, and make it bigger whenever you are ready.

MAINTAINING OBJECT CREATION LISTS

It is very important to keep track of all object creation scripts (see Chapter 17, "Managing the Audit System," for standards). This will save your life during migration, version control, and disaster recovery.

You learned earlier that it is conceivable for a database to be unrecoverable for a variety of reasons. It is occasionally necessary to rebuild from scripts. For this reason, maintain a complete script of everything that goes into your database, including the following:

- Rules
- Defaults
- User-defined datatypes
- Tables
- Views
- Indices
- Triggers
- Stored procedures (make sure these can be retrieved in dependency order)
- Users
- Aliases
- Groups
- Permissions

In master, you also need to record scripts that manipulate the following elements:

- Logins
- Devices
- Databases
- Roles

If you do not have scripts, or are taking over a server or database that does not have scripts, there are several third-party tools that do this efficiently and correctly.

TABLE-LEVEL MAINTENANCE

At the table level, you can do the following:

- Update distribution statistics
- Monitor space utilization of volatile tables

UPDATING DISTRIBUTION STATISTICS

The single most important thing that a Sybase DBA can do to ensure consistent, positive query performance is to keep index statistics up to date.

Remember that statistics are not kept current dynamically because it would cause too much overhead. That's why you have to issue the following:

```
update statistics table_name [(index_name)]
```

for each table (or index) periodically. As the data skews, you must update the statistics.

Note

If you have lots of tables or your list changes frequently, it is best to use a tool that creates a dynamic list of tables and update all the statistics sequentially. You can do this with isql by writing a script something like this:

```
select "update statistics " + name
from sysobjects
where type = 'U'
```

U is the type for user tables in the sysobjects table. S is used for system tables.

Here is the output of the script:

```
----------------------------------------------
update statistics pt_sample
update statistics pt_tx
update statistics pt_sample_CIkey2
update statistics pt_sample_CIcompany
update statistics pt_sample_CIidNCk
update statistics pt_tx_CIamountNCamount
update statistics pt_tx_NCamount
update statistics pt_tx_CIid
( 8 rows affected)
```

Now you can run the output from this script as a script itself.

MONITORING SPACE UTILIZATION OF VOLATILE TABLES

If you have a table that is by its nature volatile (for example, a live data feed), put it on its own segment to control growth of the table and avoid having a rapidly growing table fill the database.

With System 10 and later, you can use threshold management to get warnings as segments fill up and as you need to alter database sizes (or make the decision to truncate some rows).

Prior to System 10, you must run `sp_spaceused` or `dbcc checktable` to keep track of table growth.

Note

It is unusual to have to track growth of an individual table.

SUMMARY

You need to develop a regimen of periodic maintenance tasks. Your personal periodic maintenance checklist might look like the Checklist at the end of this chapter if you are in production and things are running smoothly.

14

PERIODIC MAINTENANCE

CHECKLIST

SERVER-LEVEL MAINTENANCE

	Frequency	Task	Notes
☐	Weekly	Monitor CPU- and I/O-busy statistics	Use sp_monitor or a third-party tool
☐	Daily	Monitor errorlog contents and use	Remember to prune the log so that it doesn't encompass all your disk space
☐	Weekly	Compare resources allocated and in use	Do not allow overallocations of databases, devices, or users to consume memory
☐	As required	Keep software current	But do not be the first on your block to put it in production
☐	After every change	Store results of buildmaster with -yall option and sp_configure	File the results in a secure place

DATABASE-LEVEL MAINTENANCE

	Frequency	Task	Notes
☐	Before every backup	Run dbcc commands	Inspect output for OAM page problems and other errors
☐	See Chapter 7	Dump databases	And get a copy off-site
☐	See Chapter 7	Dump transaction logs	This is the only way to prune the logs in production
☐	Monthly	Make sure you can load from backup	Tapes go bad, dumps go awry

DATABASE-LEVEL MAINTENANCE

Frequency	Task	Notes
☐ Daily	Monitor space utilization of data and log	Use `sp_spaceused`, `dbcc checktable`, or a third-party tool
☐ After every change	Maintain all your object creation lists	Essential for documentation and disaster recovery

TABLE-LEVEL MAINTENANCE

Frequency	Task	Notes
☐ As data changes (see Chapter 12)	Update distribution statistics	The single most important thing you can do for performance
☐ Daily	Monitor space utilization of volatile tables	So they don't grow to encompass your entire database unexpectedly

14

PERIODIC MAINTENANCE

CHAPTER 15

What Do You Do When Things Go Wrong?

If you have read this far in the book, you should be ready to handle most problems that would not require a call to Sybase Technical Support. If a problem occurs and you're really stumped, use this section like the back of your auto owner's manual.

Note

> I remember the owner's manual of my 1982 Volkswagon Scirrocco. Under the symptom heading of "Engine Overheating," the probable cause was listed as "Driving uphill at high speeds pulling a trailer." Now that's confidence.
>
> Once you've identified what the error message really means, and to what it is attributed, resolving the problem is usually simple. Not necessarily fast, but simple.
>
> This chapter should be a bit more useful than the Scirrocco owner's manual.

There are two basic principles of disaster preparedness. The first principle is emotional; the second is practical.

◆ Law of Disaster Recovery: Don't Panic. This was blatantly plagiarized from Douglas Adams' *Hitchhiker's Guide to the Galaxy*.

◆ Law of Database Administration: The less you prepare for a disaster, the more likely it is to happen. (Curiously, the more you prepare for a disaster, the more likely it is to happen.)

This law is a combination of two other laws: Murphy's Law—Anything that can go wrong will, and at the worst possible time; and the Buttered Bread Law—The chances of a dropped piece of buttered bread landing butter side up is inversely proportional to the cost of the carpeting.

What we are really trying to say is this: Disasters are going to happen. It is best to be prepared. The server typically knows what is wrong with it; sometimes, it even clues you in.

After most types of extreme disaster, you will need to restore a database (see Chapter 16, "Tools for Sybase Administrators"). For more minor problems, and everyday types of phone calls, this chapter tells you some possible symptoms, likely causes, tools for understanding the problems, and some possible resolutions.

SYMPTOMS

There are a variety of typical complaints that will be called in to you, as a production DBA. Many are quickly recognizable. For example, there's the caller who announces in a sing-song voice, "The server's hung. Again!" This chapter presents a variety of symptoms and typical causes, as well as the basic tools you'll use. Here is a summary of the symptoms:

- The server will not come up.
- Users claim the server is hung.
- The server is up, but not all users can gain access.
- Processing slows or stops.
- A database or databases cannot be accessed.
- Users cannot access objects.

BASIC TOOLS

You typically will use only a few tools to evaluate problems, including the following:

- `sp_who`
- `sp_lock`
- `sp_monitor`
- the system errorlog

Depending on the nature of the problem, your first line of attack probably should be to run `sp_who` to see who is doing what to whom. If the call implies locking and/or contention problems, you also will use `sp_lock` to find out what is being locked. If performance is an issue, run `sp_monitor` or any other Sybase or third-party utility you have available to try to determine where the bottleneck lies. If you want to find out whether a problem has been ongoing, check the system errorlog (you may need to shut down the system to flush the last few messages from the OS buffer—the errorlog is written to a file system).

You have already spent ample time on all of these topics, so there is no reason to cover old ground here.

Typically, you can resolve problems in a familiar way. First, verify that a problem exists. If it does, try to identify the scope of the problem: is it local to a user, to a network, to a database, or is the entire server affected? Next, identify the nature of the problem, and get as much information as you can regarding the symptoms.

SERVER WON'T COME UP

When the server won't come up, there are several things you can check to determine the cause.

Make sure you are signed in to the host operating system as the Sybase user, who has the permissions to start the server. If you signed in as any other user, the server process fails because it does not have access to any other necessary resources. (Even the UNIX root user cannot start a SQL Server process.)

Check the system errorlog. (Remember, the default location is in the sybase/install directory, but the actual location may be changed. Another location may be specified at startup with the -e option; check the runserver file for the server, which is in the sybase/install directory.) Once you find the errorlog, the information there is usually specific enough to identify a problem. There may be a problem with the master device or you may not have enough available resources (check server configuration).

Check to see if network drivers are available within the host operating system; if they are not, the Sybase SQL Server will not come up. This is a particular problem at system boot time. If you start the network synchronously, and then start the SQL Server process, the network may not have come up before the server looks for it, causing the server to fail to come up. You may be able to simply restart the SQL Server.

Check resource availability as follows:

◆ Is the master device offline? You may need to check the physical drive.

◆ Is there enough memory for the server? You may need to terminate some applications. Some versions of UNIX cause boot problems when the amount of memory configured exceeds the size of the swap space of your operating system. (See "Troubleshooting Guide," in Chapter 1.)

◆ Alternatively, you may need to run buildmaster with the -R option to reset the configuration to the default. This is especially common after you reset the maximum number of users, locks, or devices with sp_configure.

USERS CLAIM THE SERVER IS HUNG

The first thing to do when users claim the server is hung is to try to sign in yourself. The users are often wrong when they say the server is hung up. If you can't sign in, see if any other users are working. If so, identify what characterizes systems that have lost access. It helps to have a schematic of the network: if half of your users lose access, a single network segment may have failed after a router or network card problem.

If the situation is specific to the user, his connection may have timed out. By the time you have started looking, he may have gotten an appropriate message. Check the errorlog for anything informative. If the server disconnected a process, it may tell you why.

If you get in, run sp_who. If the number of rows approaches or exceeds the number of configured user connections, there's a problem (reconfigure the server with sp_configure). Next, identify the user's process, and look in the blk column. Anything other than zero in this column indicates a blocked process. The server process ID of the blocking process will appear in this column. Try to determine how the blocking process is creating the blocking "live" lock. (Remember that SQL Server does not time out processes that are blocked by live locks. That's the responsibility of the client application.)

If nobody can sign in, the software may be stopped. You can run showserver at the operating system level to see if there is actually a process running. (If you can't log in to the operating system, the entire machine may have locked up.) If you get desperate, you might need to shut Sybase down at the operating system level, or even cold boot the host on which it's running. If you do, your chances of coming up clean are much better if you are using raw partitions for database devices.

SERVER IS UP BUT CAN'T BE ACCESSED

When the server is up, but not all users can gain access, verify that the number of user connections used and configured are not overlapping. If this is not an issue, call the network administrator, because it is an SEP (Somebody Else's Problem—expression used by Douglas Adams in his book, *Hitchhiker's Guide to the Galaxy*).

PROCESSING SLOWS OR STOPS

On a single-processor (non-SMP) box, slowed or stopped processing is frequently caused by a batch process being run during online hours. This problem occurs because swapping resources in and out increases beyond the allocated time slice, so the batch process gets a time slice that is disproportionately large. Either buy an SMP box, run the batch job during a processing lull, or try another application alternative. Also, check all of the locked process suggestions just discussed.

Finally, look for system stored procedures, index creations, or dbcc processes that are running. These may temporarily lock tables or indexes.

ONE OR MORE DBs CAN'T BE ACCESSED

When users can't access a database, run sp_helpdb on the database. Check the status column to see if the database has been marked corrupt or suspect. If it has, you will probably need to use dbcc dbrepair (dbname, dropdb) to get rid of the database, then re-create it and load from backup.

If nothing is wrong, run sp_who and count the number of different databases being accessed. If the number is equal to the number of configured databases, reconfigure.

USERS CANNOT ACCESS OBJECTS

When users can't access objects, the first question to ask is this: Is the user using the correct database? If so, there is a remote possibility of a corrupt table or index, but most likely the permission scheme has broken down. Use the sp_helpprotect command to check permissions. Remember to check permissions not only for the individual, but also his group and public.

DBCC ERRORS

If you are running into problems identified by the Database Consistency Checker, you will find messages in the dbcc output, as well as the system errorlog. Typically, these messages tell you the exact nature of the problem, along with what to do. Running dbcc with the fix option is covered thoroughly in Appendix A, "dbcc Commands."

For example, dbcc checkalloc will sometimes return allocation errors. On SQL Servers prior to System 10, run dbcc fix_al. Subsequently, run checkalloc with the fix option.

Note

This problem happened frequently in versions 4.8 through 4.9.1, but it is unusual to observe in System 10 dbcc output.

Another common problem when you can't access a database is when the sybsecurity database is full. If you have "use database" auditing turned on and the sybsecurity database fills, any user attempting to use the audited database will hang until space is free in the sybsecurity database.

UNUSUAL MESSAGES

Sybase error messages are informative about 60 to 80 percent of the time. You have to guess the meaning of the other 20 to 40 percent. Typically, anything cryptic has to do with system configuration variables. For example, a message may mention insufficient kernel allocation rather than a need to increase the open databases parameter.

If you run into something inexplicable, check the troubleshooting guide. Alternatively, you can look in the sysmessages table in the master database to see if there is more text to the message you are looking for, as shown in the following example:

```
Select * from sysmessages where error = 607
error  severity dlevel description                            langid sqlstate
-----  -------- ------ -------------------------------------- ------ ----------------------
607          21      2 Insufficient room was allocated in the session descriptor
                       for object '%.*s' for search arguments. Only %d search
                       arguments were anticipated.
                       ( 1 row affected)
```

NAMED CACHES DON'T IMPROVE PERFORMANCE

You've read the section on named caches, have tried implementing large buffer pool sizes, and you are still not getting a performance benefit.

It may be that your task was not I/O bound. In order to get a benefit from a cache, you must first have determined that there is an I/O bottleneck.

You may also not be using an appropriate fetch strategy. If you are creating large buffer pools and not getting a performance benefit from what you expect to be large block writes (for example, a table scan or long-running batch update process), try setting the prefetch parameter to your select statement. Use sp cachestrategy to turn on a strategy for an index (see Chapter 10, "Optimizing SQL Server Configuration Options").

If you have not set a cache strategy, try using the prefetch in the select statement, as in this example:

```
select * from authors (index aunmind prefetch 16384 mru)
```

If lru is not effective for the prefetch, try mru.

15

LOG IS A HOT SPOT

With System 11, you now have a separate cache for each user. The cache size is configurable by the DBA on a server-wide basis (See Chapter 9, "Configuring and Tuning the SQL Server").

You may find that "Right out of the Box," System 11 makes your log bottlenecks vanish. If it doesn't, it is probably because the user log cache is too small for your transaction volumes. If you use `sp configure` to reset the `User log cache size` parameter, you may be able to reduce this contention.

Alternatively, if this value is too high, you may increase the needed spinlocks on your system and end up waiting for same.

Don't make your log cache size greater than the size of your actual transactions.

SUMMARY

Most problems can be resolved by using a little common sense. You now have the basics to resolve most types of problems.

Don't panic. Gather all the data to which you have access before acting. Resolve the problem and not the symptoms.

When in doubt, check the basics. And remember, this is fun!

- Installation Programs

- Server Administration
  Executables

- Invoking a Backup
  Server

- Copy and Interface
  Tools

CHAPTER 16

Tools for Sybase
Administrators

Sybase provides several command-line tools to manage the database server. You may have used several of these utilities in the past, but it can be helpful to understand their full capabilities. For example, did you know you could encrypt your SQL Server password when using tools such as bcp, defncopy, and isql? Or that you can increase the network packet size to make the bulk copying routine perform faster?

This chapter considers the utilities in three categories: installation programs, server administration executables, and copying and interface tools. These tools are used to perform activities such as install languages and server databases, start and report on servers, and copy data and definitions from the server.

Note

You can execute all these tools from the operating system where SQL Server resides. Some (isql and bcp, in particular) may be run from client workstations as well.

As with everything else about SQL Server, the syntax for the tools may vary slightly among host operating systems and will certainly provide different capabilities with different release levels. You need to check the detailed release information that came with SQL Server to be sure about the names, syntax, and capabilities of the utilities you have installed.

Here's a summary of the tools covered in this chapter and what they do:

buildmaster	Builds (or rebuilds) the master database. Run once during install, this utility is subsequently run after a disaster or configuration error. You also use buildmaster to tune parameters that are not available from sp_configure.
langinstall	Installs a new language on the server.
startserver	Executes a runserver file, which causes a specific SQL Server engine to run.
showserver	Displays any running SQL Servers on the current host.
dataserver	Starts the actual SQL Server engine. It usually is not run by itself.

backupserver   Initiates the backup server process on the current server.

bcp   (bulk copy program) Initiates a data transfer session, enabling the administrator to copy data between SQL Server tables and operating system files.

defncopy   Enables the reverse engineering of existing database objects whose definitions are stored in syscomments (rules, defaults, procedures, triggers, and views).

isql   (interactive SQL) An interactive tool for issuing SQL commands and retrieving result sets.

Installation Programs

Use buildmaster to build and rebuild server-based databases (master, model, and tempdb) and langinstall to install a language.

Building and Rebuilding Databases (BUILDMASTER)

The sybinit script invokes buildmaster as part of installation. During a server install, you specify many things, including the master device location and master database size. This information is passed to buildmaster as parameters. These parameters are used by buildmaster to determine the information necessary to write the configuration block and to create the master, model, and tempdb databases. You probably won't even realize that buildmaster is running.

Syntax

buildmaster [-d *devicename*] [-c *controller_#*] [-s *size_in_pages*] [-r] [-m] [-x]

Options

Table 16.1 presents detailed descriptions of each parameter of buildmaster.

16

TABLE 16.1. buildmaster PARAMETERS.

Parameter	Value	Description
-d	devicename	If you are using a raw device, this is the full pathname of that device. It must be owned by Sybase (for example, /dev/rid001f). If you are using a file for the master device, this is the full pathname for the file (for example, /home/sybase/devices/master.dat).
-c	controller_#	This is the controller number for the master device, normally 0. Do not change this value unless directed to.
-s	size_in_pages	This is the size of the master device in 2KB blocks. The size should be at least 10MB, although more is recommended. (For a 40MB master device, use 20480.)
-r		This rewrites the configuration block with the default values and is used when a value is set too high for the server to come up.
-m		This rewrites the master database only. Use when only the master database is corrupt (other databases on the master device are okay). The current configuration values remain unchanged unless the -r option is also provided.
-x		This rewrites the model database only. Use to "restore" model to original condition after unwanted changes. It cannot be used for corrupt model databases.

If you're lucky, the initial installation is the only time you will run buildmaster. It also is used, however, to resolve problems in certain situations:

♦ Is your master database corrupted? Run buildmaster with the -m parameter to rebuild the master database; then load the current version from backup:

```
buildmaster -d/home/sybase/devices/master.dat -m
```

♦ Did you set the number of connections to 250 instead of 25? Did the server not come up because it couldn't grab enough memory? Run buildmaster with the -r parameter to rewrite the configuration block with the default values; then reset the values (using a reasonable value for the one you set too high!):

```
buildmaster -d/home/sybase/devices/master.dat -r
```

◆ Did a user "playing around" accidentally change data or drop a table in the model database? Run `buildmaster` with the `-x` parameter to rebuild only the model database:

```
buildmaster -d/home/sybase/devices/master.dat -x
```

INSTALLING A LANGUAGE (*LANGINSTALL*)

Use `langinstall` to install a language on SQL Server. This is run automatically during installation or can be run at the command line to install a new language. It adds data to the syslanguages table and modifies the data in the sysmessages table in the master database.

SYNTAX

```
langinstall  [-S servername] [-I interfaces_file] [-R release_number]
             [-P sa_password][-v] language character_set
```

OPTIONS

Table 16.2 presents detailed descriptions of each parameter of `langinstall`.

TABLE 16.2. langinstall PARAMETERS.

Parameter	Value	Description
-S	servername	This is the name of the server in which to install the new language. If this option is not specified, it uses the value of DSQUERY. If no value exists, SYBASE is used.
-I	interfaces_file	This is the name of the interface file to use when trying to find a server to which to connect. If this option is not provided, bcp looks for a file named interfaces in the directory identified by the SYBASE environment variable (SYBASE home directory).
-R	release_number	Use only when you think the sysmessages table in the master database is out of date. It tells the server the release number to use to upgrade messages.
-P	sa_password	This is the password of the sa login. If this is not provided, it will be prompted for.

continues

16

TOOLS FOR ADMINISTRATORS

Table 16.2. continued

Parameter	Value	Description
-v		Do not use with any other option. This option tells langinstall to print the version number and copyright information, then exit.
	language	This is the official name of the language you are going to install. A language must be specified when using langinstall.
	character_set	This is the name of the SQL Server's default character set.

Examples

Run langinstall to install a new language (german), as in the following example. The default character set remains cp_850. Note that you must purchase additional languages separately from Sybase.

```
langinstall -SSYBASE1 -Pfrance german cp_850
```

Get the version number and copyright information for the SQL Server and make no changes, as in this example:

```
langinstall -SSYBASE -Pfrance -v
```

Note

langinstall is run as part of a new installation or as part of an upgrade to a new release and must be run by the system administrator login (sa).

Server Administration Executables

There are several executables used either to start a server or to report on currently running servers. The startserver command is passed runserver files that execute either the dataserver or backupserver programs. The result is an up-and-running SQL Server or backup server. showserver is then used to report on the servers running on a particular machine.

Starting the Server

The `startserver` command is used to start any number of SQL Servers or backup servers. The `startserver` executable is passed a runserver file as an argument. A runserver file is a file containing all the commands necessary to run (start) a server. `startserver` reads the runserver file and it provides the executable with the information it needs.

Syntax

```
startserver [ [ -f runserver_file] [-m] ] ...
```

Options

Table 16.3 presents detailed descriptions of each parameter of `startserver`.

Table 16.3. `startserver` parameters.

Parameter	Value	Description
-f	runserver_file	This is the name of the file to use to start up a server. The runserver file contains the calls to either `dataserver` or `backupserver`. If this option is not specified, `startserver` tries to start the default server, named SYBASE.
-m		Use this to start SQL Server in single-user mode, which enables only one system administrator to log in.

Notes

Runserver files normally are named with the convention RUN_{SERVERNAME}. For example, if you have a SQL Server name TEST and a two backup servers named BACKUP1 and BACKUP2, you will have the following runserver files: RUN_TEST, RUN_BACKUP1, and RUN_BACKUP2. To start all three servers in one command, execute the following:

```
startserver -f RUN_TEST -f RUN_BACKUP1 -f RUN_BACKUP2
```

16

Tools for Administrators

Here is an example of a generic runserver file:

```
#!/bin/csh -f
# name:        SYBASE
# master device:      /dev/rsd01
# errorlog       /home/sybase/install/errorlog
# interfaces      /home/sybase
# shared memory file location      /home/sybase/install
# replication enabled:      FALSE
setenv DSLISTEN SYBASE
/home/sybase/bin/dataserver -d /dev/rsd01
```

For an explanation of the options provided to the `dataserver` executable, see the next section, "Invoking a SQL Server."

Remember to use `startserver` whenever possible.

INVOKING A SQL SERVER

`dataserver` is the executable used to run the SQL Server program. This executable can be invoked at the command line or embedded in scripts for ease of use. Normally, a SQL Server is started from other scripts (usually a runserver file that is read by the `startserver` program).

Note

In some releases of SQL Server, including the System 10 release for Windows NT, `dataserver` is called `sqlserver`.

SYNTAX

```
dataserver [-d devicename] [-e errorlog_file] [-r master_mirror_dev]
           [-M shared_mem_dir][-p sso_login_name ] [-m] [-T trace_value]
```

OPTIONS

Table 16.4 presents detailed descriptions of each parameter of `dataserver`.

TABLE 16.4. `dataserver` PARAMETERS.

Parameter	Value	Description
-d	devicename	If you are using a raw device, this is the full device pathname of the master device. It must be owned by SYBASE (for example, /dev/rid001f).

Parameter	Value	Description
		If you are using a file for the master device, this is the full pathname (for example, /home/sybase/devices/master.dat)
-e	errorlog_file	This is the full pathname to place messages and errors encountered by SQL Server.
-r	master_mirror_dev	This is the device used to mirror the master device (listed in the -d option).
-M	shared_mem_dir	This tells Sybase to put any shared memory files in the directory specified. The default directory used is defined by the environment variable $SYBASE.
-p	sso_login_name	This is used to regenerate a password for a login with the sso_role. The password is displayed when dataserver is run, and it is encrypted and saved in the syslogins table in the master database.
-m		This starts the server is single-user mode.
-T	trace_value	This starts the server using the indicated trace value.

Start a SQL Server using the provided startserver command whenever possible.

Most sites place either a call to startserver, or the commands contained in the appropriate runserver file(s), into an operating system startup file. This ensures that the database is started every time the hardware is booted. Placing the commands in a startup file avoids the annoying calls to database administration complaining that the SQL Server is down after a reboot.

If the last system security officers (logins with the sso_role) forgot their passwords, generate a new one using the -p option. It creates, displays, encrypts, and stores the new password for the login specified. Now the login can be used to access the server and administrate passwords (that is, this login can give any other person a new password, if needed). If deadlocking is a problem, start the server with the 3605 and 1204 trace flags. The 3605 trace flag tells the server to place messages in the errorlog, and the 1204 trace flag tells the server to write out extended information about the processes involved in a deadlock. The call to dataserver looks something like this:

```
/usr/sybase/bin/dataserver -d/dev/rid001g -e/usr/sybase/install/errorlog
                           -r/dev/rid002g -T 3605 -T 1204
```

> ## Tip
>
> Add the traceflags to your runserver file and use `startserver` to start the server.

Limit permissions on the `dataserver` executable to the `sybase` user only, ensuring that only SYBASE will start the server. This avoids annoying permission problems that occur when someone other than SYBASE starts the server. (Even the UNIX root user should be blocked from starting the SQL Server.)

Once a server has been started, it can be shut down by logging in to the server and executing the `shutdown` or `shutdown with nowait` commands. In extreme cases, if you cannot access the server you might have to kill the SQL Server process from the operating system.

INVOKING A BACKUP SERVER

The `backupserver` executable is used to run the backup server program (System 10 only). This executable can be invoked at the command line or embedded in scripts for ease of use. Normally, the backup server is started from other scripts (usually a runserver file that is read by the `startserver` program).

SYNTAX

```
backupserver [-C #_of_connections] [-S backup_servername]
             [-I interfaces_filename] [[-e errorlog_file]
             [-M sybmultbuf_file] [-N network_connections]
             [-T trace_value] [-v]
```

OPTIONS

Table 16.5 presents detailed descriptions of each parameter of `backupserver`.

TABLE 16.5. `backupserver` PARAMETERS.

Parameter	Value	Description
-C	#_of_connections	This is the maximum number of server connections to be used by `backupserver`. The default value is 20.
-S	backup_servername	This is the name, as listed in the interfaces file, of the backup server to start. (Note that the interfaces file location and name can be passed as an option.) The default name is SYB_BACKUP.

Parameter	Value	Description
-I	interfaces_filename	This is the full pathname of the interfaces file to use to find the server specified with the -s option, or SYB_BACKUP by default.
-e	errorlog_file	This is the full pathname of the errorlog file to use for backup server messages and errors. The types of errors contained in this file include internal errors, sybmultbuf errors, disconnected session errors, and errors that stop the execution of the backup server.
-M	sybmultbuf_file	This indicates the location of the sybmultbuf executable. It is used when invoking a backupserver from a directory other than $SYBASE/bin or when you want to use a different executable than the one contained in the standard SYBASE directory.
-N	network_connections	This gives the total number of connections the backup server can originate. The default value is 25.
-T	trace_value	This is the trace flag to be set at the server level.
-v		Do not use this with any other option. This option tells backupserver to print the version number and copyright information, then exit.

16

NOTES

Start a backup server using the provided startserver command whenever possible.

Most sites place either a call to startserver, or the commands contained in the appropriate runserver file(s), into an operating-system startup file. This ensures that the database is started every time the hardware is booted. Placing the commands in a startup file avoids the annoying calls to database administration complaining that the backup server or SQL Server is down after a reboot.

If you are striping your database dumps (System 10), you need more than one backup server. In this case, it is necessary to have the -s option specified, because only one of the backup servers will have the default name of SYB_BACKUP.

Limit permissions on the backupserver executable to the sybase user only, ensuring that only SYBASE will start the server.

Note

The method for shutting down a backup server depends on your platform. In Windows NT, Sybase provides a graphical services manager, enabling the system administrator to run startup utilities such as backupserver and startserver by clicking on an icon. On other platforms that do not provide a graphical user interface on every server, you need these utilities to initiate and stop servers.

To shut down a backup server process on most platforms, you log in to the backup server using ISQL or other client and issue the shutdown command. You can also shut down a backup server from the SQL Server with shutdown *<backup_server_name>*.

REPORTING ON RUNNING SERVERS

showserver is used to report on currently running servers. This is a shell script that executes operating system commands. For example, in the UNIX environment, the process status command (ps) is run and the existence of certain strings is checked (backupserver, dataserver, and so forth). If it finds this information, it prints a line for that process. For example, if you have a SQL Server and a backup server running, it should report two server processes running. The format for this command is simple:

```
showserver
```

There are no arguments to be passed to this command. It simply runs operating system commands and shows you the output. Although the actual command executed in the showserver script varies, based on things such as operating system, vendor, and platform, it usually is a fairly simple command.

Occasionally, this command encounters errors. In that case, break the showserver command into its individual operating system commands to analyze.

COPY AND INTERFACE TOOLS

There are three major tools provided by Sybase for administrating the server. bcp is used to import and export data between a SQL Server table and an operating system file. defncopy is used to import and export object creation statements for views, triggers, rules, defaults, and procedures. isql is the standard interface provided by Sybase, which also is often used for batch program execution.

THE BULK COPY PROGRAM

The bulk copy program (bcp) is a tool to transfer data between a table and an operating system file at high speeds. It is the most common way to load large amounts of data into a Sybase table. It also is frequently used to transfer data from other database vendors, spreadsheet applications, and other SQL Servers. Often bcp is fully integrated into an overall system design. Initially, bcp is used to load existing data from other data sources. Then incremental data is bulk-copied on a nightly, weekly, or monthly basis using a scheduling program (crontab in UNIX).

The bcp program has over 25 options available. It is important to understand the capabilities and shortcomings of bcp especially if you plan to use bcp as part of a production system design.

SYNTAX

```
bcp [ [ database_name.]owner.]table_name { in ¦ out } datafile
    [ -m maxerrors ] [ -f formatfile ] [ -e errfile ]
    [ -F firstrow ] [ -L lastrow ] [ -b batch_size_in_rows ]
    [ -T text_or_image_size ] [ -n ] [ -c ]
    [ -t field_terminator ] [ -r row_terminator ]
    [ -U username ] [ -P password ] [ -I interfaces_file ]
    [ -S server ] [ -a display_charset ] [ -q datafile_charset ]
    [ -J client_charset ] [ -z language ] [ -v ] [ -A size ] [ -E ] [ -X ]
```

OPTIONS

Table 16.6 presents detailed descriptions of each parameter of bcp.

16

TABLE 16.6. bcp PARAMETERS.

Flag	Option	Description
	database_name	This is the database in which the table exists.
	owner	This is the owner of the "table name" table.
	table_name	This is the name of the table to import or export.
	in ¦ out	This indicates the direction of data flow—out to copy rows from a table to a file, in to copy rows from a file to a table.
	datafile	This is the name of the source or target datafile (depending on whether the bcp is in or out). It should include a complete pathname and file specification.
-m	maxerrors	This is the maximum number of errors before bcp aborts a batch; the default is 10. (Tip: if you want to make sure all rows in a batch are tried, set maxerrors equal to batch size in rows.)
-f	formatfile	Use this to indicate that you have an existing format file, which was probably created earlier during a bcp out without the -c or -n options. This file is normally created in the directory you invoke bcp from, although a full pathname could be provided. (See more on format files later in this chapter.)
-e	errorfile	This is the file (full path or relative) where the bcp program stores rows that failed to be copied into a table. The types of errors are usually conversion problems (can't convert from int to datetime, for example). Duplicate rows rejected by an index are not considered errors, so they are not placed in the error file.
-F	firstrow	This is the number of the first row in the file or table to copy (default is 1). This can be used for both in and out, and usually is combined with the -L option to specify file boundary (in) or table boundary (out).
-L	lastrow	This is the last row for bcp to copy; the default is the last row. This can be used for both in and out, and is usually combined with the -F option to provide a specific boundary.

Flag	Option	Description
-b	batch_size_in_rows	This specifies the number of rows to be used for each batch; the default is all rows. (Tip: Use this option when copying large amounts of data so that the checkpoint process has a chance to remove rows in the log. Use this option with a batch size of 1 row if you want each row to be treated separately.) (See the section on batches, later in this chapter, for more on batch sizes.)
-T	text_or_image_size	This is the size (in bytes) of text or image data; the default is 32KB. The value provided to bcp is converted to a 2KB increment. If data is longer than the value provided (or larger than 32KB if no value is provided), bcp will not send any data after the maximum has been reached.
-n		This indicates send or receive data in native format. bcp will not prompt for input. The output file is in operating system format and is not easily readable.
-c		This indicates send or receive data in character format. The output file contains readable data. Fields are separated by a tab (\t), with a newline at the end of the row (\n). This is probably the easiest way to use bcp, but beware of conversion issues.
-t	field_terminator	This specifies the delimiter used to indicate the end of a field; the default is tab, \t. This is useful if you are copying data from another product and the fields are separated with a character other than a tab.
-r	row_terminator	This specifies the delimiter used for the end of a row; the default is newline, \n). This is useful if you are copying data from another product and the rows are terminated with a character other than newline.
-U	username	This is the login name for bcp to use when connecting to the server. The default is the username identified by your environment.

continues

TABLE 16.6. CONTINUED

Flag	Option	Description
-P	password	This is the password for the login name specified. If this option is not specified, bcp prompts for it. (It is recommended that logins with no passwords specify the -P option at the end of the command line with no value provided.)
-I	interfaces_file	This is the name of the interface file to use when trying to find a server to which to connect. If this option is not provided, bcp looks for a file named interfaces in the directory identified by the SYBASE environment variable (SYBASE home directory).
-S	server	This is the name of the server to which to connect. If it is not provided, it uses the DSQUERY value if it exists or SYBASE. This name must be found in the interfaces file used by bcp. The location of the interfaces file is explained in the -I option.
-a	display_charset	This is the character set used by the display device. The bcp program can be running on a different machine than the display. This is used normally with the -J option to specify the complete conversion information. Use -a without -J if the client character set is the same as the default. This option is seldom used.
-q	datafile_charset	Use this option when the file to be created or read uses a character set other that the client character set. This option is seldom used.
-J	client_charset	This is the character set to use on the client machine. bcp filters all rows in or out, translating between the SQL Server character set and the client character set. This option is seldom used.
-z	language	Use this option if you want messages and prompts to be in a language other than the default language for the server.
-v		Use this to display the version number of bcp and copyright information.

Flag	Option	Description
-A	size	Use this to change the network packet size for this bcp session. The network packet size boundaries are determined from the configuration options default network packet size and maximum network packet size. The value must be a multiple of 512. This option is used on large bulk copy operations to improve performance.
-E		Use this only if the table contains an identity column. Without the -E option, bcp ignores the identity column during a bcp out so that it will not be part of the output file. During a bcp in, bcp sets the identity value, starting with 1 for the first row in the file. When you specify -E, the identity value is copied into the output file during a bcp out. During a bcp in, bcp uses the identity value in the file if it exists or prompts you for a value for each row in the file. (Do not forget there is a maximum identity value dictated by the number of numeric digits specified for the identity column at creation time.)
-X		This is for password encryption. If -X is specified, bcp attempts to connect to the server and requests an encryption string. The server sends the encryption code to the client and the client encrypts the password using the provided code. The client sends the encrypted password to the server where it is decoded and verified. Use this option if security needs dictate.

NOTES

You should use the database_name option to specify a database. You can rely on the default database mechanism for a login, but if a name is not provided to bcp, a connection is made to the server and bcp looks for the table in the current database only. The current database is the designated default database (or master, if none is specified in syslogins).

16

You rarely use the owner option. Remember that the server identifies objects first by looking for a table owned by the database user name (determined when the database is "used"), then for a table owned by the database owner (dbo). Therefore, the owner name does not need to be provided unless the object you want is owned by someone other than yourself or dbo.

One of the few places you specify an owner is during development, when two different users of a database own identically named tables and want to transfer data between them. To transfer data from a table owned by "mark" to a table owned by "dave," you specify mark on the bulk copy out and dave on the bulk copy in.

The login name parameter is critical, because your login name can be mapped to a user name within a database. For data being copied out, the user must have "select" permission. For copying data in, the user must have "insert" permission.

The interfaces file is seldom specified, except in those cases where DBAs create a "super" interface file for administrative use and the default interface file contains only a subset of entries.

CHARACTER SETS

If the -J option is included without a value, bcp assumes that the client uses the same character set as the default SQL Server character set. If no value is specified, bcp assumes a default for the platform of the client where bcp is running (remember that bcp can run on the server itself or on a network-connected client). There are four default character sets:

iso_1:	Sun, DEC, Pyramid, NCR, others
roman8:	HP
cp850:	RS6000/AIX and OS/2
max:	

Note

In MS Windows/DOS environments, cp850 is the default character set. if you are importing data from the PC to a server (Sun, DEC, HP), you should specify the client character set.

MODES OF OPERATION

The bcp program has two modes of operation: fast and slow. Modes of operation apply only to bulk copying data into a table, because a bcp out essentially executes a select.

The fast bcp does not log the insert of individual rows into the transaction log. It logs only the allocation of pages and extents. To achieve fast bcp, several conditions must apply:

◆ The select into/bulkcopy option must be set on for the database.

◆ The table in question cannot have triggers or indexes.

◆ The rows inserted by the bcp are not recoverable. Transaction logs cannot be dumped after nonlogged bcp; dump database has to be used instead.

Slow bcp is used when a table has one or more indexes or triggers. Each insert is logged, but triggers are not kicked off. Log activity may be intense. If you are using slow bcp to import a large file, the log must be dumped frequently. Either set the truncate log on checkpoint option on or have a script dump the transaction log at short intervals (every five or ten minutes).

Note

Setting truncate log on checkpoint automatically prunes the transaction log every time the system issues an automatic checkpoint. Manual checkpoints issued by the dbo do not truncate the transaction log.

Here is an example:

```
/* SQL to dump the transaction log
   of the customer database every 5
   minutes until 4:00 PM. */
while (getdate() < "1/1/95 4:00:00 PM)
begin
    dump transaction customer with truncate_only
    waitfor delay "00:05:00"
end
```

FORMATS

The bulk copy program can be run interactively or can be fully executed at the command line. An interactive bcp prompts you to enter information about each column. An interactive bcp gives you an option to save your selections in a format file. This format file can be used for later imports or exports to avoid having to respond to prompts every time you want to copy data. There also are two default formats, native and character, which act in a predefined manner.

The field terminator can be specified using the -t option, and the row terminator can be specified using the -r option. If the interactive mode is used, the values supplied using the -t and -r options are used as the default input value for the field. In character (-c) or native (-n) mode, these values override the default values of the tab character for the end of a field and the newline indicator for the end of a row. For example, if you want to copy the data out of the titles table in native format with ¦ as the field terminator and carriage return (\r) as the row terminator, this is the command:

```
bcp pubs2..titles out titles.bcp -Uuser1 -Ppasswd -n -t\¦ -r \\r
```

Note

Because the pipe character (¦) is used to pipe output from one UNIX process to another and the backslash (\) is used to escape characters, they both have special meaning to UNIX. The ¦ and the \ are escaped using the backslash. The first \ in each case tells bcp to interpret the next character literally.

INTERACTIVE *BCP*

If you do not specify native format (-n) or character format (-c) or do not provide a format file (-f format_*filename*), bcp enters interactive mode. Interactive mode prompts you for the storage type, prefix length, storage length, and field terminator for each column in a table. This provides flexibility for importing and exporting data.

FILE STORAGE TYPE

The file storage type tells bcp how to store (or expect) the data in a file. You can select from any of the valid SQL Server datatypes. bcp writes the data to the file in an operating system format, and noncharacter data is not readable. bcp provides default storage type values as part of the prompt. The datatype specified by bcp normally provides the most compact way to store your data.

Accept the default datatype values if possible. If you specify a datatype different than the default, make sure the datatype can accommodate the value without truncation. During bcp in, if the type is too small, bcp prints an overflow message and aborts the insert of the row.

PREFIX LENGTH

Prefix length is used to specify the length of a field. Use the default value if possible. The prefix length defaults are shown in Table 16.7.

TABLE 16.7. DEFAULT LENGTHS FOR EACH DATATYPE WHEN USED WITH BULK COPY.

Description	Default Value
Fixed-length columns	0
Variable-length characters	1
Text or image columns	4
Binary or varbinary column (defined in table) and character data in file	2

Note that prefix lengths are stored in a native (noncharacter) format, causing the output file to have nonprintable characters. For more information on prefix length, see the *Sybase SQL Server Utility Program* manual for your operating system.

STORAGE LENGTH

The storage length always refers to the operating system file. When specifying this value, be aware that this is the number of bytes it will use to represent the data in your operating system file.

Tip

Use the default storage length, if possible, because making this number too small can lead to truncation and loss of data or overflow errors in the output file.

FIELD AND ROW TERMINATORS

A terminator marks the end of a column. The terminator for the last column is considered the row terminator. The terminator can be any printable character, or string of characters, as well as null terminators (\0), backslash (\), carriage return (\r), newline (\n), or tab (\t). The default terminator for character data is the tab character (\t). Your terminator should be something that does not appear in your data (for example, ¦ or ,). bcp looks for this terminator to determine whether it is at the end of a field or at the end of a row.

Do not forget which column is the last in your table. bcp will ask you to Enter field terminator, even though this terminator actually does double duty by specifying that it is the end of the row. A newline (\n) is normally used to terminate a row, although carriage return (\r) is sometimes used.

FORMAT FILES

After you answer all the questions about how to store each column of data, bcp asks whether you want to save these values in a format file. Unless this is a one-time bulk copy, you should save your values for later use. If you save your format file, a later bcp can run without requiring field-by-field information. Merely specify the -f option followed by the name of the format file.

Tip

Format files are usually created by running bcp out from the target table into an operating system file. Once the file is created, you know that any data you copy out using that file can be read in using that file.

If your file was not created by the SQL Server bcp out program, you need to understand how the input file is formatted before starting your interactive bcp in.

The following output is a sample bcp session run on a Windows NT System 10 SQL Server. In the example, the user is retrieving (out) data from the pubs06..publishers table into a file named publ.out. The user is the system administrator. Because no password is provided, the bcp program prompts for one.

After each column is defined, the utility prompts for a filename for the format file. Finally, the copy starts:

```
C:\users\default>bcp pubs06..publishers out publ.out -Usa
Password:

Enter the file storage type of field pub_id [char]:
Enter prefix-length of field pub_id [0]:
Enter length of field pub_id [4]:
Enter field terminator [none]:

Enter the file storage type of field pub_name [char]:
Enter prefix-length of field pub_name [1]:
Enter field terminator [none]:

Enter the file storage type of field city [char]:
Enter prefix-length of field city [1]:
Enter field terminator [none]:

Enter the file storage type of field state [char]:
Enter prefix-length of field state [1]:
Enter field terminator [none]:

Do you want to save this format information in a file? [Y/n]
y
Host filename [bcp.fmt]: publ.fmt
```

```
Starting copy...

3 rows copied.
Clock Time (ms.): total = 1      Avg = 0        (3000.00 rows per sec.)
```

Here's the format file automatically generated by bcp:

```
10.0
4
1      SYBCHAR      0      4        " "      1       pub_id
2      SYBCHAR      1      512      " "      2       pub_name
3      SYBCHAR      1      512      " "      3       city
4      SYBCHAR      1      512      " "      4       state
```

There are seven columns in the format file:

- ◆ Position in the operating system file
- ◆ Data type
- ◆ Prefix length
- ◆ Data length
- ◆ Column terminator
- ◆ Position in the SQL Server table
- ◆ Column name in the SQL Server table

NATIVE FORMAT

If you want your data in operating-system–specific format and want the server to make all the default choices for file storage type, prefix length, and storage length, use the -n option to indicate native format. Terminators are the defaults (tab for field, newline for row) unless the -t or -r options are specified.

CHARACTER FORMAT

Bulk copying data in character format is one of the easiest and least troublesome ways to bulk copy data. When the -c option is specified, it tells bcp that all data is to be represented in character format. Fields are terminated with tabs, and rows are terminated with the newline. Data in character format can be easily read and modified using text editors. This makes it easy to change the data in the input file, which can help when creating test data. Terminators are the defaults (tab for field, newline for row) unless the -t or -r options are specified.

BATCHES

A bcp batch is a logical unit of work. If you do not use the -b option, the entire data set is considered a single transaction. Encountering a fatal error results in having the entire load aborted. By setting the batch size, you enable bcp to commit fewer rows per transaction. Fatal errors during bcp sessions may still enable partial results; you can fix the problem and continue where you left off.

If you set your batch size properly, log entries pertaining to the insert can be deleted when the log is truncated, even while the bcp is still running. If you do not set the batch size, your transaction log must be able to accommodate the logging of all rows added to your table in a session.

Tip

If your batch size is too large, you need to rerun large amounts of data when you encounter a fatal error. If your batch size is too small, the additional overhead in managing more numerous, smaller transactions slows bcp down noticeably. Experiment with batch sizes between 100 and 50,000, depending on your requirements.

PERMISSIONS

The permissions needed to run bcp depend on whether you are copying data in or out. If you are copying data into a table, you need insert permission on that table. If you are copying data out of a table, you need select permission on that table (as well as select permission on sysobjects, syscolumns, and sysindexes, and the permission to create the operating system file).

TEXT OR IMAGE DATA

When copying data out to an operating system file, bcp likes to enable enough characters to handle any possible value in a field. That is why variable-length character fields are stored as their maximum value. Text and image columns, however, can be of almost unlimited length. At present, a single column of this type can contain almost 2 billion characters per row.

By default, the server limits how much data to copy out of a text or image column to 32KB per row. Any data after 32KB is not copied to the output file. If it is possible that your fields contain more that 32KB (16 pages) of data, override the default value by specifying a new maximum value with the -T option.

NETWORK PACKET SIZE

Use the -A option to specify the size of the network packet to use when transferring data between SQL Server and the operating system file. The default network packet size is determined by the configuration variable, default network packet size, and the maximum network packet size is determined by the value of `maximum network packet size`. The size specified must be between these values and must be a multiple of 512. This packet size is used only for the duration of the `bcp`.

Tip

Benchmark your system by executing a large `bcp` several times, using different values for network packet size. This helps determine what value is appropriate for your architecture.

ERROR FILES

Error files are used to store rows that `bcp` is unable to copy. To create an error file, specify a filename after the `-e` flag. If you don't provide a full path, `bcp` attempts to create the error file relative to your current directory. An error file is created only if an error is encountered. The error file contains information on the row number and the type of error encountered on one line and the actual data on a second line. The data itself is copied in the default character format (file data is character and readable, tab for field terminator, newline for row terminator). You should always specify the `-e` option because the error file can be very helpful in analysis.

The error file actually can be used as an input file for a future `bcp`. Because the data is in character format, you can determine the reason why the insert failed and modify the error file with data that is acceptable. The information lines inserted by `bcp` can be deleted by hand or by using an operating system facility to exclude data (`grep -?` in UNIX). The file can then be copied into the table, but make sure to specify the `-c` option.

ERRORS DURING *BCP IN*

When you copy data to a table, these are the types of errors you might encounter:

◆ Data conversion errors (input data of `000000` for a datetime field; `bcp` cannot format a valid date from this string and the insert will fail)

◆ Nullability errors (no value in input file, column defined as `not null`)

◆ Format errors (more bytes in input file than were expected by `bcp`)

Duplicate rows are not discovered until the batch is submitted, and they are caught by SQL Server, not `bcp`. Duplicate data is not written to the error file. If the `ignore_dup_key` option is specified for the index, `bcp` does not interpret the rejection of that row as a fatal error. Additionally, the rejection is not included in the count of errors for the batch. There is a message indicating there were duplicate rows in the batch. Set this option when creating the index if duplicate data is not considered to be a serious business error warranting the aborting of a batch.

16

TOOLS FOR ADMINISTRATORS

Tip

Specify the -m option for the maximum number of errors. The default value of 10 is not always adequate if you want to insert all the input rows. Set the value for -m equal to the value of -b (batch size) to ensure that all input rows are attempted.

ERRORS DURING *BCP OUT*

When copying data out of a table, the -e option is not as useful. The types of output errors you might encounter include the following:

- Data conversion errors
- I/O errors in writing to the host bcp output file

These errors are somewhat rare, especially when using the -n or -c options.

Note

This book does not cover the following issues:

- Translations based on differences in languages or terminal types. See the -J, -a, -q, and -z options in your *SQL Server Utility Programs* manual for more information on this problem.

- Programming using the bcp db-library and CT-library routines. There are several bcp functions available in db-library to enable you to write your own programs to handle the bulk transfer of data. Your programs will have access to the same bcp functions as the bcp utility. See the *Open Client db-library Reference Manual* or *CT-library Reference Manual* for more information.

DATA INTEGRITY ISSUES

When you are running bcp, you need to be aware of several data integrity issues. These issues are most important if you are loading data directly into existing tables which are used in production. Here are the highlights, then we will look at each issue in detail. During a bcp the following are true:

- Triggers are not fired.
- Rules are not enforced.
- Constraints are not enforced.

◆ Defaults are enforced.

◆ Money columns are truncated to 2 digits with the -c option.

Note

Many organizations bulk copy data into load tables, then use insert statements to load data into the production tables. In that case, any integrity that works for common insert statements works with an insert from the load table.

BCP and Triggers

bcp does not fire triggers, even in slow mode, so your trigger code is completely bypassed. Triggers are often used to implement referential integrity, complex rule, or default enforcement, or for keeping derived values in sync with detail records. When bulk copying data into a table with triggers, decide how you are going to resolve this issue. To make sure the new data is valid, run the trigger code at the command line for referential integrity or complex rule and default enforcement. Decide how invalid rows are to be handled. If you are using triggers to keep summary and detail values in sync, the trigger code to perform this activity is likely to be invalid at the command line.

Validate the bcp data by executing the integrity pieces of the pertinent trigger SQL after a bcp. This enables you to validate the existing data. For example, if you have a trigger on the table named purchase indicating that a customer_number inserted into a table must exist in the customer table, execute the SQL to validate all customer numbers that exist in the purchase table. That SQL might look like this:

```
select cust_id, line_no
from purchase
where cust_id not in
   (select cust_id
    from customers)
```

Sometimes triggers are used to keep summary values in sync. For example, the pubs2 database has a salesdetail and a titles table. The quantity value (qty) in salesdetail table for a particular title is summarized to establish the total sales for a book (total_sales column in the titles table). In this case, your trigger code is structured to handle the incremental adding of data. The overall total value for the sales cannot be determined by the trigger code. You may have to recalculate fully all summary values for detail rows. Determine the SQL necessary to accomplish this task and execute the code. Here is the SQL statement to reestablish the relationship between titles.total_sales and salesdetail.qty:

```
update titles
set total_sales =
   (select sum(qty)
   from salesdetail sd
   where titles.title_id = sd.title_id
   group by sd.title_id)
```

BCP AND RULES

bcp does not invoke rules. Compare the count of rows that matches the domain criteria to the total number of rows in the table. For example, the following queries check how many drivers are of legal driving age (16 years or older) versus the total number of drivers in the table:

```
select count(*)
from drivers
where age < 16
```

If they are not equal, you have some values that do not conform. Determine which rows violate your rule criteria and decide whether to change the rule, remove the rows, or change the invalid data.

BCP AND CONSTRAINTS

bcp does not invoke constraints (System 10). Handle check constraints as you would rules, and referential integrity constraints (primary key or foreign key declaration) as you would referential integrity code in triggers.

You must export all columns when using bcp. The identity column, available in System 10, is the only exception to this rule (see the -x option). When importing data, using the -n or -c option also requires you to copy all columns (identity column exception still applies). If you do not want to copy all columns, you must use a format file and specify a 0 for the server column order.

BCP AND TRUNCATION

A bcp out of data using the character mode (-c) automatically rounds money columns to two decimal places. If this is unacceptable, you should not use the -c option to copy out any tables that contain money columns.

BCP AND DEFAULTS

bcp does kick off defaults, if appropriate. Note that defaults are checked once, at the beginning of the bcp process, and applied to every row in the run.

BCP AND CHARACTER CONVERSION

When using the `-c` option to specify character data, it is important to know what your input file contains for those unknown pieces of data. `bcp` reads characters until it detects a delimiter. The default delimiter is the tab character (`\t`), although you can specify a different delimiter if desired (`¦`, `@`, `#`, and so forth). All the characters up to the delimiter are considered part of that field. Many programmers (mainframe programmers especially) are accustomed to padding a field with spaces if no data exists at the source. Note that Sybase considers spaces to be different than null. The spaces are converted to the appropriate column datatype:

- ◆ For numeric datatypes, spaces convert to a 0 equivalent (0 for int, 0.00 for float, and so forth)
- ◆ For datetime datatypes, spaces convert to the default Sybase date of 1/1/1900.
- ◆ For character datatypes, a string of spaces is inserted as a single space.

Note

Sybase stores actual data length in variable length and nullable columns (not maximum length).

If you truly want no value for a column (null), do not pad the field with any characters. Merely follow a delimiter with another delimiter. `bcp` interprets this as no data, and the row is inserted with that field being null.

Warning

Don't learn the date conversion issue the hard way! It is very frustrating to find out that 40 percent of your customers were born on January 1, 1900, after you have loaded 10 million customer records.

FORMAT FILES VERSUS STANDARD FORMAT

One of the key elements in everyday use of `bcp` is whether format files are used. Format files are used when the input or output file needs to exist in a format other than the standard character or native formats.

Try to avoid using format files whenever possible. Format files are a nuisance to maintain, and the extra file is another possible point of failure, which you should minimize. Whenever possible, use the `-n` or `-c` option, although `-c` is preferable because the operating system file contains data you can read and change with a text editor.

IS FAST *BCP* REALLY POSSIBLE?

The fast mode for bcp is attempted when data is copied into a table with no indexes or triggers. It requires the select into/bulkcopy option to be set on for the database. It is the fastest way to load data, but it is often difficult to use this mode when importing data. The issues that affect your approach are table distribution within databases and data availability to users. It is important to consider these issues based on whether the load is of initial data or incremental data.

INITIAL LOAD

Initial load data must be considered when the SQL Server is to contain information that exists in some other source. Consider a new customer support application. You may require that all existing customers be copied into the customer table as part of the necessary startup data for the application. When a customer calls in, the record already exists in the Sybase table. Your initial load of the customer table includes all customers as of a certain point in time. You write programs or use an export facility to copy the data from the source into an operating system file. This file is then loaded into the customer table using bcp.

Initial load data implies that the table is not truly usable until the data is loaded. The table is not accessed until the load is finished. This gives you the luxury of deciding how the data will be loaded because data availability is not an issue.

INCREMENTAL LOAD

Incremental data is data that represents a roll-up of existing data. Incremental data is any new data that has been added to a source since a point in time (the time of the initial extract or last incremental extract of data).

Incremental data implies that the table is currently being used and needs to be available for business use. Therefore, availability of the data is the big concern. Normally, there is a certain period of time in which to load incremental data without worrying about people using the system. This is normally referred to as the "batch window."

Another major concern, especially for production databases, is recoverability. Rows inserted using slow bcp are logged like a normal insert. Fast bcp does not log row inserts and causes the dump transaction capability to be turned off. Fast bcp may not be prudent because the capability of recovering up to the minute is jeopardized.

ACHIEVING FAST *BCP*

To achieve fast bcp, the table cannot have triggers or indexes. Almost every table you deal with in a production environment contains at least one index (for uniqueness) and probably a trigger (especially if used to enforce referential integrity). The trigger is not an issue here; it is not executed anyway. See the sections on data integrity and triggers in this chapter for information on how to handle trigger code. Indexes have a much greater impact on your ability to use fast bcp.

Indexes are needed by the application for the table to perform in a reasonable amount of time. Therefore, all indexes should be created before users access the table and impact the table's availability. Indexes have three important issues to be addressed:

◆ Creation time. The creation of an index can take a great deal of time, which is proportional to the amount of data on the table and size of the index. The time to create all indexes easily can be greater than the actual time available in a batch window.

◆ Space requirement. Clustered indexes need available database space estimated at 120 percent of the size of the table. If the table you are copying data into is the only table in a database, it may not be possible to create the index after the data is loaded. For example, take a 2G table. If you want to use fast bcp, you need 2G for the table and 2.4G for the creation of the index. You then have to size the database to at least 4.4G (without accounting for the size of the log). If this table is not going to grow over time, the 2G will never be used. If disk space is at a premium, this is not a valid option.

◆ Locking. Nonclustered indexes perform shared locks on a table, and clustered indexes perform exclusive locks. During clustered index creation, the table will not be available to users. Because clustered index creation can take a lot of time, fast bcp is not normally an option for an incremental load of data. Although nonclustered indexes can be created while the system is in use, online modifications of the data may conflict with the index creation.

A summary of what mode to use based on the type of data to be loaded is shown in Table 16.8.

16

TABLE 16.8. A COMPARISON OF bcp MODES.

Mode	Initial Load Data	Incremental Load Data
Fast bcp	Use if there is no clustered index on table or if space required for clustered index is not an issue.	This is usually not possible due to space availability constraints caused by index creation. Use only on small tables or tables whose indexes could be re-created in the available time.
Slow bcp	Use if space restrictions require that the clustered index exists before data is loaded.	This is the normal mode. Distribution of data in the table can be affected by the bulk load of data. The distribution statistics for the indexes on the table should be updated using the update statistics command.

Tip

Be sure the input file data is sorted in clustered index order if a clustered index already exists. This avoids page splits and decreases the amount of time and space needed for the load.

DEALING WITH NO TERMINATORS

Often an input file contains data in fixed-length character format with no termina-tors. In this case, use interactive bcp to specify the format of the input file. The prefix length for each field should be 0, indicating the absence of a value for the width of the row. The storage data type should be character, and the length should be the number of characters specified for that field in the input file.

UPDATING STATISTICS

The optimizer uses the distribution page for an index to determine the number of rows affected by an operation. It is used to determine the query plan, which specifies the order the tables will be accessed and the index used to retrieve the data. The distribution page is created at index creation time and updated only when the update statistics command is executed.

During initial load, space conditions may mandate that data be loaded into a table with an existing index. This implies that the index was created when the table was empty. If so, no distribution page is created.

Warning

If you load data into a table with an existing clustered index, run the `update statistics` command after the data is loaded to create the statistics page.

During incremental loads, tables usually have existing indexes (clustered and/or nonclustered). An incremental load can change the actual distribution of data in a table. It is a good idea to run the `update statistics` command after an initial load to ensure that the table has valid statistics. Because this activity may take a long time, consider updating the statistics when the batch window is larger (weekends or holidays).

It's considered a basic tool because it is somewhat limited in functionality. You must export and import all columns (System 10 has an identity column exception to this rule). Error processing can be troublesome.

REPLACEMENT DATA

When adding data to a table, you must ensure that all data is "new," meaning it is a new row to be added to the table. If the input file contains data for existing rows, `bcp` does not have the capability of replacing the existing row with the row in the `bcp` input file. To replace a row in a table with a record in a file, you must use a different facility or write a data loading routine to perform the delete and insert or update of the row.

DEFINITION COPY (*DEFNCOPY*)

Use `defncopy` to copy object creation statements from the database system tables into an operating system file, or use it to create an object in a database using an existing file. `defncopy` can be used to copy defaults, rules, stored procedures, triggers, or views, but cannot be used for tables or indexes. `defncopy` works on all those objects on which you can perform an `sp_helptext`. Remember, you can copy any objects you create "as" SQL Statements (create default as "5," create rule as `@value > 0`, and so forth).

This tool is invoked much like `bcp`, on the command line with a variety of options. However, the database name is listed separately for `defncopy`, unlike `bcp`, which accepts a database name only as part of fully qualifying the name of a table. `defncopy in` assumes an object does not exist, and `defncopy out` assumes an object does exist.

SYNTAX

```
defncopy [ -U login_name ] [ -P password ] [ -S server ] [ -v ]
         [ -I interfaces_file ] [ -a display_charset ]
         [ -J client_charset ] [ -z language ] [ -X ]
         { in ¦ out } datafile database_name
         { [owner.]object_name [ [owner.]object_name] ...}
```

Note

Specify object names for defncopy out only.

OPTIONS

Table 16.9 presents detailed descriptions of each parameter of defncopy.

TABLE 16.9. defncopy PARAMETERS.

Flag	Option	Description
-U	login_name	This is the login name for defncopy to use when connecting to the server. The default is the username identified by your environment.
-P	password	This is the password for the login name specified. If this option is not specified, defncopy prompts for it. (It is recommended that logins with no passwords specify the -P option at the end of the command line with no value provided.)
-S	server	This is the name of the server to which to connect. If it is not provided, it uses the DSQUERY value if it exists or SYBASE. This name must be found in the interfaces file used by defncopy. The location of the interfaces file is explained in the -I option.
-v		This is used to display the version number of defncopy and copyright information.
-I	interfaces_file	This is the name of the interface file to use when trying to find a server to which to connect. If this option is not provided, defncopy looks for a file named interfaces in the directory identified by the SYBASE environment variable (SYBASE home directory).

Flag	Option	Description
-a	display_charset	This is the character set used by the display device. The defncopy program can be running on a different machine than the display. This is used normally with the -J option to specify the complete conversion information. Use -a without -J if the client character set is the same as the default. This option is seldom used.
-J	client_charset	This is the character set to use on the client machine. defncopy filters all definitions in or out, translating between the SQL Server character set and the client character set. This option is seldom used. (See the previous material on character sets under bcp for more on character sets.)
-z	language	Use this option if you want messages and prompts to be in a language other than the default language for the server.
-X		This is for password encryption. If -X is specified, defncopy attempts to connect to the server and requests an encryption string. The server sends the encryption code to the client and the client encrypts the password using the provided code. The client sends the encrypted password to the server where it is decoded and verified. Use this option if security needs dictate.
	in ¦ out	This indicates the direction of data flow—out to copy definitions from a database to a file, in to create an object using a creation script as input.
	datafile	This is the fully qualified path name of the datafile to be created (in) or used as a source (out).
	database_name	When copying out, this is the database where the object resides. For copying in, this is the target database where you want the object copied.

continues

16

TOOLS FOR ADMINISTRATORS

TABLE 16.9. CONTINUED

Flag	Option	Description
	owner	(out only) This is the owner of the object (rarely used). The mechanism used to identify objects is first to look for a table owned by the database user name (determined when the database is "used"), then look for a table owned by the database owner (dbo). Therefore, the owner name does not need to be provided unless the object you want is owned by someone other than yourself or dbo.
	object_name	(out only) This is used to identify the object name to copy out. defncopy first searches sysobjects to determine whether it is a valid object; then it extracts the definition from the syscomments table. Regardless of the number of objects listed, their creation statements are copied into the indicated output file.

NOTES

Note that the login name is critical, because your login name can be mapped to a user name within a database (or you can be a guest). For definitions being copied out, the user must have select permission on syscomments and sysobjects. For copying definitions in, the user must have create <object>, where <object> is either default, rule, trigger, procedure, or view.

The interfaces option (-I) is seldom used, except in those cases where DBAs create a super interface file for administrative use and the default interface file contains only a subset of entries.

PERMISSIONS

When copying a definition out of a table, you do not need the capability of accessing the object in question. defncopy first identifies the existence of an object based on the database (required), owner (optional), and object_name (required). Using this information, defncopy queries the sysobjects table to determine whether an object exists in the database with the specified name. It searches only the following types:

- ◆ V (view)
- ◆ R (rule)
- ◆ D (default)
- ◆ TR (trigger)
- ◆ P (procedure)

If a match is made, `defncopy` captures the internal `object_id` and selects the definition from the syscomments table. Therefore, you need to select permission only on the sysobjects and syscomments table, which is normally granted to public by default.

When using `defncopy` to create an object based on an existing file, you must be able to perform that function within the specified database. For example, if your script has a rule creation statement, you must have create rule command permission in the target database. The types of command permissions that may be needed include create view, create rule, create default, create trigger, and create procedure.

Dealing with Comments

`defncopy` constructs an output file from the data in the syscomments table. When commenting creation text, people often place all comments before the create statement. When there are more than 100 characters of text before a create statement, `defncopy` may fail or it may construct a script that cannot be used without modification. To avoid this problem, embed all comments inside your create statement or keep comments before a create statement to a minimum.

`defncopy` places a comment in all the scripts it creates. This comment must end the definition for `defncopy` to be able to execute the script. If you are creating your own scripts to use with `defncopy`, make sure you place the following comment at the bottom of your script:

```
/* ### DEFNCOPY:  END OF DEFINITION  */
```

If your script file does not have this comment at the bottom, `defncopy` is unable to execute your code.

Tips

You can easily use `isql` to create a `defncopy` command to create backup scripts for most existing objects (rule, default, trigger, view, and procedure) other than tables or indexes. Because you can list your current objects by querying the sysobjects table, you easily can concatenate a string to generate the necessary creation syntax.

For example, suppose you are given a database called marketdb and standards such as the following:

- ◆ Trigger script files should have a suffix of .trg.
- ◆ Procedure script files should have a suffix of .prc.
- ◆ Rule script files should have a suffix of .rul.
- ◆ Default script files should have a suffix of .def.
- ◆ View script files should have a suffix of .vew.

You can execute the following code:

```
1>  use marketdb
2>  go
1>  set nocount on
2>  go
1>  select "defncopy -Uuser1 -Ppasswd out " + name + ".trg marketdb " + name
2>  from sysobjects where type = 'TR'
3>  and uid = user_id()
4>  go
1>  select "defncopy -Uuser1 -Ppasswd out " + name + ".prc marketdb " + name
2>  from sysobjects where type = 'P'
3>  and uid = user_id()
4>  go
1>  select "defncopy -Uuser1 -Ppasswd out " + name + ".rul marketdb " + name
2>  from sysobjects where type = 'R'
3>  and uid = user_id()
4>  go
1>  select "defncopy -Uuser1 -Ppasswd out " + name + ".def marketdb " + name
2>  from sysobjects where type = 'D'
3>  and uid = user_id()
4>  go
1>  select "defncopy -Uuser1 -Ppasswd out " + name + ".vew marketdb " + name
2>  from sysobjects where type = 'V
3>  and uid = user_id()
4>  go
```

The output from these five selects can be used to create an operating system script to run the necessary defncopy commands. This is a very easy way to give yourself a warm fuzzy feeling about your ability to re-create an object in the case of a problem.

INTERACTIVE SQL (*ISQL*)

isql is the generic interactive SQL parser for SQL Server. It is often referred to as "working at the command line." isql is used to execute activities such as creating objects, testing, inserting data, and selecting information. However, it is somewhat limited in its formatting and scrolling capabilities. isql often is run as a batch command interpreter rather that an interactive tool. Files are created that are read into isql for processing, with the output being directed into mail or some other file.

SYNTAX

```
isql [ -U login_name ] [ -P password ] [ -S server ] [-H hostname ]
     [-E editor] [ -I interfaces_file ] [-y sybase_dir]
     [-c command_end ] [-h headers] [-s col_separator]
     [-w column_width] [-i inputfile] [-o outputfile] [-m errorlevel]
     [ -J client_charset ] [ -a display_charset ] [ -z language ]
     [-l login_timeout] [-t timeout] [ -A size]
     [-e] [-F] [-p] [-n] [-v] [-X] [-Y]
```

OPTIONS

Table 16.10 presents detailed descriptions of each parameter of isql.

TABLE 16.10. isql PARAMETERS.

Flag	Option	Description
-U	login_name	This is the login name for isql to use when connecting to the server. The default is the username identified by your environment.
-P	password	This is the password for the login name specified. If this option is not specified, isql prompts for it. (It is recommended that logins with no passwords specify the -P option at the end of the command line with no value provided.)
-S	server	This is the name of the server to which to connect. If it is not provided, it uses the DSQUERY value if it exists or SYBASE. This name must be found in the interfaces file used by isql. The location of the interfaces file is explained in the -I option.
-H	hostname	This is used to set the host name for the client.
-E	editor	This is used to specify an editor other than the default editor. For example, if vi is the default editor and you want to use emacs, invoke isql with the argument -E emacs.
-I	interfaces_file	This is the name of the interface file to use when trying to find a server to which to connect. If this option is not provided, isql looks for a file named interfaces in the directory identified by the SYBASE environment variable (SYBASE home directory).
-y	sybase_dir	This is the directory in which to look for the interfaces file, if other than the default $SYBASE directory.

continues

TABLE 16.10. CONTINUED

Flag	Option	Description
-c	command_end	This is used to specify a command terminator other that the word go. For example, if you have a script that uses a semicolon to indicate the end of a command, invoke isql with the argument -c;.
-h	headers	This is used to identify the number of rows to print between column headings. The default mode of operation is to list column headers only once for a result set.
-s	col_separator	This specifies a column separator other than the default (space).
-w	column_width	This is used to set the screen width for output. This is often used so that output is not broken into several lines. A good value to use is 120 or 160.
-i	inputfile	This is the name of a file to be read into isql for processing. This file must contain command terminators (go or a character specified by -c option).
-o	outputfile	This is the name of the file to use for standard output of the isql commands. This is normally used with the -i option.
-m	errorlevel	This is used to set the minimum level of error required to print error data on your screen. Currently, all errors go to your screen. If you want to suppress messages below an error level of 17, specify the value -m 17.
-J	client_charset	This is the character set to use on the client machine. defncopy filters all definitions in or out, translating between the SQL Server character set and the client character set. This option is seldom used.
-a	display_charset	This is the character set used by the display device. The defncopy program could be running on a different machine than the display. This is used normally with the -J option to specify the complete conversion information. Use -a without -J if the client character set is the same as the default. This option is seldom used.

Flag	Option	Description
-z	*language*	Use this option if you want messages and prompts to be in a language other than the default language for the server.
-l	*login_timeout*	This specifies the maximum timeout value allowed when connecting to SQL Server. The default value is 60 seconds.
-t	*timeout*	This is the number of seconds before a command times out. Without setting this value, a command can run indefinitely.
-A	*size*	This is used to specify the network packet size for this connection. The value provided must be a multiple of 512 and between the configured values for default network packet size and maximum network packet size.
-F		This is used to enable the FIPS flagger, which alerts the user to any SQL that is considered nonstandard.
-p		This tells isql to print out performance statistics after completion of each batch. It lists clock time (the entire transaction, from db-library building the query to receiving of results, could be several transactions) and the average per transaction (clock time/# or commands).
-n		This removes prompt (line number and >) from input lines.
-v		Use this to display the version number of isql and copyright information.
-X		This is for password encryption. If -x is specified, isql attempts to connect to the server and request an encryption string. The server sends the encryption code to the client, and the client encrypts the password, using the provided code. The client sends the encrypted password to the server where it is decoded and verified. Use this option if security needs dictate.
-Y		This tells SQL Server to use chained transactions (required for some application development environments—might be helpful in testing embedded SQL code).

16

TOOLS FOR ADMINISTRATORS

NOTES

The login name is critical, because your login name can be mapped to a user name within a database (or you can be a guest).

The interfaces option (-I) is seldom used, except in those cases where DBAs create a super interface file for administrative use and the default interface file contains only a subset of entries.

OPTION RECOMMENDATIONS

isql has about as many options as bcp (25+). Aside from the familiar ones such as -U and -P, there are several other options that can help you use isql:

◆ Use the -e option to echo input when reading in files. This option is useful when you are using isql as a batch command interpreter. There are several commands you can execute in SQL Server that do not have output or in which the output does not contain enough information to define fully the activity that encountered the error. When you are working interactively, you know what commands an error applies to because the error information is displayed after you type go to execute the query. When working with files, however, this can be very frustrating, especially when you are rebuilding the database or performing an activity across a number of tables. By specifying the -e option, isql echoes input lines after they are read by SQL Server. Then your output file will contain all input commands, which may make the output file more readable and useful.

◆ The -w option is used to change the column width of your output from 80 characters to a user-defined value. This command is often used when the output from a command such as sp_help *tablename* is broken across several lines and is difficult to read. By increasing the column width size, the server uses that number of characters when deciding how much of a line of output can fit on a screen.

◆ The -c option is used to specify a command terminator other than go. This is extremely useful for those people migrating to a Sybase environment from some other database vendor. Often a semicolon (;) is used to indicate the end of a command, even in GUIs such as PowerBuilder. A script exported from this environment has a semicolon to indicate the end of a command. Rather than editing all your source files, turning each ; into go, you can simply invoke isql and provide the terminator using -c;.

◆ The -X option is important for any sites that are worried about security. Because a knowledgeable person with a network sniffer is able to capture a userid and password from the raw network packets, it is important to encrypt passwords to make an environment more secure. The -X option requests that encryption be used. Provide a command alias to redefine `isql` to `isql -X` if security is an issue.

♦ The `-A` option may provide some performance gains if you are sending or receiving large amounts of data in `isql`. Use this option when you are executing `readtext` or `writetext` commands or when you are extracting a lot of information using `isql` in a batch mode.

Warning

Beware of the security dangers of using the `-P` option on the three commands discussed. For instance, using `-P` on a UNIX system makes the password visible to anyone executing a `ps`.

IMPORTANT COMMANDS

When using `isql`, there are several commands that have special meaning. These words are typed at the `isql` command line and are interpreted by the `isql` program (see Table 16.11).

TABLE 16.11. IMPORTANT `isql` COMMANDS.

Command	Description
go [*number*]	This indicates to the server that the contents of the buffer are to be sent to the server. The word `go` must be on a separate line from the other statements in the batch. A number can be specified after the word `go` to indicate the number of times to execute the SQL in the batch. For example, `go 100` tells the server to execute the SQL in the buffer 100 times.
reset	This clears the command buffer, and is used when you want to `<cntrl>-C` clear your work and start over. It is sometimes used to clear the buffer before invoking a text editor.
vi (or other)	This enters an editing session using the contents of the command buffer. The UNIX default is `vi`, but other editors can be used by defining the `EDITOR` environment variable or the `-E` option to `isql`.
quit or exit	This is used to break the connection to SQL Server and end the `isql` process. This word must be the only command on the line and can be typed at any time.

continues

16

TOOLS FOR ADMINISTRATORS

Table 16.11. continued

Command	Description
!!os_cmd	This is used to shell out to the operating system to run a command at the operating-system level. For example, if you want to see what scripts you have in the current directory, you execute !! ls (UNIX) or !! dir (DOS) to obtain a listing of files in the current directory. Upon completion of the operating system command, you still will be at the same isql command line as before execution.
:r filename	This reads the contents of *filename* into the command buffer. The buffer will not be displayed. For example, if you have a file with 10 lines in it and you read in that file starting at line 1 in isql (1> :r filename), you immediately see an indicator of the 11th line (11>) showing that isql read in 10 lines and is awaiting additional input. This file cannot contain a command terminator (go). If your files contain terminators, you have to edit the buffer content using an editor before executing the query.

Command-line Redirection

Often isql is used as a batch interpreter, where input and output files are specified as isql options or using standard redirection syntax. To use the isql options, specify -i for the input file and -o for the output file. When using normal redirection commands, use < to direct a file into isql and > to direct the output into an output file. Therefore, the following two commands are equivalent:

```
isql -Uuser1 -Puser1 -i mytext.sql -o mytext.out
isql -Uuser1 -Puser1 < mytext.sql > mytext.out
```

There also is a way to tell isql to accept data as input until a certain character or combination of characters is detected. This normally is used as a scripting technique, although it can be used interactively. When used interactively, it essentially acts like the command quit or exit. Note this example, where isql is invoked at the command line with the option telling it to look for the string !@! as an indicator to exit isql:

```
% isql -Uuser1 -Puser1 << !@! > outputfile
use pubs2
go
select * from titles
go
!@!
```

Clearly this is not as useful on an interactive basis—it is much easier to type `quit` or `exit`. This capability is wonderful for scripting, though. It can be used in a shell script to invoke `isql` and pass data without having to deal with an input file.

SUMMARY

The Sybase administrative utilities are a nuisance to learn and most administrators only learn what they need to know to get by. It's especially difficult for administrators who are unaccustomed to the UNIX command style to learn to use these commands well.

It's very important to use utilities to simplify the tasks that are performed by the basic Sybase utilities. Using `bcp` properly can save you hours in a load, and knowing how to automate scripts with `isql` can allow you to simplify administrative tasks that were previously impossible.

If you use Windows or Windows NT on your client workstation, take a look at the Script Manager included with Aurora Utilities (in this book). The Script Manager does everything `isql` does with greater flexibility and has many additional capabilities, including reverse engineering of objects and multiple concurrent server connections.

`bcp` is a good basic tool to use for extracting and importing data. It does have shortcomings—for example, rules, defaults, and constraints are bypassed (perhaps this should be an option)—but with some extra work you can feel confident about the integrity of your data. It is important to understand how loading large amounts of data affects table distribution.

`defncopy` gives you the capability of re-creating the creation text for most objects in your database. `bcp` can be used for data, and third-party tools are available to recreate your table and index creation syntax (Erwin and so forth). If you do not currently have your object creation scripts stored away, the SQL shown in this chapter can have you covered in a matter of minutes. You can decide whether to use `defncopy` or a third-party tool, but make sure you have a way to re-create your database at any point in time.

`isql` is a tool that is used heavily in the industry. It is the standard means of interactive access, and is often a critical part of a DBA's toolset. It doesn't have a great deal of formatting capabilities, but it does a good job as a standard interface.

16

TOOLS FOR ADMINISTRATORS

CHAPTER 17

Managing the Audit System

The audit system was introduced as part of the System 10 release. It is an Open Server 2.0 application and is compatible with previous versions of the server (to version 4.2). Audit system is like Big Brother: with auditing enabled, you can keep tabs on most SQL Server activities. For years, Sybase system administrators have needed auditing to address security, data integrity, and performance questions.

If you are unfamiliar with auditing in Sybase, consider the following scenarios:

◆ You suspect there are people trying to break in to the server and wonder how they are trying to get in.

◆ Rows are being deleted from a table, but users all say they never delete rows. Who's been deleting these rows?

◆ Bob in marketing has not been himself lately. Management is nervous that he may try to sabotage the system. How can Bob's activities be monitored?

◆ Someone ran the purge procedure and deleted active data. Who committed this most grievous offense?

◆ The mix of activity on our consumer table is estimated at 80 percent selects, 10 percent inserts, 5 percent updates, and 5 percent deletes. Is this an accurate estimate?

◆ Ellen is running ad hoc queries from a report generator that doesn't display any SQL to the user. The reports are taking forever and sometimes even providing questionable results. How can you find out the SQL actually being provided to the server?

The audit system product can provide answers to all of these questions, as well as many others. The capabilities available in audit system help a database administrator (DBA) understand how and when SQL Server is being used. These capabilities give a DBA a powerful new tool that can be utilized to gather historical information or to conduct point-in-time analysis.

The following shows some practical reasons to use auditing:

◆ To detect unauthorized attempts to log in to the server, use a database, or access objects within a database

◆ To track the use of potential "hot spots" or suspected trouble areas in the server

◆ To analyze applications by monitoring the execution of stored procedures or the use of objects

◆ To determine the effect of adding new views or tables to the system by tracking the access to those new objects to determine actual use

◆ To gather specific data on selects, inserts, updates, and deletes to a table to determine volatility

◆ To monitor a specific user's activities in SQL Server

Note

The release of the audit system product was welcome news to long-time administrators of SQL Server. This new capability has been needed for years.

Analysis was a much more crude activity before the audit system. In many cases, administrators would collect `iostat` data (I/O statistics from the UNIX operating system) from a disk on the database server, map that disk to a database device, and map those devices to tables on the database. Many administrators would try to infer how `iostat` data related to actual activity. As you can see, this was a very imperfect science.

What's more, trying to track individual usage statistics was practically impossible. The audit system can provide detailed answers to many database administrator questions.

This chapter covers the types of specific events that can be tracked by the audit system, but first you will learn what type of data is collected as part of an audit system record. You can collect the following information for each audited event:

◆ The name of the user

◆ The action for the event (select, insert, update, and so on)

◆ The fully qualified name of the object (`dbname.owner.objectname`)

◆ The type of object

◆ The time the event occurred

◆ The authorization status (was it authorized?)

◆ The number of rows returned or affected

◆ The stored procedure arguments or command options provided (`grant/revoke`)

Note

When Sybase released System 10 and provided auditing, they also provided a method for existing SQL Server sites using earlier versions for implementing auditing through the audit system open server application.

The audit system is similar in many ways to the audit system implemented as a part of the server under System 10 and later. This chapter discusses how to implement the audit system. Please refer to the Sybase documentation for more information on the specifics of the audit system.

INSTALLING AND ENABLING AUDITING

The audit system is normally installed by the system administrator (sa) login as part of the sybinit program (or equivalent on non-UNIX platforms) in a System 10 and later installation. You can install auditing during the initial installation of SQL Server or after the server is up and running.

Tip

> At many sites system administrators choose not to install auditing during initial installation because they believe that auditing introduces overhead and hurts performance. Go ahead and install auditing during server installation: auditing only collects data (introducing overhead and requiring maintenance) when it is enabled. By installing auditing but not enabling it, you can experiment with the system and become familiar with its capabilities.

When you install the audit system, a database called sybsecurity is created. The truncate log on checkpoint option is automatically turned on in the database. The transaction log in this database is somewhat useless, because the rows added to the sysaudits table are not logged. Also, the data added to the sysaudits table can be considered a much more detailed readable version of the transaction logs from the other databases in your system. The rows added to the audit database are not considered critical, because they report on activity, and are not essential to the integrity of the system.

Auditing is not enabled after you install the audit system. To enable auditing, you must execute the sp_auditoption stored procedure, as in the following example:

```
sp_auditoption "enable auditing", "on" /* enable auditing */
```

This procedure also is used to disable the auditing system:

```
sp_auditoption "enable auditing", "off" /* disable auditing */
```

SYBSECURITY

When you install the audit system, the sybsecurity database is automatically created. This database contains all database-level system tables (copied from the model database) and the sysaudits and sysauditoptions auditing tables. When you install the audit system, several auditing stored procedures also are created in the sybsystemprocs database.

Note

Auditing also creates an audit queue, which is an in-memory holder of audit records used to buffer audit rows before they are written to the actual sysaudits table. For more about the audit queue, see the section titled "How Large Does the Audit Queue Need To Be?" later in this chapter.

Warning

Because the sybsecurity database is just another database, it is possible to create user objects (tables, procedures, views, and so on). Don't do it! Once you add user objects to the sybsecurity database, you may need to save the transaction log (it is normally marked trunc. log on checkpoint), which will increase the complexity and maintenance requirements of this database.

SYBSECURITY TABLES

You use only the following two tables when you do auditing:

◆ sysauditoptions contains a row for each global audit option (see the section titled "sp_auditoption" later in this chapter).

◆ sysaudits contains the records generated as part of audited activities.

When sysauditoptions is installed, it contains a row for each global option; the default value for each option is zero, which means off. Change the value settings for each option with sp_auditoption. The structure of the sysauditoptions table is outlined in Table 17.1.

TABLE 17.1. SYSAUDITOPTIONS TABLE LAYOUT.

Column	Datatype	Description
num	smallint	Option number. See Table 17.3 for values and descriptions.
val	smallint	Current value configured. Initially set to zero.
minval	smallint	Minimum valid value for this option.
maxval	smallint	Maximum valid value for this option.

continues

TABLE 17.1. CONTINUED

Column	Datatype	Description
name	varchar(30)	Name of the option, corresponds to the value in the column named optn.
sval	varchar(30)	Short string description corresponding to the value of the val column.
comment	varchar(255)	Full description of the option.

The val column defines the state of the auditing feature. It ranges from 0 to 3. The sval column decodes val, as shown in Table 17.2.

TABLE 17.2. SYSAUDITOPTIONS: val VERSUS sval.

val	sval
0	off
1	ok (nonfatal for optn=13)
2	fail (fatal for optn=13)
3	both (where applicable)

SYBSECURITY SYSTEM PROCEDURES

There are six new system procedures (procs) used to manage the auditing system. This may not seem like a lot of new procs, but each procedure accepts a wide variety of parameters and can have very wide implications. Each procedure enables you to audit activity at a specific level: the server, a database, an object, a stored procedure, or a login. You can also add a user-defined message to the sysaudits table.

The following are the auditing stored procedures:

sp_auditoption	Enables server-level or "global" options
sp_auditdatabase	Enables database-level auditing options
sp_auditobject	Enables auditing for a particular object, all objects (tables or views), or all future objects in a database
sp_auditsproc	Enables auditing for a particular procedure, all current procedures, or all future procedures in a database
sp_auditlogin	Enables auditing of activity to be specific logins to SQL Server
sp_addauditrecord	Creates a comment record in the sysaudits table

SP_AUDITOPTION

Use sp_auditoption to enable, disable, or report on server-wide auditing and global audit options. There are many options, and each has its place in an overall audit strategy. As discussed previously, this proc enables the audit function (enable auditing). Typically, you will set all of your audit options, then turn auditing on and off as necessary.

The format for sp_auditoption is

```
sp_auditoption ["option_name" [, "value"] ]
```

If you do not provide the value parameter, this procedure will report on the particular option. A full list of options and acceptable value settings for sp_auditoption is found in Table 17.3.

TABLE 17.3. VALUE SETTINGS FOR THE STORED PROCEDURE
sp_auditoption.

Option	Values (if no value supplied, proc reports on option)	Description
enable auditing	{on ¦ off}	Enable/disable auditing.
logins	{ok ¦ fail ¦ both ¦ off}	Enable/disable authorized and/or unauthorized login access to the system for all users.
logouts	{on ¦ off}	Enable/disable monitoring of normal logouts from the system and lost connections.
server boots	{on ¦ off}	Enable/disable logging of reboots to the system in the audit log. Works like an effective check point in the log to indicate all future activity in the log was on a clean server (memory flushed, no users, and so on).
rpc connections	{ok ¦ fail ¦ both ¦ off}	Enable/disable logging of access to the server from other servers.
roles	{ok ¦ fail ¦ both ¦ off}	Enable/disable logging of authorized and/or unauthorized use of set role command. Useful in determining who is using special roles (sso, oper, and so on).

continues

TABLE 17.3. CONTINUED

Option	Values (if no value supplied, proc reports on option)	Description
{ sa ¦ sso ¦ oper ¦ navigator ¦ replication} commands	{ok ¦ fail ¦ both ¦ off}	Enable/disable logging of the use of commands that need the `sa_role`, `sso_role`, `oper_role`, `navigator_role`, or `replication_role` to execute.
errors	{nonfatal ¦ fatal ¦ both ¦ off}	Enable/disable logging of fatal and/or non-fatal errors in the server. Includes fatal errors by a client resulting in a restart of the client program, but not internal errors.
adhoc records	{on ¦ off}	Enable/disable capability to use the `sp_auditrecord` procedure, which adds user-defined records to the sysaudits table.
all	{on ¦ off}	Enable/disable of the preceding options except `enable auditing`. Options will be set to `on` or `both` (options that can detect success or failure will be set to detect both).

RECOMMENDATIONS

The following are some useful server-level audit settings:

◆ To audit unauthorized login attempts to the SQL Server: `sp_auditoption "logins", "fail"`

◆ To gather information on server logouts: `sp_auditoption "logouts", "on"`

Although this command also reports on normal logouts, its real usefulness comes in capturing information on lost connections. This is almost impossible to track unless you audit it.

◆ To write a record in the audit log when you boot SQL Server: `sp_auditoption "server boots", "on"`

You should set this on so you know that all activity that occurs after this record has happened after a fresh reboot of the server.

◆ To monitor remote access: `sp_auditoption "rpc connections", "ok"`

◆ To track fatal and non-fatal errors: `sp_auditoption "errors", "both"`

This may be very helpful in problem analysis if these types of errors become a problem in your system.

◆ To allow user-defined records to be added to the sysaudits table: `sp_auditoption "adhoc records", "on"`

Use this to set reference points in your audit log before you start a specific test, or to indicate that a certain option has been set on and why.

To report on server-wide and global options, you can execute either of the following two commands:

```
sp_auditoption
sp_auditoption "all"
```

The output from `sp_auditoption` indicates the state of each global audit option, as shown in the following example. No audit options are set for this server.

```
name                               sval
- - - - - - - - - - - - - - - - - - - - - - - - - - - - - - - -
enable auditing                    off
logins                             off
logouts                            off
server boots                       off
rpc connections                    off
roles                              off
sa commands                        off
sso commands                       off
oper commands                      off
navigator commands                 off
errors                             off
adhoc records                      off
replication commands               off
```

If you only want information about a certain option, supply an option name but do not provide a `value`.

```
sp_auditoption "errors" /* report on the "errors" global option */
```

SP_AUDITDATABASE

Use `sp_auditdatabase` to report on database-level activity.

Note

sp_auditdatabase is not intended to focus on object access within a database. Use sp_auditobject for that purpose.

The dropping of objects, truncating tables, granting permissions to objects, and using the database (directly or indirectly) are the types of activities that you can audit. The format for this command is

```
sp_auditdatabase [ "db_name" [ , "value" [ ,"option(s)" ] ] ]
```

The value parameter can be set for successful attempts (ok), failed attempts (fail), all attempts (both) or turned off (off).

For example, to track both successful and unsuccessful grant statements in the testdb database, execute

```
sp_auditdatabase "testdb", "both", "g"
```

where g indicates that grants and revokes should be tracked.

Database-level auditing information is stored in bitmap form in a column, audflags, of the master..sysdatabases table. The following query from spt_values returns a results set outlining the bitmap for the audflags column in sysdatabases.

```
select number, name
from master..spt_values
where type = "Q"

number      name
----------------------------------------
-1          DATABASE AUDITING
1           successful drop
2           failed drop
4           successful use
8           failed use
16          successful outside access
32          failed outside access
64          successful grant
128         failed grant
256         successful revoke
512         failed revoke
1024        successful truncate
2048        failed truncate
```

The next example provides a listing of the dbid, name, and audflags from sysdatabases. Note that audflags for the system databases (master, model, tempdb) is null. The following listing of databases shows only one database, testdb, with auditing enabled (audflags is not 0):

```
select dbid, name, audflags
from master..sysdatabases
```

```
dbid    name                            audflags
------  ------------------------------  ----------
1       master
3       model
7       sybsecurity                     0
4       sybsystemprocs                  0
2       tempdb
5       testdb                          192
6       testdb2                         0
```

The audflags value of 192 for testdb means that failed grant statements (128) and successful grants (64) are enabled. A full list of the options available to the sp_auditdatabase proc is provided in Table 17.4.

TABLE 17.4. OPTIONS AVAILABLE TO THE sp_auditdatabase STORED PROCEDURE, FOLLOWING sp_auditdatabase "db_name", "{ok ¦ fail ¦ both ¦ off}", ...

Value	Description
d	Audits dropping of tables, views, procedures, triggers, or the database itself by any user
u	Audits execution of the use dbname statement
g	Audits execution of the grant statement
r	Audits execution of the revoke statement
t	Audits execution of the truncate table statement
o	Audits execution of SQL that references this database (for example, a user in the master database executes a query that references the pubs2 database: select * from pubs2..publishers)

SETTING OPTIONS

When you execute sp_auditdatabase, you can set an option or list of options in a single statement. If you specify a database and a value (without any options), the procedure will set that value for all six options. Consider the following examples:

```
/* audit failed attempts of dropped objects in the pubs2 database */
sp_auditdatabase pubs2, "fail", "d"

/* audit all attempt to execute the use command, grants, and
revokes in the master database */
sp_auditdatabase master, "both", "ugr"

/* audit failed attempts for all options */
sp_auditdatabase pubs2, "fail"
    or
sp_auditdatabase pubs2, "fail", "dugrto"
```

REPORTING ON DATABASE OPTIONS

If no parameters are passed to sp_auditdatabase, it reports the audit status of all databases in a server.

```
/* report on all databases */
sp_auditdatabase
```

If a database is specified but the value and option parameters are not provided, the procedure reports all options set for that database.

```
/* report on the pubs2 database */
sp_auditdatabase pubs2
```

RECOMMENDATIONS

The following are a few options and values you should set as part of an auditing strategy in a production environment. Most of these options would create a high volume of fairly uninformative audit transactions in a typical development environment because these types of activities happen all the time (dropping objects, granting permissions, and so on). I like to set the following database-level settings in production systems:

- To log any attempts to drop objects within a database:

  ```
  sp_auditdatabase "dbname", "both", "d"
  ```

  This helps you determine how certain objects "disappear" (as in, "I don't know where it went, it just disappeared!") with no person to claim responsibility.

- To log any unauthorized attempts at using a database in a system:

  ```
  sp_auditdatabase "dbname", "fail", "u"
  ```

  This helps you identify users in your system who are trying to access databases they should not be able to access.

- To log any attempts to truncate a table within a database:

  ```
  sp_auditdatabase "dbname", "both", "t"
  ```

  Truncating a table in production is as serious as dropping a table. This will provide data on the table that was truncated and the user who performed the action.

- To log failed attempts at accessing data within a database from some other database:

  ```
  sp_auditdatabase "dbname", "fail", "o"
  ```

  Use this command along with the command to audit failed attempts to use the database (fail, u). I only like to audit failed attempts, because this provides information on unauthorized access attempts.

SP_AUDITOBJECT

One of the most valuable capabilities of audit system is being able to audit access to objects. Use the `sp_auditobject` command to audit any or all of the four basic operations (`select`, `insert`, `update`, `delete`). You can monitor successful attempts (`ok`), failed attempts (`fail`), all attempts (`both`), or turned off (`off`).

You can also use `sp_auditobject` to define auditing for future tables and views. This can simplify your maintenance for auditing objects. For example, you may want to track deletes on all tables in your system. By defining the auditing parameters for future objects, you are assured that any new table or view will be tracked in the manner you define. The format for this command is

```
/* audit an existing object */
sp_auditobject <object_name>, <db_name>
 [, "{ok¦fail¦both¦off}" [, "{d i s u}" ] ]

/* audit a future object */
sp_auditobject {"default_table"¦"default_view"}, <db_name>
 [, "{ok¦fail¦both¦off}" [, "{d i s u}" ] ]
```

For example, to audit all successful selects from the table testdb..product, execute the following statement:

```
sp_auditobject "product", "testdb", "ok", "s"
```

You can use a single command to set several auditing values. For example, to audit failed and successful attempts to select, insert, or update the titles table in the pubs2 database, you would execute the following command:

```
sp_auditobject titles, pubs2, "both", "siu"
```

REPORTING ON OBJECT OPTIONS

If the `access success (ok¦fail¦both¦off)` and `access type (d i s u)` parameters are not provided, this procedure will report on the options set for that object or future objects.

```
/* report on the titles table in the pubs2 database */
sp_auditobject titles, pubs2

/* report on future views created in the pubs2 database */
sp_auditobject "default view", pubs2
```

Note

In the past, it was almost impossible—or a crude science, at best—to try to track activity to a table. You can implement limited object auditing capability by combining table design with triggers and a few built-in functions.

17

MANAGING THE AUDIT SYSTEM

> When I transform a logical model into a physical implementation, I add columns for "modified_by" and "modification_date" to each table. Then, I create triggers for insert and update to change the values in these columns to the login name (using the `suser_name()` function) and current date (using the `getdate()` function).
>
> This approach enables you to use an insert trigger to record the name of the person adding the row and the date on which it was added. You can then use the update trigger to maintain these values, recording the user name and modification date.
>
> This approach would at least let you track some information for the most recent activity to a row. It is limited because you are not able to track selects or deletes and it only provides for the activity about that particular row, not overall activity to the table. This approach is still useful and can be combined with audit system capabilities. However, `sp_auditobject` should satisfy most of your needs.

SQL Server stores object auditing information in a bitmap column, `audflags`, in sysobjects. A breakdown of that bitmap value is provided in the following output. This query retrieves the values of the bitmap flags in `audflags` in the sysobjects table.

```
select number, name
from master..spt_values
where type = "M"

number      name
----------  ------------------------
-1          OBJECT/SPROC/TRIGGER
1           successful deletes
2           failed deletes
4           successful updates
8           failed updates
16          successful selects
32          failed selects
64          successful inserts
128         failed inserts
256         successful sproc/trigger
512         failed sproc/trigger
```

The following statement will enable you to audit failed deletions and insertions (`di`) for the marketing_table in testdb:

```
sp_auditobject marketing_table, "testdb", "fail", "di"
```

The following output requests a listing of all objects except system tables. (This database includes a single table, marketing_table.)

```
select id, name, audflags
from sysobjects
```

```
where type != "S"
id          name                          audflags
- - - - - - - - - - - - - - - - - - - - - - - - - - - - - - - - - - - - - - -
144003544   marketing_table               130
```

In the bitmap provided earlier for `audflags` in the sysobjects table, the value of 130 in the `audflags` column means that failed inserts (128) and failed deletes (2) will be tracked by the audit system (128 + 2 = 130).

Keep the following in mind when you are auditing objects:

◆ An audit record is written only when command-line SQL or application-embedded SQL is sent to the server. Auditing will not capture object access when the command is issued by a stored procedure.

◆ A user who accesses a view which, in turn, acts on an audited table will only generate an audit record when permissions are different between the two objects.

◆ `sp_auditobject` might be too cumbersome to put on all tables or views. Specific volatile tables that need additional analysis are good candidates for auditing.

◆ Use `sp_auditobject` as part of an overall analysis approach by tracking specific tables for a short period of time (usually one hour) during peak and normal operations. This gives you real distribution statistics and enables you to develop a benchmark plan for that table. A good benchmark test should produce data on normal operations as well as peak activity periods (the beginning of the day, end of a shift, end of the day).

◆ Use `sp_auditobject` sparingly to gather statistics on specific, secure objects.

◆ Set the `fail` option for most auditable activities to provide data on possible unauthorized attempts to access data. To avoid the nuisance of having to execute this command for all existing tables and views, set the `fail` option on for all future tables before you create any objects in your database.

```
sp_auditobject "default_table", dbname, "fail"
sp_auditobject "default_view", dbname, "fail"
```

SP_AUDITSPROC

Use `sp_auditsproc` to audit access to stored procedures. It enables you to specify an existing procedure, all procedures, or any future procedure. The format for this command is

```
/* audit a specific (or all) existing procedure(s) */
sp_auditsproc [ proc_name ¦ "all", dbname
               [ , "{ ok ¦ fail ¦ both ¦ off }" ] ]

/* audit future procedures */
```

```
sp_auditsproc "default", dbname
 [ , "{ ok ¦ fail ¦ both ¦ off }" ]
```

SETTING PROCEDURE OPTIONS

You can specify auditing for specific, all, or future stored procedures in a database. You can request audit records after successful attempts (ok), failed attempts (fail), all attempts (both) or turned off (off). The following are a few examples:

```
/* audit all attempts to execute the sp_addlogin command
 in the sybsystemprocs database */
use sybsystemprocs
go
sp_auditsproc sp_addlogin, sybsystemprocs, "both"
go

/* audit failed attempts to execute any existing proc in customerdb */
sp_auditsproc "all", customerdb, "fail"

/* audit failed attempts to execute any future proc in pubs2 */
sp_auditsproc "default", pubs2, "fail"
```

REPORTING ON PROCEDURE OPTIONS

You can report on procedure options in a single database only. If the dbname parameter is not specified, the command will report on the current database you are using. The following code shows a few examples:

```
/* provide a list of all procs being audited in the current db */
sp_auditsproc

/* report on the auditing status for all procs in the current db */
sp_auditsproc "all"

/* report on auditing status for the sp_addlogin command */
use sybsystemprocs
go
sp_auditobject sp_addlogin, sybsystemprocs
go
```

RECOMMENDATIONS

You can use the sp_auditobject stored procedure to track SQL access to tables. Unfortunately, you will not be able to set this option to capture the access of a table through a stored procedure. I have administered several sites that dictate that all access to a table or views must be done through stored procedures. If you are using stored procedures to manage most or all access to objects, sp_auditobject becomes essentially useless at handling the brunt of activity and you will need to audit stored procedures.

If you enable auditing of all stored procedures, you can gather actual usage statistics of the procs in your database. This is also very useful in developing a benchmark plan, because you can use these statistics to choose representative stored procedures for a test.

Keep the following in mind when you are auditing objects:

◆ It might be too resource-expensive to continuously audit all stored procedures in your database, especially in an online transaction processing (OLTP) environment that uses stored procedures heavily. The overhead of recording a high volume of audit records could damage performance, or the sheer mass of audit records may turn out to be less useful than a simpler record of failed attempts.

◆ Set this option as part of an overall analysis approach by tracking all procedures for a short period of time (usually one hour) during peak and normal operations. This gives you real distribution statistics and enables you to develop a benchmark plan that includes a representative suite of stored procedures. Note that a good benchmark test should produce data on normal operations, as well as peak activity periods (the beginning of the day, end of a shift, end of the day).

◆ The `dbcc memusage` command is not as useful as `sp_auditsproc` in determining procedure distribution or usage. The `dbcc memusage` command has a section for the top 20 stored procedures in memory. This, however, is the largest 20 stored procedures in memory, not the 20 most often accessed.

◆ Set this option sparingly to gather statistics on a particularly secure or sensitive procedure.

◆ Set the `fail` option for most auditing capabilities to provide data on unauthorized attempts:

```
sp_auditsproc "all", dbname, "fail"
```

◆ If your database is still undergoing changes, it is useful to set the `default` option to ensure that any new procedures that are created will be audited:

```
sp_auditsproc "default", dbname, "fail"
```

Note

It's especially important to set `sp_auditsproc` to track future stored procedures while stored procs are in development. Remember that stored procs cannot be modified, but must be dropped and re-created. Make the resetting of `sp_auditsproc` part of the standard procedure creation script if you are not automatically enabling auditing for all new stored procedures.

SP_AUDITLOGIN

Use `sp_auditlogin` to track the work of a specific individual. This is the most "Big Brother" of all the auditing functions; you will normally execute this command when you suspect the activities of a particular person in your organization.

Using login-level auditing, you can track table or view access using this format (an example follows):

```
audit access to tables or views by a particular login */
sp_auditlogin [ "login_name" [ , "table ¦ view"
                [ , "{ ok ¦ fail ¦ both ¦ off }" ] ] ]

/* audit failed table access by "user1" */
sp_auditlogin "user1", "table", "fail"
```

Using an alternative format, you can record every SQL batch issued by a user:

```
/* capture all SQL passed to the server by a login */
sp_auditlogin [ "login_name" [ , "cmdtext" [ , "on ¦ off" ] ] ]

'/* capture all SQL text sent by "mary" */
sp_auditlogin "mary", "cmdtext", "on"
```

REPORTING ON PROCEDURE OPTIONS

You can obtain a list of all logins being audited, the auditing status of a login, or whether a particular type of auditing is set for a login. The following shows several examples:

```
/* provide a list of logins being audited */
sp_auditlogin

/* report on the auditing status for bob */
sp_auditlogin "bob"

/* determine if the SQL is being captured for mary */
sp_auditlogin "mary", "cmdtext"
```

RECOMMENDATIONS

Keep in mind the following when you are auditing logins:

◆ Use this option when you suspect the activities of a particular person.

◆ The table and view option are usually sufficient for initial tracking of a login. Because this only generates rows when a select, insert, update, or delete is executed against a table, it does not cover stored procedure access. Use the `cmdtext` option when you are very concerned with a person's activities.

◆ The `cmdtext` option will generate a row in the sysaudits table and the SQL text will be placed in the extrainfo column. I consider this high-maintenance auditing because you must search the extrainfo column to gather data about a person's activities.

Note

Some products are so user-friendly that you can't figure out what they are doing. Companies purchasing third-party applications, report generators, or other front-end applications may find that they have too little control or understanding of the SQL being generated by these systems.

Tracking the `cmdtext` for a test user is a good way to observe the generated SQL from a closed application. It is also useful for catching datatype mismatches and other quirks that prevent good optimizations and slow performance.

You may also use the `cmdtext` option to find out who is generating queries that generate a Cartesian product (a join query that fails to set sufficient join criteria). You can't suppress those queries, but finding out who is executing them is the next best thing.

The query in the following output examines some sample rows in sysaudits, after login-level auditing was established for the sa login so he could track all commands. This output displays all audit records related to the sa login.

```
select event, spid, suid, dbid, loginname, extrainfo
from sysaudits
where suid = 1

107     8     1     5      sa                    select * from master..syslogins
107     1     1     4      sa                    use  sybsecurity
107     1     1     7      sa                    select user_name()
107     1     1     7      sa                    select * from sysaudits
```

Note

If the `cmdtext` is longer than the maximum 224 characters per audit record, the server will append multiple audit records to record the entire SQL statement.

SP_ADDAUDITRECORD

Use `sp_addauditrecord` to add a user-defined comment into the sysaudits table. The format for this command is

```
sp_addauditrecord [ @text = "<message text>" ]
                  [ , @db_name = "<db_name>" ]
                  [ , @obj_name = "<object_name>" ]
                  [ , @owner_name = "<object_owner>" ]
                  [ , @dbid = "<database_id>" ]
                  [ , @objid = "<object_id>" ]
```

Refer to Table 17.5 for a list of the available parameters and how they are used and the affected columns in the sysaudits table.

TABLE 17.5. `sp_addauditrecord` PARAMETERS.

Parameter Name	Usage	Affected Column
@text	The text of the message to be added. It should be descriptive and provide an understanding of why a message is added. This is often the only parameter specified.	extrainfo
@db_name	The database to which the message applies. If the message applies to the server or to several databases, do not specify this parameter.	dbname
@obj_name	The object to which the message applies. If the message does not pertain to a single object, do not use this parameter.	objname
@owner_name	The owner of the object specified in @obj_name. Use only if the @obj_name parameter is specified.	objowner
@dbid	The database ID corresponding to the @db_name. Use only if the @db_name parameter is specified.	dbid
@objid	The object ID of the object specified in @obj_name. Use only if @obj_name is specified.	objid

SETTING PROCEDURE OPTIONS

Because you use `sp_addauditrecord` to add a user-defined message to the sysaudits table, the `@text` parameter is the most useful of the available parameters. You can use the other parameters, but they are not validated (the server will not verify object IDs, database names, and so on). Anyone can be granted permission to use this procedure, once both auditing and adhoc records have been enabled.

```
exec sp_auditoption "enable auditing", "on"
exec sp_auditoption "adhoc records", "on"
```

The following shows two examples of how to use `sp_addauditrecord`:

```
/* make a notation regarding temporary system-wide privileges */
sp_addauditrecord @text = "SSO privileges temporarily granted to Bob
between 10 and 11 AM", @db_name = "master"

/* enter a checkpoint before commencing system test */
sp_addauditrecord @text = "Beginning of system test.
All records to the next checkpoint are based on a system with 20 users
using the new billing application", @db_name = "test_db"
```

RECOMMENDATIONS

Use the `sp_addauditrecord` command for the following types of activities:

◆ To set a boundary when you are conducting a test. For example, if you are going to audit some activities during a stress test, add a record just before the test starts and after the test completes to indicate that the records in the table between these entries pertain to that test.

◆ To enter a record before you grant a certain privilege as a reminder and/or log of the event. Use it before granting temporary sensitive access to a login. (For example, Bob needs `sa_role` capabilities to set up a database, but will only have the access for a short period of time).

◆ To identify the point in time a certain auditing function is enabled (to serve as a logbook entry for further reference).

MANAGING THE AUDIT QUEUE

The audit queue is an in-memory area used to buffer audit rows that are to be added to the sysaudits table. The queue decreases the performance burden from auditing server activity by avoiding physical writes during transaction processing. You can set the audit queue size by executing the `sp_configure` procedure.

```
sp_configure "audit queue size", <number_of_audit_records>
```

The size of an audit record on disk can range from 22 bytes to 424 bytes, but in memory each audit record always requires 424 bytes. To determine how much memory auditing needs, multiply the configured number of audit queue records by 424 bytes.

The server stores audit records first in the audit queue, then writes them to a buffered page from sysaudits as time allows. No more than a single page of audit data will remain in cache at any time, so buffered pages are flushed to the disk copy of sysaudits at least every 20 records, depending on the size of the audit records (see Figure 17.1).

Figure 17.1.
Audit records are
stored in the audit
queue until the system
has time to write them
to buffered audit pages.
Audit pages are flushed
after no more than 20
records are written
from the queue.

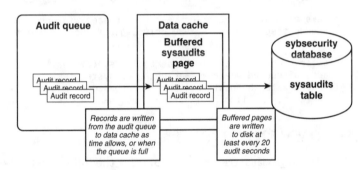

HOW LARGE DOES THE AUDIT QUEUE NEED TO BE?

The trade-off in setting audit queue size is transaction performance versus the risk of losing audit data.

Note

There are situations in which audit data could be lost, but auditing does not change the transaction logging mechanism and should not put you at risk of actual production data loss. Keep this in mind throughout this discussion.

Although SQL Server writes transactions to disk as part of the commit process, audit records associated with your transaction are inserted in the audit queue. Audit queue records are written to the audit pages in buffer as the server has available time, or when it is necessary because the queue is full.

When the queue fills up, audited activities waiting for audit queue space are held off until the queue can write to the buffer pages. Under load, it is clear that the audit queue could be a substantial bottleneck. To reduce the bottleneck, you could make the audit queue very large, enabling the system to prioritize transactions until there are enough cycles to move the queue to the buffer and flush the buffer.

The problem is, the larger the queue, the more audit records are in memory waiting to be written to disk. After an unmanaged server shutdown (power failure, system lock-up), the audit data will be lost. Your total exposure in any case will be the number of records in the audit queue plus no more than 20 additional buffered audit records in the data cache.

The solution is to start with a small audit queue. After introducing auditing, if you see a steep performance drop-off under load, the audit queue is a bottleneck. You will need to increase the size of the queue until the bottleneck is eliminated for your site. If audit integrity is critical to your site, you could try adding an additional CPU engine to an SMP version of SQL Server instead of increasing the size of the queue.

Growth of Audit Tables on Disk

You must closely manage the available space in the sybsecurity database. When there is no space available, the server is unable to flush the contents of the audit queue to the sysaudits table. Therefore, the audit queue will fill. This produces a serious domino effect.

◆ Any audited command or activity is suspended until space becomes available in the audit queue.

◆ If an audited activity performs modifications on a table in a database, the implicit or explicit transaction involved in this modification remains open.

◆ Any locks that are acquired are held until the transaction is complete.

◆ The number of locks in the server will soon multiply, because other activities are likely to be blocked waiting for locks to release, causing their locks to be held.

At this point, server concurrency is completely shot.

Worst-Case Scenario

In your worst nightmare, the sybsecurity database becomes full (followed almost immediately by the in-memory audit queue) and audited activities cannot be performed. If logins are audited (sp_auditoption "logins"), no new connections to the server will be granted. If no login with the sa_role or sso_role is currently logged in to the server, the database cannot be altered to allocate more space and the sysaudits table cannot be archived to free up existing space. If activities by users with the sso_role are being audited (sp_auditoption "sso_role", "on"), the sso_role becomes powerless.

IS IT THE END OF THE WORLD?

It is not the end of the world. The server detects this situation and immediately makes changes to rectify the situation.

◆ Any login with the sso_role will gain executive privileges. The server will not generate audit records for any activity performed by a login with the sso_role and a person with this role will be able to log in to the server even if logins are audited.

◆ A login with the sso_role can then archive and truncate the sysaudits table.

◆ A login with the sso_role will be able to shut down the server, normally a capability reserved for the sa (or sa_role).

◆ Error messages will be placed in the errorlog to document the situation.

RECOMMENDATIONS

Obviously a complete end to all audited work would be devastating to a production server. To prevent this, you must take necessary precautions. The following are some tips to help you prevent sybsecurity from filling up:

1. Create a simple script to check the space available in the sybsecurity database. Run this script every day to track the growth in the sybsecurity database. Listing 17.1 shows an example of a possible UNIX script.

LISTING 17.1. THIS UNIX SCRIPT TRACKS THE GROWTH OF THE OBJECTS IN THE SYBSECURITY DATABASE.

```
#!/bin/ksh
/*      The following command will invoke isql
and input lines to the specified delimiter "!!".
The output will be placed in an output file.
You may need to list the full path of the isql executable,
located in the bin subdirectory of the SYBASE home directory.
If the SYBASE home directory is /usr/local/sybase,
the isql executable's full path is /usr/local/sybase/bin/isql

     The output file named "audit_space.out"
could also be given a full path filename.
Make sure this file is placed somewhere safe.
The ">>" is specified so the file will be
continuously appended to, to save the historical data */

isql -Uusername -Ppassword << !! >> audit_space.out
use sybsecurity
go
declare @curdate datetime
select @curdate=getdate()
print "-----------------"
```

```
print "Space Availability as of %1!", @curdate
go
sp_spaceused
go
print " "
print " "
!!
```

2. To avoid the nuisance of having to run this script by hand, place it in a scheduling program to run at the same time each day. UNIX systems have a scheduling utility called crontab. Windows NT has a system scheduler. Other environments may need a client application to use its own timer to initiate a similar process.

3. Gather enough data to establish a realistic growth rate for audit records in the sysaudits table. It is helpful to create a spreadsheet or document that lists the date and time, the size of sysaudits, and the growth from the previous day.

4. Divide the amount of space allocated for data for the sybsecurity database by the average growth rate from step 3. This gives you an estimate of the number of days you can audit activity before having to archive the sysaudits table. I recommend you archive this table before the database becomes 75 percent full, to insulate the system from sudden unforeseen surges in audited activity.

SYSTEM 10 AND LATER USERS

System 10 and later users should use the threshold facility to provide even more information about the space available in the sybsecurity database. A threshold is a marker you set in a segment to execute a stored procedure once a specified amount of available space has been crossed. I highly recommend that you install a threshold, because it is easy to do and provides the peace of mind of knowing that you have done all you can to insulate the system from a temporary catastrophe. For more on creating thresholds, see the section titled "Thresholds" in Chapter 5, "Defining, Altering, and Maintaining Databases and Logs."

To decide on the amount of space available when the threshold is crossed, determine how many days in advance you want to be notified about the filling of the sybsecurity database. Take this number and multiply it by the average growth per day found in step 1. Use this total to determine the value of the number of pages parameter for the sp_addthreshold procedure. The format for this procedure is

```
sp_addthreshold dbname, segment, free_pages, proc_name
```

If you add 2MB of audit data per day, and you want four days notice, set the number of pages to 8MB × 512 2k pages / MB = 4096 pages.

Create a simple procedure. When you are using thresholds, any `print` statements in a procedure will be placed in the system errorlog. You should review the errorlog daily, and these comments will alert you to the impending fill. Here is a sample procedure:

```
create proc audit_fill
as
print "WARNING:  The sybsecurity database has only 8MB of space left!"
print "          This is enough space for about 4 days more of activity."
print "          Archive the sysaudits table as soon as possible!!!"
go
```

Now that you have the procedure (`audit_fill`) and the number of free pages (4096) you can set the threshold. The database name is sybsecurity and the segment name is system (because the sysaudits table is a system table). The procedure with parameters would be

```
sp_threshold sybsecurity, system, 4096, audit_fill
```

Note

For much more detail on setting up log and data space thresholds, see Chapter 5, "Defining, Altering, and Maintaining Databases and Logs."

ARCHIVING THE AUDIT QUEUE

The sysaudits table will fill until it is truncated by a person with the `sso_role`. (Note: `truncate` is the only command you can use to remove rows from this table; you cannot use `delete sysaudits`.) Before truncating this table, you can archive the data by

◆ Inserting this data into a different table in another database, as in the following example, where the contents of the table are copied to an audit_archive table in the database, archive_db:

```
use sybsecurity
go
select *
into archive_db..audit_archive
from sysaudits
go
```

(Of course, you could insert this data into a different table in the sybsecurity database, but that would defeat the purpose of freeing up space.)

◆ Bulk copying the archive data to an operating system file using the `bcp` command.

```
bcp sybsecurity..sysaudits out aud_archive.bcp -c -Usso_login -Ppswd
```

◆ You could then save the operating system file to tape for long-term storage.

Summary

The auditing features of System 10 and later provide a welcome facility to help manage a database, to look for problems before they become crises, and to monitor system usage. The many levels of auditing provide you with the flexibility to focus on a specific problem or to get broad statistics about system use.

Be certain to decide in advance on the purpose of auditing, and make certain that the usefulness of the auditing outweighs the potential performance cost. And finally, don't forget that auditing requires its own maintenance as well.

Table 17.6 summarizes the stored procedures used to maintain auditing.

TABLE 17.6. SYSTEM PROCEDURES USED TO MANAGE AUDITING OPTIONS.

Procedure	Description
sp_auditoption	Enables and disables system-wide auditing and global audit options.
sp_auditdatabase	Establishes auditing of different types of events within a database, or of references to objects within that database from another database.
sp_auditobject	Establishes selective auditing of accesses to tables and views.
sp_auditsproc	Audits the execution of stored procedures and triggers.
sp_auditlogin	Audits a user's attempts to access tables and views, or the text of commands that the user executes.
sp_addauditrecord	Enables users to enter user-defined audit records (comments) into the audit trail.

CHAPTER 18

Defining Systems Administration and Naming Standards

As the amount of work you do with the Sybase product increases, you will see the need to develop standards to be able to approach administration in a consistent manner. Most companies that succesfully implement SQL Server have good standards in place. Standards are created to provide a foundation for administrative tasks and often result in establishment of the infrastructure necessary to enable the creation of procedures and scripts to automate activities.

What if you don't have standards in place? The cost of application development without standards is usually very high. The price is paid in effort and delay, as well as credibility. Let's face it: client/server is really no different from any other application environment. Success comes from the right mix of discipline and creativity. Thoughtful standards provide the discipline within which creativity can thrive.

This chapter focuses on those core standards that are needed to enable you to further develop procedures at your environment. You will look at two core activities: first, approaches to organizing databases and servers, especially regarding the development environment, and second, naming standards, from both a Sybase and operating-system level. Once you decide on names, directory structure, and how you are going to approach development, you can start building those site-specific procedures and scripts to automate activities in your organization.

SQL SERVER ENVIRONMENT APPROACH

You must approach development in a Sybase environment in a consistent fashion, or each development project is destined to waste time performing certain activities. The approach should be focused on providing flexibility for the developer and structure for the database administrator. It also should be built to enable portability of code from the development environment to the potentially many levels of your test environment, and eventually to the production environment.

DEFINING ENVIRONMENTS

Most people who purchase Sybase are using it to develop new production applications. When developing production software, you should assume there will be a development environment, at least one test environment, and a production environment. You must decide how each environment will be supported by SQL Server.

Note

Typical environments include development, system test, volume/stress test, user acceptance test, and production. Because there can be several test environments, this book considers them conceptually as a single environment called test.

For each environment, you must determine the following:

◆ Is the environment supported by a separate (dedicated) SQL Server or does it share the server with some other function?

◆ Is it the only SQL Server running on a piece of hardware (dedicated server on dedicated hardware) or are there many servers running on a single machine?

◆ How are the databases organized on the server? Is there a database for an environment rather than a server per environment?

The most restrictive environment is a single SQL Server with databases for development, test, and production. As the details will show, the needs of each environment conflict with the other environments. The development environment may require the SQL Server to be rebooted often, but the production environment is likely to have up-time as an important business requirement. The testing environment often is constructed to be able to gather performance statistics. The requirements of the development and production environments, however, might skew these performance statistics, and testing might ruin performance for production. It is strongly recommended that development, test, and production activities take place on separate SQL Servers.

DEVELOPMENT ENVIRONMENT

The development environment requires the maximum flexibility for developers while enabling the necessary control structures to provide for consistent promotion of code. In designing this environment, several issues should be considered:

◆ The SQL Server used for development may or may not be dedicated. A dedicated SQL Server is strongly preferred because "bouncing" (shutdown and restart) of the SQL Server is a very common activity in development. If the SQL Server is shared by several development groups, frequent reboots of the system may have a significant impact on the productivity of developers.

18

ESTABLISHING STANDARDS

◆ The SQL Server may or may not be running on dedicated hardware. Dedicated hardware is preferred because occasionally the database hardware must be rebooted. Although dedicated hardware enables developers maximum control, it may not be cost-effective. Because this environment is used to unit-test individual modules for functionality and not performance, dedicated hardware is not a requirement.

◆ Although flexibility is at a maximum for the developer, so is developer responsibility. A developer has much more responsibility for administrative activities. Developers often create their own objects (tables, indexes, procedures, triggers, and so forth) in the pursuit of satisfying a business problem. Developers often are responsible for managing their own test data. Organized database administration (the DBA group) still has some responsibilities, however. A DBA may create a base set of objects or manage a core set of data. As always, DBAs still get calls about any problems a developer cannot handle (killing processes, adding space, and so forth).

◆ Developers must have a set of tables to use when developing. Define how many tables will be organized to meet the needs of all developers. (This is discussed in detail later in this chapter.)

◆ Occasionally, a single logical database is physically implemented as several Sybase databases in production. The distribution of tables to databases should match the production model. (Remember that relating tables from two different databases requires that at least one of the table names be qualified by the database name. If the development environment does not have the same database structure, SQL has to be modified before production implementation, which is likely to introduce new bugs.) Your development environment should look exactly like the production environment in the base structure (database, tables, and objects).

If other projects share the development server, create a document to provide information about all groups. It should contain information such as project name, manager, contact name, phone, and specific instructions. Development environments are volatile. You may need to reboot the server to continue development. Because a reboot affects all users on the system, you should contact user representatives to prepare them for this situation.

A DETAILED APPROACH

The development environment is the area where developers first attempt to create new modules of an application. Development is an iterative process. Multiple revisions of code are normally created in the process of correctly satisfying design requirements. Consequently, the code may have unexpected results on tables.

During the refinement of a module, database activities such as delete, insert, or update may need several modifications before they are deemed to work correctly. This requires the developer to create test conditions to test individual pieces of functionality. Additionally, new requirements may necessitate the addition or deletion of columns from tables to test the new pieces of code. These changes may become permanent modifications to the existing structures, validated by the iterative testing of an application. The development environment needs to be structured to minimize contention between developers.

Due to the nature of development, it is assumed that the development environment will use a SQL Server separate from the test and production environments. Based on that assumption, you can then determine an approach to development at a database and object level.

There are three main approaches to development in a Sybase environment. The differences between the approaches are based on whether the developers share a database and whether they have their own copies of objects and data.

The development approach is greatly impacted by the number of actual SQL Server databases used to represent the single logical database. An initial approach is to put all tables in a single database. However, experience shows that grouping tables into several databases can have significant performance and administrative benefits. The definition of databases in the development environment should be identical to the ultimate production environment to minimize code changes from development to production. If the production environment is organized using several databases, the development environment should also contain several databases.

Let's look at these three approaches to handling development in a Sybase environment.

SHARED DATABASE AND SHARED OBJECTS AND DATA

In the shared database/shared objects and data approach, a single database (or databases) exists for development. All developers use the same objects and data. This approach is sometimes used in very small developments (one or two developers). Once the number of developers increases, this approach quickly breaks down.

ADVANTAGES

◆ It simplifies administration. There are fewer objects (tables, indexes, stored procedures, triggers, and so forth) to manage.

◆ There are reduced storage requirements. There is only one database and one copy of objects and data.

◆ It is a viable option if your tables are grouped into multiple databases. The development environment is assumed to use a separate SQL Server. The names used for databases can be identical between development, test, and production environments. Therefore, code that is developed does not have to be modified to be promoted to the next level.

DISADVANTAGES

◆ There is an almost unavoidable contention for data. Developer 1 might be testing a delete activity on the same row that Developer 2 is using to test an update activity. Development will be impeded as confusion results from "unexpected" changes to data.

◆ There is a significant decrease in a developer's capability of changing the underlying structure to support a hypothesis or test condition. Additionally, Developer 1 might want to add a column that would negatively affect Developer 2's testing.

◆ Development flexibility is greatly reduced.

INDIVIDUAL DATABASE AND INDIVIDUAL OBJECTS AND DATA

With the individual database/individual objects and data approach, each developer has a dedicated database for development. Because objects are created in the context of a database, the developer therefore has a personal copy of all objects and data. Normally, developers are responsible for all activities with their databases, including data creation and backups.

ADVANTAGES

◆ The developer has the capability of changing data or structures without affecting other developers.

◆ Because object names are created in the context of a database, all the SQLs can be created to assume the database name and contain only object names.

DISADVANTAGES

◆ If tables are grouped into several databases, using this development approach likely will require code changes to promote code to production. In a single database approach, code is consistent from development to production because there is never a need to qualify the name of a table with the database name. In a multiple database scenario, if a query is executed that refers to tables in different databases, at least one of the tables has to be qualified with the database name.

Consider an example with five developers. The first developer writes code against customerdb_1 and purchasedb_1, the second developer writes code against customerdb_2 and purchasedb_2, and so on. The following is an example of SQL access across databases:

```
select *
from customerdb_1..customer c, purchasedb_1..purchase p
where c.cust_id = p.cust_id
```

Migrating this code into the test or production environments requires changes because these environments likely would contain different database names (customerdb, purchasedb). You have to modify the code to arrive at the following statement:

```
select *
from customerdb..customer c, purchasedb..purchase p
where c.cust_id = p.cust_id
```

◆ Changing code from one environment to the next is not recommended. Do not use the private database approach for multiple database implementations.

◆ The amount of space required to support development increases. Each database will require the space necessary to hold a copy of all objects, procedures, and data. In addition, the minimum size of any SQL Server database is the larger of the default database size (normally configured for 2MB) or the size of the model database.

◆ The number of databases in the server increases. This complicates administrative tasks. It also can affect the recovery process.

Note

I was teaching a class once when the SQL Server was rebooted. Our training databases had dbids of 70 to 80. It took about an hour for our training environment to become usable.

SHARED DATABASE AND INDIVIDUAL OBJECTS AND DATA

In the shared database/individual objects and data approach, a single database (or databases) is used for development. Developers do not share objects or data. Each developer is a true user of the database. Objects are created, and owned, by the developer. The production objects are created by the user dbo. Code written by the developer does not refer to user name. The normal Sybase procedure of looking for an object owned by you before looking for an object owned by dbo is leveraged. The SQL that is written acts against the developer's tables when executed in the development environment and the dbo's tables when executed in the test and production environments.

ADVANTAGES

- ◆ Each developer has an individual set of data. A developer has complete freedom to update, delete, and insert data without affecting other developers.

- ◆ Migration from development environment to the production environment is eased. All developers work with the same database and object names. This ensures that any SQL created is identical in all environments. No code changes due to different database or object names is necessary.

- ◆ Systems spanning multiple databases do not require modifications to promote to production (unlike the Private Database development approach) because the development environment database structure is identical to the production database structure.

DISADVANTAGES

- ◆ The number of tables in a single database can be large. A system with 100 tables and 10 developers will have 1,000 tables in the development database.

- ◆ Storage requirements are magnified by the number of developers as compared to the shared object approach.

Note

Each table and index requires 16KB (one extent) regardless of the amount of data in the table. Therefore, the storage requirements between a private database and a shared database/individual object approach should be equal.

In a private database approach, however, each developer database has its own free space. On average, the total amount of free space required in the private database approach is much greater than the shared free space in the shared database/individual object approach.

Normally, a shared database/individual objects and data approach to development is recommended for multiple and single database installations. The individual database/individual objects and data approach is recommended for single database installations only.

Warning

Your production requirements may not surface until after development has started. This approach does not work with a multiple database installation. If the decision to implement with multiple databases occurs after development starts, the shared database/ individual objects and data approach is able to adapt to the new structure much easier. You may be forced to change your development environment structure completely if you choose the individual database approach. Choose your approach carefully.

TEST ENVIRONMENT

There can be several test environments used in the Software Development Lifecycle (SDLC). You will test for function or performance. Functional testing is used to confirm that elements of an application or several distinct applications can work together. Performance testing is conducted to verify how the database performs under peak numbers of users, data size, or both.

FUNCTIONAL TESTING ENVIRONMENT

Most functional testing can be handled by a single SQL Server. Consider the following when planning this environment:

- ◆ A SQL Server used only for testing is strongly preferred because SQL Server should be configured for testing, and the configuration for your application may be different than the configuration needed for the testing of some other application.

- ◆ The hardware in which the SQL Server is running may or may not be dedicated. Dedicated hardware is useful in analysis because performance statistics gathered at the hardware level can be related easily to SQL Server, but you are testing functionality and usability across modules here, not performance.

- ◆ Objects are created by database administration. Often the files necessary to build the databases structures (DDL scripts) are part of a source code control system.

- ◆ There is only one copy of each object necessary to support the system. (A development environment may have several copies of each table.)

- ◆ If the tables in the system are physically organized into several databases for performance, recovery, or security reasons, there is only one copy of each database.

◆ All objects should be owned by the database owner, dbo. This supports the seamless migration of code from the development to the testing environments.

◆ A core set of data is created that is representative of production data. The amount of data does not need to represent production volumes, because it will be used to support feature, integration, and system testing.

◆ Logins and users of the test system should be representative of production users. This enforces the testing of the system in the same manner as it would be used by the actual production users. By simulating real users, potential problems such as improper permissions can be identified.

Development logins may be added to enable developers to add specific system test data or to assist in the creation of a core set of data. However, developers should not have the capability of changing the structure of tables or adding, dropping, or modifying any other existing object. Although developers may have access to tables to add or modify data, testing should be conducted using the logins of users representative of production users.

PERFORMANCE TESTING ENVIRONMENT

Performance (or stress) testing should be handled by a different SQL Server than your functional testing environment. This environment will have similar features to the functional test environment, except for the recommendations for servers, hardware, and data:

◆ The SQL Server used for testing must be configured as it would be in production. Using an identically configured SQL Server is necessary because performance data captured is used to estimate production performance.

◆ The hardware wherein SQL Server is running should be configured identically to the production hardware so that statistics gathered can be considered representative of production performance. This environment is used to validate the system's capability of handling production loads.

◆ A core set of data, representative of production volumes and content, is created and loaded. The data in this environment is used to test the performance of the system under varying loads. To capture performance and load statistics that are representative of production, production type data must be used.

◆ Development logins are normally not added to the performance testing server. Logins are representative of production, and all modifications (data or structure) are conducted by database administration.

PRODUCTION ENVIRONMENT

The production environment is the last and most important environment in the SDLC. The production environment is under maximum control of database administration, and all defined production controls must be implemented and observed. This environment should have the following features:

◆ The SQL Server and database hardware used for production should be dedicated. A dedicated SQL Server is preferred because it greatly simplifies analysis of performance statistics captured at the SQL Server or hardware level. Most production implementations use dedicated hardware for the production SQL Server.

◆ An initial load of data may be required. Database administration normally is responsible for loading the core supporting data (code tables) as well as any other production data needed to support production use of the application.

◆ Logins and users are the actual production users. The only other logins added to this server should be for administration reasons. All modifications (data or structure) are conducted by database administration. Security standards and procedures are in place and enforced.

Note

More and more sites have multiple SQL Servers running for different groups of apps. Because more companies are using packaged solutions, it is often required to run different versions of Sybase in production. For example, vendors will certify at different rates under System 11. If you are running only one production SQL Server, you can't upgrade anyone until all applications support System 11.

NAMING STANDARDS

What's in a name? The answer to this simple question often takes organizations months—or years—to define. Names should be chosen in a consistent manner across all Sybase systems in your organization; for example, a word should not be abbreviated two different ways in two different places. Consistency with names is one of the building blocks of an infrastructure to which employees and users can become accustomed. Consistent naming enables employees to move from system to system (or software to software) and have basic expectations regarding names. This can help in the transition when learning a new environment.

Note

> Naming standards are like filing standards. You have to think about the person who is storing the information and the person who will retrieve it. For the person defining the name, the choice should be automatic. For the person retrieving or accessing an object, the name should completely define its content without ambiguity.

Naming standards can be broken into two areas: Sybase names and operating system names. Sybase names are the names you specify in the Sybase environment (databases, objects, and so forth). Operating system names are the names you specify for files and directories.

SYBASE NAMES

In Sybase, you are responsible for naming the server, each user database, each object in the database (tables and columns, indexes, views), and any integrity constraints (rules, defaults, user datatypes, triggers, declarative constraints). Device names (disk and dump) have different parameters governing their names because they can be somewhat operating-system-related.

Capitalization standards must be defined for each type of name. (Should names be in all capital letters, all lowercase letters, or mixed case?) This decision can be different for different groups of names (for example, server names could be in all capital letters and object names could be in mixed case).

Consider also whether to use an indicator of the item being named. For example, does the word database or the abbreviation DB get included in a database name? In the end, your standard should identify whether the customer database will be named Customer, CUSTOMER, CustomerDB, or CUSTOMERDB. For most database objects, the structure of names is the personal preference of the person writing the standard.

INDICATORS

An indicator is a string of characters embedded in a name to indicate something about the type of object. In Sybase, they are often used to indicate an object type. For example, CurrDate_Def could be used as a name for a default setting a column to the current date and time. There are two schools of thought on the use of indicators:

♦ An indicator is not needed because it can be retrieved from the system tables (the type column in the sysobjects table) or is indicated by the table you are selecting from (sysdatabases, sysservers). Including it in the name is redundant and a waste of valuable characters. Names are usually constrained to 30 characters in length and an indicator can easily take 4 or 5 characters (_tbl or _view, for example). This limits the number of available characters in an object name. Indicators can propagate (Customer_Tbl_CIdx), further reducing the number of available characters. When users need to use a name frequently, indicators also mean extra typing.

◆ An indicator is needed because it simplifies reporting—a DBA can tell the type of object from just a listing of object names. Application designers are cognizant of what type of objects they are accessing (for example, the name tells them whether they are selecting from a table or view). Indicators also enable you to use similar, meaningful names for two objects, once with each indicator (for example, price_rule and price_default).

Note

All object names within a database must be unique for the owner. In other words, the dbo may own only one object of any name. If you have a rule named price_check, you cannot create a constraint named price_check. This restriction applies to tables and views as well as rules, defaults, constraints, procedures, and triggers. To avoid being constrained by these names, use indicators, especially for objects that users do not interact with and whose names they will never type (rules, defaults, constraints, and triggers).

Entries in sysindexes and syscolumns must be unique by table (only one index per table named name_index, only one column per table named price).

User-defined types are not objects: they are stored in systypes instead. Names of types will not clash with objects, but it makes sense to qualify them by type.

If you decide to put an indicator in a name, it is best to make that indicator as short as possible. For object names based on an underlying table (constraints, triggers, indexes), the length of the indicator has an effect on the number of available characters used for the table name. For example, if you decide insert triggers will be identified by adding the indicator _InsertTrigger after the table name, the number of available characters that can be used for the table name can be no greater than 16 (30 characters minus 14 for the indicator). To give as much flexibility to the naming of an object, consider using an abbreviated indicator (such as _tri).

Indicators sometimes are placed at the beginning of the name, but you do not usually use this approach. Given an indicator of tbl_, a list of all object names groups the tables together. Although it's sometimes useful to list objects by type, you can do that in your SQL:

```
select name, type
from sysobjects
order by type
```

Table 18.1 lists the most common indicators used by Sybase installations throughout the world. Consider that many sites choose no indicators at all.

TABLE 18.1. COMMON SYBASE INDICATORS.

Item	Possible Indicators	Preferred
Server	Server, _Server, _SERV, _serv, SERV, SRV	None
Database	_Database, _DATABASE, _DB, DB	DB
Table	Table, TABLE, T, TBL, _TBL, _tbl, _t, _T	None
Column	_col	None
Index	Clustered: ClusIdx, Cidx, _clus, _C, _CI, CI	
	Nonclustered: _Idx[#], Idx[#], NCIdx[#], NCI[#], _I[#]	_CI, _Idx[#]
View	V_, _V, _View, _VIEW	None
Rule	_Rul, _rul, _RUL, _rule, _RULE, R, _R,	_Rul
Default	_Def, _def, _DEF, _default, _DEFAULT, D, _D	_Def
User-defined datatype	_TYPE, _Type, TYPE, Type, _TYP, _Typ, TYP, Typ	_TYPE
Trigger	InsertTrigger, InsTrig, ITrg, _ITrg	_ITrg
Check constraint	_Check, _constraint, _con, _CkCon, _Chk	_Check
Primary key constraint	_PK, PK, _Pk, Pk	_PK

Item	Possible Indicators	Preferred
Unique constraint	_UniqueCons, _Unique, _Uniq, _UN, _UQ	_Uniq
Foreign key constraint	_FK, RI	_FK
Data device	_DISK[#], _Disk[#], _DATA[#], _Data[#], _LOG[#], _Log[#],_IDX[#], _Idx[#]	_Data1, _Log1, _Idx1
Dump device	TAPE[#], _Dump, _Tran, _Log, _Tape[#], _Disk, _DUMP, _TRAN, _LOG, _TAPE[#], _DISK	_Dump, _Tran, TAPE[#]

AN OVERALL APPROACH

One approach is outlined in Table 18.2. You can use these standards at your site or develop your own. Make sure you produce a matrix such as this to distribute to application development projects.

TABLE 18.2. SAMPLE SYBASE NAME STANDARDS.

Item	Capitalization	Include Type Name?	Example
Server	ALL CAPS	No	CUST_DEVEL
Database	Mixed case	Yes	CustomerDB
Table	Mixed case	No	CustomerPurchase
Column	Mixed case	No	Age, Name, Address, FaxNumber, HomeNumber
Index	Mixed case CustomerCIdx (clustered) CustomerIdx3 (3rd nonclus)	Yes	(Formatof "TableName[C]Idx[#]")
View	Mixed case	No	CaliforniaCustomer PartialCustomer

continues

Table 18.2. continued

Item	Capitalization	Include Type Name?	Example
Rule	Mixed case	Yes	ValidSSN_Rul, NonNegative_Rul
Default	Mixed case	Yes	Zero_Def, CurrDate_Def, CurrUser_Def
User-defined datatypes	ALL CAPS	Yes	SSN_TYPE, ADDRESS_TYPE, NAME_TYPE, PHONE_TYPE, COMMENT_TYPE, STATE_TYPE, ZIP_TYPE
Triggers	Mixed case	Yes	Customer_ITrg, Customer_DTrg, Customer_UTrg
Constraints	Mixed case	Yes	NonNegative_Check (check), Customer_Uniq (Uniqueness) Customer_PK (Primary Key) CustomerPurchase_RI (RI)
Data devices	Mixed case	???	Customer_DATA1, Customer_LOG1, Customer_Data1, Customer_Log1, DISK1, DATADISK1, LOGDISK1
Dump devices	Mixed case	???	Customer_Dump, CustomerDB_Tran, TAPE1

The standards outlined in this table are used throughout this chapter.

Note

It is probably not a good idea to use indicators in the names of tables or views. Many sites use the table name in the name of other objects. The inclusion of _tbl increases the number of redundant characters in the dependent object name (trigger, index, and so forth). In addition, views exist to give users the feel that their queries are acting against a real table, although they actually are accessing a view. Therefore, the names should be identical in format, and should not contain anything that would distinguish one from the other (_tbl or _view, for example).

Your standards likely will be different, but the important thing is to be consistent in your implementation of names. Knowing the standards up front can save you days or weeks of costly name conversion changes (with SQL code, administration activities, and so forth).

NAMING THE SERVER

Name servers according to function. For example, you would much rather have a server named development rather than a server named RSR8_AB100. Several companies name their servers according to cartoons or movies. There are Snow White servers (DOPEY, GRUMPY, DOC, and so forth), Batman servers (BATMAN, ROBIN, JOKER, PENGUIN), and Mickey Mouse servers (MICKEY, MINNIE, GOOFY, DONALD). Although these names are fun, they should be used only for development or general server names. Servers intended to support applications should be named in a consistent manner across all applications. The following is a good format:

```
systemname_environmentname
```

For the development of a Customer system, you might use CUST_DEVEL, CUST_TEST, AND CUST_PROD servers.

NAMING DATABASES

Databases should be named according to their contents—for example, the type of data (customer or product) or activity (security or administration). A database containing security tables could be named SecurityDB, and a database that contains customer data could be called CustomerDB. The name selected should be intuitive. (If a document is required to relate a database's name to its contents, it probably is not intuitive.) Some databases are named using a letter followed by three numbers. Would you rather have a database named B123 or ProductDB? Avoid nondescriptive database names.

TABLES, VIEWS, AND COLUMNS

Table and view names should be representative of the underlying data. A customer table should be called Customer; a view of the California customers should be called CaliforniaCustomer. Some organizations like to use nondescriptive table names (TBL0001). Again, avoid nondescriptive table and view names. If names are not intuitive, a decode document may be required to relate the table name to its contents. This delays development and makes it harder to write SQL statements. Column names should indicate the data in the column. Name a column containing the age of a customer Age or CustomerAge.

INDEXES

A table can have one clustered index and up to 249 nonclustered indexes. Index names should contain the table name and an indicator of the type of index. Some DBAs like to include the column as part of the index name, but compound indexes make this naming scheme difficult to implement. The following are examples of possible index names for the Customer table:

Index Type	Identifier	Index Name
Clustered (max of 1)	_CIdx	Customer_CIdx
Nonclustered (up to 249)	_Idx[#]	Customer_Idx1, Customer_Idx2

Tip

Some application development tools enable you to perform database administration activities. These tools may already have standard ways to construct names of indexes. Check whether you can modify the format or change your standards to accommodate this new format.

RULES AND DEFAULTS

Rules and defaults are implemented at the database level and can be used across tables. Their names should be based on the function they are providing. A rule that checks for a valid age range could be called ValidAge_Rul, a default placing the current date in a field could be called CurrDate_Def.

User-Defined Datatypes

Here is a good format for user-defined types:

CONTENTS_TYPE

Because user-defined datatypes normally are targeted at certain types of columns, the name should contain the type of column it is to be used for (SSN, PRICE, ADDRESS) followed by the indicator _TYPE.

Triggers

Trigger names should consist of the table name and an indicator of the trigger action (insert, update, delete). A good format is TableName_[IUD]Trg:

Object Type	Object Name
Table name	Customer
Insert trigger	Customer_ITrg
Delete trigger	Customer_DTrg
Update trigger	Customer_UTrg
Update and delete trigger	Customer_UDTrg

Note

The indicator consists of seven characters maximum (_IUDTrg, for example). To avoid abbreviation problems, no table name should be greater than 23 characters (30 – 7).

Constraints

Constraint names vary based on the scope of the constraint. Constraints can be used to check for valid values, add unique or primary keys, and establish relationships between tables (foreign keys).

A check constraint checks for valid values in a column or number of columns. Its name should indicate the column(s) and type of check.

Unique and primary key constraints are based on a table and should contain the table name and an indicator (_PK or _Uniq).

A foreign key constraint implements referential integrity between two tables. Its name should contain the tables or columns involved in the relationship and an indicator (_FK or _RI). Table 18.3 shows a sample list of constraint indicators and names for the customer table.

TABLE 18.3. SAMPLE CONSTRAINT INDICATORS AND NAMES.

Constraint Type	Indicator	Name Based On	Constraint Name
Check constraint	_Check	Column or columns	ValidAge_Check
Primary key constraint	_PK	Table	Customer_PK
Unique key constraint	_Uniq	Table	Customer_Uniq
Foreign key constraint	_FK	Related tables and/or columns	CustomerPurchase_FK

Warning

Remember that constraints are objects; for an owner, their names must be unique among all objects within the database. You may want to qualify the constraint name by including the table name as well. (In Table 18.3, different tables might contain columns named ValidAge and their check constraint names would clash.) If you decide to include table names in your constraint names, you face a serious limitation in the length of table and column names.

For example, if you have a table called Institution and a check constraint on the column Date_of_Enrollment, the constraint might be named with the following:

```
Institution_Date_of_Enrollment_Check
```

which is much longer than the name length limit. The only realistic solution is to abbreviate the name, but that requires having both the person creating the constraint and the person retrieving information about it know the abbreviation rules.

Table-level constraints can evaluate many columns. Include in your naming standard the method of naming table-level constraints. For example, the constraint requiring an invoice amount to be greater than zero whenever the type is "SALE" might look like this:

```
constraint Invoice_AmtType_Check
check ((amt > 0) or (type <> "SALE"))
```

Keep table and column names fairly short, yet descriptive, especially if you plan to use table names in check constraints.

DATABASE DEVICE NAMING STANDARDS

A database device is physical space that is initialized with the `disk init` command. Once a device is initialized, it is available for use by any database (except for master and model). Selecting the logical name for a device is dependent on what may exist on that device and a DBA's confidence factor of the eventual use of that device. Devices can be named generically, by database, or by database contents.

GENERIC NAME

Devices can be named generically according to their number or general contents. For example, if you want to name a device according to number, you can (DEVICE1). This approach is flexible, because any part of any database can be placed on the device without confusion. Tracking the databases created on a certain device cannot be easily inferred, however. It often is useful in performance analysis if the device can be easily mapped to a database, type of activity, or type of activity for a database.

Devices can be generically named to represent the type of data that will exist on that device (DATA1, LOG1, INDEX1). This provides a DBA with a guideline as to what portion of a database to place on each device. However, indicating the type of data expected on the device in the name can cause confusion if space constraints force you to create the data portion of a database on a device named LOG1.

Note

> Once you begin placing database log segments on a device, the SQL Server prevents you from mistakenly placing database data segments on that same device. Go ahead and call a device "log-something" if you are planning to put a log on it immediately.

DATABASE NAME

Devices can be named to represent the database that will be using the device. The device name can consist of the database name and a device number. For example, the four devices for the customer database might be named CustomerDB_dev1, CustomerDB_dev2, CustomerDB_dev3, and CustomerDB_dev4. The name indicates the database intended to be created on the device, but does not indicate the type of data. Therefore, log, data, and index data can be created on a device without confusion based on the device name. However, indicating the database expected on the device in the name can cause confusion if space constraints force you to create a different database on that device.

18

ESTABLISHING STANDARDS

DATABASE CONTENTS

Devices can be named to represent the database and the expected contents to be created on that device. The device name can consist of the database name and the type of contents (data, log, index). For example, the four devices for the customer database could be named CustomerDB_Data1, CustomerDB_Data2, CustomerDB_Log1, and CustomerDB_Idx1. The name indicates the database and the type of data expected to exist on the device. This naming scheme requires you to be very confident about the placement of databases.

Note

> Experience has shown that early estimates of index, log, and data requirements are usually way off.

Name devices in the most appropriate manner for your environment, based on the number of databases, whether certain data is placed on separate devices (log, index, data, and so forth), and your confidence that the intended use of the device will not change. (It's probably best if a device named CustDB_Data1 not be used for expansion of the ProductDB database.) VLDB environments are more likely to use the database-contents approach to naming, because databases normally span multiple disks and there is more flexibility for placement.

DUMP DEVICE NAMING STANDARDS

Recall from Chapter 8, "Backing Up and Restoring the Database and Transaction Logs," that a dump device is created using the sp_addumpdevice command. A dump device is used to back up an entire database or transaction log of a database to some type of media. Normally, this media is a local disk or a local tape device. You are required to provide the logical name and physical name of each dump device. This logical name is linked to the physical name. When dumping a database or transaction log, you can dump the database to the logical name (although the physical name can be supplied). The following are examples of three dump commands for the CustomerDB database:

```
dump database CustomerDB to CustomerDB_Dump
```

```
dump transaction CustomerDB to CustomerDB_Tran
```

```
dump database Customer DB to TAPE1
```

The logical name given to a dump device is normally based on the device type—tape or disk.

TAPE DEVICES

A tape device is usually attached or integrated with your database server hardware. These devices normally take 8mm or 4mm tapes, and the tape capacity can be as great as 20GB. Tape devices have simple names. The string TAPE followed by a number is a common approach to a generic tape device name. For example, if you have three tape devices, they could be named TAPE1, TAPE2, and TAPE3.

DISK DEVICES

Disk device names should be selected with care. Dumping a database or log to disk creates a file on your file system. Each time a dump is executed to a disk device, a file is created whether a file exists or not. If you have not moved the previous dump to a new filename, the file will be overwritten and lost. Databases or logs dumped to disk should be copied off to a tape. Disk devices often are used in a development situation, due to the frequency of dumps and the inconvenience of tapes.

It is wise to create two disk dump devices for each database in your system—one for database dumps, one for transaction log dumps. Use the following format for the logical name:

```
DatabaseName_Dump
```

```
DatabaseName_Tran
```

Therefore, the CustomerDB database would have two dump devices created: CustomerDB_Dump and CustomerDB_Tran. Here is an example of the possible commands used to create these devices:

```
/* create a disk dump device for database dumping
** of the CustomerDB database*/
sp_addumpdevice "disk", CustomerDB_Dump,
    "/dbdump/CustomerDB/CustomerDB_Dump"

/* create a disk dump device for transaction log dumping
** of the customer database*/
sp_addumpdevice "disk", CustomerDB_Tran,
    "/dbdump/CustomerDB/CustomerDB_Tran"
```

This approach has a number of benefits. Each database will have separate names for each type of dump. This eliminates the possibility of accidentally dumping the CustomerDB dump over the ProductDB dump. Additionally, a consistent naming standard enables you to create operating system scripts (normally some type of command shell) to automate the backup process.

For example, a general dump script can be created. The script can be passed the database name as an argument. Because the device name is based on the concatenation of the database name and _Dump, the entire dump command can be dynamically created. Functionality also can be written into the script to move the dump to a safe location as soon as it completes successfully.

OPERATING SYSTEM NAMES

You need to establish a naming standard for operating system files and directories. This standard normally is needed to organize DDL files. You need a DDL file for every important action and object that exists in SQL Server. This includes device creation, configuration changes (sp_configure), adding users and logins, creating and altering databases, creating objects (tables, views, indexes, and so forth), and granting permissions. Place the files in directories organized to enable you to recreate an entire environment from scratch.

DIRECTORY-NAMING STANDARDS

Specifying and organizing directory names should be based on your environment. Here are some important questions to answer:

◆ How many environments are you supporting (CUSTOMER_DEVEL, CUSTOMER_SYSTEST, CUSTOMER_PERF)?

◆ How many user databases exist in each server?

◆ Is there only one database or are multiple databases supported by the server?

◆ What is the approach to handling Data Definition Language files?

◆ Are all the creation statements in a single file or is there a file per object?

◆ Are index creation statements located in the same file as table creation statements?

◆ How do you intend to grant permissions?

For this discussion about naming directories, we assume the greatest complexity and level of detail—a directory structure that can handle multiple SQL Servers and individual creation files for each object.

BASE DIRECTORY: SERVER NAME

All DDLs for a server/environment should be stored relative to a base directory named according to the server name. For example, if you have three SQL Servers named CUSTOMER_DEVEL, CUSTOMER_TEST, and CUSTOMER_PROD, the base directories would be /CUSTOMER_DEVEL, /CUSTOMER_TEST, and /CUSTOMER_PROD, respectively.

The base directory should contain every necessary DDL statement to re-create the entire SQL Server. Separating the files from different SQL Server environments by directory enables different environments to contain different versions of the same file. This is helpful in regression testing.

FIRST SUBDIRECTORY: DATABASE NAME

Under the base directory for the server are subdirectories for each of the databases supported by the server. This includes all user databases and the system databases (master, model, and sybsystemprocs).

USER DATABASES

User databases are created to support applications. The name of the subdirectory should be identical to the database name. For the CustomerDB database in the CUST_DEVEL server, this is the directory name:

`/CUST_DEVEL/CustomerDB`

For each user database in the server, there are a number of subdirectories that can be created to hold the various DDL files. Table 18.4 lists possible subdirectories under the user database subdirectory.

TABLE 18.4. SAMPLE SUBDIRECTORY NAMES.

Object or Activity	Subdirectory Name
Table	../tbl
Index	../idx
View	../view
Rule	../rul
Default	../def
User-defined datatypes	../type
Triggers	../trg
Constraints	../con
Permissions	../grant
Stored procedure	../proc
Remote procedure	../rproc
Users	../user
User-defined error messages	../error
Threshold	../thresh

The directory containing the table creation statements for the CustomerDB database in the CUST_DEVEL server is the following:

```
/CUST_DEVEL/CustomerDB/tbl
```

The number of subdirectories under the database subdirectory is based on the level of granularity of your DDL files. Some sites like to put all creation statements in a single file. This gives you the least amount of control. To change the creation statement for a particular index, you might have to edit a 70,000-line file. The portion of the file for the index creation is copied into some temporary file or directly into an isql session for execution.

The next level of granularity is to put all creation statements of a particular type into a file—all the table creates in one file, the index creates in another. You still have the same problems with modification and execution, but you have a greater level of control (object type).

The last approach is to have a separate operating system file for each object in your system. This provides you with the maximum amount of control. Sites that use this approach normally save DDL files in a source code control system.

MASTER DATABASE

The master database subdirectory should contain all files necessary to re-create the base server and all user database structures. After the execution of the scripts in this subdirectory, the server is configured, disk devices are initialized, dump devices are added, logins and users are added, and all user databases are created.

You can use the following subdirectories for the master database:

Object or Activity	Subdirectory Name
Configuration commands	../config
Device creation (disk and dump)	../device
Database creation, alter, and setting of options	../dbcreate
Addition of logins and users	../user

The file used to create the dump devices in the CUSTOMER_DEVEL server is /CUSTOMER_DEVEL/CustomerDB/device/CustomerDB.dmp.

MODEL DATABASE

The model database subdirectory should contain all files necessary to re-create any applicable objects and/or users. The model database normally contains generic users, rules, defaults, user-defined datatypes, and user-defined error messages. These are the types of items you might want propagated to a new database.

You can use the following subdirectories for the model database:

Object or Activity	Subdirectory Name
Rules	../rul
Defaults	../def
User-defined datatypes	../type
User-defined error messages	../error
Generic users	../user

SYBSYSTEMPROCS DATABASE

The sybsystemprocs database contains the system stored procedures. The base set of procedures can be easily re-created from Sybase-provided scripts. DDL files to create any new custom system procedures should be maintained in a subdirectory (/CUST_DEVEL/sybsystemprocs/sysproc).

These guidelines should be able to be implemented, in some form, in your own organization. Note that user databases are handled differently than system databases.

FILE-NAMING STANDARDS

Name DDL files identically to the object names they are creating, with a concatenated indicator. Of course, the name of the DDL file should be based on its contents. The content of each file is based on the granularity of control needed in your system. A file that contains the create statements for all the objects in a database should not be run to re-create the Order table only. All DDL statements that do not pertain to Order should be deleted before running the script. However, if you have individual files for each object in your system, the Order table can be re-created easily.

For example, a file containing the create statement for the Order table in the CustomerDB database in the development environment has this full path filename:

```
/CUST_DEVEL/CustomerDB/tbl/Order.tbl
```

FILE EXTENSIONS

It is common to name a file with an extension indicating the type of object or activity. The philosophy is similar to indicators in Sybase names. The extension is redundant because you know the type of object being created by the name of the subdirectory (../tbl, ../rul, and so forth). However, a file extension is normally provided as a matter of habit. The filename should be the concatenation of the object name and the extension. A rule called ValidPrice_Rul has a filename of ValidPrice_Rul.rul. Notice the triple redundancy. A rule is created in the ../rul subdirectory with a filename of ValidPrice_Rul and a file extension of .rul. Consider that some sites do not use file extensions to indicate file type. Table 18.5 lists examples of filenames and extensions.

TABLE 18.5. SAMPLE FILENAMES AND EXTENSIONS.

Object or Activity	Subdirectory Name	Extension
Table	../tbl	.tbl
Index	../idx	.idx
View	../view	.vew
Rule	../rul	.rul
Default	../def	.def
User-defined datatypes	../type	.typ
Triggers	../trg	.trg
Constraints	../con	.con
Permissions	../grant	.gnt
Stored procedure	../proc	.sp
Remote procedure	../rproc	.rpc
Users	../user	.usr
User-defined error messages	../error	.err
Threshold	../thresh	.thr
Configuration commands	../config	.cfg
Device creation (disk and dump)	../device	.dsk .dmp
Database creation, altering, and setting of options	../dbcreate	.cre, .alt, .opt
Addition of logins and users	../user	.lgn, .usr

SOURCE CODE CONTROL

Source-code-control software has been used for a number of years in the development of software to manage changes to application code (COBOL, C, and so forth). Source-code-control software also can be used to manage changes to DDL. It often acts as a logbook, enabling only one person to check out a file at a time. Checking in a file normally requires text to be provided to indicate why the file was checked out. The version number of the file is incremented each time a file is checked in. Some sites decide to cross-reference the check-in statement with a database change request document.

Capabilities of "cutting a version" of a group of related files should be available. For example, 20 different source code files (each having its own revision number based on the number of times it was changed) can be used to create a C application. Cutting a version relates these 20 files together and logically groups them. Database changes happen for a reason. These changes usually parallel application changes that can be listed as part of the check-in comment.

Source code control gives DBAs a mechanism to manage distinct versions of the database effectively. Through use of this tool, a DBA can identify what versions of DDL files to load to recreate a specific version of a database, object, or stored procedure.

SUMMARY

A number of Sybase names must be defined in your environment. Too many Sybase customers approach development without standards. This is likely to result in costly rework to bring an existing system up to standard once the standards are defined. Sometimes, customers decide not to change the database due to the cost of conversion. This results in a nonstandard Sybase implementation in your environment.

Application standards are also important, but are not the focus of this book. You need to develop application standards to be able to build high-performing Sybase applications consistently. The construction of SQL statements can have striking effects on query performance, and the uniform implementation of triggers, procedures, rules, defaults, and constraints is important in providing a consistent approach to developing Sybase systems. This enables developers to develop more efficiently because a base structure is provided. It is important that you define standards as early as possible and monitor the adherence.

It also is important to define naming standards as early as possible and stick with them. Naming standards apply to the operating system as well as to Sybase. With a consistent approach to naming, you can build upon the underlying structure. Scripts can be written to automate activities on the server, decreasing the overall workload.

APPENDIX A

The Database Consistency Checker (*dbcc*)

Below is the list of Database Consistency Checker (dbcc) commands that are used by database administrators to perform consistency checks against items within a Sybase SQL Server. These commands run at different levels, including database, table, index, and page. Most of these checks are used to ensure that a database is not corrupt before dumping it; however, some of these commands are executed as part of a language upgrade, to target suspected items, or to just get more information.

Note

There are a wealth of other, undocumented dbcc commands used by Sybase Technical Support personnel to assist in database analysis and fixing corruption problems. Some of the more useful (and non-destructive!) commands are presented for your reference in this appendix because I have found them to be very useful and helpful.

PREVENTIVE *DBCC* COMMANDS

Table A.1 briefly summarizes many commonly used dbcc commands. The remainder of this appendix describes each command in detail, along with its syntax and examples of usage.

TABLE A.1. PREVENTIVE dbcc COMMANDS FOR TABLE AND PAGE CONSISTENCY CHECKS, AND OTHER ACTIONS.

Command	Action
	TABLE CONSISTENCY CHECKS
checkcatalog*	Check system tables
checkdb*	Check all tables for a database
checktable	Check a specific table's consistency
	PAGE ALLOCATION CONSISTENCY CHECKS
checkalloc*	Check page allocations
indexalloc	Check index page pointers
tablealloc	Check table allocation pointers
	OTHER dbcc COMMANDS
dbrepair	Drop a corrupt database
fix_text	Upgrade text to multi-byte character set, language upgrade
help	Display syntax help for dbcc commands

Command	Action
memusage	Review memory-usage information
reindex	Correct indexes as part of sort-order conversion
log	Display contents of transaction log
page	Review header (and possible contents) of a page
pglinkage	Display page chain linkage information
prtipage	Display index row pointer information
traceon/traceoff	Set trace flags on or off for a session

Tip

Sybase recommends that you perform at least those dbcc commands marked with an asterisk (*) before backing up (dumping) the database or transaction log.

TABLE CONSISTENCY *DBCC* COMMANDS

Because bad data tends to snowball, it pays to periodically verify that your data has integrity. Also, when you suspect table corruption (because messages are in the error log or queries do not act as expected), it's nice to be able to tell the server to go take a look.

CHECKCATALOG

The dbcc checkcatalog command checks for consistency problems between system tables and within a system table in a database. For example, some of the checks performed include:

◆ Verifying that a table or view in the sysobjects table has at least one row in the syscolumns table (all tables or views must consist of at least one column).

◆ Verifying that a type in the syscolumns table has a row in the systypes table (each column must be defined with a valid type).

◆ Checking that the last checkpoint in the syslogs table is valid.

◆ Checking the segment definitions in the syssegments table.

checkcatalog performs these types of checks for all of the system tables within the specified database or the current database.

SYNTAX

```
dbcc checkcatalog [ ( database_name ) ]
```

EXAMPLES

```
dbcc checkcatalog /* check system tables for current database */
dbcc checkcatalog (master) /* check system tables for master database */
```

CHECKDB

The dbcc checkdb command performs a dbcc checktable on each of the tables within a database.

SYNTAX

```
dbcc checkdb [ ( database_name [ , skip_ncindex ] ) ]
```

EXAMPLES

Check tables in current database:

```
dbcc checkdb
```

Check tables in database pubs2:

```
dbcc checkdb (pubs2)
```

Check database pubs2, skip checking of non-clustered indexes:

```
dbcc checkdb (pubs2, skip_ncindex)
```

The dbcc checkdb command performs a dbcc checktable for every table in the specified database. See the following section "checktable" for a description of what dbcc checkdb performs.

The skip_ncindex parameter enables you to skip the checking of nonclustered indexes. Use this option, especially in an EIS/DSS environment, to check only the data and ignore potentially huge nonclustered indexes. Use this option on large databases to speed up dbcc time when you are performing dbccs before dumping a database. It enables you to shorten your maintenance window so you can perform at least a minimal check of the database before dumping it.

CHECKTABLE

The checktable command (and, correspondingly, checkdb for each table in the database) verifies the following information for a table:

- Page linkages: making sure previous page, current page, and next page are consistent throughout the page linkage
- Index sort (that is, making sure indexes are in the correct order)
- Consistency of all pointers (that is, the index pointer to the page and row are valid)
- Data rows on each page have entries in an object allocation map (OAM) page

The OAM pages in SQL Server maintain information on rows and pages used by the tables. The `checktable` command also updates the information in the OAM pages that potentially can become inaccurate.

> *Note*
>
> The built-in `rowcnt()` function, used in the system procedure `sp_spaceused`, reads the OAM page to provide quick counts. The `dbcc` `checktable` command ensures that the OAM page is accurate, providing better data for `sp_spaceused`.

In System 11, `checktable` reports page linkage information on table partitions.

SYNTAX

```
dbcc checktable ( { table_name ¦ table_id } ) [ , skip_ncindex ] )
```

The `skip_ncindex` parameter enables you to skip the checking of nonclustered indexes. This may be quite a useful option, especially in an EIS/DSS environment, because it enables you to check only the data and ignore potentially voluminous nonclustered indexes. It is recommended for large sites so that you can check tables quickly.

EXAMPLES

Check table syslogs, ID is 8:

```
dbcc checktable (8)
```

Check table titles:

```
dbcc checktable (titles)
```

Check titles table, skip checking of nonclustered indexes:

```
dbcc checktable (titles, skip_ncindex)
```

Check authors table in the pubs2 database from a different database:

```
dbcc checktable ("pubs2..authors")
```

PAGE ALLOCATION *DBCC* COMMANDS

Use the page allocation dbcc commands to check allocation information. These commands check allocation pages to ensure that pages that are allocated actually are a part of a page linkage, and that pages in a page linkage have been marked as allocated.

Object allocation map problems seemed most prevalent in SQL Server version 4.9.1 and early 4.9.2. They would crop up for no apparent reason, which was often a source of DBA frustration. Eventually, Sybase fixed whatever error was causing the problems, which are once again unusual—but still annoying when they crop up.

If an OAM page error does crop up, you must run the page allocation dbcc commands with the fix option to attempt to correct them. To do so, the database must be in single user mode.

CHECKALLOC

The dbcc checkalloc command checks to see if the page allocation for a database is consistent. It basically executes the following command for every table and index in your database:

```
dbcc tablealloc ( table_name, full, nofix )
```

(See the section "tablealloc" for a discussion on that command.) dbcc checkalloc checks to see that all pages have been correctly allocated, that no page is allocated that is not part of a page linkage, and that no page is part of a page linkage that has not been marked as allocated. In addition to checking page allocation for all tables, checkalloc also checks all allocation pages in a database to ensure that they contain valid information.

The output of checkalloc can be useful, because it reports the number of pages and extents that have been allocated to the table (indid of 0, or 1 if the object is a clustered index) and any nonclustered indexes. For example, it reports information such as *n* Data Pages in *n* extents. A DBA could use this information to see if there has been significant shrinkage of data in a table. Each extent represents eight pages. If you divide the number of pages reported by eight and round to the next-highest integer (finally, a use for the built-in ceiling function), you will have the minimum number of extents that would be required to hold the specified data pages. If the number you come up with is off by a large margin from the number of extents reported, you probably have had page shrinkage.

Output such as `100 Data Pages in 25 extents` indicates that 15 extents have been allocated to the table, but there may be an overabundance of free pages. Optimally, only 13 extents would be needed to hold 100 data pages, with four pages available for use:

$13 \times 8 = 104$ pages
$104 - 100 = 4$

If you are using 25 extents, that means you have a total of 200 pages allocated ($8 \times 25 = 200$), of which only 100 are in page linkages. Logic would dictate that the reason the extents are only half full is because of page shrinkage (voluminous deletes) or the table was created with a low fill factor. If space is an issue, you may want to consider dropping and re-creating the clustered index on this table (if one exists), or creating a "dummy" clustered index that you drop after creation. Either of these methods will consolidate your data into the minimum number of needed extents.

SYNTAX

```
dbcc checkalloc [ ( database_name [ , fix ¦ nofix ] ) ]
```

The `fix` option fixes allocation errors, as described in the section "`tablealloc`" later in this chapter, but it is not recommended that you use this option as part of `checkalloc`. Because `dbcc checkalloc` checks system tables, it needs the database to be set to single-user mode. Setting a database to single-user mode for the duration of a `checkalloc`, especially for large databases, is prohibitive. Use `checkalloc` to locate errors, and then use `tablealloc` to fix those errors. This will help limit the amount of time a database is unavailable to a user.

EXAMPLES

Check allocation for current database:

```
dbcc checkalloc
```

Check allocation for database pubs2, default is "`nofix`":

```
dbcc checkalloc (pubs2)
```

Check allocation for database pubs2, fix allocation errors—not recommended (database must be in single-user mode):

```
dbcc checkalloc (pubs2, fix)
```

INDEXALLOC

The `dbcc indexalloc` command applies to a single-index structure. It can check (with the `full` option) that all pages have been correctly allocated, that no page that is not part of a page linkage is allocated, and that no page is part of a page linkage that has not been marked as allocated. It also can check only certain pieces of an index structure, as described in the "Options" section.

SYNTAX

```
dbcc indexalloc ( {table_name¦table_id}, index_id [, {full¦optimized¦fast¦null}
                 [ , { fix ¦ nofix ] ] )
```

OPTIONS

The `dbcc indexalloc` command is much more flexible than the `dbcc checkalloc` command, which essentially executes a `dbcc tablealloc` for all of the tables, and `dbcc indexalloc` for all of the indexes in a database. The `dbcc indexalloc` command enables you to target an index by itself, which is helpful in segmenting `dbcc` activity. The following options are available to `dbcc indexalloc`:

full	Widest scope, checks all pages for all types of allocation errors. This is the method used by `dbcc checkalloc`.
optimized	Checks only allocation pages referenced in the OAM pages. An extent not referenced in the OAM page is not detected. This is the default option if null is specified or this option is omitted.
fast	Checks whether all index pages that are part of page linkages have been allocated.
fix	Fixes allocation errors detected by the consistency check. This option is the default for indexes on user tables. If you select `fix` for indexes on system tables, the database must be in single-user mode.
nofix	Does not fix any allocation errors. This is the default for indexes on system tables.

EXAMPLES

Check index allocation pages (defaults to "optimized") of index with an ID of 2 on the titles table, fix errors (defaults to `fix` for user tables):

```
dbcc indexalloc (titles, 2)
```

Fully check index page allocation of the sysobjects table, fix errors (database must be in single user mode):

```
dbcc indexalloc (sysobjects, 2, full, fix)
```

Check index allocation pages for the sysobjects table, do not fix errors (null defaults to optimized and nofix is default for system tables):

```
dbcc indexalloc (sysobjects, null)
```

Check index OAM pages for the titleauthor table, fix errors:

```
dbcc indexalloc (titleauthor, 2, fast, fix)
```

TABLEALLOC

The dbcc tablealloc command applies to a single table structure. It can check (with the full option) that all pages have been correctly allocated, that no page is allocated that is not part of a page linkage, and that no page is part of a page linkage that has not been marked as allocated. It also can check only certain pieces of a table structure, as described in the "Options" section.

SYNTAX

```
dbcc tablealloc ( {table_name ¦ table_id} [ , {full ¦ optimized ¦ fast ¦ null}
                [ , { fix ¦ nofix ] ] )
```

OPTIONS

The dbcc tablealloc command is much more flexible than the dbcc checkalloc command, which essentially executes a dbcc tablealloc for all of the tables and dbcc indexalloc for all of the indexes in a database. The options available to dbcc tablealloc include the following:

full	Widest scope; checks for all types of allocation errors. This is the method used by dbcc checkalloc.
optimized	Checks only allocation pages referenced in the OAM pages. An extent not referenced in the OAM page is not detected. This is the default option if null is specified or this option is omitted.
fast	Checks whether all pages that are part of page linkages have been allocated.
fix	Fixes allocation errors detected by the consistency check. This option is the default for user tables. If you select fix for system tables, the database must be in single-user mode.
nofix	Does not fix any allocation errors. This is the default for system tables.

EXAMPLES

Check allocation pages (defaults to "optimized") of titles table, fix errors (defaults to "fix" for user tables):

```
dbcc tablealloc (titles)
```

A

Fully check allocation of the syslogs table, fix errors (database must be in single user mode):

```
dbcc tablealloc (8, full, fix)
```

Check allocation pages for the syslogs table, do not fix errors (null defaults to optimized and nofix is default for system tables):

```
dbcc tablealloc (8, null)
```

Check OAM pages for sales table, fix errors:

```
dbcc tablealloc (sales, fast, fix)
```

SEGMENTING THE ALLOCATION-CHECKING WORKLOAD

You can use the dbcc indexalloc command with dbcc tablealloc to effectively segment the workload performed by the dbcc checkalloc command. Because the dbcc checkalloc command sequentially checks each table (and its indexes) in object ID order, it is a serial process. To speed up an overall consistency check, a DBA could run several dbcc tablealloc or dbcc indexalloc commands in parallel. This has a negative effect on overall activity on the server, but can effectively reduce the overall amount of time you spend performing this type of consistency check. Hardware capable of Symmetric MultiProcessing (SMP) would definitely be helpful in this type of scenario.

OTHER *DBCC* COMMANDS

These dbcc commands are not used as often as the standard preventive maintenance batch, but you'll probably use them eventually.

DBREPAIR

To drop a database that has become corrupt, use the dbcc dbrepair statement. This drops a database that you were unable to drop with a standard drop database command.

SYNTAX

```
dbcc dbrepair (db_name, dropdb)
```

EXAMPLES

```
dbcc dbrepair (customerdb, dropdb)
```

> ## Warning
>
> Do not use `dbcc dbrepair` without first trying to dump the database, sending Sybase Technical Support the tape, and asking for an explanation as to why the problem occurred in the first place.

FIX_TEXT

The `dbcc fix_text` command is used to upgrade text values after converting the server to a multi-byte character set. This command makes sure that any existing text fields work correctly with the new multi-byte character set.

SYNTAX

```
dbcc fix_text ( { table_name ¦ table_id } )
```

EXAMPLE

```
dbcc fix_text (publishers) /* adjusts the publishers table */
```

HELP

The `dbcc help` command probably is one of the more useful `dbcc` commands in SQL server. `dbcc help` displays the syntax for a `dbcc` command passed as a parameter. This is helpful for commands such as `dbcc log`, which has a lot of esoteric options. Note that you need to issue the `dbcc traceon(3604)` command to send the output from `dbcc help` to the user terminal.

SYNTAX

```
dbcc help (cmd_name)
```

EXAMPLE

```
dbcc traceon(3604)
dbcc help(log)
go

log( [dbid][,objid][,page][,row][,nrecords][,type={-1..36}],printopt={0¦1} )

DBCC execution completed. If DBCC printed error messages, contact a user with
System Administrator (SA) role.
```

LOG

Another useful command is the dbcc log command. This command lets you view, in hex data format, the contents of your transaction log. One good use of the dbcc log command is to verify that updates in place are occurring.

Warning

Do not run dbcc_log in a database if you have the trunc. log on chkpt. option set to true for that database. There apparently is a rare situation where, if you are running dbcc log at the same time that the SQL Server is attempting to truncate the log, you could end up with a corrupted transaction log, and your database is marked suspect.

If your log ever gets corrupted, you'd better hope you have a fairly recent backup of your database. There is no way to fix a bad transaction log other than to restore your database to a point prior to the log getting corrupted.

SYNTAX

```
dbcc log [( dbid ¦ dbname [,objid][,page][,row][,nrecords][,type={-1..36}],
          printopt={0¦1} )]
```

To view the entire contents of the log, execute dbcc log with no options. Be forewarned, however, that if your transaction log hasn't been truncated recently, the output can be rather voluminous.

For this reason, you may want to use these additional parameters to limit the records retrieved:

objid	Display only log records associated with the specified object. 0 indicates all objects.
page	Display only log records associated with the specified page. 0 indicates all pages.
row	Display only log records associated with the specified row id. 0 indicates all rows.
nrecords	Display the specified number of records. 0 indicates all records.
type	Display log records for the specified transaction operation type code. (See Table A.2 for a list of some of the more useful operation types.) A type of -1 indicates all records.
printopt	Print all or part of the log record. A 0 indicates the entire log record; a 1 indicates only log record header information.

TABLE A.2. TRANSACTION LOG OPERATION TYPE CODES.

Type	Description
0	BEGIN TRANSACTION
4	INSERT
5	DELETE
6	INSIND (indirect insert)
7	IINSERT (index insert)
8	IDELETE (index delete)
9	MODIFY (update in place)
11	INOOP (deferred insert)
12	DNOOP (deferred delete)
13	ALLOC (page)
15	EXTENT (allocation)
16	PAGE SPLIT
17	CHECKPOINT
30	END TRANSACTION (commit or rollback)

EXAMPLES

The first example shows dbcc log output with no parameters. The output has been edited down to help save a tree or two:

```
dbcc log
go

LOG SCAN DEFINTION:
    Database id : 5
    Forward scan: starting at begining of log

LOG RECORDS:
    BEGINXACT     (3652,0)
    attcnt=1 rno=0 op=0 padlen=2 sessionid = (3652,0) len=60 status=0x0000
    masterxsid=(empty)
    xstat=XBEG_ENDXACT,
    spid=1 suid=1 uid=1 masterdbid=0 mastersite=0
    name=$ins   time=Jan 17 1996 12:37PM

    INSERT        (3652,1)
    attcnt=1 rno=1 op=4 padlen=2 sessionid = (3652,0) len=72 status=0x0000
    oampg=2360 pageno=2419 offset=1660 status=0x00 cid=0
    old ts=0x0001 0x0000426d   new ts=0x0001 0x00004273
    xrow:
2094808c:  004a0100 00000100 00000100 00000789  .J..............
2094809c:  0000f320 d000                         ... ...
```

```
ENDXACT        (3652,2)
attcnt=1 rno=2 op=30 padlen=0 sessionid = (3652,0) len=28 status=0x0000
endstat=COMMIT time=Jan 17 1996 12:37PM

BEGINXACT      (3652,3)
attcnt=1 rno=3 op=0 padlen=2 sessionid = (3652,3) len=60 status=0x0000
masterxsid=(empty)
xstat=XBEG_ENDXACT,
spid=1 suid=1 uid=1 masterdbid=0 mastersite=0
name=$ins    time=Jan 17 1996 12:37PM

INSERT         (3652,4)
attcnt=1 rno=4 op=4 padlen=2 sessionid = (3652,3) len=72 status=0x0000
oampg=2360 pageno=2474 offset=1638 status=0x00 cid=0
old ts=0x0001 0x0000426e    new ts=0x0001 0x00004275
xrow:
2094812c:  00490100 00000100 00000100 00000789   .I..............
2094813c:  0000fd20 d000                          ... ...

ENDXACT        (3652,5)
attcnt=1 rno=5 op=30 padlen=0 sessionid = (3652,3) len=28 status=0x0000
endstat=COMMIT time=Jan 17 1996 12:37PM

CHECKPOINT     (3652,6)
attcnt=1 rno=6 op=17 padlen=0 sessionid = (3652,6) len=60 status=0x0000
rows=0, pages=0 extents=0
timestamp=0x0001 0x00004276  xstat=0x0040  no active xacts

...


Total number of log records 24
DBCC execution completed. If DBCC printed error messages, contact a user with
System Administrator (SA) role.
```

The following example displays all log records for page 2170:

```
dbcc log (perftune, 0, 2170)
go

LOG SCAN DEFINTION:
    Database id : 5
    Forward scan: starting at beginning of log
    log records for page 2170

LOG RECORDS:
    IDELETE        (3652,12)
    attcnt=1 rno=12 op=8 padlen=1 sessionid = (3652,7) len=60 status=0x0000
    oampg=2184 pageno=2170 offset=516 status=0x00 cid=0
    old ts=0x0001 0x00001611    new ts=0x0001 0x00004277
    xrow:
209482c8:  00ee0300 000b0900 003c00          .........<..

    IDELETE        (3652,14)
    attcnt=1 rno=14 op=8 padlen=1 sessionid = (3652,7) len=60 status=0x0000
    oampg=2184 pageno=2170 offset=516 status=0x00 cid=0
    old ts=0x0001 0x00004277    new ts=0x0001 0x00004279
    xrow:
2094834c:  00ee0300 000b0900 003d00          .........=..
```

```
PREVIOUS PAGE:
    SALLOC      (3652,17)
    attcnt=1 rno=17 op=24 padlen=0 sessionid = (3652,7) len=92 status=0x0000
    Pagehdr: pageno=2162 nextpg=2172 prevpg=2170
          ts=0x0001 0x0000427e stat=130, objid= 240003886, oampg= 1992
    cid = 0
    old next ts=0x0001 0x00001611 new next ts=0x0001 0x0000427d
    old prev ts=0x0001 0x00004279 new prev ts=0x0001 0x0000427c
    extent oampage= 1992

    SPLIT       (3652,18)
    attcnt=1 rno=18 op=16 padlen=0 sessionid = (3652,7) len=52 status=0x0000
    oampg=2184 pageno=2170 offset=1022 status=0x03 cid=0
    old ts=0x0001 0x0000427c   new ts=0x0001 0x0000427f

    IINSERT     (3652,20)
    attcnt=1 rno=20 op=7 padlen=1 sessionid = (3652,7) len=60 status=0x0000
    oampg=2184 pageno=2170 offset=516 status=0x00 cid=0
    old ts=0x0001 0x0000427f   new ts=0x0001 0x00004281
    xrow:
209484dc:  00ee0300 000b0900 003c00             .........<..

    IINSERT     (3652,22)
    attcnt=1 rno=22 op=7 padlen=1 sessionid = (3652,7) len=60 status=0x0000
    oampg=2184 pageno=2170 offset=527 status=0x00 cid=0
    old ts=0x0001 0x00004281   new ts=0x0001 0x00004283
    xrow:
20948554:  00ee0300 000b0900 003d00             .........=..


Total number of log records 6
DBCC execution completed. If DBCC printed error messages, contact a user with
System Administrator (SA) role.
```

Another good use of the dbcc log command is to determine how many page splits
(op=16) are occurring in a database since the last time the log was truncated. To get
a count of all the page splits, execute the following:

```
dbcc log (perftune, 0, 0, 0, 0, 16, 1)
go
LOG SCAN DEFINTION:
    Database id : 5
    Forward scan: starting at begining of log
    Log operation type SPLIT (16)

LOG RECORDS:
    SPLIT       (3652,18)
    attcnt=1 rno=18 op=16 padlen=0 sessionid = (3652,7) len=52 status=0x0000
    oampg=2184 pageno=2170 offset=1022 status=0x03 cid=0
    old ts=0x0001 0x0000427c   new ts=0x0001 0x0000427f


Total number of log records 1
DBCC execution completed. If DBCC printed error messages, contact a user with
System Administrator (SA) role.
```

In this example, you can see that there is only a single page split in the transaction log. This is because I recently truncated it and have only run one update statement since.

MEMUSAGE

The dbcc memusage command output is extremely useful for validating your SQL Server memory configuration. dbcc memusage reports three pieces of information:

◆ The current allocation of memory within SQL Server

◆ Up to the 20 largest tables and/or indexes currently in data cache

◆ Up to the 20 largest stored procedures currently in procedure cache

The first section of output, the current memory allocations, provides the following information:

◆ Configured Memory. This should be the same as what you configured for total memory using sp_configure.

◆ Code Size. This is the amount of memory required for the SQL Server executable.

◆ Kernel Structures and Server Structures represent the memory requirements for the fixed overhead and configurable options (for example, user connections).

◆ Cache Memory. This is the amount of memory available for data cache.

◆ Proc Buffers and Proc Headers. This is the total amount of memory available as procedure cache. Proc Buffers represents the size of the memory structures set aside for managing compiled objects in procedure cache. Proc Headers is the actual amount of procedure cache space available.

You must use the dbcc memusage command with a traceon (3604) if you want to see the output on your screen.

Tip

On some platforms or releases of the server, dbcc traceon (3604) must be in its own batch to take effect for the subsequent memusage. If you can't get trace flag 3604 to send data to your screen, use 3605 to send the data to the error log.

SYNTAX

```
dbcc memusage
```

EXAMPLE

```
dbcc traceon (3604)
go
dbcc memusage
go
```
Memory Usage:

	Meg.	2K Blks	Bytes
Configured Memory:	400.0000	204800	419430400
Code size:	3.4259	1755	3592296
Kernel Structures:	5.9769	3061	6267212
Server Structures:	13.9494	7143	14627040
Cache Memory:	357.0625	182816	374407168
Proc Buffers:	0.6974	358	731272
Proc Headers:	18.8848	9669	19802112

Buffer Cache Memory, Top 8:

Cache	Buf Pool	DB Id	Object Id	Index Id	Meg.
default data c		2	8	0	0.1035
	2K	2	8	0	0.1035
default data c		6	8	0	29.0000
	2K	6	8	0	29.0000
default data c		1	8	0	3.0000
	2K	1	8	0	3.0000
default data c		10	99	0	2.0000
	2K	10	99	0	2.0000
default data c		1	31	1	1.0000
	2K	1	31	1	1.0000
default data c		3	8	0	1.0000
	2K	3	8	0	1.0000
default data c		3	99	0	1.0000
	2K	3	99	0	1.0000
default data c		10	0	0	1.0000
	2K	10	0	0	1.0000

Procedure Cache, Top 6:

```
Database Id: 1
Object Id: 672005425
Object Name: sp_configure
Version: 1
Uid: 1
Type: stored procedure
Number of trees: 0
Size of trees: -0.000000 Mb, 0.000000 bytes, 0 pages
Bytes lost for alignment 0 (Percentage of total: -INF)
Number of plans: 4
```

```
Size of plans: -INF Mb, 667416.000000 bytes, 328 pages
Bytes lost for alignment 100832 (Percentage of total:
➡ -303894856385275468835337216.000000)


- - - -
Database Id: 4
Object Id: 1776009358
Object Name: sp_spaceused
Version: 1
Uid: 1
Type: stored procedure
Number of trees: 0
Size of trees: 0.000000 Mb, 0.000000 bytes, 0 pages
Bytes lost for alignment 0 (Percentage of total: 0.000000)
Number of plans: 1
Size of plans: 0.107710 Mb, 112942.000000 bytes, 56 pages
Bytes lost for alignment 8739 (Percentage of total: 7.737600)


- - - -
Database Id: 4
Object Id: 1440008161
Object Name: sp_lock
Version: 1
Uid: 1
Type: stored procedure
Number of trees: 0
Size of trees: 0.000000 Mb, 0.000000 bytes, 0 pages
Bytes lost for alignment 0 (Percentage of total: 0.000000)
Number of plans: 1
Size of plans: 0.037201 Mb, 39008.000000 bytes, 20 pages
Bytes lost for alignment 1660 (Percentage of total: 4.255537)


- - - -
Database Id: 1
Object Id: 656005368
Object Name: sp_getmessage
Version: 1
Uid: 1
Type: stored procedure
Number of trees: 0
Size of trees: 0.000000 Mb, 0.000000 bytes, 0 pages
Bytes lost for alignment 0 (Percentage of total: 0.000000)
Number of plans: 1
Size of plans: 0.028290 Mb, 29664.000000 bytes, 15 pages
Bytes lost for alignment 850 (Percentage of total: 2.865426)


- - - -
Database Id: 4
Object Id: 1872009700
Object Name: sp_who
Version: 1
Uid: 1
Type: stored procedure
Number of trees: 0
Size of trees: 0.000000 Mb, 0.000000 bytes, 0 pages
Bytes lost for alignment 0 (Percentage of total: 0.000000)
Number of plans: 1
```

```
Size of plans: 0.023853 Mb, 25012.000000 bytes, 13 pages
Bytes lost for alignment 1059 (Percentage of total: 4.233968)

....
Database Id: 4
Object Id: 1728009187
Object Name: sp_server_info
Version: 1
Uid: 1
Type: stored procedure
Number of trees: 0
Size of trees: 0.000000 Mb, 0.000000 bytes, 0 pages
Bytes lost for alignment 0 (Percentage of total: 0.000000)
Number of plans: 1
Size of plans: -INF Mb, 9924.000000 bytes, 5 pages
Bytes lost for alignment 248 (Percentage of total:
➥-204377558912439736709353472.000000)

....
DBCC execution completed. If DBCC printed error messages, contact a user with
System Administrator (SA) role.
```

Note

For a detailed discussion on using and interpreting the output of the
`dbcc memusage` command for tuning your SQL Server memory configuration, refer to Chapter 10, "Optimizing SQL Server Configuration
Options."

Warning

If you are running SQL Server in an SMP environment with multiple
engines configured, running `dbcc memusage` can cause other processes
within the SQL Server to time out and die. Do not run `dbcc memusage`
while other processes are active in a multiple engine environment.

PAGE

The `dbcc page` command enables you to view a page header and, optionally, the data
on a page. It has limited use, but it can provide further insight during lock analysis
by determining the exact type of page where locking occurred.

The page numbers you may want to check using this command are those indicated
in the output of the `sp_lock` command. By using `dbcc page`, you can tell if a page is a
data or index page (and which level it is in the index). The things to look for in the
`dbcc page` command output include the following:

| indid | The index ID, which indicates the type of page: 0 = data page, 1 = clustered index page, 2-250 = non-clustered index page, 255 = text/image page |
| level | the level within the index in which the page is found |

There also is an indication of the previous page, next page, and current page. If a zero is listed for previous page, you are looking at the first page in a page linkage. If a zero is listed for next page, you are looking at the last page in the page linkage. (If zero is listed for both, this is the only page in the page linkage.)

You can determine page ranges for a database by looking in the sysusages table. Remember that the high-level byte of the low column is the virtual device number. Also, the sysindexes table provides values for the following:

first	The first data page or leaf page in an index or table
root	The last page in a table linkage (table) or text chain (text/image), or the root index page if it is an index
distribution	The location of the distribution page for an index

Syntax

```
dbcc page( dbid¦dbname, pagenum [, printopt={0¦1¦2¦3} [, cache={0¦1}
                                [, logical={1¦0} [, cachename ¦ -1 ]]]] )
```

> ## *Note*
>
> If you've used dbcc page in the past, notice that the syntax has changed slightly for System 11. You now must provide the named data cache where the page can be found in memory. If you haven't set up named data caches, all pages come from the "default data cache." If you provide the -1 option instead of a cache name, SQL Server will search all data caches to find the page in memory.

The display options (0, 1, 2, 3) determine how the page contents will be displayed. 0 is the default and displays only the page header without the page contents. 1 displays the page header and a hex dump of the page contents individually by row. 2 displays the same information as 1, but displays the page contents as a single block of data. 3 is used when displaying the contents of a control page for a partitioned table.

Note

You need to run the `dbcc traceon(3604)` command prior to running `dbcc page`, or `dbcc page` will print its output to the SQL Server error log rather than to the user's screen.

The `cache` option indicates whether to fetch the page from disk (0) or from memory (1, the default). The `logical` option indicates whether the page number specified is the virtual page number (0) or the logical page number in the database (1, the default).

EXAMPLES

Check page header of page 402 in database 6:

```
dbcc page (6, 402)
```

Review page header and data, segmented by row, on page 402 in database 6, look for page in the default data cache:

```
dbcc page (6, 402, 1, 1, 1, "default data cache")
```

Review page header and data, rows displayed as a single block, on page 402 in database 6, search all data caches:

```
dbcc page (6, 402, 2, 1, 1, -1)
```

Tip

For more information on the contents of pages within SQL Server databases and interpreting the output of `dbcc page`, see Chapter 10.

PGLINKAGE

You can use this command to display the page chain and check the consistency of page pointers for a table or index page chain. You may find this command useful to traverse a page chain, or to determine whether the pages in the table are contiguous.

SYNTAX

```
dbcc pglinkage ({dbid ¦ dbname}, startpage#, #ofpages, printopt,
    target_page#, direction [, cachename ¦ -1 ])
```

The startpage# option specifies the page number you want to start scanning the page linkage from. The #ofpages option specifies how many pages you want to scan in the linkage (0 scans to the end of the page linkage). The target_page# lets you specify a logical page address where you want the scan to stop (0 will cause prtipage to scan to the end of the page linkage or until #of pages value is reached). direction is either 0 (descending) or 1 (ascending).

Here are the available print options:

0   Print only a count of the pages in the chain.

1   Print the last 16 pages in scan.

2   Print each page number in scan.

EXAMPLE

This example examines the first eight pages for the pt_sample_CIcompany table, starting at the first page in the table (which you can get from the sysindexes table).

```
dbcc traceon(3604)
dbcc pglinkage (perftune, 1616, 8, 2, 0, 1)
go

Page : 1616
Page : 1617
Page : 1618
Page : 1619
Page : 1620
Page : 1621
Page : 1622
Page : 1623

8 pages scanned.  Object ID = 112003430.  Last page in scan = 1623.
```

This output shows that the pages belong to the pt_sample_CIcompany (object ID = 112003430), and that all eight pages are sequential, from 1616 to 1623.

PRTIPAGE

You can use the prtipage command to display the page pointers for each row on a clustered index page or non-leaf nonclustered index page or the page and row pointers on a leaf level nonclustered index page.

SYNTAX

```
dbcc prtipage (dbid ¦ dbname, object_id ¦ object_name, index_id, page_#)
```

EXAMPLE

To examine the pointers for the first leaf index page retrieved from the sysindexes table for the nonclustered index, NCamount, on the pt_tx_NCamount table in the perftune database, enter the following command:

```
dbcc traceon(3604)
dbcc prtipage (perftune, pt_tx_NCamount, 2, 2096)
```

The output appears as follows:

```
*** INDEX LEVEL 0 - PAGE # 2096

Leaf row at offset 32 points to data page 771, row number 67
Leaf row at offset 47 points to data page 771, row number 62
Leaf row at offset 62 points to data page 770, row number 18
Leaf row at offset 77 points to data page 771, row number 16
Leaf row at offset 92 points to data page 772, row number 22
Leaf row at offset 107 points to data page 771, row number 28
Leaf row at offset 122 points to data page 771, row number 47
Leaf row at offset 137 points to data page 771, row number 32
Leaf row at offset 152 points to data page 770, row number 17
Leaf row at offset 167 points to data page 771, row number 73
Leaf row at offset 182 points to data page 771, row number 52
...
```

From this output, you can determine to which rows on which data pages the index rows on this index page point.

REINDEX

If the sort order of the server is changed, you should use the dbcc reindex command to make sure the indexes on a table are in sync with the new sort order of the system.

SYNTAX

```
dbcc reindex ( { table_name ¦ table_id } )
```

EXAMPLE

Perform a "fast" version of dbcc checktable, and drop and rebuild any indexes that do not comply with the new sort order:

```
dbcc reindex ( publishers )
```

TRACEON/TRACEOFF

Many trace flags are covered in this book; two common ones are 3604 and 3605. The 3604 flag directs output to the local session. The 3605 flag directs output to the error log. These trace flags are used primarily for commands such as `dbcc memusage` and `dbcc page`. There are other trace flags, such as `201`, `302`, and `310`, that you can set to display detailed information to augment performance analysis. Table A.3 provides a list of useful trace flags.

TABLE A.3. USEFUL `dbcc` TRACE FLAGS YOU CAN SET WITH THE `traceon/traceoff` OPTION OF `dbcc`.

Trace Flag	Information to Display
200	"Before" image of query tree
201	"After" image of query tree
302	Information on index selection
310	Information on join selection
317	Complete information on join select
1204	Deadlock trace information
3604	Send output to screen
3605	Send output to the SQL Server error log

SYNTAX

```
dbcc traceon ( traceflag [, traceflag …] )
dbcc traceoff (traceflag [, traceflag …] )
```

EXAMPLES

Send `dbcc` output to screen:

```
dbcc traceon (3604)
```

Send `dbcc` output to SQL Server error log:

```
dbcc traceon (3605)
```

Turn off trace flag output:

```
dbcc traceoff (3604)
```

Turn on printing of deadlock trace information to the SQL Server error log:

```
dbcc traceon (3605)
dbcc traceon (1204)
```

COMPARISON OF COMMANDS

Table A.4 compares the various dbcc checking commands.

TABLE A.4. COMPARISON OF dbcc COMMANDS.

Command	Action	Usage
dbcc checkdb	Check all tables for a database	Run before a database dump (or if you suspect inconsistencies)
dbcc checktable	Check a specific table's consistency	Run if a certain table is suspect, or as part of a maintenance plan (check half the tables on Sunday, the other half on Wednesday)
dbcc checkcatalog	Check rows in system tables for consistency	Run before a database dump (or if you suspect inconsistencies)
dbcc checkalloc	Check allocation for all tables and indexes in a database	Run before a database dump (or if you suspect inconsistencies)
dbcc tablealloc	Check allocation for a specific table (or clustered index)	Run with fix option when a table is identified by checkalloc, or as part of a maintenance plan (check half the tables on Sunday, the other half on Wednesday)
dbcc indexalloc	Check index page pointers	Run with the fix option when an index is identified by checkalloc, or as part of a maintenance plan (check half the tables on Sunday, the other half on Wednesday)

Table A.5 shows the scope of the dbcc checking commands.

Table A.5. Scope of dbcc checking commands.

Command/Option	Scope of Check	Locking	Performance/Speed	Coverage
`checktable` `checkdb`	Page chains, sort order, data row checks for all indexes	Shared table lock, one at a time (lock A, release A, lock B, release B)	Slow	Full coverage
`checktable` `checkdb` `with skip_ncindex`	Page chains, sort order, data rows for tables and clustered indexes	Same	Potentially much faster than without the `skip_ncindex` option, dependent on number of non clustered indexes	Partial coverage; nonclustered indexes ignored
`checkalloc`	Page chains	No locks, heavy I/O, only allocation pages cached	Slow	Full coverage
`tablealloc full` `indexalloc full`	Page chains	Shared table lock, heavy I/O, only allocation pages cached	Slow	Full coverage; essentially distributed `checkalloc`
`tablealloc optimized` `indexalloc optimized`	Allocation pages	Shared table lock, heavy I/O, only allocation pages cached	Medium	Partial coverage; only allocation pages checked
`tablealloc fast` `indexalloc fast`	OAM pages	Shared table lock	Fast	Least coverage; only OAM pages checked
`checkcatalog`	System table rows	Shared page locks on system tables, released after data on page is checked; not much cached	Fast	Detailed check of consistency of rows of certain system tables

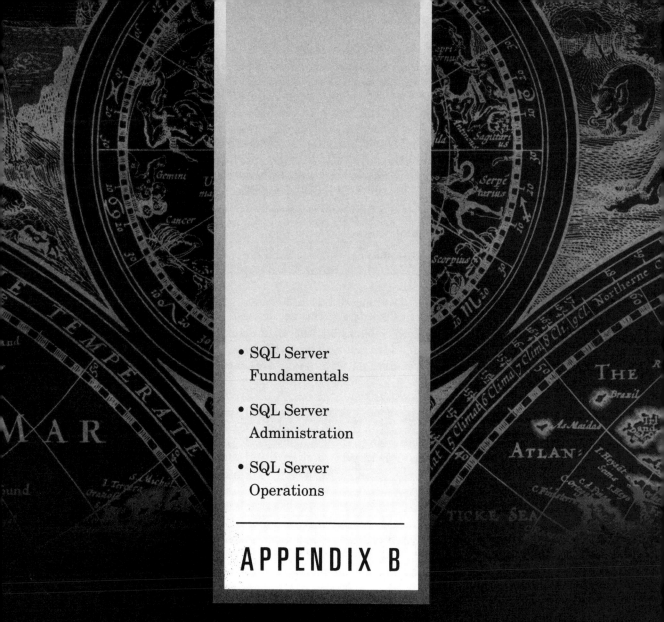

- SQL Server
  Fundamentals

- SQL Server
  Administration

- SQL Server
  Operations

APPENDIX B

Sample Certified Sybase Professional DBA (CSP DBA) Test

Sybase certifies individuals' (programmers, DBAs, system administrators) knowledge about SQL Server operation and maintenance. To become a Certified SYBASE Professional Database Administrator (CSP DBA), you will need to pass three tests on the operation, administration, and tuning of SQL Server. To help you prepare for that test sequence, we have provided a fairly comprehensive test of your knowledge of SQL Server, which is divided into three sections:

◆ SQL Server Fundamentals
◆ SQL Server Administration
◆ SQL Server Operations

Use this test to prepare for the examination, or to identify areas where you need to improve your knowledge.

Most of the questions in the first and third sections of this chapter are not covered in this book. To learn more about SQL Server fundamentals and performance and tuning, you may want to look at *Sybase SQL Server 11 Unleashed* from SAMS Publishing, or attend courses on SQL Server Transact-SQL and performance and tuning.

Note

We cannot guarantee that passing our test will automatically make you pass the CSP DBA examination, but if you do well on this test, you are certainly on your way to being a qualified Sybase system administrator.

SQL SERVER FUNDAMENTALS

Questions 1–9 are based upon the following table definition:

```
create table mytable (a int not null, b int default 10 null)
go
create rule b_rule as @bval  between  0 and 100
go
sp_bindrule b_rule, "mytable.b"
go
create view sample_view as select * from mytable
go
alter table mytable add c varchar(20) null
go
alter table mytable add constraint b_check
check (b between -10 and  10)
go
```

1. What value will be added to the table for column b by the following `insert` statement:

   ```
   insert mytable (a, b) values  (1, null)
   ```

2. If there were 50 rows already in the table when the default was bound to column b and 20 of the rows contained NULL for column b, what value will those rows contain for column b after the default is bound?

3. If a file containing 20 rows is bulk copied into the table and 5 of the rows do not have values for column b, what value will those rows have for column b after the `bcp` has completed?

4. Will a file containing rows that have negative values for column b be added during a bulk copy load?

5. What columns will a user see if he runs the following `select` statement:

   ```
   select * from sample_view
   ```

6. What values are allowed in column b for inserts/updates?

7. What methods can be used to enforce a business rule requiring a value in column b to be greater than a value in column a for an insert/update?

8. What would be the result of running the following commands:

   ```
   create default b_dflt as 10
   go
   sp_bindefault b_dflt, 'mytable.b'
   go
   ```

9. If the following command was run, what would happen during an insert if no value was supplied for column b?

   ```
   alter table mytable replace b default -1
   ```

10. What is the role of a client in a client/server architecture?

11. What is the role of the server in a client/server architecture?

12. What system table contains information about objects within a database such as tables, defaults, triggers, etc.?

13. How many pages are allocated when a table is created?

14. How is a clustered index different from a non-clustered index?

15. Can a clustered index be placed on a separate device than a table?

16. Can a column be deleted from a table?

17. What command allows you to add columns to a table?

    What is the `null` property of columns added to a table using this command?

18. What is the result of creating a column on a table with the `identity` property?

How many columns with the identity property can be created in a table?

What system datatype must be used for identity columns?

19. How are identity columns updated and by whom?

20. What global variable can be queried to determine the last identity value inserted into a table?

21. Explain the difference between char and varchar datatypes.

How is the string "ABC" stored differently in a char(10) not null column from a varchar(10) not null column?

22. Define what is meant by null.

How are null values handled by aggregate functions?

23. What SQL Server function can be used to substitute a value for null in a query?

24. What is the restriction on updating base tables through a view, if the view is defined on multiple tables?

25. What is the restriction on inserting data into a base table through a view if the view only contains a subset of the columns in the base table?

26. What is the restriction on deleting rows through a multi-table view?

27. What is the maximum number of triggers that can be created on a table?

28. If an update on table_a fires a trigger which updates table_b, and table_b has an update trigger defined on it, will the trigger on table_b be executed?

29. If an update of a row in table_a fires a trigger which updates another row in table_a, will the trigger on table_a execute again?

30. What are the names of the tables that are normally accessible from within a trigger when a trigger is executed?

What structure do they have?

Where are these tables located?

31. What is the statement that can be used inside a trigger to check whether a specific column has been modified by the insert or update statement which caused the trigger to fire?

32. An insert trigger is created on a table that validates whether one of its column values exists in another table before allowing the insert to succeed. A file is bulk copied into the table that contains invalid values for that column. Will the rows be inserted by the bulk copy?

33. If a table is created with a unique constraint on a column, can that column allow null values?

What if the column is created with a primary key constraint?

34. If a view is created on table `mytable` and that table is renamed to `newtable`, will the view still work?

35. If a column is added to a table after a view has been defined on the table, what must be done to make the column accessible through the view?

36. Under which of the following circumstances will a stored procedure automatically be recompiled?

    a. Creating an index on a table referenced in the stored procedure

    b. Dropping an index on a table referenced in the stored procedure that is being used to satisfy the query

    c. Renaming a table referenced in the stored procedure

    d. Dropping and recreating, with the same name, a table referenced in a stored procedure

37. What three methods can be used to force a stored procedure to recompile a new query plan?

38. What system table contains information on system and user-defined datatypes?

39. Describe how the `@@trancount` global variable is incremented and decremented.

40. What type of lock is held on a page during a `select`?

41. What type of lock is held on a page during an `insert`?

42. By default, how many page locks must be accessed by a single data modification statement before it is upgraded to a table lock? How can you change this value in System 11?

43. What global variable contains the number of rows affected by your last executed SQL statement? Which SQL statements affect that variable?

44. What is the difference between Server cursors and Language cursors?

45. What is the proper sequence of statements to use and process a cursor?

46. What statement is used to delete the currently fetched row in an updatable cursor?

47. What type of lock does an updatable cursor obtain by default as it is fetching rows? A read-only cursor?

48. What is the difference between the following two `select` statements?

```
select title, type, price from titles
    order by type
    compute avg(price) by type

select title, type, price from titles
    order by type
    compute avg(price)
```

49. Assume the following four users have each executed the following set of statements in different databases (assume all users are running in unchained mode):

```
User 1: begin tran
        delete mytab
        commit tran
        go

User 2: begin tran
        delete mytab
        checkpoint
        go

User 3: begin tran
        delete mytab
        commit tran
        go
        checkpoint
        go

User 4: begin tran
        delete mytab
        go

User 5: delete mytab
        go
```

If the SQL Server were to crash at this point, which of these transactions would be rolled back during recovery? Rolled forward? No recovery required?

50. A user executes the following set of statements:

```
create table sample_tab (a int)
go
begin tran mytran
insert sample_tab (a) values (1)
save tran mysavept
insert sample_tab (a) values (2)
rollback tran mysavept
insert sample_tab (a) values (3)
commit tran
```

What rows will be displayed by a `select * from sample_tab` statement?

51. What global variable can be checked to determine the current status of a transaction?

52. Describe a deadlock scenario.

What SQL statement is notorious for causing deadlock situations?

What steps can be taken to avoid deadlocks?

53. What is the definition of a transaction?

54. Describe the differences between chained transaction mode and unchained transaction mode. When does a transaction begin/end in chained mode? unchained mode?

55. What global variable can be queried to determine whether you are running in chained or unchained transaction mode?

56. What will be displayed by the following SQL statements

    a. if the average price after update is greater than $50

    b. if the average price after update is less than $50

```
begin tran mytran
print "Updating titles"
update titles set price = price * $1.25
if (select avg(price) from titles) > $50
    print "Avg price exceeds $50"
    rollback tran mytran
    print "Update rolled back"
    return
commit tran mytran
print "Update successful"
go
```

What changes would you recommend for this code?

57. How are local variables defined? How are global variables defined?

58. How are values assigned to local variables?

59. How are values assigned to global variables?

60. What is the duration of local variables?

61. What are the two ways to change the displayed column headings for a `select` statement?

62. What statement can be used to create a table in SQL Server other than the `create table` statement?

63. What will be the effect of the following statement:

```
select * into newtitles from titles where 1 = 2
```

64. What data values would the following `where` clause match:

```
where name like "%_[Cc]omputer"
```

65. What function is used to display the value of a datetime column in the format dd/mm/yyyy?

66. What requirements must be met before a table can be referenced by a foreign key reference constraint?

Consider the following table definition for questions 67 and 68:

```
create table titles
    (title_id char(6) not null,
     title varchar(60) not null,
     pub_id char(4) not null
     references publishers(pub_id)
     total_sales int null,
     pubdate)
```

67. What happens if you attempt to delete a row from `publishers` where there is an existing `title(s)` in the `titles` table for that `pub_id`?

    What if you attempt to update a `pub_id` for a publisher that has related rows in the `titles` table?

    What if you attempt to insert a new publisher into the `publishers` table?

68. What happens if you attempt to insert a row into `titles`?

    Update a `pub_id` in `titles`?

    Delete a row from `titles`?

69. Describe the difference between a table-level constraint and a column-level constraint.

    When must you define a constraint as a table-level constraint?

70. What value will be displayed for `@var` when the following statements are executed:

    ```
    create proc myproc (@parm1 int output)
    as
    select @parm1 = @parm1 + 50
    go
    declare @var int
    select @var = 50
    exec myproc @var output
    select @var
    go
    ```

71. What data values can be returned by the `return` statement from within a stored procedure?

    What data values are reserved for use by Sybase?

72. What statement is used to generate system-like error messages?

    What is the minimum error number that can be used?

73. If a rule is bound to a user-defined datatype, what happens to any existing columns which are defined with that user-defined datatype?

    What if those columns already had a rule bound explicitly to the column?

74. If a column already has a rule bound to it, and you attempt to bind another rule to that column, what happens?

75. How are database objects fully qualified?

76. What is the purpose of the `syskeys` table?

77. What command can you execute to view the total logical and physical I/O for a query? What is logical I/O?

78. What command can you execute to view the query plan chosen by the SQL Server to execute a query?

    What is the component of SQL Server which determines the best query plan?

79. What command do you need to execute periodically to keep the distribution pages for the indexes on a table up to date?

    What information is contained on a distribution page?

80. What is the size of a data page in SQL Server?

    How much of this space is available for data? If a row is 100 bytes wide, including overhead, how many rows will fit on a single data page?

81. What is the maximum number of columns in a row?

    What is the maximum row width?

82. If a table contains no clustered index, where are new rows added?

83. Describe how a page split occurs when adding rows to a table with a clustered index.

    When is an overflow page created instead?

84. What is the difference between a deferred update and a direct update?

    What is the difference between a direct update in place and a direct update not in place?

85. What information is contained in the leaf rows of a nonclustered index? In the leaf and non-leaf rows of a clustered index?

86. Describe what is meant by index covering.

87. How is text and image data stored within a SQL Server database?

88. Which of the following where clauses are considered optimizable Search Arguments (SARGs) by SQL Server:

    a. where age > 21

    b. where "1/2/94" > pubdate

    c. where name not like "Sm%"

    d. where name like "%son"

    e. where substring(name, 1, 1) = "P"

    f. where t.pub_id = p.pub_id

    g. where dept = 2 or dept = 3

    h. where pub_id in ("1234", "2345", "3456")

    i. where price > $10.0 and price < $15.0

    j. where salary between 10000 and 30000

    k. where bonus > salary * .5

    l. where salary/2 > 10000

    m. where 100 between lo and hi

    n. where dept != 20

B

If not an optimizable SARG, which of these can be turned into an optimizable SARG?

89. Describe the OR Strategy used by SQL Server for resolving queries with OR clauses.

90. A primary key constraint by default will create what type of index? A unique key constraint by default will create what type of default? A foreign key constraint?

SQL SERVER ADMINISTRATION

1. What command do you use to configure the server?

2. What command do you use to start SQL Server in a UNIX environment?

3. How are remote procedures invoked?

4. What needs to be setup/configured on the local server to implement remote procedure calls?

    What needs to be setup on the remote server?

5. What command do you use to shut down the server gracefully? Unconditionally?

    What steps does the SQL Server perform during a graceful shutdown?

6. What buildmaster option do you use to recreate the master database?

    What buildmaster option do you use to recreate the model database?

7. What buildmaster option allows you to report on the system configuration?

8. What utility is used to install SQL Server on most platforms?

9. What isql scripts need to be run after a manual rebuild of the master device?

10. Describe how the model database is used by SQL Server.

11. Where are system stored procedures located in System 10 and later?

12. Which stored procedure reports on current connections to the SQL Server?

13. What command is used to allocate disk space to the SQL Server?

14. What device can be mirrored to ensure non-stop SQL Server operation?

15. Name the three segments created by SQL Server during a create database statement.

16. What stored procedure is executed when the last-chance threshold is reached?

    Where is this stored procedure located?

17. Name the two types of data devices that can be initialized by SQL Server.

18. What command provides information on the current roles you have been assigned in SQL Server?

19. What role must you have to add logins to the SQL Server?

20. What commands are used to define security on objects in a database?

21. Explain the relationship between the `sysusers` and `syslogins` tables.

22. What command do you use to grant the `sso_role` role to `User1`?

23. If you wanted all future databases to contain a `guest` account and have the `select into/bulk copy` option turned on, what would be the easiest way to do this?

24. List the steps and commands you would need to take to allocate a new device to a database, create a user-defined segment on the device, and limit that device to only objects explicitly created/placed on that segment (assume the log is on its own device).

25. How do you create a non-clustered index on a device separate from the table?

26. What is an easy method, without having to drop and recreate the table, to move a table to a different segment?

27. If a server is expected to have three devices (in addition to the `master` device), and all four devices are to be mirrored, what is the minimum number of devices the server needs to be configured for?

28. A SQL server is expected to have 100 total users. There is expected to be 30 concurrent users at any one time running an Open-Client application which opens two connections to the SQL Server. In addition, two DBAs will be monitoring the system with an application which requires one SQL Server connection, and an on-line batch process will be running 24 hours a day (possible during normal activity) which requires three user connections. Backups are performed via Backup Server, and there are three devices defined for this SQL Server, including the master device. What is the recommended minimum number of `user connections` this SQL Server should be configured for?

29. Consider the following fragments of the `sysusages`, `syssegments`, `sysdevices`, and `sysdatabases` tables for the `mydb` database:

```
mydb..syssegments
    segment name          status
    ------- -----------   ------
          0 system             0
          1 default            1
          2 logsegment         0
          3 Seg1               0
```

```
sysusages
    dbid   segmap   lstart        size        vstart      ...
    ------  ------   ----------   ----------   ----------  ...
        6        3            0         2048   51556616 ...
        6        4         2048         1024   77714249 ...
        6       10         3072          512       9044 ...

sysdevices
    low          high        ... name               ...
    ----------   ----------  ... --------------     ...
    5156616      5166856     ... data_dev1          ...
    7711177      7716296     ... log_dev1           ...
    9044         19283       ... data_dev2          ...

sysdatabases
    name               dbid   ...
    ----------------   -----  ...
    master                0   ...
    model                 1   ...
    tempdb                2   ...
    sybsystemprocs        3   ...
    mydb                  6   ...
```

What were the commands used to create `mydb`?

30. In the previous question, what segments are mapped to the `data_dev2` device?

31. What role must you have to grant the OPER role?

32. What command is used to grant roles?

33. What command is used in System 10 and later to change a user's default database?

34. What permissions will the users Mary and Fred have on the `employee` table after the following commands are executed:

```
grant all on employee to public
revoke insert, update, delete on employee from Mary, Fred
revoke select on employee (salary) from public
```

35. What steps/commands must be executed to grant `user1 create database` permission? Who can grant `create database` permission?

36. Describe the outcome of the following command:

```
grant select on accounts to Fred with grant option
```

37. Based upon the previous question, what command would you need to issue if you wanted to remove `select` permission on the `accounts` table from Fred and all users Fred granted permissions to?

38. If a user owns objects in a database, what must be done if you wish to drop the user's login from the SQL Server?

How can you prevent a user from logging into SQL Server without dropping the user's login?

39. Who can run the `sp_modifylogin` procedure?

40. Which SQL Server user(s) can perform database dumps and loads?

41. Which SQL Server user(s) can perform DBCC commands in a database?

42. What command do you execute to set SQL Server passwords to expire 30 days after the last time they were modified?

    Who can execute this command?

    What happens when a user's password expires?

43. You want to set up mirroring of the `Device1` device on `/dev/rdsk2`. What is the syntax of the command you need to execute to implement this setup?

    What must be true of `/dev/rdsk2` for this to be successful?

    How can you mirror the `master` device on `/dev/rdsk3`?

44. What command do you use to start SQL Server in single user mode?

45. Which system table contains the current SQL Server configuration? Which system table contains configuration values the SQL Server will use upon the next SQL Server restart?

46. Name four configuration variables which require a SQL Server restart to take effect.

    Why is a SQL Server restart required?

47. What system table is used to map multiple logins to a single user ID within a database?

    What command is used to add entries to this table?

48. Examine the following object ownership chain:

    a. `ProcA` (owned by `joe`)

    b. Executes `ProcB` (owned by `mary`)

    c. which inserts data into `ViewA` (owned by `mary`)

    d. `ViewA` is defined on `TableA` (owned by `joe`)

    e. `TableA` has an insert trigger defined on it which updates `TableC` (owned by `mary`)

    Assuming all object creators have the necessary access to all objects in the database, what permissions must be granted for user `Fred` to successfully execute `ProcA`?

49. You are managing a SQL Server which contains two databases. Each database is on a separate physical device and has its log on a separate physical device. `DatabaseA` is used for an OLTP application which updates over 10,000 records per day. `DatabaseB` is used for running management reports and is updated twice a month. You only have two devices available

to use for mirroring. If you can only mirror two devices, in order to maximize system availability and minimize data loss, which two devices would you recommend mirroring?

50. Identify in which database(s) each of the following system tables appears:

```
syssegments
sysroles
sysprocesses
sysmessages
sysalternates
sysobjects
sysprocedures
sysdevices
sysservers
syslogs
syscomments
sysusers
syslogins
syslocks
sysusages
sysusermessages
sysaudits
```

51. What command(s) do you use to install the auditing system in SQL Server?

52. How can you verify if auditing has been installed on a SQL Server?

53. What command do you use to determine if auditing is enabled?

54. What happens to audited processes if the audit queue fills up?

    How do you increase the size of the audit queue?

55. What permissions and password does the sa login have after SQL Server installation?

56. Describe how a system stored procedure is different from a user-defined stored procedure.

57. If a login has been created in SQL Server without specifying a default database, what database will the user be in after a successful login to SQL Server?

58. What will happen if a default database is specified, but the user is not a valid user in that database?

59. Identify which role or special user can perform the following tasks:

    a. Install SQL Server

    b. Drop database users

   c. Grant/revoke access to an object

   d. Reset passwords

   e. Add dump devices

   f. Manage the audit system

   g. Grant/revoke command permissions

   h. Modify login information (default database, full name, default language)

   i. Set server configuration options

   j. Set database options

60. What are the steps SQL Server performs to verify user access to a database?

61. How do you create a group within a database?

   What two ways can you add a user to a group in a database?

62. What information is returned by the system function `suser_id("fred")`? `user_name(10)`? `db_id()`?

63. If you were to grant the `sa_role` to user `fred`, when would that role take effect?

64. What command would you use to temporarily disable a role for your session?

   To revoke a role for a user permanently?

65. When configuring SQL Server memory, what unit of measurement is used to specify the amount of memory to allocate to SQL Server?

   If the SQL Server is supposed to be configured to allocate 20MB of memory, what value would you specify to `sp_configure`?

66. If the SQL Server is configured to use 16MB of memory, 4MB of which are used by the SQL Server executable and server and kernel structures, and procedure cache is set to 30, how large would the procedure cache be in megabytes?

   How large would the data cache be?

67. What command can be used to display how SQL Server has allocated memory internally?

   Where else can you look to determine the number of pages allocated to the data and procedure cache?

68. When creating freespace thresholds on a segment, how far apart should you create them?

69. Describe what it means when `nested triggers` is configured to `1`.

   When `recovery flags` is set to `1`.

70. Describe `fillfactor`. What two ways can you control the `fillfactor` to be used when creating indexes?

    What does a `fillfactor` of `0` mean? `100`?

71. What configuration option must also be configured if the maximum network packet size is set higher than the default network packet size?

72. The `mydb` database was initially created with the log and data segments on the same single device. You have a separate device available for log use called `logdev` which is 100MB in size. You would like to create a 50MB log segment for your database on the `logdev` device. What steps would you take to accomplish this?

73. If a database is created with the log and data on the same device, what is the maximum size the transaction log can grow to?

74. You have four devices available to a database (`dev1`, `dev2`, `dev3`, `dev4`). You want to maximize performance by minimizing disk I/O contention within your database. Each device is 100MB in size and you will use all of each device for your database (300MB for data, 100MB for log). Your database primarily contains two high-use tables, `TableA` and `TableB`. You want to avoid I/O contention between them by placing each on a separate device. In addition, a large amount of update activity will be occurring on `TableA`, so you want to place its nonclustered index on columns `Fkey1` and `Fkey2` on a separate, relatively quiet device. List the commands and syntax you would use to set up your database and create these tables/indexes to meet these requirements.

75. What types of locks does SQL Server use during creation of a clustered index?

    A nonclustered index?

76. If four users are running the same stored procedure concurrently, how many copies of the stored procedure's query plan will be in procedure cache?

77. If you run `disk init` to create a database device on an operating-system file and the file already exists, what happens?

78. What is the result of running the `set transaction isolation level 3` command?

79. What command can be used to display permissions for an object? A user?

80. What command can be used to list all stored procedures which reference a specific table?

SQL SERVER OPERATIONS

1. What system procedure do you use to monitor the SQL Server? What information does it report?

2. What command do you use to start the Sybase Backup Server?

3. What is the maximum number of dump devices Backup Server can use for one database dump?

4. What directory is the SQL Server error log located in?

5. The master database has become corrupted, but fortunately you have a backup of the master database. What must you do before loading this backup?

6. You've restored the backup of the master database, but it does not contain the device you added and database you created on that device since the last dump of the master database. What commands do you need to issue to recover the device and database?

7. The data device for your database has failed, but the log device is still available. What command would you use to capture the log records available?

   What steps would you then take to restore the database?

   What would be the state of the database once the restore is complete?

8. The log device for your database has failed, but the data devices are still available. What operations can you perform on this database?

   To what point can you recover this database?

   What if the log device was mirrored?

9. In System 10 and later, the state of the database contained in the backup is at what point during the backup process?

10. How does SQL Server identify the local backup server?

    Information on the local backup server must be contained where?

    Information on remote backup servers must be set up where?

11. You have been hired to replace a DBA who left abruptly, leaving no notes. How do you identify the network names of your local and remote backup servers?

12. In System 10 and later, what commands/tools are available to monitor the size of the transaction log if the log is on a separate device?

13. You want to back up three databases, db1, db2, and db3, to a single tape on device tapedev1. You do not wish to have any other backups contained on this tape. What commands would you issue to perform this backup?

14. What command is used in SQL Server to abort a stranded or runaway process?

15. `print` statements inside a threshold procedure are displayed where?

16. You performed a full database dump of your database at midnight and transaction log dumps every four hours. At 9PM, you lose your database device. You have the full backup from midnight and all five regular transaction log dumps plus the final one dumped after the loss of the data device. During the restoration process, you discover that the tape containing the dump for 8AM has gone bad and cannot be read. To what point can you recover your database?

17. You perform full database dumps at midnight and noon and transaction log dumps every four hours in-between. At 5PM you lose your log device and it is not mirrored. When you try to restore the database, you discover that the tape containing the database dump from noon has gone bad and cannot be read. Assuming all your log dumps are okay, to what point can you recover this database?

18. If you wish to load a database dump into a new database, what must be true of the new database for the load to be successful?

19. If you are loading a database dump from one server to another server, what potential conflicts should you be aware of?

20. What command should you run on a regular basis to verify the integrity of the system tables within a database?

21. How do you verify that all pages within a database are correctly allocated?

22. How do you verify that all pages are correctly allocated for a table? For an index?

23. What command do you run to check that all index and data pages are correctly linked in a table?

    What command will run the same checks for all tables in a database?

24. What command do you need to use to drop a database if it is marked suspect and cannot be dropped with the `drop database` command?

25. What happens if the log fills up in a System 10 or later database if the log is not on a separate segment?

    If the log is on a separate segment from the data?

26. What commands can you issue to truncate the transaction log without writing it to a dump device?

27. What happens if a table fills up the segment it is defined on?

    What can you do to make more space available?

28. What information is contained in a normal RUN_*SERVERNAME* runserver file?

29. Where is the Backup Server error log located and what is the name of the file by default?

30. What type of information is contained in the SQL Server error log?

31. What stored procedure can you execute to display space usage within a database?

32. Where can you look to verify the last time the SQL Server was started?

33. Where can you look to determine the sort order and character set that a SQL Server is configured to use?

34. Where can you look to check for SQL Server startup error messages?

35. What command can you execute to determine the largest stored procedures which have been recently executed?

36. List four reasons that could cause the SQL Server not to start up.

37. List six common reasons why users may not be able to access a SQL Server which is up and running.

38. List three reasons why a user may not be able to access a database.

39. What commands would you normally execute to identify a cause why a user's SQL Server process appears to be hung?

40. What could be some possible causes for a query that used to take two minutes to run taking over 10 minutes to run?

41. What could cause the transaction log to still be full even though you just dumped the log and truncated it?

42. Your network is configured with a remote backup server called SYB_DUMPHOST. This backup server has access to two tape drives for performing backups called /dev/nrmt1 and /dev/nrmt2. List the proper syntax you would use to perform a multivolume dump of mydb to both tape drives.

43. What command can you use to define logical device names for your dump devices?

44. What command do you execute to get information on the dump devices defined to SQL Server?

45. The error log should be monitored for error messages of at least what severity level?

46. What utilities does Sybase provide to perform a logical database rebuild (e.g., moving a database from one platform to different platform)?

47. Errors of severity 10–16 are typically what type of error? Where are these errors displayed?

48. If dumping a database to an operating-system file on disk and the file already exists, what happens?

49. You've run sp_who and it indicates that process 6 is blocking other processes. What command can you run to determine what resources process 6 is holding that are blocking the other processes?

   If it indicates that the contention is on a specific page for a particular table, i.e., a "hot spot," what are some possible solutions to minimize the contention for this data page?

50. You cannot kill a process in SQL Server if it has what status?

51. What are some standard guidelines to minimize deadlock and locking contention problems for transactions?

52. If you've run out of room on a segment and need to increase its size by allocating space on another device to the database, what would be the steps/commands you would need to carry out to perform this task?

53. What permission do database users need to be able to create temporary tables in tempdb?

54. If a database backup to a single dump device spans multiple tapes, what stored procedure do you need to execute to instruct Backup Server that a new tape has been inserted?

55. If you attempt to load transaction log dumps out of order, what will happen?

56. In System 11, what stored procedure is used to create named data caches?

57. In System 11, how can you force the optimizer to use a particular index for a table when processing a query?

58. In System 11, when executing a query, how can you force the optimizer to use 16KB I/Os when performing physical reads? What condition must be met in order for 16KB I/Os to be performed?

59. What stored procedure is used to create buffer pools for large block I/O?

60. How do you associate an object with a named cache in System 11?

61. In System 11, how do you disassociate an object from a named cache? Disassociate all objects from a named cache?

62. What are the allowable buffer pool and prefetch I/O sizes in System 11?

63. In System 11, when is a newly defined named cache available? When do changes to a named cache buffer pool take effect?

64. How do you partition a table in System 11? What is the primary performance benefit of partitioning a table? What restrictions are there on partitioned tables?

65. In System 11, what must you do first before dropping a partitioned table?

66. How do you add standard user-defined error messages to a database?

67. Describe transaction isolation level 0. How can you run a query at this isolation level in System 11?

68. Describe the difference between the LRU and MRU buffer replacement strategies in System 11.

69. In System 11, what command must be executed after a database is loaded from a backup before the database can be accessed by database users?

70. In System 11, what command can you execute so operations on tables will not escalate to table-level locks until at least 500 page locks are acquired, rather than the default 200?

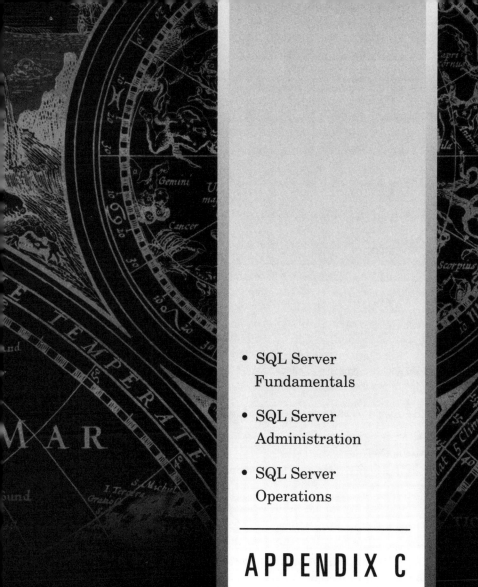

- SQL Server Fundamentals
- SQL Server Administration
- SQL Server Operations

APPENDIX C

Answers for the Sample CSP DBA Test

This appendix presents the answers for the CSP DBA Preparation Exam contained in Appendix B. For the sake of convenience in grading your test, the questions are repeated for you in this appendix.

SQL SERVER FUNDAMENTALS

Questions 1–9 are based upon the following table definition:

```
create table mytable (a int not null,
    b int default 10 null)
go
create rule b_rule as @bval  between  0 and 100
go
sp_bindrule b_rule, "mytable.b"
go
create view sample_view as select * from mytable
go
alter table mytable add c varchar(20) null
go
alter table mytable add constraint b_check
check (b between -10 and  10)
go
```

1. What value will be added to the table for column b by the following insert statement:

   ```
   insert mytable (a, b) values  (1, null)
   ```

   Answer: Null. Explicitly providing null overrides the default. The default will not be used.

2. If there were 50 rows already in the table when the default was bound to column b and 20 of the rows contained null for column b, what value will those rows contain for column b after the default is bound?

   Answer: Null. Defaults (and rules) only apply to future rows added to the table. Existing rows are unaffected.

3. If a file containing 20 rows is bulk copied into the table and 5 of the rows do not have values for column b, what value will those rows have for column b after the bcp has completed?

   Answer: 10. Defaults are applied during bcp load.

4. Will a file containing rows that have negative values for column b be added during a bulk copy load?

   Answer: Yes. Rules, triggers, and constraints are not applied during bulk copy loads.

5. What columns will a user see if he runs the following select statement:

   ```
   select * from sample_view
   ```

Answer: Columns a and b. Although the view executes a `select *`, which is all columns, the actual column list is resolved during view creation, not during execution. Column c did not exist when the view was created.

6. What values are allowed in column b for inserts/updates?

   Answer: Null and 0 to 10. The rule is checked first (between 0 and 100), then the constraint will be checked (-10 to 10). The valid range of values is the intersection of the two.

7. What methods can be used to enforce a business rule requiring a value in column b to be greater than a value in column a for an insert/update?

   Answer: A table-level check constraint or an insert/update trigger.

8. What would be the result of running the following commands:

   ```
   create default b_dflt as 10
   go
   sp_bindefault b_dflt, 'mytable.b'
   go
   ```

   Answer: This would cause an error, as column b already has a default bound to it and only one default can be bound to a column.

9. If the following command was run:

   ```
   alter table mytable replace b default -1
   ```

   what would happen during an `insert` if no value was supplied for column b?

   Answer: The `insert` would fail because SQL Server would apply the default and then check the constraint/rule on column b. The default value is incompatible with the constraint.

10. What is the role of a client in a client/server architecture?

    Answer: Submit requests, process/display results, handle user interface.

11. What is the role of the server in a client/server architecture?

    Answer: Respond to client requests, process data, and manage data.

12. What system table contains information about objects within a database such as tables, defaults, triggers, etc.?

    Answer: The `sysobjects` table.

13. How many pages are allocated when a table is created?

    Answer: An extent, which is 8 pages.

14. How is a clustered index different from a non-clustered index?

    Answer: Clustered indexes dictate the physical order of data, i.e., maintain the data in sorted order. The leaf level of the index is the data itself. A non-clustered index has rows in the leaf level of the index containing a pointer for every data row in the table.

C

15. Can a clustered index be placed on a separate device than a table?

    Answer: No, because the leaf row of the clustered index is the table itself, they cannot be separated from one another.

16. Can a column be deleted from a table?

    Answer: No. (Not officially, although there is an undocumented System 10 feature: `alter table t1 drop c1` drops column `c1` from table `t1`. The implementation is interesting: the column is undefined, but all the data remains untouched until the rows are modified. As each row is modified, the column is nullified.)

17. What command allows you to add columns to a table?

    Answer: `alter table`

    What is the `null` property of columns added to a table using this command?

    Answer: They must be declared as `null` since no value can be provided for existing rows in the table.

18. What is the result of creating a column on a table with the `identity` property?

    Answer: During inserts, the value for the `identity` column is not supplied. SQL Server will automatically insert the next available sequential number into the `identity` column.

    How many columns with the `identity` property can be created in a table?

    Answer: One.

    What system datatype must be used for `identity` columns?

    Answer: `Numeric`, with a definition of `(N,0)`, where N is the number of digits.

19. How are `identity` columns updated and by whom?

    Answer: `identity` columns cannot be updated.

20. What global variable can be queried to determine the last identity value inserted into a table?

    Answer: `@@identity`

21. Explain the difference between `char` and `varchar` datatypes.

    Answer: `char` is a fixed-length datatype; `varchar` is a variable-length datatype. A `char` column that allows nulls is stored like `varchar` because it is variable length—it is either no length or the declared length.

    How is the string "ABC" stored differently in a `char(10) not null` column from a `varchar(10) not null` column?

    Answer: As a `char(10)`, the column would be padded with seven spaces so that it is 10 bytes in length. The `varchar(10)` would store just the three bytes plus an additional byte of overhead to store the actual column width.

22. Define what is meant by `null`.

    Answer: The absence of a value, and unknown value. It is not the same as a zero (0) or an empty string (" "), as these are actual values.

    How are `null` values handled by aggregate functions?

    Answer: Nulls are not considered in the calculation of aggregates.

23. What SQL Server function can be used to substitute a value for `null` in a query?

    Answer: `isnull` (`expression`, `value`)

24. What is the restriction on updating base tables through a view, if the view is defined on multiple tables?

    Answer: The columns being updated must exist in only one of the base tables.

25. What is the restriction on inserting data into a base table through a view if the view only contains a subset of the columns in the base table?

    Answer: The columns not part of the view must allow `null` or have a default bound to them.

26. What is the restriction on deleting rows through a multi-table view?

    Answer: Deletes are not allowed on multi-table views.

27. What is the maximum number of triggers that can be created on a table?

    Answer: 3—up to one trigger each for `insert`, `update`, and `delete`. (NOTE: There is a column called `seltrig` in `sysobjects`, but it is not currently used.)

28. If an `update` on `table_a` fires a trigger which updates `table_b`, and `table_b` has an update trigger defined on it, will the trigger on `table_b` be executed?

    Answer: Yes, in the default server configuration. If the `nested triggers` configuration value is set to 0, the trigger on `table_b` would not fire.

29. If an `update` of a row in `table_a` fires a trigger which updates another row in `table_a`, will the trigger on `table_a` execute again?

    Answer: No, by default. If nesting is allowed and `set self_recursion on` has been executed, the trigger would fire.

30. What are the names of the tables that are normally accessible from within a trigger when a trigger is executed?

    Answer: `inserted` and `deleted`

    What structure do they have?

    Answer: The exact structure of the table the trigger is created on.

    Where are these tables located?

Answer: In memory—they are actually a special view of the record(s) in the transaction log for the modification statement which caused the trigger to fire.

31. What is the statement that can be used inside a trigger to check whether a specific column has been modified by the `insert` or `update` statement which caused the trigger to fire?

    Answer: `if update(column_name)`

32. An insert trigger is created on a table that validates whether one of its column values exists in another table before allowing the insert to succeed. A file is bulk copied into the table that contains invalid values for that column. Will the rows be inserted by the bulk copy?

    Answer: Yes. `bcp` bypasses triggers, rules, and constraints (but not defaults).

33. If a table is created with a `unique` constraint on a column, can that column allow null values?

    Answer: Yes, but only one row may contain a null value for that column.

    What if the column is created with a `primary key` constraint?

    Answer: No. The `primary key` constraint requires the column to be declared as `not null`.

34. If a view is created on table `mytable` and that table is renamed to `newtable`, will the view still work?

    Answer: Yes. During creation of the view, SQL Server resolves an object's name to its object ID. The rename changes only the name of the table. The view can still reference the table through the table's ID.

35. If a column is added to a table after a view has been defined on the table, what must be done to make the column accessible through the view?

    Answer: Drop and recreate the view.

36. Under which of the following circumstances will a stored procedure automatically be recompiled?

    a. Creating an index on a table referenced in the stored procedure

    b. Dropping an index on a table referenced in the stored procedure that is being used to satisfy the query

    c. Renaming a table referenced in the stored procedure

    d. Dropping and recreating, with the same name, a table referenced in a stored procedure

    Answer: b and d.

37. What three methods can be used to force a stored procedure to recompile a new query plan?

Answer:

```
sp_recompile table_referenced_in_proc
create procedure procname … with recompile
exec procname with recompile
```

38. What system table contains information on system and user-defined datatypes?

Answer: `systypes`

39. Describe how the `@@trancount` global variable is incremented and decremented.

Answer: Each `begin tran [tran_name]` increments `@@trancount` by `1`, `commit tran` decrements `@@trancount` by `1`, `rollback tran` rolls the transaction back and returns the value of `@@trancount` to `0`.

40. What type of lock is held on a page during a `select`?

Answer: A shared lock.

41. What type of lock is held on a page during an `insert`?

Answer: An exclusive lock.

42. By default, how many page locks must be accessed by a single data modification statement before it is upgraded to a table lock? How can you change this value in System 11?

Answer: 200. System 11 allows changing the default lock promotion threshold points for the SQL Server with `sp_configure`, or at the server, database, or table level with `sp_setpglogpromote`.

43. What global variable contains the number of rows affected by your last executed SQL statement? Which SQL statements affect that variable?

Answer: `@@rowcount`; all SQL statements except `declare` change the value of `@@rowcount` (many change its value to zero).

44. What is the difference between server cursors and language cursors?

Answer: A server cursor is declared and processed in a stored procedure. A language cursor is declared and executed using SQL, but not Open Client calls.

45. What is the proper sequence of statements to use and process a cursor?

Answer:

```
declare cursor_name cursor
open cursor_name
fetch cursor_name …
close cursor_name
deallocate cursor cursor_name
```

46. What statement is used to delete the currently fetched row in an updatable cursor?

Answer: `delete tablename where current of cursor_name`

47. What type of lock does an updatable cursor obtain by default as it is fetching rows? A read-only cursor?

Answer: An updatable cursor uses update locks; a read-only cursor uses shared locks.

48. What is the difference between the following two `select` statements?

```
select title, type, price from titles
    order by type
    compute avg(price) by type

select title, type, price from titles
    order by type
    compute avg(price)
```

Answer: The first `select` statement will report the average price for each `type` after listing its detail rows (subtotals); the second statement returns all detail rows followed by the average price for all non-null `prices` (grand total).

49. Assume the following four users have each executed the following set of statements in different databases (assume all users are running in unchained mode):

```
User 1: begin tran
        delete mytab
        commit tran
        go

User 2: begin tran
        delete mytab
        checkpoint
        go

User 3: begin tran
        delete mytab
        commit tran
        go
        checkpoint
        go

User 4: begin tran
        delete mytab
        go

User 5: delete mytab
        go
```

If the SQL Server were to crash at this point, which of these transactions would be rolled back during recovery? Rolled forward? No recovery required?

Answer: Assuming an internal checkpoint was not activated by the server immediately prior to the crash,

Rolled back: User2—Data changes were checkpointed, but not commited.

Rolled forward: User1, User5—these transactions have been commited, but not checkpointed.

The remaining transactions require no recovery because they were either commited and checkpointed prior to server crash, or if not commited, were also not checkpointed. A `commit` writes the log records; a `checkpoint` writes both log records and data changes. If log records are written to disk, but not the data changes, a roll forward needs to be done. If the data changes are written to disk, but no commit record for the transaction, those data changes need to be rolled back.

50. A user executes the following set of statements:
```
create table sample_tab (a int)
go
begin tran mytran
insert sample_tab (a) values (1)
save tran mysavept
insert sample_tab (a) values (2)
rollback tran mysavept
insert sample_tab (a) values (3)
commit tran
```
What rows will be displayed by a `select * from sample_tab` statement?

Answer:
```
a
--
1
3
```

51. What global variable can be checked to determine the current status of a transaction?

Answer: `@@transtate`

52. Describe a deadlock scenario.

Answer: User 1 locks page A, User 2 locks page B. User 1 requests page B (process will be blocked waiting for the lock on page B to be released). If User 2 requests page A, a deadlock has occurred.

What SQL statement is notorious for causing deadlock situations?

Answer: `select ... holdlock`

What steps can be taken to avoid deadlocks?

Answer: Accessing tables in the same order in transaction, decreasing the duration of transactions, spreading data across data pages, avoiding use of `holdlock`.

53. What is the definition of a transaction?

Answer: A logical unit of work.

54. Describe the differences between chained transaction mode and unchained transaction mode. When does a transaction begin/end in chained mode? unchained mode?

Answer: In chained mode, an implicit `begin tran` statement is issued before the first SQL statement (`insert`, `update`, `delete`, or `select`, `open`,`fetch`). An explicit `commit transaction` must be specified. No data modifications are implicity committed. In unchained, explicit `begin tran` and `commit tran` statements are required to define a multi-statement transaction. Single statement transactions (i.e., an `update` not within a `begin tran`/`commit tran` pair) are implicitly commited.

55. What global variable can be queried to determine whether you are running in chained or unchained transaction mode?

Answer: `@@tranchained`

56. What will be displayed by the following SQL statements

    a. If the average price after update is greater than $50

    b. If the average price after update is less than $50

```
begin tran mytran
print "Updating titles"
update titles set price = price * $1.25
if (select avg(price) from titles) > $50
    print "Avg price exceeds $50"
    rollback tran mytran
    print "Update rolled back"
    return
commit tran mytran
print "Update successful"
go
```

Answer:

a.

```
Updating titles
Avg price exceeds $50
Update rolled back
```

b.

```
Updating titles
Update rolled back"
```

What changes would you recommend for this code?

Answer: Add a `begin` after the `if` statement, and an `end` after the `return` statement. As written, this code will never reach the `commit` statement.

57. How are local variables defined? How are global variables defined?

Answer: Local variables are defined using the `declare` *variable_name* *datatype* command. Global variables are defined by the system.

58. How are values assigned to local variables?

    Answer: With the `select` statement (e.g., `select @varname = value`).

59. How are values assigned to global variables?

    Answer: Values for global variables are set by the SQL Server only, based upon server configuration or current session status. Users cannot explicitly set global variable values.

60. What is the duration of local variables?

    Answer: Local variables exist for the duration of a stored procedure or for the duration of a batch.

61. What are the two ways to change the displayed column headings for a `select` statement?

    Answer:
    ```
    select "HEADING"=col_name …
    select col_name HEADING …
    ```

62. What statement can be used to create a table in SQL Server other than the `create table` statement?

    Answer: `select into`

63. What will be the effect of the following statement:
    ```
    select * into newtitles from titles where 1 = 2
    ```

    Answer: A new table will be created with the same structure as `titles`, with no rows copied in.

64. What data values would the following `where` clause match:
    ```
    where name like "%_[Cc]omputer"
    ```

    Answer: Any string that ends in the word "Computer" or "computer", with at least one character before the word.

65. What function is used to display the value of a datetime column in the format `dd/mm/yyyy`?

    Answer: The `convert` function, specifying the appropriate style parameter.

66. What requirements must be met before a table can be referenced by a foreign key reference constraint?

    Answer: The table being referenced must have a primary key constraint or a unique index defined on the column(s) being referenced.

Consider the following table definition for questions 67 and 68:

```
create table titles
    (title_id char(6) not null,
     title varchar(60) not null,
     pub_id char(4) not null
     references publishers(pub_id)
     total_sales int null,
     pubdate)
```

67. What happens if you attempt to delete a row from `publishers` where there is an existing `title(s)` in the `titles` table for that `pub_id`?

    Answer: The `delete` will fail because of the foreign key constraint on the `pub_id` column in the `titles` table, but processing will continue. You must check `@@error` and roll back manually if the statement is part of a multi-statement transaction.

    What if you attempt to update a `pub_id` for a publisher that has related rows in the `titles` table?

    Answer: The update will fail because of the foreign key constraint.

    What if you attempt to insert a new publisher into the `publishers` table?

    Answer: The row is inserted. Foreign key constraints do not affect primary key inserts.

68. What happens if you attempt to insert a row into `titles`?

    Answer: It will check the `pub_id` value to see if it exists in the `publishers` table. If not, the insert fails.

    Update a `pub_id` in `titles`?

    Answer: It checks to see if the new `pub_id` value is in the `publishers` table. If not, the update fails.

    Delete a row from `titles`?

    Answer: The row is deleted. Foreign key constraints do not affect foreign key deletes.

69. Describe the difference between a table-level constraint and a column-level constraint.

    Answer: A constraint is considered table level if it is defined after the column definitions in the `create table` statement or is defined using `alter table`.

    When must you define a constraint as a table-level constraint?

    Answer: When the constraint references two or more columns in that table.

70. What value will be displayed for `@var` when the following statements are executed:

```
create proc myproc (@parm1 int output)
as
```

```
select @parm1 = @parm1 + 50
go
declare @var int
select @var = 50
exec myproc @var output
select @var
go
```

Answer: 100.

71. What data values can be returned by the `return` statement from within a stored procedure?

    Answer: Any integer value.

    What data values are reserved for use by Sybase?

    Answer: -1 through -99.

72. What statement is used to generate system-like error messages?

    Answer: `raiserror`.

    What is the minimum error number that can be used?

    Answer: 20001.

73. If a rule is bound to a user-defined datatype, what happens to any existing columns which are defined with that user-defined datatype?

    Answer: The rule will also be bound to those columns.

    What if those columns already had a rule bound explicitly to the column?

    Answer: An explicit bind to a column overrides a bind to a datatype. The bind to the datatype would have no effect on those columns.

74. If a column already has a rule bound to it, and you attempt to bind another rule to that column, what happens?

    Answer: The new rule will replace the old one (the existing rule does not have to be unbound first).

75. How are database objects fully qualified?

    Answer: `dbname.username.objectname`

76. What is the purpose of the `syskeys` table?

    Answer: To document, within the database, the primary, foreign, and common key relationships between tables. `syskeys` contains a row for every primary, foreign, or common key in a database if this information is added manually using `sp_primarykey`, `sp_foreignkey`, or `sp_commonkey`.

77. What command can you execute to view the total logical and physical I/O for a query? What is logical I/O?

    Answer: `set statistics io on`. Logical I/O are page reads from data cache rather than physical reads from disk.

78. What command can you execute to view the query plan chosen by the SQL Server to execute a query?

    Answer: `set showplan on`

    What is the component of SQL Server which determines the best query plan?

    Answer: The SQL Server query optimizer.

79. What command do you need to execute periodically to keep the distribution pages for the indexes on a table up to date?

    Answer: `update statistics`

    What information is contained on a distribution page?

    Answer: Distribution steps representing a histogram of the data based on the first index key column, and the index density (i.e., the percentage of duplicate values in the index).

80. What is the size of a data page in SQL Server?

    Answer: 2KB (4KB for Stratus)

    How much of this space is available for data? If a row is 100 bytes wide, including overhead, how many rows will fit on a single data page?

    Answer: 1962 bytes. 19 rows.

81. What is the maximum number of columns in a row?

    Answer: 250.

    What is the maximum row width?

    Answer: 1962 bytes—a single row cannot exceed the maximum available space on a data page.

82. If a table contains no clustered index, where are new rows added?

    Answer: At the end of the table.

83. Describe how a page split occurs when adding rows to a table with a clustered index.

    Answer: If a new row must be added to the middle of the page and the page cannot accommodate the row, the server will allocate an additional page and place approximately equal amounts of data on each page.

    When is an overflow page created instead?

    Answer: If the index value of a row being inserted into a table with a clustered index which allows duplicate values matches the index value of the last row on the page, and the addition of that row cannot fit on that page, an overflow page will be created.

84. What is the difference between a deferred update and a direct update?

Answer: A direct update modifies the rows in the table itself. A deferred update moves the rows to be modified into the transaction log and modifies them there and reinserts them back into the table. Deferred updates are performed when a data modification can have a cascading effect (e.g., update mytab set col1 = col1 + 1 and mytab has a unique index on col1, or insert into mytab select * from mytab).

What is the difference between a direct update in place and a direct update not in place?

Answer: A direct update not in place requires two log records to perform the update, a delete of the old row and a reinsert of the new row into the table. With a direct update in place, the row is modified right in place, requiring only a single (MODIFY) log record. Direct updates in place require that no variable-length or nullable columns be modified and that the column being modified is not a clustered-index column or a column of an index used to satisfy the query, and that the optimizer can determine the number of records to be modified at query compile time. System 11 allows updates in place on variable-length columns if the row width remains the same.

85. What information is contained in the leaf rows of a nonclustered index? In the leaf and non-leaf rows of a clustered index?

    Answer: The leaf level of a nonclustered index contains a page pointer and row number for each row in the table. The non-leaf rows are page pointers to the index pages at the next level down and the index data value for the first row on that page.

    Answer: The leaf level of a clustered index is the data page itself, so the leaf rows are data rows. The non-leaf rows are page pointers to the data or index pages at the next level down and the index data value for the first row on that page.

86. Describe what is meant by index covering.

    Answer: Index covering occurs when all the columns referenced by a query (columns in the select list and the where clause) can be found in the nonclustered index itself. SQL Server can satisfy this query at the nonclustered index leaf level without having to access the data page itself.

87. How is text and image data stored within a SQL Server database?

    Answer: For a row that contains text or image data, the value placed in that column is actually a pointer to a linked list of pages containing the text or image data.

88. Which of the following where clauses are considered optimizable Search Arguments (SARGs) by SQL Server:

C

CSP DBA TEST ANSWERS

a. `where age > 21`

b. `where "1/2/94" > pubdate`

c. `where name not like "Sm%"`

d. `where name like "%son"`

e. `where substring(name, 1, 1) = "P"`

f. `where t.pub_id = p.pub_id`

g. `where dept = 2 or dept = 3`

h. `where pub_id in ("1234", "2345", "3456")`

i. `where price > $10.0 and price < $15.0`

j. `where salary between 10000 and 30000`

k. `where bonus > salary * .5`

l. `where salary/2 > 10000`

m. `where 100 between lo and hi`

n. `where dept != 20`

Answer: a, b, i, j, and m are optimizable SARGs. f is a join, e and l contain operations on a column, k compares against another column instead of a constant, d doesn't contain a constant as the first character in the `like` string, g and h are OR clauses, and c and n contain "not equal" comparisons.

If not an optimizable SARG, which of these can be turned into an optimizable SARG?

Answer:

e. `where name like "P%"`

l. `where salary > 20000`

89. Describe the OR Strategy used by SQL Server for resolving queries with OR clauses.

    Answer: If an OR clause is used in a query, and SQL Server can satisfy both sides of the OR clause with an index (e.g., `where title_id = "BU2075" or pub_id = "9999"`, and the table has indexes on both `title_id` and `pub_id`), SQL Server will run two separate `select` statements internally, putting the row IDs of the matching rows into a work table in `tempdb` (a "dynamic" index). It will then remove any duplicate row IDs and use the row IDs to retrieve the actual data rows from the table itself. This method will be used only if its estimated cost is less than that of a full table scan to resolve the OR clause.

90. A primary key constraint by default will create what type of index? A unique key constraint by default will create what type of default? A foreign key constraint?

Answer: A primary key constraint creates a unique, clustered index by default. A unique key constraint creates a unique, nonclustered index by default. Foreign key constraints do not create indexes.

SQL Server Administration

1. What command do you use to configure the server?

   Answer: `sp_configure`. System 11 also allows direct modification of the configuration file, now located in the Sybase home directory by default.

2. What command do you use to start SQL Server in a UNIX environment?

   Answer: `startserver -f RUN_SERVERNAME`

3. How are remote procedures invoked?

   Answer: By fully qualifying the procedure name to include the server name. The format is *servername.dbname.owner.procedure_name*.

4. What needs to be set up/configured on the local server to implement remote procedure calls?

   Answer: Remote access must be turned on and the local and remote server names must be added to the `sysservers` table (using `sp_addserver`) and the remote server connection information must be added to the local server's `interfaces` file.

   What needs to be set up on the remote server?

   Answer: Remote access must be turned on, the remote server and the server issuing the remote procedure call must be added to the `sysservers` table (`sp_addserver`), connection information for the server issuing the remote procedure call must be added to the interfaces file, and remote logins must be set up.

5. What command do you use to shut down the server gracefully? Unconditionally?

   Answer: `shutdown`; `shutdown with nowait`

   What steps does the SQL Server perform during a graceful shutdown?

   Answer: It disables all non-SA logins, waits for currently executing SQL statements to finish, checkpoints each database, then ends the SQL Server executable.

6. What `buildmaster` option do you use to recreate the master database?

   Answer: `-m`

   What `buildmaster` option do you use to recreate the model database?

   Answer: `-x`

7. What `buildmaster` option allows you to report on the system configuration?

   Answer: `-yall`

8. What utility is used to install SQL Server on most platforms?

   Answer: `sybinit`

9. What `isql` scripts need to be run after a manual rebuild of the master device?

   Answer: `installmaster, installmodel`

10. Describe how the `model` database is used by SQL Server.

    Answer: The contents of the `model` database are copied into any new database created in the server.

11. Where are system stored procedures located in System 10 and later?

    Answer: The `sybsystemprocs` database.

12. Which stored procedure reports on current connections to the SQL Server?

    Answer: `sp_who`

13. What command is used to allocate disk space to the SQL Server?

    Answer: `disk init`

14. What device can be mirrored to ensure non-stop SQL Server operation?

    Answer: The `master` device. To ensure non-stop operation of the entire SQL Server, all devices containing databases should be mirrored. (First mirror the `master` device, then any log devices, then data devices.)

15. Name the three segments created by SQL Server during a `create database` statement.

    Answer: `default, system, logsegment`

16. What stored procedure is executed when the last-chance threshold is reached?

    Answer: `sp_thresholdaction`

    Where is this stored procedure located?

    Answer: It can be located in the local database; however, the normal placement is in the `sybsystemprocs` database. It must be created by the `dbo` or a SQL Server System Administrator—Sybase does not provide a default `sp_thresholdaction` stored procedure.

17. Name the two types of data devices that can be initialized by SQL Server.

    Answer: raw and file.

18. What command provides information on the current roles you have been assigned in SQL Server?

    Answer: `sp_displaylogin`

19. What role must you have to add logins to the SQL Server?

    Answer: sso_role

20. What commands are used to define security on objects in a database?

    Answer: grant and revoke

21. Explain the relationship between the sysusers and syslogins tables.

    Answer: The syslogins table is located in the master database and contains all login names and suids (server user ID). The sysusers table is located in all databases and maps a database user ID to a server login ID (uid to suid).

22. What command do you use to grant the sso_role role to User1?

    Answer: sp_role "grant", sso_role, User1

23. If you wanted all future databases to contain a guest account and have the select into/bulk copy option turned on, what would be the easiest way to do this?

    Answer: Perform these activities in the model database.

24. List the steps and commands you would need to take to allocate a new device to a database, create a user-defined segment on the device, and limit that device to only objects explicitly created/placed on that segment (assume the log is on its own device).

    Answer:
    ```
    use master
    go
    alter database mydb on newdevice = 5
    go
    use mydb
    go
    sp_addsegment myseg, mydb, newdevice
    go
    sp_dropsegment system, mydb, newdevice
    go
    sp_dropsegment "default", mydb, newdevice
    go
    ```

25. How do you create a non-clustered index on a device separate from the table?

    Answer: Add on *segment_name* at the end of the create index statement.

26. What is an easy method, without having to drop and recreate the table, to move a table to a different segment?

    Answer: Drop the clustered index (if it exists). Re-create the clustered index on the desired segment by specifying on *segment_name* in the create index statement.

27. If a server is expected to have three devices (in addition to the master device), and all four devices are to be mirrored, what is the minimum number of devices the server needs to be configured for?

Answer: Four. Mirrored devices are not added with `disk init`, and therefore do not need to be counted.

28. A SQL server is expected to have 100 total users. There is expected to be 30 concurrent users at any one time running an Open-Client application which opens two connections to the SQL Server. In addition, two DBAs will be monitoring the system with an application which requires one SQL Server connection, and an on-line batch process will be running 24 hours a day (possible during normal activity) which requires three user connections. Backups are performed via Backup Server, and there are three devices defined for this SQL Server, including the master device. What is the recommended minimum number of `user connections` this SQL Server should be configured for?

Answer:

   60 for 30 users times 2 connections
 + 2 for 2 DBAs times 1 connection
 + 3 for 1 batch process times 3 connections
 + 1 for each master network listener
 + 1 for Backup Server
 = 67 as a minimum number; generally round up to 70 as a fudge factor. Devices do not need to be counted in the user connection configuration.

29. Consider the following fragments of the `sysusages`, `syssegments`, `sysdevices`, and `sysdatabases` tables for the `mydb` database:

```
mydb..sysegments
     segment name         status
     ------- ----------- ------
          0 system           0
          1 default          1
          2 logsegment       0
          3 Seg1             0


sysusages
     dbid    segmap  lstart         size          vstart      ...
     ------- ------- ------------- ------------- ----------- ...
          6       3             0          2048  51556616 ...
          6       4          2048          1024  77714249 ...
          6      10          3072           512      9044 ...


sysdevices
     low         high       ... name            ...
     ----------- ---------- ... --------------- ...
     5156616     5166856    ... data_dev1       ...
     7711177     7716296    ... log_dev1        ...
     9044        19283      ... data_dev2       ...


sysdatabases
     name             dbid    ...
     ---------------- -----   ...
     master              0    ...
```

```
model            1  ...
tempdb           2  ...
sybsystemprocs   3  ...
mydb             6  ...
```

What were the commands used to create `mydb`?

Answer: `mydb` has three fragments, as there are three rows in `sysusages` for `mydb` (dbid = 5). A segmap in `sysusages` of 3 indicates the `system` and `default` segments on that device, a segmap of 4 indicates the `logsegment` is on that device. The `size` in `sysusages` is in pages. The number of pages/512 = the number of megabytes for each device fragment. The order of the rows in `sysusages` indicates the order the devices were allocated to the database. Therefore, the `mydb` database was created as:

```
create database mydb on data_dev1 = 4
   log on log_dev1 = 2
go
alter database mydb on data_dev2 = 1
go
```

30. In the previous question, what segments are mapped to the data_dev2 device?

    Answer: `Seg1` and `default`. `segmap` is a bitmap field mapped as follows:

bit	bitmap value	segment ID
1	1	0
2	2	1
3	4	2
4	8	3
5	16	4
...		

    Therefore, a bitmap value of 10 indicates bits 2 and 4, which map to segment IDs 1 and 3, which in this case are the segments `default` and `Seg1`.

31. What role must you have to grant the `OPER` role?

    Answer: `sso_role`

32. What command is used to grant roles?

    Answer: `sp_role`

33. What command is used in System 10 and later to change a user's default database?

    Answer: `sp_modifylogin` *login_name*, `defdb`, *new_default_database*

34. What permissions will the users `Mary` and `Fred` have on the `employee` table after the following commands are executed:

```
grant all on employee to public
revoke insert, update, delete on employee from Mary, Fred
revoke select on employee (salary) from public
```

Answer: `select` permission on all columns except `salary`.

35. What steps/commands must be executed to grant `user1` `create database` permission? Who can grant `create database` permission?

    Answer: The following must be executed by a login with the `sa_role`:

    ```
    use master
    go
    grant create database to user1
    go
    ```

36. Describe the outcome of the following command:

    ```
    grant select on accounts to Fred with grant option
    ```

    Answer: `Fred` would be able to `select` from all columns of the `accounts` table and could also grant that permission to other database users.

37. Based upon the previous question, what command would you need to issue if you wanted to remove `select` permission on the `accounts` table from `Fred` and all users `Fred` granted permissions to?

    Answer: `revoke select on accounts from Fred`

    SQL Server, by default, will cascade the `revoke` to any users Fred granted `select` on accounts to. If you just wanted to revoke Fred's ability to grant `select` permission on `accounts`, but not his `select` permission, issue the following statement:

    ```
    revoke grant option for select on account from Fred cascade
    ```

    In this case, the `cascade` option is required to revoke `select` from any users `Fred` may have granted `select` permission on `accounts` to.

38. If a user owns objects in a database, what must be done if you wish to drop the user's login from the SQL Server?

    Answer: Any object created in a database by the user associated with the login must be dropped, the user must be dropped from the database, and then the login can be dropped.

    How can you prevent a user from logging into SQL Server without dropping the user's login?

    Answer: `sp_locklogin` *login_name*, `"lock"`

39. Who can run the `sp_modifylogin` procedure?

    Answer: Any login can execute `sp_modifylogin` to modify their own login information. Only a login with the `sa_role` can modify login information for other logins.

40. Which SQL Server user(s) can perform database dumps and loads?

    Answer: The `dbo` or any login with the `sa_role` or `oper_role`.

41. Which SQL Server user(s) can perform DBCC commands in a database?

    Answer: The `dbo` or any login with the `sa_role`.

42. What command do you execute to set SQL Server passwords to expire 30 days after the last time they were modified?

    Answer: `sp_configure "password expiration interval", 30`

    Who can execute this command?

    Answer: Any user with the `sso_role`.

    What happens when a user's password expires?

    Answer: The user will be allowed to log in to SQL Server, but the only command they will be able to execute is the `sp_password` stored procedure to change their password.

43. You want to set up mirroring of the `Device1` device on `/dev/rdsk2`. What is the syntax of the command you need to execute to implement this setup?

    Answer: `disk mirror name = "Device1", mirror = "/dev/rdsk2"`

    What must be true of `/dev/rdsk2` for this to be successful?

    Answer: It must be owned by the `sybase` user account and be at least as large as `Device1`.

    How can you mirror the `master` device on `/dev/rdsk3`?

    Answer: Add `-r /dev/rdsk3` to the `dataserver` command in the RUNSERVER file (UNIX).

44. What command do you use to start SQL Server in single user mode?

    Answer: Provide the `-m` option to the `dataserver` command (normally placed in a RUNSERVER file) or to the `startserver` command.

45. Which system table contains the current SQL Server configuration? Which system table contains configuration values the SQL Server will use upon the next SQL Server restart?

    Answer: `syscurconfigs` contains the current system configuration; `sysconfigures` contains the config values the SQL Server will use upon the next SQL Server restart. In System 11, the configuration values used for the next SQL Server restart can also be viewed by examining the contents of the SQL Server configuration file.

46. Name four configuration variables which require a SQL Server restart to take effect.

    Answer: `devices, locks, memory, user connections, open databases, open objects, default network packet size, additional netmem, recovery flags, extent io` buffers, audit queue size—essentially, all the configuration options which require memory structures to be allocated or affect the memory configuration.

Why is a SQL Server restart required?

Answer: SQL Server only allocates and configures memory structures upon startup.

47. What system table is used to map multiple logins to a single user ID within a database?

Answer: sysalternates

What command is used to add entries to this table?

Answer: sp_addalias

48. Examine the following object ownership chain:

    a. ProcA (owned by joe)

    b. Executes ProcB (owned by mary)

    c. which inserts data into ViewA (owned by mary)

    d. ViewA is defined on TableA (owned by joe)

    e. TableA has an insert trigger defined on it which updates TableC (owned by mary)

Assuming all object creators have the necessary access to all objects in the database, what permissions must be granted for user Fred to successfully execute ProcA?

Answer: The server will check permissions whenever there is a change in the ownership chain. Therefore:

    a. joe must grant execute permission to fred on ProcA and

    b. mary must grant execute permission to fred on ProcB and

    c. joe must grant insert permission on TableA to fred and

    d. mary must grant update permission on TableC to fred (access to tables within triggers is based upon the current user context).

49. You are managing a SQL Server which contains two databases. Each database is on a separate physical device and has its log on a separate physical device. DatabaseA is used for an OLTP application which updates over 10,000 records per day. DatabaseB is used for running management reports and is updated twice a month. You only have two devices available to use for mirroring. If you can only mirror two devices, in order to maximize system availability and minimize data loss, which two devices would you recommend mirroring?

Answer: It is usually recommended that the `master` database be mirrored first, and then the most active log devices, in this case the log device for `DatabaseA`.

50. Identify in which database(s) each of the following system tables appears:

    syssegments
    sysroles
    sysprocesses
    sysmessages
    sysalternates
    sysobjects
    sysprocedures
    sysdevices
    sysservers
    syslogs
    syscomments
    sysusers
    syslogins
    syslocks
    sysusages
    sysusermessages
    sysaudits

    Answer: `master` only: `sysroles, sysprocesses, sysdevices, sysservers, syslocks, sysusages`

    `sybsecurity` only: `sysaudits`

    All other system tables are in all databases.

51. What command(s) do you use to install the auditing system in SQL Server?

    Answer: Auditing is installed via `sybinit`. It is enabled by running:

    `sp_auditoption "enable auditing", "on"`

52. How can you verify if auditing has been installed on a SQL Server?

    Answer: Check to see if the `sybsecurity` database exists and whether an audit process is running (via `sp_who`).

53. What command do you use to determine if auditing is enabled?

    Answer: Execute `sp_auditoption` or

    `sp_auditoption "enable auditing"`

    Check to see if it reports "on" or "off".

54. What happens to audited processes if the audit queue fills up?

    Answer: A process will wait until space is available in the queue.

How do you increase the size of the audit queue?

Answer: `sp_configure "audit queue size", #_of_records`

55. What permissions and password does the `sa` login have after SQL Server installation?

    Answer: `sa` has the `sa_role` and `sso_role`. Password is `null` upon installation.

56. Describe how a system stored procedure is different from a user-defined stored procedure.

    Answer: A system stored procedure is prefixed with `sp_` and is placed in `sybsystemprocs`. Upon execution of a procedure with this prefix, SQL Server will first look for the procedure in the database you are currently in, then `sybsystemprocs`. The procedure can be accessed from any database in your server. (Do not forget to grant `execute` permission to `public`.)

57. If a login has been created in SQL Server without specifying a default database, what database will the user be in after a successful login to SQL Server?

    Answer: `master`

58. What will happen if a default database is specified, but the user is not a valid user in that database?

    Answer: A message is displayed indicating the login is not a valid user in that database, and the user is placed in the `master` database as `guest`.

59. Identify which role or special user can perform the following tasks:

    a. Install SQL Server

    b. Drop database users

    c. Grant/revoke access to an object

    d. Reset passwords

    e. Add dump devices

    f. Manage the audit system

    g. Grant/revoke command permissions

    h. Modify login information (default database, full name, default language)

    i. Set server configuration options

    j. Set database options

    Answer:

    a. Install SQL Server—the `sybase` user in the operating system

    b. Drop database users—the `dbo` or login with `sa_role`

    c. Grant/revoke access to an object—object owner only

d. Reset passwords—any login can change their own password; only a login with sso_role can change any login's password

e. Add dump devices—any login with the sa_role

f. Manage the audit system—any login with the sso_role

g. Grant/revoke command permissions—dbo or any login with sa_role

h. Modify login information (e.g., default database, full name, default language)—any login can modify their own login information; only a login with the sa_role can modify the login information of other logins.

i. Set server configuration options—sa_role

j. Set database options—sa_role or dbo

60. What are the steps SQL Server performs to verify user access to a database?

Answer:

a. Checks to see if the login is mapped to a valid database user ID (syslogins.suid = sysusers.suid)

b. Checks to see if the login is aliased to a valid user ID in the database (syslogins.suid = sysalternates.suid)

c. Checks to see if a guest user has been added to the database

61. How do you create a group within a database?

Answer: sp_addgroup

What two ways can you add a user to a group in a database?

Answer:

```
sp_adduser user_name, name_in_db, group_name
sp_changegroup group_name, name_in_db
```

62. What information is returned by the system function suser_id("fred")? user_name(10)? db_id()?

Answer: suser_id("fred") returns fred's system user ID from the syslogins table.

user_name(10) returns the database name associated with user ID 10.

db_id() returns the database ID of the current database.

63. If you were to grant the sa_role to user fred, when would that role take effect?

Answer: The next time fred logs into the server, or if fred executes:

```
set role "sa_role" on
```

64. What command would you use to temporarily disable a role for your session?

Answer: `set role "role_name" off`

To revoke a role for a user permanently?

Answer: `sp_role "revoke", role_name, login_name`

65. When configuring SQL Server memory, what unit of measurement is used to specify the amount of memory to allocate to SQL Server?

    Answer: # of pages.

    If the SQL Server is supposed to be configured to allocate 20MB of memory, what value would you specify to `sp_configure`?

    Answer: 10240—512 2KB pages/MB * number of MB (5120 for Stratus—4KB pages)

66. If the SQL Server is configured to use 16MB of memory, 4MB of which are used by the SQL Server executable and server and kernel structures, and procedure cache is set to 30, how large would the procedure cache be in megabytes?

    Answer: The procedure cache refers to the percentage of available cache memory. Therefore, 12MB x 30% = 3.6MB.

    How large would the data cache be?

    Answer: The remaining cache memory—8.4MB.

67. What command can be used to display how SQL Server has allocated memory internally?

    Answer:

    ```
    dbcc traceon(3604)
    go
    dbcc memusage
    go
    ```

    In System 11, the `sp_configure` stored procedure also reports the memory requirements of each individual configuration parameter.

    Where else can you look to determine the number of pages allocated to the data and procedure cache?

    Answer: The SQL Server startup messages in the error log.

68. When creating free-space thresholds on a segment, how far apart should you create them?

    Answer: Two times the `@@thresh_hysteresis` value.

69. Describe what it means when `nested triggers` is configured to `1`.

    Answer: When triggers perform activities on other tables with a trigger defined on them for that activity, the trigger on that table will also be fired. The maximum number of nesting levels is 16.

    When `recovery flags` is set to `1`.

Answer: The server will report the name of each individual transaction resolved during recovery and whether it was rolled forward or back.

70. Describe `fillfactor`. What two ways can you control the `fillfactor` to be used when creating indexes?

    Answer: `fillfactor` specifies how full to make each page when creating a new index. For nonclustered indexes, this refers only to the index pages. For clustered indexes, the data pages are also affected. The number specified is a percentage each page should be filled. A default `fillfactor` is specified for the SQL Server and can be changed using `sp_configure`. This value can be overridden by the `fillfactor` option of the `create index` syntax.

    What does a `fillfactor` of `0` mean? `100`?

    Answer: `0` creates the leaf-level pages 100% full (data pages for clustered, leaf index pages for non-clustered) and the non-leaf pages at approximately 80% full.

    A `fillfactor` of `100` will completely fill all leaf and non-leaf pages.

71. What configuration option must also be configured if the maximum network packet size is set higher than the default network packet size?

    Answer: `additional netmem`

72. The `mydb` database was initially created with the log and data segments on the same single device. You have a separate device available for log use called `logdev` which is 100MB in size. You would like to create a 50MB log segment for your database on the `logdev` device. What steps would you take to accomplish this?

    Answer: To perform the move:
    ```
    alter database mydb log on logdev = 50
    go
    dump tran mydb with no_log  [to truncate all existing log records]
    go
    sp_logdevice mydb, logdev
    go
    ```

73. If a database is created with the log and data on the same device, what is the maximum size the transaction log can grow to?

    Answer: The amount available space in the database.

74. You have four devices available to a database (`dev1`, `dev2`, `dev3`, `dev4`). You want to maximize performance by minimizing disk I/O contention within your database. Each device is 100MB in size and you will use all of each device for your database (300MB for data, 100MB for log). Your database primarily contains two high use tables, `TableA` and `TableB`. You want to avoid I/O contention between them by placing each on a separate device. In addition, a large amount of update activity will be occurring on `TableA`, so

you want to place its nonclustered index on columns Fkey1 and Fkey2 on a separate, relatively quiet device. List the commands and syntax you would use to set up your database and create these tables/indexes to meet these requirements.

Answer: Recommended solution:

```
create database mydb on dev1 = 100, dev2 = 100, dev3 = 100, log on dev4 = 100
go
use mydb
go
sp_addsegment seg1, mydb, dev1
go
sp_addsegment seg2, mydb, dev2
go
sp_addsegment seg3, mydb, dev3
go
create table TableA (Pkey int, Fkey1 int, Fkey2 char(3), …) on seg1
go
create table TableB (…) on seg2
go
create nonclustered index idx1 on TableA(Fkey1, Fkey2) on seg3
go
```

75. What types of locks does SQL Server use during creation of a clustered index?

    Answer: Exclusive table lock.

    A nonclustered index?

    Answer: Shared table lock.

76. If four users are running the same stored procedure concurrently, how many copies of the stored procedure's query plan will be in procedure cache?

    Answer: Four.

77. If you run disk init to create a database device on an operating-system file and the file already exists, what happens?

    Answer: The disk init fails and the vdevno specified cannot be used until the server is cycled.

78. What is the result of running the set transaction isolation level 3 command?

    Answer: All select statements will implicitly use a holdlock.

79. What command can be used to display permissions for an object? A user?

    Answer: sp_helprotect *objectname*; sp_helprotect *username*

80. What command can be used to list all stored procedures which reference a specific table?

    Answer: sp_depends *tablename*

SQL Server Operations

1. What system procedure do you use to monitor the SQL Server? What information does it report?

    Answer: sp_monitor

    sp_monitor reports information on how busy the SQL Server has been regarding CPU usage, disk I/O, and network I/O since the server was started and since the last time sp_monitor was run.

2. What command do you use to start the Sybase Backup Server?

    Answer: If Backup Server was installed with the default name SYB_BACKUP, a runserver file named RUN_SYB_BACKUP will be created. Execute:

    ```
    startserver -f RUN_SYB_BACKUP
    ```

3. What is the maximum number of dump devices Backup Server can use for one database dump?

    Answer: 32.

4. What directory is the SQL Server error log located in?

    Answer: $SYBASE/install (where $SYBASE is the Sybase home directory) by default, or in the directory specified by the -e option to the dataserver command.

5. The master database has become corrupted, but fortunately you have a backup of the master database. What must you do before loading this backup?

    Answer: Shut down the SQL Server, run buildmaster -m to rebuild a default master database, start the SQL Server in single user mode, load the backup of the master database, and then restart the SQL Server.

6. You've restored the backup of the master database, but it does not contain the device you added and database you created on that device since the last dump of the master database. What commands do you need to issue to recover the device and database?

    Answer: disk reinit and disk refit

7. The data device for your database has failed, but the log device is still available. What command would you use to capture the log records available?

    Answer: dump database *dbnbame* to *dumpdevice* with no_truncate

    What steps would you then take to restore the database?

    Answer: Drop the affected database. Create a new database with the same size and number of devices as the original with the for load option. Load the database dump and all transaction log dumps, including the one you executed after losing the data device.

What would be the state of the database once the restore is complete?

Answer: The database would be restored up to the point at which the data device failed.

8. The log device for your database has failed, but the data devices are still available. What operations can you perform on this database?

    Answer: None, except `drop database`.

    To what point can you recover this database?

    Answer: The database can be recovered up to the last available log dump.

    What if the log device was mirrored?

    Answer: The database would still be operational.

9. In System 10 and later, the state of the database contained in the backup is at what point during the backup process?

    Answer: The state of the database is near the END of the database dump.

10. How does SQL Server identify the local backup server?

    Answer: SQL Server will look up the `SYB_BACKUP` entry in the `sysservers` table to identify its network name.

    Information on the local backup server must be contained where?

    Answer: In the `interfaces` file and the `sysservers` table.

    Information on remote backup servers must be set up where?

    Answer: In the `interfaces` file.

11. You have been hired to replace a DBA who left abruptly, leaving no notes. How do you identify the network names of your local and remote backup servers?

    Answer: The local backup server network name will be defined in the `sysservers` table (run `sp_helpserver` and examine the network name for the local name `SYB_BACKUP`). Remote backup servers will be defined in the `interfaces` file, but unless a naming scheme was used to distinguish backup servers from other servers, there is no definitive way of identifying them.

12. In System 10 and later, what commands/tools are available to monitor the size of the transaction log if the log is on a separate device?

    Answer: `sp_spaceused syslogs`, `dbcc checktable(syslogs)`, or thresholds.

13. You want to back up three databases, db1, db2, and db3, to a single tape on device `tapedev1`. You do not wish to have any other backups contained on this tape. What commands would you issue to perform this backup?

Answer:

```
dump database db1 to tapedev1 with init
dump database db2 to tapedev1
dump database db3 to tapedev1 with unload
```

14. What command is used in SQL Server to abort a stranded or runaway process?

    Answer: `kill spid`

15. `print` statements inside a threshold procedure are displayed where?

    Answer: The SQL Server error log.

16. You performed a full database dump of your database at midnight and transaction log dumps every four hours. At 9 PM, you lose your database device. You have the full backup from midnight and all five regular transaction log dumps plus the final one dumped after the loss of the data device. During the restoration process, you discover that the tape containing the dump for 8 AM has gone bad and cannot be read. To what point can you recover your database?

    Answer: You can load the database dump and the 4 AM transaction log dump. (All other log dumps after the bad 8 AM log dump cannot be loaded.)

17. You perform full database dumps at midnight and noon and transaction log dumps every four hours in between. At 5 PM you lose your log device and it is not mirrored. When you try to restore the database, you discover that the tape containing the database dump from noon has gone bad and cannot be read. Assuming all your log dumps are okay, to what point can you recover this database?

    Answer: You can load the valid database dump from midnight and all valid transaction log dumps up to and through the bad noon database dump to the last log dump at 4 PM. Database dumps do not truncate the transaction log so no log records are lost with the loss of the noon database dump.

18. If you wish to load a database dump into a new database, what must be true of the new database for the load to be successful?

    Answer: It must be at least the size of the database that was dumped.

    No one can be using the database when the `load database` command is executed.

    You also must be the `dbo`, or have the `sa_role` or `oper_role`.

19. If you are loading a database dump from one server to another server, what potential conflicts should you be aware of?

    Answer: Mapping of login IDs to database user IDs (`syslogins.suid` to `sysusers.uid`) and different sort orders.

20. What command should you run on a regular basis to verify the integrity of the system tables within a database?

   Answer: `dbcc checkcatalog`

21. How do you verify that all pages within a database are correctly allocated?

   Answer: `dbcc checkalloc`

22. How do you verify that all pages are correctly allocated for a table? For an index?

   Answer: For a table—`dbcc tablealloc`; for an index—`dbcc indexalloc`.

23. What command do you run to check that all index and data pages are correctly linked in a table?

   Answer: `dbcc checktable`

   What command will run the same checks for all tables in a database?

   Answer: `dbcc checkdb`

24. What command do you need to use to drop a database if it is marked suspect and cannot be dropped with the `drop database` command?

   Answer: `dbcc dbrepair (`*`dbname`*`, dropdb)`

25. What happens if the log fills up in a System 10 or later database if the log is not on a separate segment?

   Answer: By default, all processes performing modifications will be suspended until the log is truncated.

   If the log is on a separate segment from the data?

   Answer: By default, all processes performing modifications will be suspended and the stored procedure `sp_thresholdaction` will be fired if it is defined.

26. What commands can you issue to truncate the transaction log without writing it to a dump device?

   Answer: `dump transaction` *`dbname`* `with no_log` or `dump transaction` *`dbname`* `with truncate_only`

27. What happens if a table fills up the segment it is defined on?

   Answer: No more rows can be added until additional space is made available.

   What can you do to make more space available?

   Answer: If this is the `default` segment, alter the database to add another device fragment (the new fragment is automatically added to the `default` segment definition). If this is a user-defined segment, extend the segment on a fragment with available space or a new fragment allocated to the database.

28. What information is contained in a normal RUN_*SERVERNAME* runserver file?

    Answer: Comments indicating the server name, the size and location of the master device, and the locations of the SQL Server error log and interfaces file, and also a call to the dataserver executable, passing as parameters the location of the master device, the server name, the location of the error log, and the mirror device (if mirroring of the master device is enabled).

29. Where is the Backup Server error log located and what is the name of the file by default?

    Answer: The Backup Server error log is normally located in the $SYBASE/ install directory, unless the -e option is specified in the Backup Server startup command to specify a different location. The default name of the Backup Server error log is backup.log.

30. What type of information is contained in the SQL Server error log?

    Answer: Startup information, reporting of execution of certain commands (kill, dump tran with no_log, etc.) and any problems encountered by the system.

31. What stored procedure can you execute to display space usage within a database?

    Answer: sp_spaceused

32. Where can you look to verify the last time the SQL Server was started?

    Answer: The SQL Server error log.

33. Where can you look to determine the sort order and character set that a SQL Server is configured to use?

    Answer: Run sp_configure or check the startup messages in the SQL Server error log.

34. Where can you look to check for SQL Server startup error messages?

    Answer: The SQL Server error log.

35. What command can you execute to determine the largest stored procedures which have been recently executed?

    Answer: dbcc memusage (Remember to execute dbcc traceon(3604) first to send output to your terminal.)

36. List four reasons that could cause the SQL Server not to start up.

    Answer: Memory is configured larger than available on the hardware; Start up executed by user other than sybase (permission denied on executables for devices); The master database is corrupt; The master device is unavailable; SQL Server is already running!; SQL Server port number is already in use by another process.

37. List six common reasons why users may not be able to access a SQL Server which is up and running.

    Answer: No more connections available; network is down; login is not valid; login is locked; invalid password typed; invalid local interfaces file information; SQL Server is in single user mode.

38. List three reasons why a user may not be able to access a database.

    Answer: User not a valid user in the database; Database is unavailable; Database is undergoing a load; Database has not been recovered yet; Database is set for DBO use only; Database is in single user mode and is already in use by a user; Database has been marked suspect; Database has not been put online following a database load (System 11 only).

39. What commands would you normally execute to identify a cause why a user's SQL Server process appears to be hung?

    Answer: `sp_who` and `sp_lock`

40. What could be some possible causes for a query that used to take two minutes to run taking over 10 minutes to run?

    Answer: Heavy activity on server; statistics are not up to date; usable index has been dropped; locking contention; less data cache is available.

41. What could cause the transaction log to still be full even though you just dumped the log and truncated it?

    Answer: A `begin tran` is on the first page of the log and the transaction is still open, preventing the log from being truncated.

42. Your network is configured with a remote backup server called `SYB_DUMPHOST`. This backup server has access to two tape drives for performing backups called `/dev/nrmt1` and `/dev/nrmt2`. List the proper syntax you would use to perform a multivolume dump of `mydb` to both tape drives.

    Answer: `dump database mydb to "/dev/nrmt1" at SYB_DUMPHOST stripe on "/dev/nrmt2" at SYB_DUMPHOST`

43. What command can you use to define logical device names for your dump devices?

    Answer: `sp_addumpdevice`

44. What command do you execute to get information on the dump devices defined to SQL Server?

    Answer: `sp_helpdevice`

45. The error log should be monitored for error messages of at least what severity level?

    Answer: Severity of 17 through 24.

46. What utilities does Sybase provide to perform a logical database rebuild (e.g., moving a database from one platform to different platform)?

Answer: bcp and defncopy

47. Errors of severity 10–16 are typically what type of error? Where are these errors displayed?

Answer: Errors of severity level 16 or less are user errors. They are displayed at the client terminal.

48. If dumping a database to an operating-system file on disk and the file already exists, what happens?

Answer: Unless the previous dump was executed with the retaindays option, the file is overwritten. If the retaindays option was specified and that number of days has not passed, a warning message is raised by the Backup Server requesting confirmation before overwriting the dump.

49. You've run sp_who and it indicates that process 6 is blocking other processes. What command can you run to determine what resources process 6 is holding that are blocking the other processes?

Answer: sp_lock

If it indicates that the contention is on a specific page for a particular table, i.e., a "hot spot," what are some possible solutions to minimize the contention for this data page?

Answer: Create a clustered index on an column that will spread out the rows across data pages to minimize the chance of "hot spots"; Create the clustered index with a low fillfactor, minimizing the number of rows in a page; Change the code to reduce the transaction time, minimizing the length of time the lock is held; System 11—Create the index specifying max_rows_per_page to minimize the number of rows per page.

50. You cannot kill a process in SQL Server if it has what status?

Answer: Status of sleeping or Bad Status or Infected.

51. What are some standard guidelines to minimize deadlock and locking contention problems for transactions?

Answer: Avoid the use of holdlock; Do not allow user interaction within transactions; Keep transactions as concise as possible; Access tables in the same order within transactions; Code transactions in stored procedures so they run faster; Use a clustered index to avoid "hot spots" in table (i.e., all updates/access occurring on a few pages); Use fillfactor or max_rows_per_page (System 11) to spread data and index rows over more pages.

52. If you've run out of room on a segment and need to increase its size by allocating space on another device to the database, what would be the steps/commands you would need to carry out to perform this task?

Answer:

```
use master
go
alter database mydb on dev4 = 50
go
use mydb
go
sp_extendsegment seg1, mydb, dev4
go
```

53. What permission do database users need to be able to create temporary tables in tempdb?

    Answer: No special permission is needed.

54. If a database backup to a single dump device spans multiple tapes, what stored procedure do you need to execute to instruct Backup Server that a new tape has been inserted?

    Answer: sp_changevolume

55. If you attempt to load transaction log dumps out of order, what will happen?

    Answer: The server will inform you the dump is out of order. Place the correct dump in the dump device and continue.

56. In System 11, what stored procedure is used to create named data caches?

    Answer: sp_cacheconfig

57. In System 11, how can you force the optimizer to use a particular index for a table when processing a query?

    Answer: Specify the index name after the table name in the FROM clause (select … from tablename (index indexname).

58. In System 11, when executing a query, how can you force the optimizer to use 16KB I/Os when performing physical reads? What condition must be met in order for 16KB I/Os to be performed?

    Answer: Specify the prefetch size in the INDEX clause after the table name in the FROM clause. For example, to force a table scan using 16KB I/Os on the mytab table, execute the following:

    select * from mytab (index mytab prefetch 16)

    In order for 16KB I/Os to be performed, the data cache used for that table must have a 16KB buffer pool configured with 16KB buffers available.

59. What stored procedure is used to create buffer pools for large block I/O?

    Answer: sp_poolconfig

60. How do you associate an object with a named cache in System 11?

    Answer: sp_bindcache cachename, dbname, tablename

61. In System 11, how do you disassociate an object from a named cache? Disassociate all objects from a named cache?

    Answer: `sp_unbindcache` *cachename, dbname, tablename*; `sp_unbindcache_all` *cachename*

62. What are the allowable buffer pool and prefetch I/O sizes in System 11?

    Answer: 2, 4, 8, & 16KB

63. In System 11, when is a newly defined named cache available? When do changes to a named cache buffer pool take effect?

    Answer: Newly defined named caches are not available until after a SQL Server restart. Buffer pool changes take effect immediately.

64. How do you partition a table in System 11? What is the primary performance benefit of partitioning a table? What restrictions are there on partitioned tables?

    Answer: To partition a table, place it on its own segment and use the `alter table` *tablename* `partition` *#_of_partitions* command to create multiple page chains. Partitioning a table helps to improve performance by providing multiple insert points (one per partition) on a heap table to minimize page locking contention on inserts. A partitioned table cannot have a clustered index defined on it, and the table cannot be dropped or truncated unless it is first unpartitioned.

65. In System 11, what must you do first before dropping a partitioned table?

    Answer: The table must be unpartitioned using the `alter table` *tablename* `unpartition` command.

66. How do you add standard user-defined error messages to a database?

    Answer: `sp_addmessage` *error_number, message_string*

67. Describe transaction isolation level 0. How can you run a query at this isolation level in System 11?

    Answer: Transaction isolation level 0 allows "dirty reads"; that is, reads of uncommitted data modifications. In System 11, dirty reads are allowed for a session by executing the `set transaction isolation level 0` command, or for a specific query by adding the `at isolation read uncommitted` clause.

68. Describe the difference between the LRU and MRU buffer replacement strategies in System 11.

    Answer: The MRU buffer replacement strategy places the buffer read in at the wash marker so it is flushed from cache as the next buffer is read in (also known as the "fetch and discard" strategy). The LRU buffer replacement strategy places the buffer read in at the beginning of the MRU/LRU chain so it stays in cache for subsequent accesses.

C

CSP DBA TEST ANSWERS

69. In System 11, what command must be executed after a database is loaded from a backup before the database can be accessed by database users?

    Answer: `online database` *dbname*

70. In System 11, what command can you execute so operations on tables will not escalate to table-level locks until at least 500 page locks are acquired, rather than the default 200?

    Answer: To prevent lock escalation until at least 500 page locks are acquired on a table, you need to set the page lock low water mark (LWM) threshold to 500 pages. To set the default locking behavior for the entire server, execute the following:

    ```
    sp_configure "lock promotion LWM", 500
    ```

    To set the lock escalation point for a specific database or table, use the `sp_setpglockpromote` stored procedure.

- Basic sa Tasks

- Database
  Management

- Monitoring CPU
  and I/O Usage

- Managing the
  Audit System
  (sso Task Only)

- Basic dbo Tasks

- System Functions

- System Tables

APPENDIX D

Quick Reference

The tables in this appendix summarize the tasks and commands of the different roles. System functions and tables also are presented. The tables are as follows:

Table D.1. Basic sa tasks.

Table D.2. Database management.

Table D.3. Monitoring CPU and I/O usage.

Table D.4. Managing the Audit System (sso task only).

Table D.5. Basic dbo tasks.

Table D.6. System functions.

Table D.7. System tables.

TABLE D.1. BASIC sa TASKS.

STARTING AND STOPPING THE SERVER

```
startserver -f runserver_file [-m] [-p]
```

runserver_file contains SQL Server command with appropriate options for locations of master device, interfaces file, SQL Server name, and so on.

d specifies master device name.

f specifies alternative runserver file.

m specifies single user mode.

p generates password for sso account.

```
shutdown [with  nowait]
```

GRANTING ACCESS TO THE SERVER

```
sp_addlogin login_name, password [ ,default_db [ ,language]]
```

password required, six characters minimum.

Note: Only user with sso_role can add logins.

```
sp_password caller_password, new_password, [ , login_name]
```

Note: Only user with sso_role should specify *login_name*.

```
sp_droplogin login_name
```

```
sp_defaultdb login_name, default_db
```

Pre-System 10, assigns or changes default database for specified user.

```
sp_locklogin login_name, {"lock ¦ "unlock"}
```

Locks the specified *login_name*.

```
sp_configure "password expiration interval", #_of_days
```

Sets number of days passwords will expire after they are changed.

A value of 0 means no password expiration.

Note: Only user with `sso_role` can set password expiration interval.

```
sp_modifylogin login_name, option, value
```

option can be `defdb`, `deflanguage`, and `fullname`.

DEFINING PHYSICAL RESOURCES

```
disk init name = 'logical_name', physname = "phys_name",
        vdevno = dev_num, size = dev_size
```

logical_name must be unique throughout server.

phys_name disk location of device.

dev_num unique integer < `sp_configure` devices.

dev_siz in pages (2KB except Stratus (4KB)).

```
disk reinit name = 'logical_name', physname = "phys_name",
        vdevno = dev_num, size = dev_size
```

Used to rebuild sysdevices to reestablish a database device after restoring a damaged master database, if the device was added since the last database dump of the master database.

```
disk refit
```

Used after `disk reinit` to rebuild sysusages and sysdatabases to reestablish databases created or altered since the last database backup of master.

```
disk mirror name = 'logical_name', mirror = 'phys_name'
```

Keeps copy of device *logical_name* on *phys_name*.

```
disk unmirror name = "logical_name"
        [ , side = {primary ¦ secondary}]
        [ , mode =  {retain ¦ remove}]
```

Defaults are side=secondary, moder=retain.

```
disk remirror name = "logical_name"
```

```
sp_adddumpdevice 'disk' ¦ 'tape', logical_name, physical_name, tape_size
```

logical_name is the unique name within server for dump device.

physical_name is the physical location of the device of disk file.

tape_size is the capacity of the tape dump device in megabytes.

```
sp_help device [logical_name]
```

Reports information about the specified or all database and dump devices.

```
sp_diskdefault logical_name, defaulton ¦ defaultoff
```

```
sp_dropdevice logical_name
```

Removes device definition if device is not in use.

TABLE D.2. DATABASE MANAGEMENT.

BASIC COMMANDS

```
create database db_name [on device_name = size [ , ...] ]
                       [log on device_name = size [, ...] ]
                       [with override]
                       [for load]
```

with override allows the specification of the same device name for the on and log on clauses. Enables dumping of transaction log even though it is not a separate device.

for load invokes a streamlined version of create database. Use when recovering from media failure, and database will be loaded from backup immediately following creation.

size is in megabytes.

device_name is any database device in sysdevices.

Separate log device is highly recommended.

```
drop database db_name
```

```
alter database db_name [on device_name = size [ , ...]]
                       [log on device_name = size [ , ...]]
                       [with override]
                       [for load]
```

```
sp_changedbowner login_name
```

```
sp_dboption database, options, true ¦ false
```

options are select into/bulkcopy, read only, single user, dbo use only, no chkpt on recovery, trunc log on chkpt, abort tran on log full, allow nulls by default, ddl in tran, no free space acctg.

```
checkpoint
```

checkpoint a database (must be in database to be checkpointed).

```
sp_helpdb [database_name]
```

GRANTING create database PERMISSION

```
use master
```

```
sp_adduser login_name
```

```
grant create database to login_name
```

MEMORY AND RESOURCE ALLOCATION

```
sp_configure [option, new_value]
```

option is any value in description column of sysconfigures.

new_value is any value in valid range for parameter.

sp_configure without arguments lists valid options and ranges.

Reconfigure after sp_configure verifies available resources.

reconfigure [with override]

Instructs server to apply changes.

TABLE D.3. MONITORING CPU AND I/O USAGE.

BASIC COMMANDS

sp_monitor

Shows CPU usage, I/O usage, and so on, since server came up and also since last sp_monitor call.

set statistics io on ¦ off

Quantity of logical and physical I/O.

set statistics time on ¦ off

Elapsed system and CPU time for parse, compile, and execute.

set forceplan on ¦ off

MANAGING REMOTE ACCESS

sp_addserver server_name, {local ¦ null}, network_name

sp_dropserver server_name [, droplogins]

sp_addremotelogin server_name [, local_name [, remote_name]]

sp_remoteoption [server_name, login_name, remote_name, 'trusted',
               true ¦ false]

sp_serveroption [servername, options, {true ¦ false}]

   options are net password encryption, time-outs.

sp_helpremotelogin [servername [, remotename]

MANAGING SYSTEM-DEFINED ROLES

sp_role {"grant" ¦ "revoke"}, {sa_role ¦ sso_role ¦ oper_role ¦
        oper_role}, login_name

login_name must be a valid SQL Server login.

User must have sa_role to grant sa_role.

User must have sso_role to grant sso_role, oper_role.

sa_role performs SQL Server management tasks:

        Server configuration
        Manage database devices

continues

TABLE D.3. CONTINUED

            Create/drop databases

            Shut down SQL Server

            Kill processes

`sso_role` performs security related tasks:

            Add/drop/lock logins

            Change passwords

            Set password expiration interval

            Manage auditing system

`oper_role` can back up and restore any database within SQL Server.

```
set role {"sa_role" | "sso_role" | "oper_role"} {on | off}
```

Disable/enable role for current session.

TABLE D.4. MANAGING THE AUDIT SYSTEM (SSO TASK ONLY).

```
sp_auditoption
```

Enables/disables auditing and global audit options.

Without arguments, displays current global audit settings.

```
sp_auditoption "{all | enable auditing | logout | server boots
            | adhoc records}" [ , "{on | off}"]
```

```
sp_auditoption " {logins | rpc connections | roles}"
            [ , "{ok | fail | both | off}"]
```

```
sp_auditoption "errors" [ , "{nonfatal | fatal | both}"]
```

```
sp_auditoption "{sa | sso | oper} commands" [ ,
            "{ok | fail | both | off }"]
```

`enable auditing` must be on before setting other audit options.

`ok` audits successful operations.

`fail` audits failed operations.

`both` audits successful/failed operations.

`on` turns on specified auditing.

`off` turns off specified auditing.

```
sp_auditdatabase [dbname [ , "ok | fail | both | off" [,
            " { d u g r t o}"]]]
```

Enable auditing of events within database or object references within data base from another database.

`d` audits `dbo` commands.

`u` audits execution of use *dbname*.

g audits grant commands.

r audits revoke commands.

t audits truncate table.

o audits outside access of *dbname*.

```
sp_auditobject table_name ¦ view_name, dbname [ ,
               "{ok ¦ fail ¦ both ¦off}" [ , "{d i s u }"]]
```

Enable auditing of access to existing tables/view.

d audits deletes.

i audits inserts.

s audits selects.

u audits updates.

```
sp_auditobject "default {table ¦ view}", dbname [ ,
               "{ok ¦ fail both ¦ off}" [ , "{ d i s u}"]]
```

Enable auditing defaults for future tables/view created in *dbname*.

```
sp_auditsproc [proc_name ¦ "all" ¦ "default"], dbname [ ,
               "{ok ¦ fail ¦ both ¦ off}"]]
```

Audit execution of existing stored procs/triggers or enable auditing defaults for future stored procs/triggers created in *dbname*.

```
sp_auditlogin [login_name [, "cmdtxt" [, "{on ¦ off}"]]]

sp_auditlogin [login_name [,"table ¦ view" [,
               "{ok ¦ fail ¦ both ¦ off}"]]]
```

Audit commands and table/view access for a login.

```
sp_auditrecord [@text="msg text"] [ , @db_name="objowner"]
               [ , @obj_name="objname"] [ , @owner_name="objowner"]
               [ , @dbid=db_id] [ , @objid=obj_id]
```

Enter user-defined audit records.

```
sp_configure "audit queue size", #_audit_records
```

Sets the number of records to be held in audit queue (default = 100).

TABLE D.5. BASIC dbo TASKS.

USER AND GROUP MAINTENANCE

```
sp_adduser login_name [ , name_within_db [ , group_name]]
```

login_name is from syslogins.

name_within_db is optional different name within database.

continues

TABLE D.5. CONTINUED

group_name is name of group to place user in. Specifying a group name requires specifying a non-null *name_within_db*.

guest is a special case of user; it gives any nonuser database access.

Adds a row to sysusers.

sp_addalias *login_name*, *current_user*

login_name is user to add to database.

current_user is existing user who *login_name* will alias to.

Adds a row to sysusers.

sp_addgroup *group_name*

Adds group *group_name* to sysusers.

sp_changegroup *group_name*, *user_name*

Places user *user_name* in group *group_name*.

sp_dropuser *user_name*

Removes user *user_name* from sysusers and any aliased users from sysalternates.

sp_dropalias *login_name*

Removes *login_name* from sysalternates.

sp_dropgroup *group_name*

Removes group *group_name* from sysusers.

sp_helpuser [*user_name*]

Displays list of database users or detailed user information.

GRANTING AND REVOKING PERMISSION

grant {all ¦ *permission_list*} on *object* [(*column_list*)]
    to {public ¦ *name_list* ¦ *role_name*} [with grant option]

grant {all ¦ *command_list*} to {public ¦ *name_list* ¦ *role_name*}

permission_list may be any combination of select, insert, update, delete.

name_list may be any combination of users and groups.

command_list may include any of the create commands (create rule, table, view, procedure, default).

with grant option enables user to grant specified permissions to other users.

revoke [grant option for] {all ¦ *permission_list* ¦ execute}
    on *object* [(*column_list*)]
    from {public ¦ *name_list* ¦ *role_name*}
    [cascade]

```
revoke {all ¦ command_list} from {public ¦ name_list ¦ role_name}
```

grant option for revokes users permission to grant specified permissions.

cascade is required with grant option for if user has granted permissions to other users.

Revoke those permissions.

SEGMENTS

```
sp_addsegment segment_name, database, device_name
```

```
sp_dropsegment segment_name, database [ , device_name]
```

```
sp_placeobject segment_name, object_name
```

Control future growth of an object.

```
sp_extendsegment segment_name, database, device_name
```

```
sp_helpsegment [segment_name]
```

```
sp_logdevice database, device_name
```

SPACE MONITORING

```
sp_spaceused [object_name]
```

```
dbcc checktable (table_name)
```

```
sp_estspace table_name, est_#_of_rows, [fillfactor [cols_to_max
            [ , textbin_length [ , iosec]]]]
```

fillfactor is the fillfactor used on index create.

cols_to_max is a comma-separated list of the variable-length columns for which to use the maximum width of the columns instead of the average width.

textbin_length is the average size of text/binary columns.

iosec is the number of disk I/Os per second for the machine (default = 30).

```
sp_addthreshold dbname, segname, free_pgs, proc_name
```

```
sp_dropthreshold dbname, segname, free_pgs
```

```
sp_modifythreshold dbname, segname, free_pgs
                  [ , new_proc] [ , new_free_pgs] [ , new_seg_name]
```

free_pgs is the number of free pages left in the segment where the threshold is placed.

proc_name is the stored procedure to execute when threshold is crossed.

```
sp_helpthreshold [segname]
```

```
sp_thresholdaction @dbname, @seg_name, @space_left, @status
```

Stored procedure is automatically called when logsegment crosses last-chance threshold.

This procedure must be defined by the sa or dbo.

D

continues

TABLE **D.5.** CONTINUED

UPDATING STATISTICS

```
update statistics table_name [(index_name)]
```
Make statistics pages current for specific table or index.

DATABASE CONSISTENCY CHECKER

```
dbcc checktable ({table_name | table_id} [, skip_ncindex])
```
Table consistency.

```
dbcc checkdb [ (dbname [ , skip_ncindex] )]
```
Check all tables in the database dbname.

```
dbcc checkalloc [ (dbname [ , fix | no fix] ) ]
```
Check page allocation.

```
dbcc checkcatalog [(dbname)]
```
Check all system tables.

```
dbcc dbrepair (dbname, dropdb)
```
Remove damaged database.

```
dbcc traceon | traceoff  (3604)
```
Make console local.

```
dbcc memusage
```
Display memory contents.

```
dbcc page (db_name, pg_num)
```
Display page contents.

```
dbcc tablealloc ({table_name | table_id}
                [ , {full | optimized | fast | null}
                [ , fix | nofix ] ] )
```
Check page allocation of specific table and its indexes.

```
dbcc indexalloc ({table_name | table_id} , index_id
                [ , {full |optimized | fast | null}
                { , fix | nofix ] ] )
```
Check page allocation of specific index.

fix option tells SQL Server to attempt to fix allocation errors found.

```
dbcc reindex ( { table_name | table_id})
```
Check and fix index integrity.

```
dbcc fix_text ( { table_name | table_id})
```
Upgrade text values after character set change to multibyte charset.

BACKING UP AND LOADING DATABASES

```
dump database dbname to dump_device [at backup_server_name]
        [ , stripe on dump_device [ at backup_server_name] . . . ]
        [with { [ dismount ¦ nodismount],
                [ nounload ¦ unload],
                [ noinit ¦ init ],
                [retaindays = #_days] ,
                [file = file-name] } ]

dump tran[saction ] dbname to dump_device [ at backup_server_name]
        [ , stripe on dump_device [ at backup_server_name] . . . ]
                [ with { [dismount ¦ nodismount],
                         [nounload ¦ unload],
                         [retaindays = #_days],
                         [file = file_name],
                         [ { truncate_only ¦ no_log ¦ no_truncate}] } ]

load database dbname from dump_device [at backup_server_name}
        [ , stripe on dump_device [ at backup_server_name]  ... ]
        [ with { [ dismount ¦ nodismount] ,
                 [nounload ¦ unload],
                 [file = file_name],
                 [listonly [= full] ] ,
                 [headeronly] } ]

load tran[saction ] dbname from dump_device [ at backup_server_name] ... ]
        [ , stripe on dump_device [ at backup_server_name] ... ]
        [ with { [ dismount ¦ nodismount] ,
                 [ nounload ¦ unload],
                 [ file = file_name],
                 [listonly [= full] ] ,
                 [headeronly] } ]
```

dismount ¦ nodismount determines whether tapes remain mounted after dump ¦ load.

nounload ¦ load determines whether tapes rewind after dump ¦ load.

no init ¦ init determines whether dumps are appended to tape or tape is overwritten.

retaindays specifies number of days Backup Server protects you from overwriting a dump.

file lets you specify a name for the dump file on the tape.

listonly lists information about dump files on tape without loading.

headeronly displays header information for a single dump file without loading.

D

continues

TABLE D.5. CONTINUED

MANAGING USER-DEFINED MESSAGES

sp_addmessage *msg_num*, *msg_text* [, *language*]

Allows adding user-defined messages to sysusermessages for use by print and raiserror calls and by sp_bindmsg.

sp_dropmessage *msg_num* [, *language*]

sp_getmessage *msg_num*, @msg_var output [, *language*]

msg_num is the user-defined message number; it must be > 20000.

@msg_var is the variable to receive returned message text.

sp_bindsmg *constraint_name*, *msg_num*

Allows binding stored message to a constraint.

sp_unbindmsg constraint_name

IMPERSONATING USERS

setuser '*user_name*'

sp_addalias login_name, name_in_db

TABLE D.6. SYSTEM FUNCTIONS.

col_length (obj_name, col_name) index_col (obj_name, index_id, key_#)

col_name (obj_id, col_id) object_id obj_name)

datalength (expression) object_name (obj_id)

db_id (db_name)suser_id (user_name)

db_name (db_id) suser_name (suser_name)

host_id (host_name) user_name (user_id)

host_name (host_id) user_id (user_name)

curunreservedpgs (db_id, page_number free_pgs)

data_pgs (object_id, {doampg ¦ ioampg})

lct_admin ({{"last chance" ¦ "logfull" ¦ "unsuspend"}, database_id}
          ¦ "reserve", log_pages)

proc_role (""sa_role", ¦ sso_role" ¦ oper_role")

reserved_pgs (object_id, doampg ¦ ioampg})

rowcnt (doampg)

used_pgs (object_id, doampg, ioampg)

tsequal (timestampl, timestamp2)

user

Note: Yes, there are no parentheses after this function.

valid_name (character_expression)

Note: A null argument retrieves current process value.

TABLE D.7. SYSTEM TABLES.

Table	Description
	DATABASE SPECIFIC
sysalternates	Aliases defined
syscolumns	Column descriptions for tables
syscomments	Original SQL definition of objects
sysdepends	Track procedure / table dependencies
sysindexes	One row for each table and index
syskeys	Keys defined (documentation only)
syslogs	Database transaction log
sysobjects	Pointers to all objects in the database; types: U - User table, P - Procedure, R - Rule, V - View, S - System table, Tr - Triggers, D - Default
sysusermessages	User-defined error messages
sysconstraints	Referential and check constraints
sysreferences	Primary / foreign keys defined in referential constraints
sysroles	maps server role IDs to local role IDs
systhresholds	Thresholds defined in database
sysprocedures	Parsed text of stored procedures
sysprotects	Protections granted and revoked
syssegments	Segment definitions
systypes	System- and user-defined data types
sysusers	Who can use the database
	THE MASTER DATABASE ONLY
syscharsets	Currently defined character sets
sysconfigures	Memory only; server-wide locks

continues

D

TABLE D.7. CONTINUED

Table	Description	
syscurconfigs	Memory only, version of sysconfigures	
sysdatabases	Defined databases	
Status:	4 Select into / BCP	1024 Read only
	8 Trunc log on chkpt	2048 DBO use only
	16 No chkpt on recovery	4096 Single user mode
	64 Crash during load	16384 db_name change
	256 Suspect	
sysdevices	Database and dump devices	
Status:	1 default disk	32 serial writes
	2 physical disk	64 mirrored device
	4 logical disk	128 read mirrored
	8 skip header	256 half mirrored
	16 dump device	512 mirror enabled
syslanguages	Available languages	
syslocks	Memory only; server-wide locks	
syslogins	Who has server access	
sysmessages	System messages	
sysprocesses	Memory-only; current server processes	
sysremotelogins	Who has remote access	
sysservers	Local and remote server names	
sysusages	Maps databases to sysdevices	
syssrvroles	Contains all server-wide roles	
sysloginroles	Maps logins to system defined roles	
sysengines	SQL Server engines currently online	

Legal Agreements
Pertaining to the CD-ROM

By opening this package, you are agreeing to be bound by the following agreement:

Some of the software included with this product is copyrighted, in which case all rights are reserved by the respective copyright holder. You are licensed to use software copyrighted by the Publisher and its licensors on a single computer. You may copy and/or modify the software as needed to facilitate your use of it on a single computer. Making copies of the software for any other purpose is a violation of the United States copyright laws.

This software is sold as is without warranty of any kind, either expressed or implied, including but not limited to the implied warranties of merchantability and fitness for a particular purpose. Neither the publisher nor its dealers or distributors assumes any liability for any alleged or actual damages arising from the use of this program. (Some states do not allow for the exclusion of implied warranties, so the exclusion may not apply to you.)

By opening this package, you are agreeing to be bound by the following agreement which applies to products supplied by Northern Lights Software:

Aurora is a copyrighted product of Northern Lights Software, Ltd., and is protected by United States copyright laws and international treaty provisions. Copyright 1994, 1995, 1996. All Rights Reserved. Aurora Utilities for Sybase, Aurora Desktop, Aurora Script Manager, Aurora Distribution Viewer, and Aurora Cost Retrieval DLL are service marks of Northern Lights Software. Sybase is a trademark of Sybase, Inc.

Period of evaluation. By installing the software, it is understood that the provided software is for the purposes of evaluation only, and cannot be used beyond a period of thirty (30) days unless the software is registered. The software can be registered only by Northern Lights Software, Ltd., or its empowered agents.

Limited Warranty. Northern Lights warrants that the SOFTWARE will perform substantially in accordance with the written description delivered with the software, usually in the form of a readme.txt, for a period of ninety (90) days. Any implied warranties are limited to the same period of ninety (90) days.

Remedies. Northern Lights and its suppliers' entire liability and your exclusive remedy shall be, at Northern Lights' option, a refund of the price paid or repair or replacement of the software. This Limited Warranty is void if the failure has resulted from accident, abuse, or misapplication. These warranties are limited to the United States unless you can provide proof of purchase from an authorized non-U.S. source.

No Other Warranties. To the maximum extent permitted by applicable law, Northern Lights disclaims all other warranties, either express or implied, including but not limited to implied warranties of merchantability and fitness for a particular purpose. This limited warranty gives you certain rights. You may have other rights which vary by state and jurisdiction.

No Liability for Consequential Damages. To the maximum extent permitted by applicable law, in no event shall Northern Lights be liable for any damages whatsoever (including without limitation, damages for loss of business profits, business interruption, loss of business information or any other pecuniary loss) arising out of the use of or inability to use this product, even if Northern Lights has been advised of the possibility of such damages. Because some states do not allow the limit or exclusion of liability for consequential or incidental damage, the above limitation may not apply to you.

Index

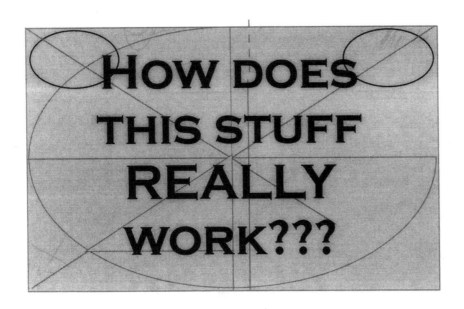

HOW DOES THIS STUFF REALLY WORK???

SYBASE AND MICROSOFT SQL SERVER ARE POWERFUL CLIENT/SERVER TOOLS.

BUT THEY CERTAINLY AREN'T...INTUITIVE. EVEN BASIC TRAINING CAN LEAVE YOU IN THE DARK ABOUT THE "REAL WORLD" OF SYBASE AND MICROSOFT SQL SERVER.

LET NORTHERN LIGHTS CONSULTING, AN INTERNATIONALLY RECOGNIZED SQL SERVER TRAINING AND CONSULTING FIRM, HELP YOU GET WHERE YOU WANT TO GO.

WE HAVE A GREAT DEAL OF EXPERIENCE HELPING FIRMS MAKE THESE TOOLS *DO WHAT THEY WANT THEM TO DO!*

BUILDING EXCELLENCE IN CLIENT/SERVER SYSTEMS

NORTHERN LIGHTS PRODUCTS & SERVICES

BOOKS

✧ "SYBASE DBA SURVIVAL GUIDE, 2ND ED"
(GARBUS, SOLOMON, RANKINS, TRETTER),
SAMS PUBLISHING, 1996

✧ "SYBASE SQL SERVER
11 UNLEASHED"
(RANKINS, GARBUS, SOLOMON, MCEWAN),
SAMS PUBLISHING, 1996

✧ "MICROSOFT SQL SERVER 6
UNLEASHED"
(SOLOMON, WOODBECK, RANKINS, GARBUS,
MCEWAN), *SAMS PUBLISHING, 1996*

COURSES

✧ SQL FOR PROGRAMMERS
✧ INTRODUCTION TO SQL SERVER
✧ PRACTICAL SQL SERVER SYSTEMS ADMIN
✧ LOGICAL DATABASE DESIGN FOR SQL SERVER
✧ SQL SERVER PERFORMANCE AND TUNING
✧ WHAT'S NEW WITH SYBASE SYSTEM 10
✧ WHAT'S NEW WITH SYBASE SYSTEM 11
✧ SQL SERVER FOR SYSTEMS ADMINISTRATORS
✧ SQL SERVER FOR DATABASE DESIGNERS
✧ GUI DESIGN
✧ OPEN SYBASE
✧ VISUAL BASIC FOR SQL PROGRAMMERS

NEW COURSES FOR 1996!!!

✧ **ADVANCED SQL TECHNIQUES**
(THREE-DAY COURSE) COVERS THE "HOWS AND WHYS" OF ADVANCED QUERY AND STORED
PROCEDURE WRITING, OPTIMIZING, AND DEBUGGING. FOR APPLICATION PROGRAMMERS
INTERESTED IN SERIOUS PERFORMANCE; INCLUDES WHEN TO BREAK UP QUERIES, FORCE A
QUERY PLAN OR INDEX, OR RESOLVE A COMPLEX QUERY, AMONG OTHER TOPICS.

✧ **DESIGNING AND IMPLEMENTING VERY LARGE DATABASES**
(FIVE-DAY COURSE) LEARN A METHODOLOGY FOR HANDLING VERY LARGE SQL SERVER
DATABASES. THIS COURSE INCLUDES A CLOSE INVESTIGATION INTO THE PHYSICAL
OPERATION OF SQL SERVER AND THE ADMINISTRATIVE IMPLICATIONS OF VLDBS.

**ALL NORTHERN LIGHTS COURSES ARE UPDATED FOR SYBASE SYSTEM 11
AND MICROSOFT SQL SERVER 6.0**

AURORA UTILITIES

✧ AURORA DESKTOP
✧ PERFORMANCE MONITOR
✧ DISTRIBUTION VIEWER
✧ STRESS TESTER
✧ COST DLL
✧ SCRIPT MANAGER

CONSULTING

✧ TUNING & OPTIMIZATION
✧ STANDARDS
✧ SYSTEM REVIEW
✧ OFF-SITE HELP DESK
✧ VLDB ARCHITECTURE

PHONE: (800) 774-6764
FAX: (518) 581-9737
E-MAIL: 72702.373@COMPUSERVE.COM
WWW: WWW.NLIGHT.COM

Northern Lights
Consulting

Visible Analyst Workbench

Integrated Enterprise CASE

Planning - Analysis - Design - Construction - Re-Engineering/BPR

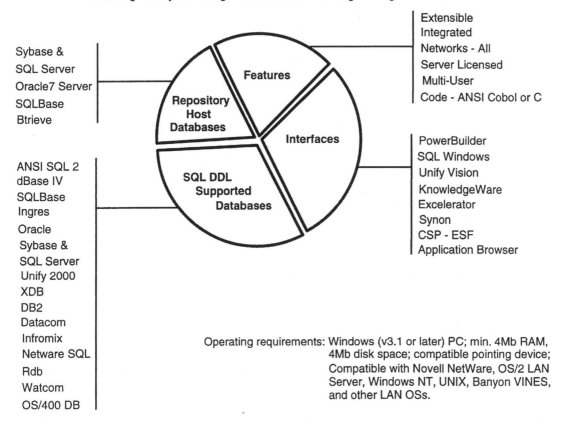

Sybase &
SQL Server
Oracle7 Server
SQLBase
Btrieve

Repository Host Databases

Features

Interfaces

SQL DDL Supported Databases

Extensible
Integrated
Networks - All
Server Licensed
Multi-User
Code - ANSI Cobol or C

PowerBuilder
SQL Windows
Unify Vision
KnowledgeWare
Excelerator
Synon
CSP - ESF
Application Browser

ANSI SQL 2
dBase IV
SQLBase
Ingres
Oracle
Sybase &
SQL Server
Unify 2000
XDB
DB2
Datacom
Infromix
Netware SQL
Rdb
Watcom
OS/400 DB

Operating requirements: Windows (v3.1 or later) PC; min. 4Mb RAM, 4Mb disk space; compatible pointing device; Compatible with Novell NetWare, OS/2 LAN Server, Windows NT, UNIX, Banyon VINES, and other LAN OSs.

The Visible Analyst Workbench® is an object based corporate workgroup CASE tool that combines data, process and objects in an integrated open repository. Powerful modeling support includes Business Modeling, Class Modeling, Entity Relationship Modeling, Data Flow Modeling, State Transition Modeling, and Program Modeling, which is synchronized and cross-balanced, allowing for all development in one singular OO environment. Migration of legacy systems, IEW/ADW and Excelerator data and designs to an OO world make for fast generation of new client/server applications.

Visible Systems Corporation
300 Bear Hill Road
Waltham, MA 02154
Phone: (617) 890-CASE (2273) Fax: (617) 890-8909
Web Page/http://www.visible.com Email: info.visible.com

Free trial copy available on CD-ROM

Add to Your Sams Library Today with the Best Books for Programming, Operating Systems, and New Technologies

The easiest way to order is to pick up the phone and call

1-800-428-5331

between 9:00 a.m. and 5:00 p.m. EST.
For faster service please have your credit card available.

ISBN	Quantity	Description of Item	Unit Cost	Total Cost
0-672-30467-8		Sybase Developer's Guide (Book/Disk)	$40.00	
0-672-30700-6		Developing Sybase Applications (Book/CD-ROM)	$39.99	
0-672-30909-2		Sybase SQL Server 11 Unleashed (Book/CD-ROM)	$59.99	
0-672-30717-0		Tricks of the Doom Programming Gurus (Book/CD-ROM)	$39.99	
1-57521-041-x		The Internet Unleashed 1996	$49.99	
0-672-30737-5		The World Wide Web Unleashed, 2E	$39.99	
0-672-30706-5		Programming Microsoft Office (Book/CD-ROM)	$49.99	
0-672-30474-0		Windows 95 Unleashed (Book/CD-ROM)	$39.99	
0-672-30602-6		Programming Windows 95 Unleashed (Book/CD-ROM)	$49.99	
0-672-30791-x		Peter Norton's Complete Guide to Windows 95	$29.99	
1-57521-014-2		Teach Yourself Web Publishing with HTML in 14 Days, Premier Edition	$39.99	
1-57521-005-3		Teach Yourself More Web Publishing with HTML in a Week	$29.99	
0-672-30745-6		HTML & CGI Unleashed	$49.99	
		Shipping and Handling: See information below.		
		TOTAL		

❏ 3 ½" Disk

❏ 5 ¼" Disk

Shipping and Handling: $4.00 for the first book, and $1.75 for each additional book. Floppy disk: add $1.75 for shipping and handling. If you need to have it NOW, we can ship product to you in 24 hours for an additional charge of approximately $18.00, and you will receive your item overnight or in two days. Overseas shipping and handling adds $2.00 per book and $8.00 for up to three disks. Prices subject to change. Call for availability and pricing information on latest editions.

201 W. 103rd Street, Indianapolis, Indiana 46290

1-800-428-5331 — Orders   1-800-835-3202 — FAX   1-800-858-7674 — Customer Service

Book ISBN 0-672-30888-6

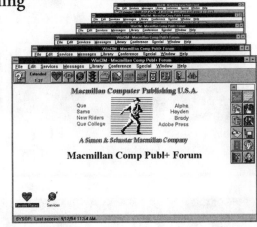

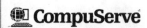

Installing the CD-ROM

The companion CD-ROM contains an assortment of trial products from third-party developers. The disc is designed to be explored using a browser program. Using Sams' Guide to the CD-ROM browser, you can view information concerning products and companies, and install programs with a single click of the mouse. To install the browser, here's what to do.

Windows 3.x/NT Installation Instructions

1. Insert the CD-ROM disc into your CD-ROM drive.
2. From File Manager or Program Manager, choose Run from the File menu.
3. Type **<*drive*>\setup** and press Enter, where <*drive*> corresponds to the drive letter of your CD-ROM. For example, if your CD-ROM is drive D:, type **D:\SETUP** and press Enter.
4. The installation creates a Program Manager group named Sybase DBA. To browse the CD-ROM, double-click on the Guide to the CD-ROM icon inside this Program Manager group.

Windows 95 Installation Instructions

1. Insert the CD-ROM disc into your CD-ROM drive. If the AutoPlay feature of your Windows 95 system is enabled, the setup program will start automatically.
2. If the setup program does not start automatically, double-click on the My Computer icon.
3. Double-click on the icon representing your CD-ROM drive.
4. Double-click on the icon titled Setup.exe to run the installation program. Follow the onscreen instructions that appear. When setup ends, double-click on the Guide to the CD-ROM icon to begin exploring the disc.

After installation, you can restart the Guide to the CD-ROM program by pressing the Start button, selecting Programs, Sybase DBA, and then Guide to the CD-ROM.

Note

The Guide to the CD-ROM program requires at least 256 colors. For best results, set your monitor to display between 256 and 64,000 colors. A screen resolution of 640×480 pixels is also recommended. If necessary, adjust your monitor settings before using the CD-ROM.